DISSENTING VOICE

OF THE

AMERICAN CENTURY

DOROTHY DAY

JOHN LOUGHERY

AND

BLYTHE RANDOLPH

SIMON & SCHUSTER

New York   London   Toronto   Sydney   New Delhi

Simon & Schuster
1230 Avenue of the Americas
New York, NY 10020

First Simon & Schuster hardcover edition March 2020

SIMON & SCHUSTER and colophon are registered trademarks of Simon & Schuster, Inc.

For information about special discounts for bulk purchases, please contact Simon & Schuster Special Sales at 1-866-506-1949 or business@simonandschuster.com.

The Simon & Schuster Speakers Bureau can bring authors to your live event. For more information or to book an event, contact the Simon & Schuster Speakers Bureau at 1-866-248-3049 or visit our website at www.simonspeakers.com.

Interior design by Carly Loman

Manufactured in the United States of America

10 9 8 7 6 5 4 3 2 1

Library of Congress Cataloging-in-Publication Data is available.

ISBN 978-1-9821-0349-1
ISBN 978-1-9821-0351-4 (ebook)

*Dedicated to Steven Roser and Thomas Orefice
and to Phil Runkel—scholar, activist, and archivist—who has done
more than anyone else to keep alive the memory of Dorothy Day
and to expand and deepen our understanding of this remarkable woman*

✌ CONTENTS ✌

DOROTHY DAY:
❧ AN AMERICAN PARADOX ❧

A NY CHRONICLE OF AMERICAN HISTORY TODAY INCLUDES THE considerable number of women of independent vision who made a mark on the modern world and raised important questions about power, economics, national identity, and social justice. Many of those women—e.g., Margaret Fuller, the Grimké sisters, Jane Addams, Ida B. Wells, Margaret Sanger, Frances Perkins, Rosa Parks, Rachel Carson, Jane Jacobs—have been the subject of fresh biographies and renewed, appreciative attention in recent years. Dorothy Day (1897–1980) is a more difficult figure to encompass.

A convert to Catholicism in her twenties, Day was the cofounder of the Catholic Worker movement, a group of autonomous communities across the country (numbering over a hundred today) that provide food and shelter to the homeless and a platform from which to remind Americans that the American Dream has not been an attainable reality for all its citizens. Day was more than the sum of her charitable endeavors, though—her corporal works of mercy, as the Church terms efforts at aiding the downtrodden. She was also a woman with an uncompromising political agenda.

Born on the eve of the Spanish-American War in the era of William McKinley, she lived to see the rise of Ronald Reagan and her country's role as a world power with a nuclear arsenal of apocalyptic potential. Coming of age when the reach of the Catholic Church and its social acceptance in the United States was at its height, she lived to see American Catholics, post–Vatican II, turn from their faith in the 1970s in daunting numbers. Both were troubling developments to a woman who was for almost fifty years a great anomaly in American life: an orthodox Catholic and a political radical, a rebel who courted controversy, challenged three generations of young admirers, and willingly went to jail for her beliefs.

An impassioned critic of unfettered capitalism, US foreign policy, the nuclear arms race, and the debacle of the Vietnam War, Day was at the same time as skeptical of many of the tenets of modern liberalism as she was of political conservatism. She was outspoken as well about what she saw as the complacent, conflicted role of religion in our national life. In large numbers, Americans regularly tell pollsters that they see themselves as a religious people. Day's concept of authentic belief, however, involved a good deal more than weekend church attendance and acceptance of an institutional creed.

The ideas Dorothy Day began to formulate in the early 1930s and exemplified to the time of her death in 1980 put her profoundly at odds with much of both secular and religious thought in the United States. She remains an outlier in that regard. The belief that material comfort—and, in particular, wealth—might actually be dangerous, putting a distance between oneself and God and one's fundamental humanity, wasn't a notion Americans were, or are, comfortable with. She came to believe that the true objects of devotion in Western culture—security, affluence, national pride, an enthrallment to innovation and technology—were the sources of our undoing as a moral society, and she was impatient with anyone who made religion seem reassuring rather than demanding and transcendent. The New Testament called on all believers to fight racism, war, and poverty, or it meant nothing at all. Faith was less about solace than a call to action and disruption. Piety and conformity to social norms had little to do with each other.

None of these values was a part of Day's upbringing. The child of a middle-class Republican family, nominally Protestant but essentially indifferent to religion and opposed to any kind of radicalism, Dorothy Day followed her own path from a young age. A precocious reader and budding intellectual, she dropped out of the University of Illinois after two years and found work in New York City as a reporter for various left-wing publications. The offices of the radical monthly *The Masses*, anarchist and socialist rallies at Union Square, the immigrant-filled streets of the Lower East Side, the avant-garde Provincetown Playhouse off Washington Square—those were the real sources of her education.

Day's romantic relationships with men such as Mike Gold, later a prominent American Communist and the author of *Jews Without Money*, and the playwright Eugene O'Neill brought her into the orbit of a group of people who were creative, inspirational, politically radical, hard-drinking, and libidinous. That was Greenwich Village in the late 1910s, a much-mythologized site of intellectual ferment and unconventional mores. For four years, it was home. It was also a world with a dark underside: her passionate and physically abusive affair with a charismatic newsman, Lionel Moise, ended with a pregnancy and abortion in 1920, a decision she regretted all of her life that was followed by two suicide attempts during a period of deep depression.

Yet Dorothy Day was never a typical bohemian. Her closest friends, including the lapsed Catholic and spiritually tormented O'Neill, knew of her clandestine visits to Catholic churches in the area. A night of carousing at the Hell Hole on Sixth Avenue, a dive of the shadiest kind, might be followed by a visit the next morning to St. Joseph's Church a block north—not to repent any misdeed but to see if she could fathom what it was the silent worshippers in the pews were feeling, what it meant to pray and seek a communion with a higher power. It was a call, inexplicable at the time even to Day herself, that she had felt in adolescence and, when she was in her late twenties, finally led to her decision to be baptized as a Roman Catholic. Her reading of William James and G. K. Chesterton was instrumental in that process.

By the mid-1920s, Day had left behind her rowdy youth and had a child in a common-law marriage with a man whom she deeply loved but who had no patience with her spiritual longings. They parted. Her life changed, her Catholicism taking on a whole new meaning, when she met a French immigrant laborer and idiosyncratic intellectual, Peter Maurin. With Maurin, she scraped together the funds to begin publishing a newspaper (*The Catholic Worker*, a still extant monthly), a publication that eventually reached more than 100,000 readers. That was the eclectic forum Day had been looking for without even realizing it, a periodical that allowed her to travel the country to report personally on labor strikes and corporate abuses, to send her reporters out to document examples of home foreclosures and racial discrimination, and to offer a lacerating critique of Americans' materialist values, all in a context that invoked Christ's teachings, the example of St. Francis of Assisi, and papal encyclicals about social issues.

Within two years, as breadlines and Hoovervilles dotted the landscape of the city, she and Maurin opened a "house of hospitality" in one of New York's poorer neighborhoods (more than fifty would exist across the country by 1940). Unlike the settlement houses of an earlier era, a Catholic Worker house required the young people who lived and worked there—like Day and Maurin themselves—to share in the poverty of the homeless men and women they served. Soon after, Day and Maurin made an effort to open self-sustaining farming communities in rural areas that were intended to be places of spiritual retreat and refuge from the pressures of city life, linked also to Maurin's special interest in fostering a "green revolution," forty years before any attention to ecology and environmental issues was a part of the public discourse in the United States.

Ultimately, though, writing about religion and injustice, providing shelter and food for the unemployed in the midst of the Great Depression, and following Maurin's lead was not enough. At heart, Dorothy Day was an activist on a far-reaching scale. The Sermon on the Mount, as she read it, would not be made a living reality simply by securing better wages for workers or putting a roof over the heads of those who had none. A revolution in thought, a new outlook that was both socially conscious and explicitly spiritual, was needed. In this sense, Day had little in common with heroes of the labor movement such as Mother Jones and Samuel Gompers or socialists such as Eugene Debs.

That way of thinking ultimately made Dorothy Day one of the most committed advocates of civil disobedience, placing her squarely in a tradition from Henry David Thoreau to Martin Luther King, Jr. In 1917, during her Greenwich Village days, she was arrested and brutalized in a Washington, DC, jail following a suffrage demonstration outside Woodrow Wilson's White House (though, when women won the vote, she never voted, having no faith in the American electoral system). She spoke before Congress in 1940 against the institution of a draft and urged young men not to register, advocated on behalf of conscientious objectors, deplored the use of the atomic bomb on Hiroshima and Nagasaki, went to jail several times in the 1950s protesting the nuclear arms race, and enthusiastically supported draft resisters who would not fight in the Vietnam War. She told college lecture audiences in 1962 that President John F. Kennedy was as much to blame for the horror of the Cuban missile crisis as Nikita Khrushchev and preached the need for a détente with Cuba and the Soviet Union long before the 1970s.

US history offers no better example of a commitment to pacifism and resistance to Cold War values than Dorothy Day, and the files J. Edgar

Hoover's FBI agents compiled against her extend over a thirty-year period. She was "Moscow Mary" to hard-line anti-Communists, including many fellow Catholics.

Church leaders were never quite sure what to make of Dorothy Day, either. The same woman who attended Mass every day of her adult life, refused to hear any criticism of the pope, and accepted Vatican teachings on all matters concerning sex, birth control, and abortion could be blistering in her remarks about priests who lived in well-appointed rectories and turned a blind eye to racial segregation in their parishes, bishops who were allies of the rich and powerful, and Catholic writers who viewed patriotism and faith as equivalent virtues, who were more concerned with the threat of "godless communism" than the needs of the poor. To her critics on the left, she was a distressingly loyal daughter of a reactionary Church, but to her critics on the right, she was a rudely outspoken woman of questionable orthodoxy. Conservative Catholic intellectuals such as William F. Buckley bristled at the mention of her name. She and New York's Cardinal Francis Spellman had, at best, a tenuous relationship.

The effort to sort out the paradoxes of a woman as many-sided as Dorothy Day continues to this day. In 2015, Pope Francis I, addressing the US Congress, named her as one of four morally exemplary Americans—along with Abraham Lincoln, Martin Luther King, Jr., and the Trappist monk and contemplative Thomas Merton—whose lives and ethical struggles offer a different way of seeing the world. Yet those who advocate her beatification and canonization, a process commenced several years after her death, have their work cut out for them. Her admirers and her enemies, Catholic and otherwise, have their own view of her, and there is enough in the record of her dramatic life to alienate anyone.

In the end, no category of common experience will neatly and precisely define this woman. She was dismayed by the Supreme Court's ruling in *Roe v. Wade*, but was never willing to condemn those women as beyond redemption who had committed that grievous sin and would have been distressed by Cardinal John O'Connor's attempts to enlist her as a posthumous leader, a "poster child," of the prolife movement. She believed in helping women find their own voice, yet had scant regard for the second wave of feminism in the 1970s. (Rather like Edith Wharton, who never saw the point of the suffrage movement, or Georgia O'Keeffe, who belittled the idea of exhibitions of "women artists," Day was of a generation who believed that strong women simply found their own way.) Her support for unionization waned as she came to believe that labor leaders were committed to securing for their members higher wages and better working conditions, but not to any larger social and spiritual change. The counterculture of the 1960s was a largely distasteful phenomenon to her, but no one was more anti-establishment than Dorothy Day. She abhorred the values of the business world, entirely committed to competition and profit, but was equally critical of Lyndon Johnson's War on Poverty and any other solution to a social ill that involved the federal government's bureaucracy and big-spending practices, leaving citizens to feel freed from their own obligations to those in need.

Dorothy Day asked hard questions—questions that are applicable to nonbelievers, but perhaps even more to those who profess some sort of faith or are seeking a resolution of their doubts. Her every statement, her every protest in the street, her lifelong rejection of comfort and respectability, ask: What kind of world do we really want to live in, and what sacrifices are we willing to make to achieve it? Do we believe that our primary concerns should be our physical ease, our family's and nation's well-being, our happiness as individuals? Can a sense of the mystical thrive in a culture that has made sacred causes of the rights of the individual, material progress, and technology? Is a flight from suffering and struggle actually a flight from God and an escape from the fulfillment of our deepest humanity? Day's life suggests answers to those complex queries, though her answers offer little to please the skeptical, the covetous, and the complacent.

⚶ ARRESTED: AGAIN ⚶

I T WOULD BE HER LAST STAY IN JAIL.

On July 30, 1973, Dorothy had flown to San Francisco from her home base at the Catholic Worker headquarters in New York City. Accompanied by her friend and colleague Eileen Egan, she was heading west to attend the fiftieth anniversary celebration of the War Resisters League. She had also been invited by the folk singer and political activist Joan Baez to make an appearance at her Institute for the Study of Nonviolence with some members of the United Farm Workers of America. When she arrived in California, however, her plans changed significantly.

Striking farmworkers in the nearby San Joaquin Valley had responded to the call of their charismatic and controversial leader Cesar Chavez to defy an injunction against mass picketing. Workers from the vineyards and the lettuce fields were being arrested in large numbers. In the farms around Fresno, 450 strikers had been taken into custody; in Tulare County, 100; and in Kern County, more than 500. Jails were filled to capacity, scuffles were taking place at every site, and the threat of serious violence was growing as one large vineyard owner promised to arm his guards with shotguns to see that the scabs he had hired were able to bring in the harvest. Most outrageous to the strikers was the court order that prohibited the use of bullhorns for more than one hour a day. How were they to appeal to the scabs to consider the strikers' plight, how were they to inform the public of the conditions they labored under, if they had to remain silent as they marched? Even the local police didn't want to enforce this ruling, leading the owners to call for the presence of the National Guard.

Hearing about the extent of the strike and the court orders, Dorothy determined that she would join the workers in their demonstration. "It appeared that I would spend my weeks in California in jail, not at conferences," she commented dryly in her diary. Her decision would provide yet more ammunition for critics who had long since branded Dorothy Day a Communist, a disloyal American, and an affront to her gender and her Church.

It was appropriate that this last arrest of a woman who had been taken into custody by police more than a few times should occur as a result of a labor dispute. Dorothy had been involved in the cause of the unfair treatment of American workers from the 1920s until well after World War II. But in the 1950s and 1960s, her interest in the labor struggle waned. Her pacifist stance and concern over disarmament had led to a shift in focus. Protesting the nuclear arms race, the Korean War, and the United States' involvement in Vietnam had claimed time and energy alongside her continued leadership of the Catholic Worker movement.

Dorothy had also been disappointed, she freely admitted, by the response of those unions which had made headway for their members; they seemed more interested in the immediate benefits of higher salaries and a shorter workweek than in making systemic changes to the social order. She had been vitally interested in Cesar Chavez and his movement, though, because of his affirmation of nonviolence and fervent religious convictions. He had visited her in New York in 1967, and two years later she had made a visit to his home in Delano, California. Though Dorothy had been writing about farm labor since the 1930s, she had long worried that the right kind of leader had not emerged. In Chavez, she thought that the movement finally had an individual to believe in, a fighter capable of effecting real change.

Dorothy was seventy-five that summer of 1973, and every one of those years was etched on her face. For decades, she had endured hard work, insufficient sleep, indifferent food, a brutal travel schedule, and occasional stints behind bars, and all of these had taken their toll. Her car had been fired on by segregationists in Georgia, and she had been excoriated by mobs at antiwar rallies and draft card–burning events. Although she stood as tall and erect as ever, she was beginning to tire physically and in the early 1970s had been diagnosed with advancing arthritis and the early stages of congestive heart failure.

Nonetheless, hours after her arrival, Dorothy rose at 2:00 a.m. and spent the day in several vineyards, pleading with the police to lay down their weapons and assist the workers. She took her folding chair-cane with her and often rested on it. In fact, one of the most famous pictures ever taken of her was shot that morning by Bob Fitch, a longtime chronicler of the peace and social justice movements. The photo shows her sitting calmly in her chair-cane while confronted by burly armed police officers. She told them she planned to return the next day and read the Sermon on the Mount to them.

That reading did not take place because the next morning Dorothy and her fellow picketers were ordered by the police to disperse. When they refused, they were herded onto buses and driven to an "industrial farm," as the authorities preferred to call it, rather than a jail or prison—although, as Dorothy observed, the difference was slight: "We are under lock and key and our barracks surrounded by barbed wire."

Her thoughts then might have drifted back fifty-seven years to the conditions of her first arrest as a twenty-year-old suffragette outside the White House, the physical abuse and her hunger strike at the infamous Occoquan workhouse, her family's indignation that she should have disgraced herself in public. Or to her second arrest in 1922, in a raid on a rooming house belonging to the anarchist organization International Workers of the World (IWW), and her humiliating treatment at the hands of the Chicago police. Both experiences had been infinitely worse.

Indeed, in comparison, the next two weeks seemed to her, despite her age, more like a retreat than a prison stay. She was surrounded by almost a hundred women, thirty of them nuns, in the two barracks reserved for them. Mass was held every evening, prayer vigils and voluntary fasting were constant, and some of the "inmates" taught small workshops and seminars on various social issues of interest to the other women. Dorothy herself taught one on the history of labor relations in the United States. Pentagon Papers defendant Daniel Ellsberg and Joan Baez visited, with Baez stopping the line in the dining room when she sang a prison song that "tore at your heart," Dorothy wrote.

Dorothy also took time to write an open letter to the Catholic bishops of California, reproving them for not visiting the prisoners. "Visiting the prisoner is a corporal work of mercy commanded by Jesus in Matthew 25 as of vital importance," she reminded them. "'Inasmuch as you did not visit the prisoners, you did not visit me.' Surely the farmworkers—Filipino, Mexican, Arab, Chinese—are 'the least of these, His brethren.'" Recognizing that the Church feared losing the financial support of the growers, she noted, "How wonderful it would be for you to embrace holy poverty by having wealth taken from you . . . forgive me for being presumptuous, but Christ's words are clear—'Sell what you have and give to the poor.'"

It had become a trademark of Dorothy Day as she aged to admonish those in power who should have known better. While she maintained a fervent allegiance to the papacy and to Catholic doctrine (she was viewed as distressingly orthodox by her more liberal Catholic friends), over the years she had frequently been at odds with the Church hierarchy, those bishops she saw as too apt to place Church politics above what she insisted was its true mission—social justice and the service of the poor and dispossessed. At bottom, Dorothy never felt that the Catholic Church did enough in this area; indeed, she could be sharply critical of its leaders for what she saw as pandering to the wealthy and the powerful.

In the same letter, Dorothy remarked about the lack of suffering that she had experienced in this latest incarceration. There wasn't any need to talk about her as a martyr. Only the absence of any privacy, with five open toilets used for all the women, was a significant problem, she noted, and she complimented her fellow prisoners, women who were "warm and loving, pure and clean of life and speech . . . women of great dignity." On the last night of her stay, several of the Mexican girls sang and taught the nuns some Mexican dances, which reminded Dorothy of one of her favorite saints, Teresa of Ávila, who had been known to play her castanets during her convent's recreation period.

The next day, after a false start and much paperwork, the prisoners were finally released, loaded into vans, and taken to Fresno, "where, with a great crowd in the park in front of the courthouse, we celebrated Mass." Dorothy had one last altercation with the warden when she refused to give up her prison smock, which had been signed by many of the other inmates as a token of gratitude for her presence with them. To her, it was going to be a treasured memento. In the end, perhaps realizing that the smock was no longer usable, the warden allowed Dorothy to keep it. Or perhaps the warden was simply the latest in a long line of individuals who came to understand that Dorothy Day was going to have things her way.

ONE

❧ BEGINNING ❧

JOHN DAY WAS A DIFFICULT MAN. A SOUTHERNER OF MODEST MEANS, he had come North in his early twenties to make a living and find a wife, which he did, but his enthusiasm over the course of his married life was often directed less toward career advancement or family and more toward his race horses, professional sports, gambling, male bonding, the bottle, and nights on the town. And, on occasion, other women.

Sharp-tongued and opinionated, "Judge Day," as he liked being called in later years (for no other reason than his demeanor and tendency to pronouncements), was used to being deferred to. Born in Cleveland, Tennessee, in 1870, he grew up in a Scots-Irish family that claimed a distant kinship to Daniel Boone and Sam Houston; his father had served the Confederacy as a surgeon and been taken prisoner in the last weeks of the conflict. In the recollection of his eldest daughter, Dorothy, John Day was a man not given to self-doubt or displays of paternal affection, and he shared many of the biases of his place of birth, his time, and his class. He was "intemperate," in her generous words, about foreigners and African Americans. He had no use for religion. As a Republican, he had even less use for political radicalism.

It was a supreme irony that John Day lived to see three of his five children—two of them his girls, no less—become as critical of capitalist America, as politically radical, as it was possible to be in the United States in the early twentieth century. Della, his youngest daughter, was a longtime supporter of Margaret Sanger's birth control crusade and walked the picket line in Boston the day the Italian anarchists Nicola Sacco and Bartolomeo Vanzetti were executed. John, his youngest son and namesake, became a Communist in the 1930s. And Dorothy, his middle child, was to follow a path entirely beyond his grasp—one for which he felt nothing but amazement and a deep revulsion.

Grace Satterlee, his wife, came from a different background and had a very different temperament. Born in 1870 in upstate New York, she was the youngest of six and was put to work in a Poughkeepsie shirt factory at the age of nine when her father died, never having fully recovered from wounds incurred fighting for the Union in the Civil War. Like John Day's father, he had been captured by the enemy and spent time in a prisoner of war camp. When a government pension belatedly came through, Grace was able to return to school.

Family finances didn't allow for any misplaced notions of gentility for this young woman in want of a career, and it was while attending a branch of the Eastman Business School in New York City that Grace met John Day. About their courtship, we know very little. Grace must have been impressed with her suitor's self-assurance, southern drawl, and sandy-haired good looks. Eight months after they were married on September 19, 1894, in an Episcopal church on Perry Street in Greenwich Village, their first child was born. Though the groom had been raised a Congregationalist and the bride an Episcopalian, neither was more than nominally religious, and their wedding day was the last occasion for some time that either set foot in a house of worship. None of their children was baptized.

The first three of those children came in rapid succession: Donald in 1895, Sam Houston in 1896, and Dorothy in 1897, on November 8. Grace Delafield, known for most of her life as Della, was born in 1899, and the last child, John, Jr., was born in 1912 after a series of miscarriages.

The family was living at 71 Pineapple Street in Brooklyn Heights when Dorothy was born, suggesting a level of gentility that Day's income as a sportswriter for the *New York Morning Telegraph* could not support for long, and they moved a year or two later to Bath Beach, a neighborhood at the other end of the borough near today's Coney Island. A good deal less expensive, Bath Beach had the additional advantage of being closer to the Gravesend Race Track, John Day's second home. Dorothy would remember frolicsome hours on the beach with her brothers when she wasn't in school, fishing for eels in a nearby creek, running through open fields, hiding with a cousin in an abandoned shack by Fort Hamilton. More vivid still were the memories that followed the family's move from the East Coast to the West Coast when her father decided to leave his job in New York, for reasons unknown, to try his luck with a San Francisco newspaper. John went on ahead to begin work and find a house; in the interim, which was longer than expected, Grace was forced to take in boarders in the Bath Beach house to make ends meet.

Finally, they were there, reunited, renting furnished lodgings in Berkeley while they waited for their own furniture to arrive by ship, living in a house with a garden filled with roses, violets, and calla lilies. The girls would fashion dolls out of the lilies, crushing flowers into a bottle of water to make perfume for themselves and their babies. "Even now," Dorothy wrote in adulthood thirty years later, "I can remember the peculiar, delicious, pungent smell" of those flowers. The move to a permanent home in Oakland, or what was supposed to be their permanent home, brought the Days into an even more bucolic setting, "near open fields and woods, where the windows looked out to the hills" and where periodic forest fires cast a delicate haze over the landscape.

For an eight-year-old with two only slightly older brothers who were a rough-and-tumble pair themselves and not averse (at that stage) to letting their sister tag along, unburdened by parents who gave much thought to their oldest daughter's pronounced lack of daintiness, freedom from convention was a source of great joy. Her closest friend in Oakland, Naomi Reed, was told by her mother to stop playing with Dorothy after hearing the language she used in an altercation with Donald over ownership of the family's guinea pigs. ("I threw things besides," Dorothy added about that incident.) The Reeds were strict Methodists and felt that their daughter's friendship with a tomboy whose parents failed to respect the Sabbath had gone far enough. Dorothy had been joining the Reeds for church on Sunday for a while, enjoying the hymns and Naomi's company, but when that came to an abrupt end, she took comfort in being adopted by the "tough gang" of the neighborhood, adolescent boys who stayed out after dark, didn't listen to their parents, and did their best to sneak into Idora Park, avoiding the ten-cent admission, to watch the Ferris wheel or cadge a ride on the mountain slide or the circle swing.

In *The Eleventh Virgin*, a somewhat autobiographical novel Dorothy would publish in 1924, she wrote about her protagonist, June, a girl at just the same age, playing in the late-summer weeds in the lots near her house, weeds "so high that June could tunnel her way through them, making large green-roofed caves here and there. One of the boys let her share his cave with him, and some afternoons when the others weren't around, he took her in his arms and kissed her, pressing himself up against her. He was one of the big boys, fourteen." Though flattered by the attention, "there was wickedness in it," she allowed. At the same time, she felt, "it was exciting."

To a child like Dorothy, life in California seemed good, or good enough to hope it would last forever. Her mother found it hard to make friends in their new home, but that wasn't something any of her children was aware of. Grace was adept at putting others' needs first and at masking her own disappointments. John was out most of the day—given his flares of temper, something everyone in the bungalow counted as a blessing. When he wasn't in San Francisco at the paper, he was at the Oakland Trotting Park or the stable where he kept a race horse. Money was flush, and he envisioned owning a string of horses. That hope ended, however, in the early morning hours of April 18, 1906.

The night before, John Day had noticed that the horses in the stable seemed unusually restless, neighing and stamping in their stalls. He thought no more about it. At 5:12 the next morning, the rumbling started and the family was awakened, Dorothy wrote, as "the earth became a sea," rocking their house tumultuously for what was less than a minute but seemed an eternity. The windmill and water tank at the back of the house started to totter, throwing water across the roof. The panicked children were hustled out of their beds and into the front yard. By the time the quake ended, the house was standing but scarcely habitable. Cracks ran from the floor to the ceiling, the chandeliers had been smashed, every glass and dish broken, the chimney toppled.

The flames visible from across the bay indicated that, bad as the damage was there, Oakland had been spared the worst of the disaster, and throughout the next few days residents greeted thousands of families from the city pouring over on the ferry and in private boats. Idora Park and the racetrack were now turned into campgrounds filled with cots, and anyone with a solid roof overhead invited strangers in to stay. Grace joined her neighbors, from morning until nightfall, cooking for the displaced San Franciscans at the refuge sites, and the family went back into the house when it seemed safe to gather up what clothes and blankets they could to give to those who had nothing.

The tragedy became personal to the Days as well when they learned that the plant in San Francisco that printed John Day's newspaper had been leveled. He was out of work. A few months before Dorothy turned nine, the family packed everything they could salvage and prepared to relocate once again. After barely three years, their California venture was over.

The move from Oakland to Chicago was a "great upheaval" for the Day family, as Dorothy remembered it, especially for the four children. There were no more vacant lots with tall weeds to play in, no more brooks to wade across, no lily-filled gardens or wide lawns or beautiful hills in the distance. Instead, there were buildings upon buildings, pavements, automobile and truck traffic, railroad tracks, soot on the windowsills—all part of urban living on a tight budget in a neighborhood that had seen better days.

John Day had sold his bungalow and horse at a loss and moved his family halfway across the country because, probably rightly, he saw no future for himself in the devastated Bay Area, but neither had he lined up a job before relocating. With more than a dozen newspapers in the United States' second largest city, he was confident he could quickly find a position, an optimism that turned out to be misplaced. Suddenly money was even tighter than it had been. The first of the Days' four moves in the city, after a brief stay in a hotel, was to a tenement apartment on the South Side above a saloon, where loud conversation came in waves at night with the smell of beer and whiskey in the air. With no girl brought in to help with the chores, as there had been in California, Dorothy and Della were pressed into service.

Genteel poverty brought out not just Grace Day's fortitude but her quirks. It was she, not her husband, who had been sent out to find the apartment; she who was left to ask the landlord's patience when the rent was overdue or the bill at the grocer's reached an embarrassing figure; she who was called upon to put a good face on a difficult situation, making a bookcase out of orange crates, hanging curtains over fishing rods, and scrubbing every surface until cleanliness took the place of refinement. Yet after a day of making beds and sweeping and shopping and doing the laundry in the building's basement, Grace would bathe and dress formally for dinner each night, whether her husband was home or not. "She reigned over the supper table as a queen," Dorothy recalled, "powdered, perfumed, daintily clothed, all for the benefit of us children." Her daughters loved to watch and assist in these early evening preparations, adding a drop of cologne to their mother's bathwater (proper bath salts being beyond the family budget), laying out her towels and kimono, combing her hair, insisting that the boys be quiet while Mother enjoyed her fifteen-minute nap before setting the table.

Grace also devoted herself to keeping from her children the mistake her marriage had been. Whatever their older brothers perceived, it wasn't until they were adults that the girls came to realize just how unsatisfying a union Grace Day had endured. Men who expected their wives to bear as many children as Nature allowed while they had no intention of helping with the child rearing, who expected their moods at the breakfast table to be tolerated no matter the pressures their wives were under to feed six mouths, who took a night at a downtown tavern or brothel to be their right: John Day was not necessarily atypical for a husband and father of his time, but his belief that his responsibility as a breadwinner was all that was required of him was unshakable. He could also be delusional and cocksure. Before he found a job, he devoted months to writing an adventure novel that was supposed to make the family fortune but, of course, was never published, if it was even completed.

Later, Dorothy would sympathize with Grace's need for a ginger ale in the afternoon livened up with a bit of "oh-be-joyful," as she liked to call it, the shot of whiskey that she sometimes added even to her elder daughter's soda, which led to a companionable feeling and her mother's desire to reminisce warmly about her grandfather and his whaling ship, her childhood in Poughkeepsie, and her life before she had met John Day. There were times, though, when even Grace reached a breaking point. *The Eleventh Virgin* tells of an incident that feels more a memory than an invented scene, when the protagonist's long-suffering mother, overcome at the state of her life, suddenly picks up every plate in the house and smashes them one by one on the kitchen floor. It was a terrifying spectacle, the manic rage and disorientation of such a normally stoical woman, and in the story the oldest son hustles his sisters out of the room while their father, equally unnerved, tries to calm his wife and later runs out for ice cream, "pathetic in his efforts" to comfort his crying daughters.

Eventually, John's fortunes improved, and he landed a job on the staff of the *Inter-Ocean*, a high-circulation daily and one of the most staunchly Republican papers in the nation. One of the strongest advocates for going to war against Spain, it was also one of the most insistent voices in journalism warning of the threat to the United States of anarchism and socialism. As one of its sportswriters, Dorothy's father was in his element: at the track reporting on the races (always his favorite assignment), at the ballpark covering the White Sox and the Cubs, at boxing matches and college football games. The job paid well, and finally the family was able to afford a home commensurate with their needs, John's aspirations, and Grace's sense of propriety.

On Webster Avenue, near Lincoln Park, the Days moved into a stately brick rowhouse with enough bedrooms to allow siblings some privacy, fireplaces in their parents' bedroom and the library, a large kitchen, plenty of comfortable furniture. Finally the children could have a dog. John could have his horses. The other boys and girls Dorothy and Della met in their new neighborhood seemed boringly well mannered after the raucous immigrant children they had known in the less genteel parts of town they'd come from, adventurous friends they could go wandering, scavenging, or swimming with when they had been expressly told not to. Her brothers seemed to have an easier time of it finding their element anywhere (Sam was of an especially pugilistic nature), and they naturally wanted less to do with their sisters as they aged. For the girls, it was different. Comfort and security came at a price.

At different times in childhood and adolescence, natural questions arose. Grace's many pregnancies was the subject of one. Learning where babies came from was something Dorothy and Della picked up from their brothers and boys in the neighborhood; that there might be any choice involved in the matter—that possibility didn't even arise as a question, though it certainly accounts for the girls', especially Della's, later intense interest in the controversial topic of family planning. Exactly how many times Grace was pregnant after the birth of her fourth child isn't clear, but it appears to have been more than a few, all but one of the pregnancies ending in a miscarriage, and the fact of John's birth thirteen years after Della's, when Grace was forty-two, indicates that contraception was unknown in the Day bedroom. The confusing part of the matter, at least in Dorothy's mind, was that John Day didn't seem to take any particular interest in his many children when they were young. He preferred to have his meals alone with his wife when that was possible, Sunday dinner being the one exception. Hating noise and clutter, he began to pay attention to the children only when they were old enough to take part in adult conversation and to hear his opinions about world affairs. And weren't four children enough, anyway? Dorothy's efforts to get some conversation out of her mother on the subject appear to have gone nowhere.

A topic about which Grace was less reticent—though her responses were no less unsatisfying to her daughter—was religion. Other families went to church, belonged to things called "denominations," said a prayer before meals. Not so at the Days'. When an Episcopal minister had visited them early in their time in Chicago, having heard from someone that they were a Protestant family new to the neighborhood, he had invited them to join his congregation, but John Day had let him know that wasn't going to happen. He wasn't necessarily telling the world he was an atheist (though he would rather proudly claim that by the time he was in his sixties), but he had no interest in setting foot in a church or having his children baptized. Nor did Grace, who was reading avidly about Christian Science as a potential cure for the headaches she was enduring so chronically of late.

Donald, Sam, and Della weren't especially troubled by the family stance on things spiritual, no more than John, Jr., was later, but Dorothy found it less easy to take her mother's nonchalance as a final word on the topic. She could clearly recall saying the Lord's Prayer in her first-grade class at Bath Beach, though that practice had no more meaning for her out of any context than many other school rituals. More vivid was her memory of coming upon a Bible, the first she had ever seen, left behind by a previous tenant in the attic of the furnished house in Berkeley they'd rented. She would recall it as a meaningful moment, the "dim attic" and the "rich, deep feeling" of holding the thick, mysterious leather-bound book in her hands at the age of eight made a strong impression—though of what exactly, she couldn't say. Observing the piety of the Reeds in Oakland, the family of her friend Naomi, Dorothy wondered if their harmony was in any way connected to their churchgoing. Mrs. Reed's warnings that the Days were not among the saved didn't rankle. None of what the lady said quite made sense. Knowing that her parents and siblings didn't want to hear about Methodism or salvation, Dorothy concluded, "I did not want to be saved alone, anyway."

In Chicago, in the working-class neighborhoods they had first called home, she met her first devout Catholics. Walking one morning into the railroad flat of a friend, Kathryn Barrett, she didn't know that all of the six children were out and she made her way to the back bedroom, where she came upon Mrs. Barrett, fresh from her chores, on her knees praying—not a posture she had ever observed her own mother in. Turning to tell the girl that her playmates weren't there, Mrs. Barrett then resumed her prayers quietly and fervently. For the moment, the sad state of this family's apartment, the blight of their poverty, had fallen away; Mrs. Barrett was clearly elsewhere, uplifted.

Another family on the block, the Harringtons, had nine children. Twelve-year-old Mary, older than Dorothy, was a close friend who talked to her, as they stretched out on the back porch after dinner, about the saints and sainthood, a concept that Dorothy had never been introduced to. It would be interesting to know how a girl Mary's age explained the idea and what saints' stories she told, but we can assume she had a gift for explanation and drama.

Dorothy felt a "lofty enthusiasm" for the "high endeavor" of suffering for a holy cause, believing in something that mattered more than one's own life, being one of a sacred elect. It was then that she went through what she described in *The Eleventh Virgin* as her protagonist's youthful "morbid" phase, telling her sister the more gruesome and glorious stories of martyrdoms that she had read about and convincing her bedmate to sleep with her on the bare floor of their bedroom in emulation of the saints who slept on the stone floors of prison cells and lived on bread and water. It was a phase—quoting snippets of the Bible to her uninterested parents and siblings, eventually derided by her sister for hectoring and posing (for Della's patience had its limits)—that Dorothy abandoned readily enough.

When she was twelve, however, she had a kind of victory: the Days allowed Dorothy to be baptized as an Episcopalian. Her mother had given in to the urging of the minister at the Church of our Savior on Fullerton Avenue, Dorothy's ally, while her father grudgingly agreed, if only out of concern that worse yet might happen—namely, that his most eccentric child would eventually be lured to the embrace of Rome by her Catholic friends. That thought was intolerable. "Only Irish washerwomen and policemen are Roman Catholic," he informed his daughter.

Dorothy went contentedly for weekly instruction, especially as one of her brother's many girlfriends was doing the same. The girlfriend turned out to be something less than a spiritual partner. She had a "precocious interest in sex," Dorothy said, combined with a Uriah Heep–like cleverness at misleading unsuspecting parents. Nonetheless, Dorothy studied her prayer book, was baptized and confirmed on the same day (describing her first trip to the Communion rail before the entire congregation as "an agony"), and began attending Sunday services, where the music, more than anything, stirred her. "I had never heard anything so beautiful as the *Benedicite* and the *Te Deum*," she later wrote. For a year she was a diligent churchgoer until the thrill of the Episcopal service wore off. Her parents were relieved.

The next two years were occupied with school and friends, caring more frequently for the new baby she adored as Grace's headaches worsened, and acknowledging her own growing awareness of the power of desire. The summer John was born, a handsome musician down the street became the focus of an erotic obsession. Dorothy dragged Della to every concert his band gave in the park, even when it was drizzling and they had to spread paper on the seats, and wheeled the baby carriage past his house at every opportunity. She fantasized about the man's wife running off with a lover, leaving him desolate and available. When she heard his violin through the open window, she convinced herself that the achingly beautiful notes were intended for her. Passing him on the street, she felt sure he knew what was going on inside her. "We never exchanged a word, but I hungered for his look!" she would write in *The Long Loneliness*, her most telling memoir.

Though Dorothy was clearly the student of the family, her public-school education doesn't seem to have held any special allure for her. In all of her writings or references to her school years, only a single teacher merits mention. Mr. Matheson at the Robert Waller High School taught Latin—a great deal more interesting to her than math, science, history, or English composition—and was sufficiently enthusiastic about how ably a small group of his students had translated *The Aeneid* that he met with them separately to read Virgil's *Eclogues* and *Georgics* and to give them lessons in Greek after school. That group included Dorothy. Her mastery of Latin would be a source of pride all her life.

If school didn't matter to Dorothy to any significant degree, pleasure reading did. The Days were a family of readers, and none so avid as Dorothy. The library at home on Webster Avenue, with its good light, fireplace, snug sofa, and ever-present bowl of apples on the center table, was a refuge. Indeed, Dorothy chose later in life to characterize the evolution of her adolescence as much by what she read as what she did. Three writers she came to on her own struck a particular chord.

Upton Sinclair had created a nationwide sensation in 1906 with *The Jungle*, in part a novel about the lives of recent immigrants living in urban poverty and in part an exposé of the horrors of the meatpacking industry. It told a long and gripping story about a Lithuanian family struggling to survive when "the lash of want," the corruption of the system, the filth and hazards of their work environment, and the exploitation of unscrupulous landlords and predatory bosses make it all but impossible. Two of the principal women, including the protagonist's wife, are eventually forced into prostitution, one at the insistence of a rapacious factory boss and the other to earn food for her family. Children comb through garbage dumps for scraps of food; a boy stupefied by liquor is killed by rats. A worker falls into a meat tank and is ground up with animal parts to be sold as part of the product. The need for the solace of alcohol and drugs in Packingtown is constant.

Dorothy was reading the novel in the right setting: Chicago itself, the meatpacking capital of the country. Some scenes are placed amid neighborhoods not so very far removed from the Days'. Dorothy took to pushing baby John in his carriage, with Della at her side, walking for miles along those "interminable gray streets, fascinating in their dreary sameness, past tavern after tavern," where she could imagine episodes from the book like the manic wedding party that opens the novel and the family's doomed efforts to find an affordable home. Yet it was also, she wrote, an area of pungent smells, "the one beauty in those drab streets . . . the odor of geranium leaves, tomato plants, marigolds; the smell of lumber, tar, of roasting coffee." A lifelong effort not to be entirely undone in the face of squalor had already started.

The success of *The Jungle* conferred a kind of immediate respectability on Upton Sinclair; everyone, after all, no matter his or her politics or party affiliation, cared about the condition of what was served to the family at dinnertime. The Federal Meat Inspection Act and the Pure Food and Drug Act were the result, in part, of Sinclair's muckraking exposé. Even President Theodore Roosevelt, who looked with a jaundiced eye upon the author and his influences—Émile Zola, Maxim Gorky, the later Leo Tolstoy—had to agree to investigate the stockyard conditions Sinclair described and grudgingly invited him to the White House. Prior to 1906, though, Upton Sinclair was a highly questionable figure in middle-class households, and certainly no one John Day wanted to see his teenage daughter reading. Sinclair was a friend of the social worker Jane Addams, the founder of Hull House in Chicago, and in New York City had organized a socialist society with the novelist Jack London as its first president.

Part of Sinclair's appeal for Dorothy was that, above and beyond the transfixing drama of *The Jungle*, he was exactly the kind of influence her father deplored. The family of the fictional Jurgis Rudkus were the very people he insisted had no business befouling his America, a view shared by her oldest brother, who was becoming as narrow in his opinions about immigrants and other races as their father. Even more pointedly, the novel took a swipe at John Day's bread and butter: racetracks are places of corruption, one character insists to Jurgis, no different from any other big business. The onetime sport of gentlemen had become a crass moneymaking enterprise, and the "doping" and doctoring of horses and the corruption of the jockeys were open secrets. Only a fool thought otherwise.

Upton Sinclair naturally led Dorothy to Jack London. She read his adventure novels, which were passed on to her brothers, as well as his essays and political diatribes in fiction, which would have been of less interest to Donald and Sam. She was especially taken with the semi-autobiographical *Martin Eden*, about the awakening of a young indigent sailor to the fact that his life need not be the one assigned to him at birth, despite the hold that class distinctions and class consciousness exert over modern America. London's protagonist is also a character of phenomenal grit. His family can doubt him all they want; he will find his own way.

Both Sinclair and London had the effect on their young reader of prompting a closer observation of her surroundings. An indefatigable walker by the time she was in her early teens, Dorothy began to take note not only of how differently people lived in Chicago but also how many of those differences were based on factors that might not be under their control and how hopeless the lot of some people seemed. Her father's newspaper insisted that the leadership and values of the Roosevelt and William Howard Taft years represented the best of all possible worlds, but in a city with a population of over two million, the contrasts were stark and painted a different picture: the Romanesque Palmer mansion on the Gold Coast so blatantly in contrast to the overcrowded Polish and Irish slums, the debutante entertainments featured in the press coexisting with Chicago's five thousand prostitutes, so numerous the city couldn't decide whether to maintain its red-light district or give up and let them wander where they might.

A third writer took Dorothy down yet another path, one more psychological than sociological, and it is somewhat harder to know what he might have meant to her. Thomas De Quincey, the author of *Confessions of an English Opium-Eater* and some brilliant, idiosyncratic essays on *Macbeth*, John Milton, his obsession with William Wordsworth, his obsession with book buying, murder as a fine art, dreams, drug taking, childhood, and literary style, was not on any high school syllabus in 1913. (For that matter, unlike so many other classic British literary figures, De Quincey is not a writer well known to most educated Americans today. He was claimed as an important influence, though, by Nikolai Gogol, Edgar Allan Poe, Charles Dickens, Fyodor Dostoevsky, Robert Louis Stevenson, Oscar Wilde, Alfred Hitchcock, Vladimir Nabokov, and Jorge Luis Borges—a list that forms a telling picture in itself.)

If it is difficult to imagine what a girl her age made of Thomas De Quincey's confessional narratives, musings, and fevered reveries, there can be no doubt that Dorothy's interest was genuine—he was her favorite writer at the time, she asserted—and that she was not in the least bit intimidated by his circuitous prose, avalanche of allusions, drollness, or extreme life experiences. The living embodiment of William Blake's credo that "the road of excess leads to the palace of wisdom," De Quincey understood both defiance and ecstasy. He also believed that our lives could best be seen as a palimpsest; beneath the erasures and the overdrawing was our experience of childhood, the events, core questions, and sensations of which would always haunt us.

For any exceptionally smart adolescent, reading need not be systematic to be meaningful, even life-changing. Personal needs, helter-skelter curiosity, and even confusion are the usual, more useful driving forces. Certainly there was no apparent consistency or programmatic order to Dorothy's voracious reading at this period of her life. Sinclair and London obviously looked to man to solve the problems of poverty and injustice; God plays no role in their thinking. They looked to socialism to make the world right. De Quincey inhabited an imaginative universe of his own, an explorer without a compass other than opium and a faith in poetry and his own intellect. For that matter, Dorothy's new love among British poets that year, Algernon Charles Swinburne, was a devout sensualist.

Yet at the same time, her thoughts were drawn in another direction that had—or seems to have—nothing to do with these admired authors. She worried in a letter to a friend with whom she shared confidences about the "lust of the flesh," the intense "cravings" that tormented her, as one crush on an attractive boy from school followed another. She debated whether it was right for her and Della to spend Sundays at the movies, the only day their father would let them attend, finally deciding that there was no need to be strict about the Sabbath if one were honoring God during the rest of the week. She made her way through the Bible in determined stages during her last year of high school and dipped into St. Augustine. Maggie Tulliver, the rebellious heroine of *The Mill on the Floss*, attempts to find solace in Thomas à Kempis's *The Imitation of Christ*, and Dorothy was inspired to do the same after reading George Eliot's novel with great enthusiasm. Alone with her baby brother in the park, especially on a desolate winter day, "under the trees and looking over the wide expanse of lake," she felt, she told her friend, an apprehension of the divine—until she returned home and the old uncertainties took over. Her mother was relentless in urging her to pay more attention to the healing powers of Christian Science, and the Episcopal minister whose church she had attended for a while came by one day to talk all afternoon to her about his wish for her to return to the fold, a prospect that held no appeal.

In hindsight, it is possible to see more similarity than conflict in Dorothy's interest in the world view of an Upton Sinclair or a Thomas De Quincey, on the one hand, and a Mark, a Matthew, or a St. Augustine on the other. None was really acceptable to her family. None suggested well-trodden paths for a child of the American middle class. Her father thought Dorothy was becoming annoyingly peculiar, and her mother was unsure of what to make of her daughter's concerns and conversational tangents. But for an intellectually inclined girl of fifteen and sixteen, these writers offered unknown possibilities and touched on a growing discontent with the life she saw around her, the injustice no less than the smug contentment. She could write an essay for her senior English class on Prince Peter Kropotkin and the Russian revolutionists, suspecting that her choice of topic and her views would shock her prim composition teacher, even as she continued to question her mother about the family's indifference to religion. The resolution of those impulses, though, would be anything but easy or imminent.

TWO

❦ AWAKENINGS ❦

THE MANAGEMENT OF THE *CHICAGO EXAMINER*, ONE OF WILLIAM Randolph Hearst's many papers, was always on the lookout for ways to increase its readership and impress Chicagoans with its importance to the community. Among them was its recently inaugurated college scholarship competition for students who could not afford the cost of tuition. On the basis of a rigorous exam, twenty Cook County high school students were awarded three hundred dollars each to get them started on their road to higher education, while the scholarship committee decided which college or university the winners would attend. Correctly sensing that this might be her only opportunity to leave home and continue her studies, Dorothy took the exam. She scored an impressive fifteenth in a field of hundreds and was told a place would be held for her in the freshman class that fall at the University of Illinois in Urbana.

Dorothy's parents, or at least her father, felt considerable ambivalence about the news. Neither of Dorothy's older brothers had gone to college (or even finished high school). John Day didn't believe in the value of too much schooling, and the award was, in effect, a public declaration of the state of the family finances. (In need of a buyer, the *Inter-Ocean* had been declared insolvent that spring, and Day's job was in jeopardy.) For the scholarship winner, though, it was a triumphant moment. Her only hesitation was about leaving her mother, her fourteen-year-old sister, and her two-year-old brother.

In September, two months shy of her seventeenth birthday, Dorothy departed from Chicago's Grand Central Station for the three-hour train ride south to Urbana. The scholarship money covered the cost of her tuition and other fees, but she would have to earn her own money for room, board, and books. The stipend her parents could afford to send would be modest and intermittent, but that was not a cause for concern. She was "happy as a lark," she proclaimed, to be leaving home for the first time—"on my own and no longer cared for by the family." The idea of earning her own living and setting her own schedule was, she decided, perhaps more thrilling even than the prospect of a degree.

Vast armies positioned themselves across the length of Europe that month to begin an orgy of death and destruction, but it wasn't an event much on the minds of American college students, certainly not Dorothy's. When she arrived, she was one of four thousand young men and women attending a school founded in 1868 in a rustic town on the prairie that now represented for many midwesterners their best hope for a good education and a promising career. The university's president had notable aspirations for his institution, judged by Harvard's president, Abbott Lawrence Lowell, to be the best state school in the country. In the 1910s, President Edmund James committed his board of trustees to a library expansion to rival the great academic collections of Europe, founded the University of Illinois Press, and launched a school of education. He worked to bring good professors to Illinois and raise academic standards, and he encouraged religious diversity. Jews were welcomed at Urbana. More hidebound trustees thought him suspiciously "advanced."

At the same time, the University of Illinois represented a predictable mixture of the liberal and the conservative. An internationalist, James had opened his campus to foreign students in a way most US institutions of higher learning had not. A third of all Chinese students studying in the United States at the time attended the University of Illinois on scholarship. In a less progressive spirit, a significant proportion of the student body, respectful of religious convention, had opposed a local petition to keep area theaters open on Sunday and tended to side with the town's supporters of prohibition, at least in public. (Athletes and fraternity brothers, a riotous bunch, took a different view of the matter and acted accordingly.) African American students were still not permitted to board on campus, and the first African American sorority had been formed in 1913, in part to deal with that housing issue.

Fraternities and sororities, with their attendant features of rushing and (among the men) vigorous hazing, played a large role in university life, an aspect of campus culture in which Dorothy had no interest. It might be more accurate to say that sorority life, when she looked into it, engendered only mild disdain. A 1914 photograph of the school's Gamma Phi Beta sorority, founded the year before, shows twenty-odd young women in white dresses and dark sashes, supervised by two matrons, on the lawn in front of their house, some with hands entwined—not a gathering in which Dorothy would ever have found herself at home. The topics that occupied the student government's time (e.g., the appropriateness of dancing the tango at on-campus social events, students' rights to attend vaudeville shows downtown) seemed petty, and the 10:30 p.m. weekend curfew in the women's dormitory meant that that comfortable place of residence was crossed off her list right away.

Dorothy's first home in Urbana, then, was the local YWCA. Her room was spartan, but clean and affordable. She took a job working in the dining hall, setting and clearing tables for the one hundred fifty students who took their meals there. Exhausting as that was, her demotion after several weeks to dishwasher was even worse. Suddenly, an intense and unexpected homesickness set in. Her separation from John—"my child and my brother" was how she thought of him—was the source of particular anguish and brought on a prolonged period of insomnia, the first she had ever suffered in her life, and bouts of uncontrollable weeping. She tried to talk herself into managing her depression by throwing herself into her studies and the work she needed to pay her bills, but that proved to be easier said than done. Determined not to show her weakness to her family, she resisted the temptation to go back to Chicago on weekends.

Calculating that she might do better away from the YWCA, Dorothy moved on to a succession of private homes where wives and mothers needed assistance in the kitchen or the nursery in return for free room and board. Her first effort along those lines didn't last long. Finding out that the man of the house was a bootlegger wasn't a problem, but his "howling troop of children" and "obvious amorous intention" were, and she packed her bags rather quickly. She did better when she moved in with the family of a language professor, John Driscoll Fitz-Gerald, in nearby Champaign. He and his wife had only three children and wanted her to be available to help prepare and clean up after breakfast and dinner, which she took with them and Dr. Fitz-Gerald's elderly mother. They were a Methodist family whose company she found congenial, whose children were bearable, and whose conversation was stimulating. In *The Eleventh Virgin*, Dorothy wrote about her time with this couple, depicting the younger Mrs. Fitz-Gerald as a woman she could talk to about sex and the older Mrs. Fitz-Gerald as someone ready to chat about her faith and the joy the Methodist Church brought to her life.

Another employer, closer to the campus but considerably less well-off than the Fitz-Geralds, was an instructor with five children and an income that barely fed his family of seven. Dorothy's compensation, sans board, was a rent-free bedroom—a dismal space, without so much as a carpet, let alone a desk or a bookcase—and a small one-burner oil stove on which to cook her own meals. She tried to keep her food allowance to forty cents a day and was forced to study in the university library at night as the room was so cold and dark. She could barely stand to get out from under her single blanket in the morning when the wind whipped off the prairie and snow or sleet covered the windowpanes. Her job was to tend to the mountains of laundry that accumulated and had to be scrubbed by hand and ironed every weekend, leaving her hands chafed red by the scalding-hot water—was it possible that babies and toddlers could go through so many clothes in one week?—and her back aching from leaning over an ironing board all Saturday afternoon.

It seems unlikely that that was what Dorothy or her parents had pictured when she learned she had won a scholarship and would be the first in her family to attend college. Yet her living arrangements and the obstacles they presented during her freshman year point to something else, something close to an emerging ascetic streak. A striking aspect of Dorothy's personality, even in adolescence, was the obstinate pride she took in the fact that she could endure so much and get by on so little. Her situation prevented her from making friends, getting to know her professors better, or becoming an integrated member of her new community. When President James gave one of his periodic speeches to the student body about the kind of young person a great university should attract and hope to mold, he wasn't thinking about a woman who could probably have found a job in the school library or an office but instead held back and looked only for work that would try the resilience of any normal person.

Another problem was that, almost from the moment she settled into her studies, the classes themselves were a disappointment for Dorothy. Neither the teachers nor the material proved stimulating, not even Latin, and she cut a fair number of lectures, leaving her homework to the last minute, when it was completed at all. She took a class in ornithology, not because she was especially interested in birds or found the textbook compelling but because it involved field trips into the woods outside of town two days a week and a boy she liked was in the class. But if freedom from direction or supervision was intoxicating, it was also dangerous, and the result was hardly surprising. Her two-year transcript is a record of B's and C's, with a F in biology. Like generations of intelligent young people before and after her, Dorothy found herself in college becoming each month less a diligent student and more an autodidact following her own random—though in her case fruitful—path.

In *Well-Read Lives: How Books Inspired a Generation of Women*, the literary historian Barbara Sicherman has argued that books had a special import for inquisitive young women born in the latter part of the nineteenth century. They were the means by which girls began to feel that they might be different from their mothers, might have a role to play in public life, might grapple with the big questions most men considered their exclusive province. Books were pathways into a larger, not always clearly defined world, a world traditionally closed to them. Certain books, certain writers, "stirred imaginations and fostered female ambition." Sicherman's examples of women so influenced include Bryn Mawr college president M. Carey Thomas, Hull House founder Jane Addams, and the African American journalist Ida B. Wells.

Though born well after those women, Dorothy Day is assuredly one of that number. The reading she had engaged in at home included the literature her parents approved of—Jane Austen, Walter Scott, Dickens, Poe, Stevenson, James Fenimore Cooper—and the "trash," as her father called it and would have discarded had he found it, the dime novels that her brothers sneaked into the house and the romance novels she borrowed from girlfriends. Away from home, under no one's guidance, reading became even more central to her life, consumed more hours, and became more wideranging: economics, labor history, political biography, American poetry, the novels of Joseph Conrad. And the Russians.

Russian literature was the true revelation. It had an impact that never waned, and the Russian novelists and playwrights she discovered during her two years in Urbana would be Dorothy's foundational authors for the rest of her life. Gorky dramatized the brutal cost of poverty and the complacency of those with the power to do something about it as effectively as any

American writer had. Ivan Turgenev understood the inevitable differences between generations and the poignancy of unrequited love. Tolstoy asked startling questions for his time: How much agency do individuals really have in trying to influence the course of history? What choices are viable when marriage and passion are in conflict? Can a sinful, selfish past ever truly be atoned for in this world? What does it mean to be prepared for death? Anton Chekhov felt and could evoke in his readers empathy for every individual he wrote about, regardless of class or temperament: aristocrats blind to the demise of their time of privilege, peasants become plutocrats, angry students, manipulative mothers, lovesick young women, landed gentry wallowing in self-pity and ennui. It was Dostoevsky, though, who made the greatest impression on the highly impressionable seventeen-year-old. She had read some of his short stories in high school, but the novels were an altogether different matter.

For a person curious about religion and what it meant to live an authentic life of faith—a curiosity matched only by an equivalent resistance to pressing that search too hard—the author of *Crime and Punishment*, *The Brothers Karamazov*, and *The Idiot* was an inevitably powerful encounter. (Dorothy's timing was right, too. Constance Garnett's translations of Dostoevsky had started appearing in the United States only two years earlier.) Sonia Marmeladov is a Mary Magdalen for the modern age, an affront to a society unrelenting in its persecution of prostitutes. The religious devotion of Alyosha Karamazov is generous, pain-filled, sustaining, unnerving, radiant in ways confusing and alienating to more worldly people. His search for "the deep flame of inner ecstasy" is everything to him. Prince Myshkin, the "idiot," is the "holy fool," a figure modern America truly had no use for.

Sonia, Alyosha, and Myshkin: imaginary but also somehow real, all followers of Christ—but how little they had in common with the well-meaning, self-satisfied Episcopalians and Methodists she knew, people for whom, in her view, religion was largely a hymn-singing, tithe-paying Sunday-morning affair. Not surprisingly, these enigmatic characters lodged in the memory of a sympathetic reader. Their trials and explorations proved worth returning to over the years, such astonishingly original individuals whose attachment to Christ's message put them at odds with every social norm, conventional belief, and bourgeois ideal that Dorothy had herself been questioning for some time. They also offered a counterbalance worth pondering to the questions raised in their different forms by the unbelievers in Dostoevsky's stories—Rodion Raskolnikov, Arkady Svidrigailov, Ivan Karamazov—about the basis of morality and the natural right to egoism, as well as Friedrich Nietzsche's call for a virility that seemed to mock the humble and the compassionate.

Yet the problem with religion, for Dorothy—what precluded for the moment an embrace of any type of faith—was just what it would be for many young people of her era, and still is today, in an even more secular age. It seemed to take one away from the exhilaration and the urgent political needs of the world as we know it, to focus on a speculative, rule-bound, otherworldly concern. "I felt so intensely alive," she noted of her college years, "that the importance of the here and now absorbed me."

Equally frustrating, she did not see around her many churchgoers interested in alleviating human suffering on a large scale, committing themselves to the struggle of a Eugene Debs or a Mother Jones. If anything, organized religion appeared to be an enemy of radicalism and change, a protector of the powerful and the well fed. Jack London had hammered that point home in *The Iron Heel* when his protagonist confronted a sympathetic clergyman to say that, if the Church insisted it did not condone capitalist abuses against the poor, it certainly did nothing to stop them. In the spirit of London, Dorothy felt the justice of the accusation and was not prepared to overlook it. "Even as I talked about religion," she wrote in her memoirs, "I rejected religion."

Long before she left the university, politics had entirely displaced religion as her great preoccupation. She even went out of her way to alienate some of the more religious students with whom she came into contact. She took up smoking, an activity banned within a hundred feet of the campus line and especially rare among the female population, and became adept at cursing, effecting a cavalier and frequently belligerent attitude toward the decorum of the Gamma Phi Beta crowd. She listened to a professor in class one day refer to religion as something that should be respected for the comfort it had historically provided people in need, though his real point (Dorothy was sure) was that the strong and clear-sighted had no such need for a crutch and the elaborate mythologies that churches espoused. Dorothy Day would be among the strong and clear-sighted, and as she saw it, that self-definition meant aligning herself with the political left.

In December 1914, the university's Socialist Club opened a women's section, the Socialist Study Club. Watched over by a nervous dean of students, the group had to be careful, and its prospectus made clear that its aim was not to win converts to the cause but to examine the topic from a theoretical angle relative to any other social science. Eugene Debs might have garnered almost a million votes for the Socialist Party in the presidential election of 1912, but alumni donors, trustees, and state legislators would have had little patience with too aggressive or proselytizing an attack on the American free enterprise system or the current state of labor relations.

In any event, the reading of scholarly papers at each session proved excruciatingly dull for the club's youngest member, and she attended only a few meetings before dropping out. More appealing was learning what she could on her own about the motley group of activists, as much anarchist as socialist, who were dominating the news: William "Big Bill" Haywood, Arturo Giovannitti, Elizabeth Gurley Flynn, Carlo Tresca, Emma Goldman. Topics never broached at home—Chicago's Haymarket bombing and the judicial travesty that ensued, the Molly Maguires taking on the Pennsylvania coal mine owners in the 1870s, the formation of the IWW—also began to inform Dorothy's sense of US history, which was not quite the streamlined narrative that had been presented at Robert Waller High School.

The university's socialist students did achieve one coup that delighted Dorothy and her like-minded peers. They invited Rose Pastor Stokes to speak on campus. Given her notoriety and her outspoken support for Margaret Sanger's still illegal efforts on behalf of birth control, Stokes was a risky guest, and the fact she was allowed to speak at all at a state-funded school says something about the liberalism of the James administration. (She had been barred from entering the grounds of Vassar and Wellesley.) A Jewish settlement worker who had married J. G. Phelps Stokes, a prominent New York City Episcopalian millionaire sympathetic to the left, Rose Pastor Stokes, in her thirties, was a dynamic spokesperson for the merits of socialism and in the 1910s was especially interested in educating college students about the nature of the economic debate she believed the nation needed to have. From New England through the South to the Midwest, her lecture tours were immensely popular among politically inclined young people. Stokes also wrote for two of New York City's most radical political organs, and it is likely that her visit to Urbana was the occasion of Dorothy's first hearing about *The Call* and *The Masses*, publications that were to play a very important role in her own life.

Understanding her need to be around charismatic, energetic, well-informed young women—frequently, Jewish women—was the real benefit of Dorothy's time in Urbana. Rose Pastor Stokes was a stirring presence, but she was gone in a day; before the end of her first year at the school, someone closer to home presented a similar, pleasing model of intelligence and dedication.

Rayna Simons came into Dorothy's life just when she desperately needed a close friend. It had become increasingly clear to Dorothy that she was, in truth, an unpopular person on campus. Nothing about her invited collegiality, let alone intimacy. She alienated people even when she didn't intend to. She was cranky and bookish (or book obsessed, and such strange books!), she rarely dated and didn't care in the least about football, she had a tart tongue. She was used to trading barbs with her brothers and had never given much thought about the need most people feel to be ingratiating.

Slightly older than Dorothy, Rayna Simons was from a wealthy family in Chicago and had come to Urbana in pursuit of a young man from a poor family whom her parents disapproved of. Unlike Dorothy, she had applied for admission to various sororities on campus but, as a Jew, hadn't been accepted by any of them. "Deliciously awkward and yet unselfconscious," Rayna had "red hair, brown eyes, and a vivid face," Dorothy later remembered, and a kind of enthusiasm and sincerity other girls lacked. Dorothy had been invited to join the school's writing club, the Scribblers, after a few of her submissions were accepted for the literary magazine, and it was there that she met and befriended both Rayna and her boyfriend, Samson Raphaelson. Dorothy was impressed by the intensity of the feeling between the two and Rayna's determination, no matter how impoverished Raphaelson's background and no matter how emphatic her parents' views, to stand by her love. (In the ironic way of such things, Rayna later became a prominent Communist buried with honors in Moscow, while the boyfriend ultimately became a successful Broadway playwright and highly paid screenwriter married to a Ziegfeld girl.)

The three friends took long walks across the prairie and enjoyed picnics, she wrote lyrically, "under the limitless sky while the sweet smell of clover filled the air and the meadow larks pierced the quiet with their songs."

Rayna thought Dorothy too obsessive on the subject of socialism and tried to talk her into a broader view of life, but despite any differences in outlook, the two quickly became close. When money was especially tight, Rayna helped her out with paying her rent and buying books, and she took it as her mission to put some flesh on her friend's increasingly thin frame. She encouraged her in her writing, too, as Dorothy published a few short pieces in the school paper, *The Daily Illini,* and even the town newspaper. They shared new authors they had discovered. Rayna let Dorothy, whose dresses were becoming noticeably frayed, wear her better clothes when she finally started to date boys on campus, and she invited her to spend the summer with her at the Simons family farm. "Rayna took me in," Dorothy would recall with gratitude.

Rayna and several of the girls she knew were living in a Jewish boardinghouse off campus, and they invited Dorothy to join them for her sophomore year. It was an agreeable arrangement, and when she contracted the flu during her second winter at school, and later when she sprained her ankle, it was a godsend to have someone to look after her. It was also pleasing to have someone to attend lectures and other outings with; together, they attended readings by poets John Masefield and Edgar Lee Masters, went to concerts, and saw the school production of *Twelfth Night.* Rayna was an influence, too, in urging her friend to be more involved with life on campus; Dorothy joined the baseball and hockey teams in her final semester, though she looks anything but enthusiastic in the hockey team photo for the yearbook. In time, "Raph," the boyfriend, became jealous of the friendship between Rayna and Dorothy, but Dorothy could feel for them only an uncritical love.

An uncritical love—and an admiration of their nerve. When Rose Pastor Stokes came to lecture, she strayed briefly from the announced topic to make a few laudatory remarks about Margaret Sanger and the growing birth control movement. She was, in essence, talking to the students about, and endorsing, something that was as yet illegal in every state. Rayna and Raph excitedly asked to meet with Stokes afterward and then submitted an interview to *The Daily Illini* that touched on that controversial aspect of radical thought. Knowing what the administration would have to say, the editors of the paper were torn about the right course to follow and, much to Rayna's and Raph's disgust, finally decided that their article was unprintable. Theirs had been a worthy effort, Dorothy felt.

Satisfying as this new friendship was, Dorothy decided not to return to the University of Illinois for her third year. After writing for the *Herald* (which had bought the *Inter-Ocean*) and the *Tribune*, John Day had been out of work for some time and had been desperately hunting for jobs elsewhere. He found one in June in New York City and went on ahead to find an apartment and take up his position as "turf editor" for the *Morning Telegraph*, the paper he had worked for when the family lived in Brooklyn. In July, as the Days were packing to leave, Dorothy decided to make the move as well. The excitement of being on her own had waned, and the thought of being so far distant from her mother, Della, and John was too much to contemplate. Her father having finagled a few book reviews for her in the *Tribune*, she wondered now if a career in writing might be possible. She left Urbana hopeful that New York would provide her with "new adventures."

THREE

❧ CAUSES ❧

D OROTHY'S PLANS WERE VAGUE AS SHE UNPACKED AND SETTLED into her parents' apartment in Manhattan, but it became clear soon enough that very little about the new arrangement was going to work. Her mother was happy to have her home. Della, sixteen and now in charge of caring for four-year-old John, was likewise happy to have her back with them. Her father, on the other hand, was not pleased with what two years of college had wrought—a daughter who smoked, didn't defer to him any more than she had before she went to Urbana, thought she was smarter than anyone in the family, and talked entirely too much about socialism, women's rights, her Jewish friends, and her future as a writer.

With an eye toward getting an apartment of her own as soon as she had an income, Dorothy made the rounds of the city's newspapers looking for work. She was met with no encouragement whatsoever, most of the time not even getting past the office boy or the city editor's secretary. As far as Dorothy was concerned, the repeated rejections she received were neither a coincidence nor an objective statement about the job market nor the predictable result of her own inexperience. In her bitterness, she was convinced that her father was spreading the word among the editors he knew that if his daughter showed up at their office, she should be talked out of her career plans or, better yet, ignored and sent on her way. That may well have been the case, but a young woman of her years with a slim college portfolio wasn't a likely candidate for work on a mainstream newspaper. The whole situation was made worse by the fact that her father had helped both her brothers get a start in journalism with far less education than she had. One editor she got in to see told her he would never let his daughter do what she was doing; another suggested a little country paper as a more feasible option.

Dorothy had other ideas. Remembering the daily newspaper Rose Pastor

Stokes had mentioned, she showed up at the offices of *The Call* on Pearl Street, in a run-down section of Lower Manhattan near City Hall, ready to make her case. Run on a shoestring budget, *The Call* had the advantage for a would-be contributor of an absence of gatekeepers or pretension. She walked right in that October morning, up a long flight of stairs, found the editor reading copy in the noisy warehouse space, and talked to him about what she felt was *The Call*'s need for more women writers. She projected energy and enthusiasm, pretending to a greater familiarity with his publication than she had. She probably mentioned her admiration for Stokes, Upton Sinclair, Eugene Debs, anything that would help. Only it didn't. The paper had no money to hire anyone else, she was told. Undaunted, she pressed an idea on the beleaguered man.

Other papers had reported on the wave of "diet squads" forming around the country in which society women claimed they could feed themselves on only a few dollars a week. Dorothy suggested she be given five dollars a week, for her food and all other expenses combined, and write a series of articles about the nitty-gritty reality of that kind of economizing, the kind sweatshop girls struggled with all of the time. Were the paper's editorial board to find her material usable, they might keep her on in some capacity. In the meantime, she would come in each day and help get that day's issue ready to go to press and even write a few articles "on spec."

The idea had a certain odd appeal to editor Chester Wright, who was finally convinced it was worth a try. It was clear enough that the young woman in front of him was of a persistent nature. She might make a decent reporter. Dorothy was thrilled to tell her parents that night that she had found employment, in a manner of speaking.

One difficulty was that *The Call* was a morning paper, which meant that most of the staff had to be at the office until midnight. Finding a room downtown, once her father made clear that a working daughter out all night had no place in his family circle, led to another experience, a first exposure to the awesome poverty of the poorest neighborhoods of New York City, worse, she thought, than anything she had seen in Chicago. She wandered south of Houston Street, stopping in any buildings that had a "Room to Let" sign in the window. Many still had backyard toilets. In a fourth-floor walk-up, in a four-room tenement apartment on Cherry Street, Dorothy found lodging— her first of many in that part of town—with an Orthodox Jewish family of six in which only the children spoke English. The bedbugs, her room lit only by candles, the air shaft by her window that blew in the most obnoxious smells, the pariah cats in the hallways—none of this, according to Dorothy's later account, mattered to her quite as much as the pious dignity of the Gottliebs, their twelve-year-old daughter's passion for books, the vibrant feel of the Lower East Side, and her independence.

Just as she hoped, things worked out at *The Call*, which proved a perfect place for someone like Dorothy to get a start in city journalism. Chester Wright was a personable, efficient editor who had plenty of reason to be proud of New York's only English-language socialist daily. Its circulation hovered around 15,000, an unimpressive figure by most standards, but the roster of men and women willing to publish in its pages was stellar and included Rose Pastor Stokes, Mary Heaton Vorse, and Upton Sinclair. Some of the best graphic artists in the city—John Sloan, Robert Henri, Robert Minor, Hugo Gellert—sent in drawings. The paper was also open to over-the-transom submissions. A few years earlier, *The Call* had published a political poem, "Fratricide," sent in from New London, Connecticut, by an utter unknown, Eugene O'Neill.

The women's page was run by one of the paper's founders, Anita Block—thirty-five, Jewish, a graduate of Barnard College—who took great pride in saying that hers was the only women's page in American journalism that never printed a recipe or a fashion tip. She also doubled as the paper's drama critic and in her columns gave free rein to her passion for modern social drama. The subject of her senior thesis at Barnard College in 1903 had been the plays of Henrik Ibsen, causing considerable discomfort to her professors, who questioned the propriety of her choice, a response that only heightened Block's excitement. She was mad for *A Doll's House* and *Hedda Gabler*. Her other great passion, beyond socialism and suffrage, was Margaret Sanger and the birth control movement. John Day's idea of a reputable newspaper and his daughter's were, from his daughter's perspective, happily worlds apart.

Dorothy's first article with a byline, published on November 11, 1916, was an account of Manhattan's judicial system replete with breezy descriptions and phonetic dialogue. "Girl Reporter, with Three Cents in Her Purse, Braves Night Court" was followed by three other features, including one on babies suffering from malnutrition, and then the promised diet squad articles, which (to no one's surprise) did not exactly establish Dorothy as a major new voice in journalism. A list of her daily food intake and its cost could be made only so interesting, and Wright let her know that four articles were more than sufficient. Efforts to be droll—one headline read "Reporter Eats Farina and Cheese and Reads Wordsworth"—fell flat. Still, *The Call*'s editors thought enough of Dorothy's nerve to take her on as a full-time reporter at a salary of ten dollars, later raised to twelve dollars, per week.

Jubilant at the prospect of seeing her words in print, with or without a byline, she eagerly went out into the city over the next few months to cover protest marches at City Hall, evictions in bad neighborhoods, Cooper Union Hall addresses by left-wing speakers, and picket lines outside government buildings, landlords' offices, and stores accused of unfair business practices. More than once Dorothy joined the picket line she was there to observe, both in approval of the cause and out of a desire to see what the experience felt like. The sneers of the police and the outraged public who crossed the picket lines were a new and unpleasant experience. She wrote with a byline about a halfway house on Beekman Place for young women recently released from prison, mainly prostitutes and drug addicts, and about educational programs at the socialist Rand School of Social Science on East 19th Street.

She was also assigned to conduct some interviews with subjects who were not always helpful. Only months before becoming a figure of international importance, Leon Trotsky had arrived in Manhattan at the start of 1917 to take up the next phase of his long exile from Russia and to work for *Novy Mir*, the city's Russian-language political paper. After hearing him lecture at Cooper Union, Dorothy and another writer were sent up to the offices of *Novy Mir* on St. Mark's Place to conduct an interview. Their time with him yielded rather little material that was printable: Trotsky took potshots at the parliamentary nature of socialism in America, and that angle wasn't judged usable for *The Call*. A large photo of Trotsky filled space that had been left for a lengthier text.

An interview with Margaret Sanger's sister turned out even worse. As Dorothy had displayed a serious interest in Sanger's campaign for family planning and had ably covered some meetings of the American Birth Control League, she was directed to get a juicy interview with Sanger's sister, Ethel Byrne, a nurse who had been arrested for attempting to open a clinic dispensing contraceptive information and then was pardoned by the governor after commencing a hunger strike in her Blackwell's Island prison cell. Dorothy showed up at Byrne's West 14th Street apartment late at night just as the presumed martyr to the cause was being delivered home. In the three minutes her interviewee allotted her, Dorothy was told that the week behind bars hadn't been all that horrendous and that the lady herself wasn't at death's door. That was not what Chester Wright or Anita Block wanted to hear, so *The Call*'s diligent questioner, with Margaret Sanger's aid, did what she could to make Byrne's experience sound rather more dramatic than she assumed it had been, but her effort was half-hearted. (Dorothy referred knowingly and grudgingly to her role at *The Call* as the paper's resident "sob sister.") The material, she felt, wasn't there.

More to Dorothy's liking than angling for sensationalism was covering events that were dramatic enough in themselves. Listening to Elizabeth Gurley Flynn addressing a crowd in Brownsville, Brooklyn, on behalf of the striking Mesabi Iron Range miners in northern Minnesota was nothing less than thrilling. A striker had been shot by a company guard, and the state's only response was to arrest Carlo Tresca, Flynn's lover and one of the IWW men organizing the strike. Flynn made an appeal for funds for the miners' destitute families, a passing-of-the-hat among the sympathetic to which Dorothy donated all that she had in her pocket, forcing her to call the office for a ride back to Manhattan. She attended a massive rally at Madison Square Garden in March 1918 at which thousands of workers cheered the political upheavals that were ending a thousand years of Russian autocracy, and at the same site covered an event from the opposite end of the political spectrum, a rally for US preparedness in anticipation of the country's almost certain entry into the debacle of the Great War.

With an eye toward that inevitability, Dorothy was sent to Washington, DC, her first trip to the nation's capital, at the end of the month with a busload of pro-peace student activists. On the way down she talked with some impressively committed undergraduates from Columbia University. Three particularly determined members of the group, Owen Cattell, Charles Phillips, and Eleanor Parker, would be arrested two months later for obstruction of the draft; Cattell's father, a Columbia professor of psychology, a chaperone on the trip, would be fired by the university for backing his son and condemning President Wilson.

That trip to Washington, DC, occasioned Dorothy's first taste of mass hysteria and the consequences of radical dissent. Along the way, the riders would stop at different towns and distribute antiwar leaflets. Most locals were not impressed, and not a few were rude and dismissive. In Baltimore, things got out of hand. Their legal gathering in a public hall was invaded by some rowdy students from a nearby Catholic college who wanted to take on the "Jew radicals from New York." In the riot that ensued, Dorothy was struck in the ribs with a policeman's billy club. The vast majority of middle-class Americans were all too ready to applaud the president's declaration of war, delivered to Congress on April 2. The United States was no longer "too proud to fight." The "Jew radicals from New York" wanted another, less acquiescent voice to be heard. John Day threw up his hands in disgust. Grace Day was filled with maternal concern.

Dorothy, however, was right where she wanted to be. She liked the camaraderie of the staff at *The Call*. At the end of their shift at midnight, they would head over to Park Row to Child's for pancakes to gossip and review the day's events and talk about politics and their favorite writers. Louis Weitzenkorn, an aspiring playwright, had a "Rabelasian tongue" that Dorothy came to appreciate, while William Radnor had a serious gambling problem. He would disappear from the office for days at a time, and everyone would understand that he was on another poker binge. He'd return with bloodshot eyes and rumpled clothes, having racked up some sizable debts, but he was too good at his job to sack. Everyone at the city desk was writing a book and envisioned a grand future, Dorothy later recalled. It was a group she wanted to be part of. Because smoking in public was still illegal for women, she had to learn to be a surreptitious indulger at those sessions. Puffing away, slipping an occasional obscenity into the conversation, pulling her weight at the office, taking pride in having suffered a cracked rib from a cop: how much easier it was than she expected to fit in with the men. It was a good moment for urban journalism, for women trying to break in. And it was a good moment—a brief good moment—for American socialism. Two big-city mayors, in Milwaukee and Schenectady, had been elected on the party ticket, as had several members of Congress and a large number of state legislators.

Another pleasing aspect of Dorothy's link to *The Call* had to do with some of the freelancers she met in the office or through the editors. The standoffishness she had manifested in college was dropping away little by little, as the

New Yorkers she came into contact with simply seemed more interesting, more complex, and easier to talk to, than anyone she had known before.

One was Mary Heaton Vorse. Though Vorse was twenty-three years Dorothy's senior, the two had a temperamental affinity and remained friends for years. Both came from families (Vorse's quite wealthy) that expected their daughters to be proper ladies; both craved adventure, cared about social injustices, and wanted to write, all of which precluded satisfying those familial wishes. Vorse had watched from the street in horror while burning shopgirls had jumped from the windows of the Triangle Shirtwaist Factory sweatshop in 1911. Having seen capitalism at its most heartless, she intended—"like a warrior scenting battles," Dorothy thought—to do something about it. She had problems, though, that someone Dorothy's age could not yet imagine. Twice widowed by forty, Vorse was a single mother attempting to do right by her children while refusing to give up her labor activism and journalism. Sinclair Lewis, a struggling writer she had befriended when he was most in need of friends, thought the world of her. John Dos Passos, impressed by her fervor, took her, loosely, as a model for a principal character in his *U.S.A.* trilogy, the idealistic and often ill-used Mary French.

A second person Dorothy met who made an even more significant difference in her life was Itzok, or Irwin as he was now calling himself, Granich, and his intentions were not solely intellectual or political. In fact, his interest in Dorothy was largely romantic, as he was pleased to tell her soon after they met. Born into a Lower East Side Romanian Jewish family in 1893, the year Stephen Crane chronicled that neighborhood in *Maggie: A Girl of the Streets*, Granich adopted the pseudonym "Mike Gold" in the 1920s (and shall be referred to by that more famous name from this point on). His shopkeeper father had died when he was eighteen, and he and his two brothers supported their Orthodox mother. A semester at the City University of New York and a semester at Harvard, the latter providing a taste of Ivy League anti-Semitism, was the extent of his higher education. He was full of stories of tenement life, bitter and comic. His days now were spent at warehouse and factory jobs with every spare minute devoted to political rallies and freelancing for *The Call* and other papers. He was a committed Marxist, though less consumed with rage about the class struggle when Dorothy knew him than he would be by the time he wrote his classic novel *Jews Without Money* in 1930. His younger brother was a Wobbly, a member of the IWW, and

Mike shared Dorothy's appreciation of Elizabeth Gurley Flynn's impassioned rhetoric at the striking miners' rally, an event he had attended with her. He had been with her in Baltimore for the riot as well.

The two had a lot in common and talked about their work for the paper, about the city and their colleagues, politics and books. If not as well-read as Dorothy, Gold was as avid to learn. His tastes ran to *Leaves of Grass*, *The Adventures of Huckleberry Finn*, and American political realism, so it is fair to assume that he and Dorothy shared responses to Upton Sinclair, Jack London, and Frank Norris. He was especially thrilled when he could report to her that winter that he had had the opportunity to meet—and bring home to dinner, no less—one of his favorite writers. Working on a play, *The Hand of the Potter*, Theodore Dreiser found himself dissatisfied with the portrayal of the impoverished Lower East Side Jewish family in his story. He asked the editors of *The Call* to suggest someone who could provide exposure to the kind of people, dialect, and environment he was writing about. They did: Mike Gold, who was thrilled to be asked. (Presumably, he had no idea what the play, which was not produced for years, was about: a Jewish pedophile.) The result was a Friday-night Sabbath dinner at his mother's table with the author of *Sister Carrie* and *Jennie Gerhardt*. Things like that happened to Mike Gold.

Dorothy would never discuss whether she and Gold actually became lovers, and Gold, who certainly wanted to marry her, died in 1967 before completing his own memoirs. Having grown up in a neighborhood overrun with pimps and prostitutes, though, he made clear, in an unpublished sequel to *Jews Without Money*, that he had been desperate as a young man for sexual relations with a "nice girl" he could court and respect. Whether he succeeded, we can't know. Dorothy wrote about their time together in a way that suggests at the very least warm memories and a deep fondness. Gold was a handsome man with a thick shock of unruly dark hair, an acid wit, energy to match hers, and an eager, confident manner. For his part, he was sure he had found his soul mate. His attentions were flattering, and he wasn't afraid to introduce her to his family and bring her to dinner on Chrystie Street. The religious differences meant nothing to him. Apparently they did to his mother, who had to endure the mournful fact that all three of her sons were dating Gentile girls. It was a tense meal. The plates Dorothy ate off of had to be smashed after she left.

When the weather was good, the two wandered where the mood took them: picnics on the Palisades, late-night walks along the piers with Gold singing Yiddish folk songs at the top of his voice, cheap dinners at Greenwich Village restaurants, ferry rides to Staten Island, where they dug for clams and relaxed on the deserted beaches. Never again would Dorothy know a man so romantically devoted to her wishes and her well-being.

Dorothy ended her association with *The Call* soon after her trip to Washington for reasons not entirely clear. One factor might have been the departure of Chester Wright, who had resigned in March over a dispute about the paper's policy on trade unions. Dorothy liked Wright and was less enthused about his successor. The office was also getting to be a dangerous place. Pro-war thugs had come up and smashed the typewriters, overturning desks, taking punches at the staff, and threatening worse.

Another potential factor was more personal. Dorothy would later tell the story of a night out with Gold at Webster Hall on East 12th Street, the site of some of downtown's more exuberant costume balls, dances, and gala fund-raisers. At the Anarchist Ball held there in April, she was spotted by someone who recognized her from the office, where he frequently stopped by. He was the type of young man, probably not entirely balanced, whom the anarchist movement attracted—disheveled, excitable, needy, lacking in social skills. He often waited until Dorothy was done at work and walked her home, to her great discomfort. That night he was delighted to see Dorothy, ran across the hall and embraced her, too ardently. Completely startled, she pushed him back and slapped him. He slapped her back. Two men, newspaper reporters covering the affair, hustled the fellow out of the hall and chucked him into the street. Dorothy was later sorry she had reacted as she did and created a needlessly embarrassing scene, but it was Mike Gold's criticism of her overreaction that stung. They got back together again after a while, but for the moment she decided she didn't want to see him, or anybody else, at *The Call*.

Three recent acquaintances Dorothy did want to stay in touch with that spring were the students she had met on the bus ride to Washington, with whom she had picketed before the Capitol and confronted the violence of the Catholic mob and the police in Baltimore. Charles Phillips, Eleanor Parker, and Owen Cattell had formed a branch of the Collegiate Anti-Militarism League with an office just off campus at Morningside Heights.

(Dorothy always misremembered the name of the group as the Anti-Conscription League.) When she told them she was done with *The Call*, they were happy to avail themselves of her typing, editing, and receptionist services for their surprisingly well-heeled organization—they offered her fifteen dollars a week, three dollars more than she made downtown—and she worked there, helping them for a few weeks to put out their fiery newsletter. The members of the Anti-Militarism League were pacifists, not only opposed to the American involvement in the war in Europe but opposed to all war. Dorothy was not a pacifist at this stage of her life, though she agreed with her friends that Wilson's declaration of war had been a moral and political blunder. She respected the group's efforts, nonetheless, and may have introduced Charles Phillips to Mike Gold, who heartily approved of the League, as the two were rooming together by the end of the year. The bravery of these student activists was incontestable. As Columbia president Nicholas Murray Butler was declaring that, with the country at war, views that had been merely wrongheaded before were now treasonous, they were putting themselves in serious jeopardy and they knew it.

Of the three students, Charles Phillips was the most taken with Dorothy and the two became good friends. His memoirs, published posthumously in 1993 under the name he later took, Charles Shipman, provide one of the most vivid portraits of Dorothy in this period. "Raw-boned, square-jawed, white-faced, and flat-chested, she was yet compellingly sexy," he recalled. "She drew men. But she was so easily involved herself and so generous with herself (as with everything) that she was often hurt." Though obviously attracted to a woman only two years younger than he was, Phillips never had an affair with Dorothy—he married Eleanor Parker later that year—but he hoped she would stay with the League for a while. Her skills were appreciated.

The two sometimes took lunch together at the Lion Saloon on West 110th Street where, for the price of a whiskey, patrons could enjoy the free noontime buffet. "She chain-smoked and made friends with everybody in the place," Phillips remembered, "especially the bums." She was also a great storyteller, "with a wonderful collection of funny stories, many involving herself, invariably ribald." Sometimes the jokes were about nuns or priests or the evangelist Billy Sunday. No matter how raucous lunch hour became, though, "in less than an hour, she would be back at the office, sober and zealous."

Dorothy didn't intend to stay long with the League, however. A woman often on the receiving end of serendipitous encounters, she was walking on 14th Street one afternoon that spring when she ran into Charles Wood, the acerbic, frolicsome drama critic for *The Masses*. Wood was a fan of Dorothy, and the feeling was mutual, though where they met is not known. It is possible that they were introduced through Anita Block. Having socialized and barhopped with him before, she accepted his invitation to join him at a German restaurant on Third Avenue where there was someone he said he wanted her to meet.

The person Wood was lunching with was Floyd Dell, associate editor of the socialist magazine Wood wrote for. Ten years older than Dorothy, he was a son of the Midwest who had started his literary career as a critic and editor in Chicago, where he had championed Sherwood Anderson. Now he was developing a reputation in New York for his own audacious short fiction and satirical drama. He was intriguing enough in appearance to be painted by some of the more talented painters of his generation, and his conversation was known to range far and wide: politics, poetry, sex, psychoanalysis, modern art, theater, economics, women's suffrage, Karl Marx and Samuel Butler, H. G. Wells and Joseph Conrad. A natural charmer, he'd have impressed someone like Dorothy the minute she sat down. Mike Gold thought highly of him, Dorothy knew, and that added to his aura.

Wood must have known that Dell was scouting about for an assistant, though nothing was said at first about that possibility. Instead, they talked about Dorothy's work experience, ate a hearty German lunch, and before going their separate ways Dell encouraged her to write a book review for *The Masses* and let him see how able a writer she was or wasn't. She accepted the offer. Her prose met with his speedy approval and, after another lunch to talk about the magazine's needs, she found she had a job as his assistant for ten dollars a week. In left-wing circles, at least in terms of her professional life, Dorothy always landed on her feet.

The Masses had an interesting history and an excellent radical pedigree. In its first iteration, it was the brainchild of a Dutch socialist, Piet Vlag, a Greenwich Village restaurateur who was funded by (of all people) an insurance company vice president, Rufus Weeks. Combining exposés, political commentary—often of a heavy-handed nature—short fiction, and illustrations, Vlag's monthly was "written *for* the masses [but] not written *down to* the masses," as an early editorial phrased it. When circulation hopes weren't realized and Weeks's subsidy dried up, Vlag announced the magazine's demise in 1912 and left New York for Florida in disgust. Some of his more enthusiastic contributors, though, weren't ready to see the enterprise fold. A few of the artists—Art Young and John Sloan, in particular—felt, rightly, that they had contributed some of their best work to *The Masses* and that the times cried out for a journal that would be as pointed but more playful than Vlag's, less blatantly propagandistic, a blend of provocation and satire. "We wanted," Young said, "one magazine in which we could gallop around in and be free." Mary Heaton Vorse and other writers wholeheartedly agreed with them.

The man they asked to helm the revived publication was Max Eastman, described by one historian as the "John Barrymore of American radicalism." Handsome and charismatic, a ladies' man and intellectual, he was a disciple of John Dewey and the kind of savvy New Yorker who knew how to finagle contributions out of potential patrons. Sloan, appointed art director, and his wife, Dolly, who came on board as the occasional business manager, concurred that in Eastman their venture had a "brilliant, untrammeled thinker," an organizational talent as likely as anyone to ensure that *The Masses* would remain a going concern. He also came as part of a team; his sister Crystal (historically never sufficiently recognized for her contribution) was an equally valued manager and editor. Dell was brought in soon after.

Over the next five years, *The Masses* did precisely what it had set out to do. Carped at by Marxists, who called it too tame, and denounced by conservatives as anti-American, its sixty-odd issues under the leadership of the Eastmans and Dell saw regular editorial essays by Max Eastman, incisive reportage by John Reed and Lincoln Steffens, short stories by Sherwood Anderson and Mary Heaton Vorse, poetry by Amy Lowell and e. e. cummings, perceptive book reviews by a range of writers, and Charles Wood's always biting, often hilarious theater criticism. No subject was off-limits. A play entitled *The Machine*, printed in its entirety (with a pungent illustration by Sloan), was about the entrapment of streetwalkers and the callousness of a judicial system that punished the women and not their patrons. Dozens of cartoons jabbed at the pretense that the teachings of Jesus actually meant anything to modern Americans. Writers and artists alike took on the themes of the hypocrisy of churchmen and congressmen in thrall to big business,

Americans' indifference to the poor, the importance of granting women the vote, the betrayal of socialists who supported the war in Europe, the gullibility of the mainstream press, and the rights—never respected in the United States—of conscientious objectors. Lacerating political cartoons by Sloan, Young, George Bellows, and Stuart Davis skewered Wilson and Roosevelt, John D. Rockefeller and Billy Sunday, the antivice crusader Anthony Comstock, army recruiters, and the idle rich. The covers of *The Masses* presented some of the most powerful examples of graphic art that American political journalism had, or has, ever seen.

By the time Dorothy joined the staff, it was obvious to everyone that the continued life of the magazine was in doubt. America's entry into the war and federal censorship made the existence of any journal as critical of the government as *The Masses* a precarious matter.

Yet for a few short months Dorothy was happily in the eye of the storm, meeting some of the most important left-wing writers and artists of the day. The office itself became yet another—better—substitute for a college campus. From Floyd Dell, she could learn about Freud and Jung; from Charles Wood, she could learn why George Bernard Shaw was the only modern playwright who mattered; from Crystal Eastman, she could learn about the history of the suffrage movement (though, in truth, she didn't find her especially approachable). Max Eastman seems not to have paid the new assistant much attention, but Floyd Dell was enamored. He thought she was an "awkward and charming young enthusiast." He admired her "beautiful slanting eyes" and would gladly have displayed the extent of that admiration in his bed. Dell at that period of his life was the city's most confirmed advocate of "free love," taking pride in his "conversion" of the poet Edna St. Vincent Millay from her lesbian sex life. Dorothy made it clear, however, that an intimate relationship was not going to happen. Boss and friend, yes; lover, no. They worked well together, in part because they had a similar sense of humor and similar taste in books, and she was comfortable in the role of protégé and wise enough not to allow for any blurring of the lines.

By summer, Eastman was away much of the time, often on fund-raising jaunts. Having enough cash on hand to pay the printers, distributors, and staff was getting to be a problem. Dell was likewise in and out (out more often than not), trying to finish the novel he had been working on. The upshot of it all was that Dorothy found herself entrusted with more responsibility than she had expected, not at all a displeasing prospect, in answering queries, sorting through submissions, and even making decisions about what might appear in the autumn issues.

With Dell's approval, she managed to make sure that a few of her own contributions found their way into print. In July, it was a short, sweet, un-rhymed poem, "Mulberry Street," about an Italian boy looking out for his sister as they sat on the curb in Little Italy and watched the world go by; in August and September, there were reviews of some pretty inconsequential new books, though one, *Doing My Bit for Ireland*, was more gripping than the inane title the author had given her work. Margaret Skinnider was an arms runner for Sinn Féin, hiding bomb detonators in her hat and trip wires in her dress, and during the famous assault on the British authorities in Dublin during Easter Week 1916, she took part in the fighting and was wounded. She wrote her lively account of the failed rebellion while in hiding. Day was rather taken with Skinnider's pluck, and the Irish effort to end British colo-nial rule, pushed even to the point of violence, was a cause that *The Masses'* book reviewer made clear she fully supported.

Within a month of the time she started work there, Floyd Dell had a proposition to make. He and two other men on the magazine's staff, Merrill Rogers and Daniel Karb, were taking an apartment on MacDougal Street, sublet from the theater designer Edna Kenton, and were looking for a fourth person to split the rent. He knew Dorothy was looking for a place to live within walking distance of the office. She liked the idea.

In one of the scenes in *The Eleventh Virgin* that sounds truest to her own life, Dorothy's protagonist is similarly housed, and her mother, while trying to be modern and supportive about the whole business, worries over what she should say if anyone asks about her daughter's living arrangements. Three men and one woman sharing an apartment is nothing anyone would have made the mistake of bringing up to John Day, to be sure. Dorothy did her best to reassure Grace that the interest of the other men, and hers to-ward them, was based on friendship and finances, nothing more.

In June, Dorothy moved into the MacDougal Street apartment. As it turned out, the men were frequently away for one reason or another, and Dorothy often had the place to herself. When everyone was at home together, the four-some enjoyed communal breakfasts and dinners eaten amid a haze of cigarette smoke and piles of newspapers, ad hoc Sunday brunches with mutual friends, poker nights, some trips to burlesque shows uptown, a day at Coney Island, an outing to Staten Island for a swim in the moonlight, everyone's clothes left on shore. Rayna Simons came for a long visit from Chicago to see New York with her college buddy. Charles Phillips would stop by to visit his "impishly profane" friend. The event that summer that was most memorable for Dorothy was the night twenty or so men gathered in the apartment—a group that included Eastman, Dell, Jack Reed, Mike Gold, and the brothers Albert and Charles Boni, the Village booksellers and publishers—to debate their response to their imminent draft call. The anguishing time was fast approaching when eligible males would have to choose: the army, prison, or flight.

In taking up residence within a stone's throw of Washington Square, Dorothy was now officially a resident of Greenwich Village. Though by middle age she hated to be discussed as a "Village habituée" and was testily unreceptive to questions on the topic, preferring that people think of her as someone whose entire preconversion life had been centered on the Lower East Side, the fact is that in the memory of everyone who knew her then she was very much a part of that other world.

The mythologizing of Greenwich Village circa 1900–1930 that occupied cultural historians for a good part of the later twentieth century has tended to downplay certain grimy realities. One encountered a fair number of bores and charlatans, hangers-on and monomaniacs—and worse. Alcoholism and drug addiction were widespread in the Village. Shady characters weren't hard to find. Bad food, inadequate plumbing, and a dearth of funds for habitable living quarters are more easily romanticized long after the fact. Casual sex, common enough, could be liberating and pleasurable, but it could also be deadening and predatory.

Yet it is true that for men and women who wanted to set themselves apart from bourgeois values, life south of 14th Street and north of Canal Street in Manhattan offered something unconventional and sustaining. In an area of low rents and relaxed mores, many Villagers perceived this as-yet-undeveloped part of New York City as a "spiritual haven," in the words of one neighborhood woman at the time—a great anomaly in God's Country, "a sort of liberal/radical small town." Political rebels, intellectuals, gay men and lesbians, and those who had been misfits among their families finally found a place. Prior to

1917, the West Village was an especially enjoyable enclave of minimal traffic and noise, as Seventh Avenue, a major thoroughfare barreling down from Midtown, still ended at Greenwich Avenue, two blocks south of 14th Street.

This was a milieu Dorothy found desirable, despite her later need, for plausible and complex reasons, to pretend otherwise. Through Mike Gold, through Floyd Dell, through friends at *The Call* and *The Masses*, she met a range of fascinating people to talk to late at night in any number of settings, including taverns—the kind of people she would not have encountered had she remained in college, the kind of people who would have appalled her parents, people with different, urgent ideas about the world. What could be more exciting to a nonconformist of nineteen, craving challenge and experience?

They were a motley bunch. Terry Carlin had known the Haymarket martyrs during the course of his vagabond wanderings, claimed a friendship with Theodore Dreiser, and was full of praise for an up-and-coming playwright he roomed with, Eugene O'Neill. The Czech-born Hippolyte Havel, another aging O'Neill buddy—"long-haired, owl-eyed, irrepressibly intellectual"—gave the impression of having served time in just about every jail in Europe for his politics and, though married, was rumored to be the lover of Emma Goldman, with whom he had edited the radical magazine *Mother Earth*. (Both Carlin and Havel were the inspirations for vivid characters in O'Neill's 1939 play *The Iceman Cometh*: Havel for the tormented, ex-movement man Larry Slade, Carlin for the aging anarchist and alcoholic Hugo Kalmar.) The poet Maxwell Bodenheim took a liking to Dorothy, though she probably had to make clear to Bodenheim that she was not interested in a liaison, as he tended, despite his lack of sex appeal, to proposition every woman who caught his fancy.

Nor was it an exclusively male domain Dorothy was entering. Mary Heaton Vorse, Anita Block, Margaret Sanger, and Crystal Eastman, all of whom she knew already, weren't the only women held in high regard. The writers Neith Boyce and Susan Glaspell, actress/directors Nina Moise and Ida Rauh, feminist reformers Henrietta Rodman and Edna Kenton, painter Marguerite Zorach, poet Edna St. Vincent Millay, and pathbreakers such as the anthropologist Elsie Clews Parsons (one of the founders in 1919 of the New School for Social Research) were a few of the many formidable women on the scene, to be met at lectures or heard lecturing or to be introduced to at parties or at the theater or after Union Square rallies, while Jessie

Tarbox Beals was everywhere with her camera, documenting their gathering places. True enough, men made unrelenting advances on attractive single, and sometimes not single, women—the atmosphere of the day was self-consciously libidinous, Victorian prudery was a subject of hearty jibes (it was "sex o'clock in America," in the much-quoted phrase of the journalist William Marion Reedy)—but the men Dorothy knew, with some notable exceptions, respected their female counterparts, and *counterparts* was very much what they were.

In the midst of this widening and enriching circle, luck played its part, and Dorothy was especially lucky in her choice of boyfriend. Mike Gold was that rare man who, when he took an interest in a woman, liked to see her enjoy her broadening horizons and all manner of new experiences. Even before she had moved to MacDougal Street, he had introduced Dorothy to a classic Village experience, the drama of the Provincetown Playhouse. *Drama* in all senses: the most original new plays being written were performed there, and the histrionics of the people involved were no less worth noting.

The fabled Provincetown Playhouse got its start in Mary Heaton Vorse's fishing wharf cottage on Cape Cod, where a group of theater-minded New Yorkers, including Vorse herself, staged some plays with their vacationing friends over two summers and then decided in 1915 that they weren't prepared to end the fun when the season ended. They had a sense they were creating something special. Relocated to Manhattan, the friends took over one floor of an 1840 brownstone at 139 MacDougal Street, a block south of Washington Square and next door to Henrietta Rodman's Liberal Club, everybody's favorite lecture and debate space.

For those with avant-garde tastes, plays—almost exclusively one-acts—were staged in the troupe's first years by Eugene O'Neill, Susan Glaspell, Floyd Dell, John Reed, Louise Bryant, Max Bodenheim, Edna St. Vincent Millay, Djuna Barnes, and Wallace Stevens. A doctor-poet from New Jersey, William Carlos Williams, acted in one; the photographer Berenice Abbott in another. Max Eastman took a turn behind the lights in one of Dell's plays. After rehearsals or performances, the actors and their friends would retire to the Samovar on West 4th Street for coffee or libations. Mike Gold was stagestruck. He thought of 139 MacDougal Street as "a house of magic."

Despite having no real talent in that direction, he dreamed of being an admired playwright. In total, he would have three one-act plays produced by the theater. In January 1917, his antiwar play *Ivan's Homecoming* had been staged in a triple bill with works on the same theme by Glaspell and Dell. He had hopes for more attention from the Players. Dorothy took to hanging about with him there, sometimes reading lines in rehearsals for absent actors. The plays she saw in those months included three one-acts by O'Neill and *The People*, Susan Glaspell's clever satire about life at the office of *The Masses* (with a wickedly funny parody of Hippolyte Havel). She might also have seen Pendleton King's *Cocaine*, about a suicidal streetwalker, her boyfriend who contemplates prostitution himself, and their addiction to a drug well known to many Villagers.

From that fervent period emerged an unlikely best friend. Peggy Baird, a louche and attractive twenty-seven-year-old, hung about with the playhouse crowd, too. She slept with a fair number of the available men, including O'Neill. A real-life version of Christopher Isherwood's Sally Bowles, she was separated, possibly already divorced, from her husband, the free-verse poet Orrick Johns. She smoked at least as much as Dorothy and drank herself into a state whenever she felt like it. Peggy, a suffragette, was purportedly the first woman in the Village to bob her hair. She liked Dorothy, invited her to her studio to see her paintings, and even talked her into posing nude one afternoon. She was also a fount of erotic advice, insisting to her considerably less experienced friend that more was always better than less in the sexual realm, that men and women understood each other better after they had coupled.

Evidence that postcoital harmony was not a universal condition was to be seen everywhere in the Village, of course, not least within the Provincetown Players circle where affairs were numerous. One woman who occasioned a good deal of talk was the journalist Louise Bryant, who lived with John Reed, everyone's favorite Village writer, the boy wonder of the left wing and a man from whom great things were always expected. Some mutual friends held against her the rumor (actually erroneous) that she had stolen him away from Mabel Dodge, who from her lower Fifth Avenue apartment ran the premier salon for New York radicals and modern artists.

Dorothy was familiar with Louise Bryant from *The Masses*. Though he published her work, Max Eastman had little personal regard for her, and Dorothy wondered how much that had to do with old-fashioned male prejudice. ("She had no right to have brains and be so pretty" was Dorothy's take on the men's reactions to Bryant at the office.) Eugene O'Neill, though, had no problem with her aspirations or her impulsiveness and professed to be madly in love with her. As she and Reed had a more or less open relationship, Bryant and O'Neill were romantically involved for a time in 1917, but Reed proved to be a little more possessive than he pretended to be. It was a torturous affair, as everything involving Bryant was. Gossipmongers hinted at Reed's alleged impotence, a pregnancy by O'Neill, an abortion. The whole prolonged, messy business ended when Bryant left for Russia with Reed to cover the great happenings there. O'Neill, less interested in the fall of the Romanovs, was crushed. Observing such incidents, Dorothy took stock of the emotional maelstrom she was entering. Never had her parents' expectations seemed so distant.

Indeed, her parents' world was becoming more remote all the time in another, quite different way. Vague stirrings were becoming less vague, though their meaning still eluded her. She would sometimes pass St. Joseph's Church under the pillars of the El on the corner of Sixth Avenue and Washington Place, one of the city's oldest Catholic houses of worship. The woman who had told Charles Phillips she was a "dedicated atheist" would walk up the steps and past the hefty white Doric pillars and look in on a Mass in progress or at parishioners who had stopped by for a few moments of quiet reflection and prayer. St. Joseph's was one of the few churches in the city that didn't affect a Gothic architecture; it had about it—and still has in the twenty-first century—an elegant simplicity. She found herself, at odd moments, drawn to the atmosphere of the church, even drawn to the impulse to pray. The old concerns of childhood and adolescence were returning. The sight of men and women in a prayerful posture exercised a draw on her imagination, even as she knew that very few of her new friends would comprehend what she was feeling any more than the members of her own family would. She understood that her curiosity was best kept to herself. Disdain for what friends called superstition and a rejection of conservative institutions, especially the Catholic Church: that was the orthodoxy of the Village she knew.

In November, the last issue of *The Masses* appeared on the newsstands—or, at least, on the very few newsstands in the city that would still stock it. None of the subscribers received a copy, as the post office had banned its delivery. Still, Dorothy had good reason to feel pleased with the issue. She had seen that Mike Gold was given space for a memoir of life on the Lower East Side, and she included her own short sketch, "South Street," an evocation of a summer's day on the Manhattan wharf on the East River. She was the author of two of the issue's book reviews as well. One was an equivocal but still generous assessment of *Marching Men*, Sherwood Anderson's dreary pre–*Winesburg, Ohio* novel about a labor organizer. Dorothy's might have been one of the few decent notices the book received. The other was a review of Upton Sinclair's newest novel, *King Coal*, about the breaking of the famous Ludlow, Colorado, miners' strike, a book she found "grim and real." Sinclair himself was given ample space in the issue in the form of his long eulogy for the recently deceased Jack London. The author of *The Jungle*, the revered writer of Dorothy's teenage years, was no favorite of Max Eastman now that he had come out in support of taking up arms against Germany, but she was insistent—and always would be—that he was a political force still worth heeding.

FOUR

❧ MOORINGS ❧

A T JUST THE MOMENT THAT THE FINAL ISSUE OF *THE MASSES* reached its few remaining readers, Peggy Baird had a request. She asked Dorothy to join her on what was supposed to be a short excursion to Washington, DC, that turned out to be anything but. The cause of woman's suffrage was the one political commitment that, after her fashion, meant something to Peggy, who otherwise seemed much more interested in art and sex, drinking and gossip. A demonstration was scheduled to be held in front of the White House, and, having participated in one earlier in the year, she was eager to take part again. Dorothy, though, had no particular feeling for the issue. (In fact, once suffrage was achieved, she never voted in her life, sharing Jack London's view that the triumph of Democrats or Republicans made little or no difference. Both parties were, as London put it, "creatures of the Plutocracy.") She also had recently started a novel that she wanted to continue working on, but Mike Gold urged her to go, and Peggy was insistent that the event would at least be interesting. That it was.

Earlier in the year, the Silent Sentinels, as they called themselves, had taken up positions in front of the White House. Women with banners proclaimed to the world, and to a supposedly progressive president, that the time for suffrage had come. The government's patience with demonstrations, especially once war was declared, was limited, and arrests were frequent. On the Friday evening Peggy and Dorothy boarded a train for Washington with a number of other women of all ages and classes, Alice Paul, one of the leaders of the movement, was already serving a seven-month jail sentence under very trying conditions. Peggy had not been, perhaps, completely forthcoming about the risks involved in this trip, but it is likely that Dorothy would not have been dissuaded, anyway, once committed to joining the protest.

On Saturday afternoon, November 10, having been given their instructions from suffragette Lucy Burns, forty-odd women began their walk, two by two, in groups of six across Lafayette Park the short distance to the White House. The police were there in significant numbers as the crowd of spectators was large, loud, and unruly. The women were jeered as they marched; boys threw stones. A sailor in uniform jumped from behind the barricades and attempted to wrestle Dorothy's banner from her hands. She held it tighter. It was like Baltimore earlier in the year, the protestors vastly outnumbered and confronting an irrational hatred. The ensuing commotion was blamed on the marchers, not their assailants, and the women were hustled into paddy wagons.

At first it probably appeared to Dorothy that the whole experience would end in an anticlimax. The women registered their names and addresses at the police precinct and were simply told to appear in court on Monday. The judge that day lectured the women about the danger of obstructing traffic on Pennsylvania Avenue, their violation of womanly decorum, and the upheavals taking place in Russia that their militancy might well lead to at home, and they were pronounced guilty but were told he would have to take some time to determine the appropriate sentences. Dismissed from court, the group promptly headed straight back to the White House, where they were arrested for a second time. This time they refused to give their names or cooperate in any way with the police, and they were carted off to a detention house. The following day, when they were brought before him again, the judge was in a much more aggressive frame of mind and not inclined to suspend anyone's sentence. He angrily handed down punishments ranging from fifteen days to six months in jail. Dorothy was sentenced to thirty days.

In windowless vans, the women were taken not to the city jail but to the outskirts of the district to the infamous Occoquan Workhouse, known for its no-nonsense warden and brutal guards. At that point, Dorothy noted, "We were afraid."

Occoquan lived up to its reputation for brutality. The warden "burst in like a tornado" to the room where the women were gathered. When one of their spokespersons informed the warden that the women considered themselves political prisoners and demanded to be treated as such—and, furthermore, would go on a hunger strike until that principle was established—he told them to shut up and called in men, suspiciously not in uniform, to drag the prisoners off to their cells. As Dorothy moved to stand next to Peggy, the warden grabbed her to hold her back. Infuriated, she sank her teeth into his hand. Two guards then grabbed her arms, twisted them high over her head, and twice slammed her down over the arm of a metal bench, bruising her back. She kicked them in the shins before they threw her into her cell, yelling condemnations at women who didn't know their place.

The cells were filthy, with no furniture other than an iron bed with a thin straw pad and an exposed toilet that had to be flushed from outside the cell. Dorothy's cellmate was Lucy Burns. Dorothy was thoroughly disconcerted by the day's events, but Burns seemed thrilled. The more cruelly the women were treated, she explained while straightening her dress and combing her hair, the better the newspaper coverage would be. That was the nature of modern political dissent. When the warden demanded that Burns be handcuffed to the door of her cell for refusing to stop calling out encouragement to the other inmates, she exclaimed to Dorothy, "Splendid! It gets worse and worse." The next morning Burns was removed to an isolation cell.

Participating in a hunger strike was a strictly voluntary action and, as everyone had heard, the process of being force-fed, if it came to that, was a physiological and psychological nightmare. Dorothy decided nonetheless to participate in that protest. After six days of gnawing hunger, isolation, inactivity, nicotine withdrawal, and terrifying dreams disrupting her efforts to sleep, she began to feel disoriented. "I lost all consciousness of any cause," she wrote. "I could only feel darkness and desolation." Unable even to cry, she just lay on her cot in "blank misery." On the sixth day, seriously weakened, she was taken to the workhouse hospital, where she had to listen to the "unutterably horrible" sounds of women in other rooms held down on their beds, struggling and gagging against the force-feeding by tubes. All that made it bearable was that she happened to be in a room adjacent to Peggy's, which enabled the friends to pass notes written on toilet paper. There was a pleasing indomitability and good sense to Peggy, which helped to carry Dorothy through the ordeal. On the eighth day, she agreed to ingest a small amount of food and urged Dorothy to do the same. Their point had been made.

Two days later, the hunger strike was called off as the women were told they would be transported back into town to the less gruesome city jail. Lucy Burns had been right; the government could stand only so much press coverage of middle-class women starving and abused. Any deaths would have made for disastrous publicity. After a few days of further incarceration, though under much better conditions, the women were pardoned and told they were free to go. Lucy Burns declined. She had committed no crime, she insisted, and therefore could accept no pardon. Dorothy and Peggy left the jail as soon as possible, settled into seats in the best restaurant they could find for a roast duck meal, bought packs of cigarettes, and then headed for Union Station.

The autumn of 1917 was a particularly hard time for all American progressives. With *The Masses* having been declared by the government unmailable as of August under the new Espionage Act (putting Eastman and Dell in the docket the next spring, acquitted on a treason charge by a narrow hung-jury vote), the magazine's days had come to an end and the office was in the process of being dismantled. Some of the old contributors, such as the artist George Bellows, had even gone over to the other side. IWW men were heinously brutalized in Oklahoma for refusing to buy war bonds, and the activist Kate Richards O'Hare was sentenced to five years in federal prison for delivering a speech in North Dakota critical of the United States' war aims. The machinery of propaganda had done its work nationwide. Socialists, anarchists, pacifists, and suffragists alike wondered about what impact, if any, they could have in a climate of suspicion, jingoism, and disdain for liberal or radical causes.

When Dorothy returned from Washington and recovered from the trauma of Occoquan, she grappled with just this confusion of purpose, this depletion of morale. "I hate being Utopian and trying to escape from reality," she wrote to a friend at the time. "Now that we are in the thick of war and there is so much work to be done, I might as well try to do some of it instead of sitting around playing at writing. And what is my writing now but book reviews, editing, playing at writing a novel of social significance? . . . What good am I doing my fellow man? It's the poor that are suffering. I've got to do something." That *something*, she decided rather impetuously, would be nursing. She submitted an application, promptly accepted, for admission to the nurse training program at Kings County Hospital in Brooklyn.

Her training wouldn't begin until April. That left almost five months to fill. Taking a cold-water flat back on the Lower East Side, she looked for freelance writing jobs, scrounged for meals among good-hearted friends, visited her worried mother when her father was out, and spent more time with Mike Gold. Gold had taken it into his head that his proletarian politics would be best served by the stage. He had written a one-act play about tenement life—earnest, preachy, autobiographical—and was able to convince the Provincetown Players to stage *Down the Airshaft* that winter. Dorothy was often at the theater while he was immersed in casting and rehearsals and even read for a part, though she quickly thought better of the idea and backed out. Her lack of thespian talent was evident, to anyone watching. She could see that not everyone thought much of Gold's didactic work, either, and the company's star among its writers was the least impressed. Turning a famous line by Thomas Grey about "the short and simple annals of the poor" into a pun, Eugene O'Neill jokingly remarked that Gold, who filled his set with rooftop clotheslines, was wont to write about "the short and simple flannels of the poor."

If O'Neill had no interest in Gold's artless play, the same couldn't be said about his view of Gold's girlfriend. And the attraction was mutual. O'Neill was just coming off a string of one-night stands after being dumped by Louise Bryant. He was the kind of man whom Dorothy would often be drawn to—difficult, oddly magnetic, morose, and in O'Neill's case, one who lost himself in drink more often than not. He had already attempted suicide once. His mother's drug addiction, eventually the subject of his finest play, weighed heavily on him. Yet he had cause to be happy even as he resisted the very notion of happiness. Dorothy was meeting him at a turning-point moment in his career. The prestigious *Smart Set*, edited by H. L. Mencken, had published *The Long Voyage Home* that October, and the *New York Times* had done a profile on him, noting that he was a talent to be watched.

Years later, Dorothy maintained that she was attracted to O'Neill's genius more than to the man himself, that although she loved his plays, she was not strongly drawn to him romantically or sexually—*strongly* being, perhaps, the operative word. Mike Gold no doubt had a different view of the matter. By the time his play opened three days after Christmas and he had time to pay attention to the situation, Dorothy and O'Neill were a couple, of a sort. They spent hours talking about books and plays and their own family sagas. He let her read a copy of his new play, *Moon of the Caribbees*. Sometimes, after a night of barhopping and wanderings through the streets of the Village and the Lower East Side, they fell into bed together, though Dorothy later maintained, not with complete plausibility to all who knew her, that theirs was a chaste relationship, with O'Neill usually wanting comfort and companionship, conversation, and understanding more than sex.

Dorothy's ultimate impression was that O'Neill "couldn't really love anybody." He was a man destined to devour anyone close to him, just as he had been devoured by his tortured family life and by his talent, "his all-consuming urge to write." For a short period at the end of 1917 and into the first weeks of 1918, however, he needed her company. Whatever the specifics of their sexual history, the drinking patterns of the two friends were clear enough to everyone who saw them together. They seemed to spend a lot of time in bars, and not always the most reputable ones. They were sometimes joined in their outings by Max Bodenheim, and one night the three of them jointly composed a poem on a tavern napkin, a relic of those bibulous nights that Dorothy kept for many years.

O'Neill's favored spot at that time was the Golden Swan, a dilapidated bar located on Sixth Avenue at West 4th Street, nicknamed "The Hell Hole" by those who frequented it. It had "a quality about it," Mary Heaton Vorse observed. "Something at once alive and deadly . . . sinister. It was as if the combined soul of New York flowed underground and this was one of its vents." It was frequented by all sorts—slumming artists (e.g., John Sloan and Charles Demuth, both of whom drew its crowded interior), working stiffs, moochers, drug pushers, streetwalkers, and outright thugs. The Hudson Dusters, in particular, were regularly employed as warehouse thieves, troublemakers on the docks, and ballot box dumpers for Tammany Hall. Nothing about the place or its patrons fazed Dorothy. One night she showed up with three questionable-looking men whom she said she had found on the steps of St. Joseph's Church across the street and had promised a drink. After buying them shots of rye and tossing back a couple of them herself, she began to sing the bawdy verses of "Frankie and Johnny" in a hard, staccato voice, which seemed to fascinate O'Neill and others in the bar.

Some acquaintances wondered about that behavior, thinking it lively and bold or, on the other hand, unhealthy, depending on the values and perspective of the observer. Village bookstore owner Samuel Roth was admiringly astounded that a woman could consume so much alcohol. The literary critic Malcolm Cowley, not yet a resident of the Village but relying on what he heard from others (probably his future wife, Peggy Baird), later speculated that the Dusters liked Dorothy because she could drink them under the table. She could also hold her liquor better than O'Neill. Yet what was she doing there and at similar dives, friends asked, night after night?

We come to know people by their attachments as much as by any other aspect of their lives. It can be—it was then, for some—a paradoxical picture, this short-lived but intense bond between a misanthropic playwright about to turn thirty and a woman almost ten years his junior who on occasion slipped into St. Joseph's Church for vespers yet sat comfortably amid gangsters and prostitutes in the appalling Golden Swan. The opinions of others didn't mean much at the moment to either party.

In O'Neill, Dorothy saw many things: a lanky, dark-haired, bitter but darkly humorous man with his own brand of charisma and a past even more rebellious than her own. After flunking out of Princeton, he had shipped as a merchant seaman to ports across South America and Europe, rough voyages that provided him with his earliest and some of his best material. An admirer of the first *S.S. Glencairn* plays she had seen at the Playhouse, Dorothy was now an object of attention from the author himself. He was smarter, or smarter in a different way, than Gold and most of the other men she associated with. He wasn't apolitical (he would write *The Hairy Ape* four years later, after all), but he was different—considerably more skeptical, less hopeful about change—than anyone she knew by way of *The Call* or *The Masses*. He had been married at twenty, had fathered a son at twenty-two, and had abandoned mother and child soon after. A touch of the poet brought with it an aura—romantic, unstable, selfish, ribald, needy—that in itself had its appeal.

Who can tell exactly what O'Neill saw in Dorothy, as he was always circumspect in discussing his relationships, but for a brief time it was something that clearly mattered to him. He enjoyed spending his evenings with an adventurous woman who seemed to live without sleep and was curious about his abandoned Catholicism, an interest she wasn't embarrassed to share with him, and simultaneously fascinated by its opposite: dissipation and what the world saw as degradation. Once, when drunk and feeling especially maudlin, he recited to her Francis Thompson's nineteenth-century poem "The Hound of Heaven" about a restless man's flight from God and ultimate capitulation.

Yet O'Neill also urged Dorothy, always voracious for suggestions, to read Strindberg and Baudelaire. Introducing his young companion to *The Dance of Death* or *Miss Julie* or *Les Fleurs du Mal* was, in effect, asking her to contemplate a different truth and a different perspective on the world than Thompson's, a social order in which men and women were irreconcilably at war, in which the assertion of power was the point of all our struggles and sensual pleasure was all that mattered—in sum, *not* a God-governed universe. One night O'Neill took Dorothy down to Fulton Street to Jimmy-the-Priest's, to see the grubby site of his suicide attempt five years before. At the tavern that provided the bleak setting for *The Iceman Cometh*, the bartender hustled them out. This isn't the place for someone your age, one of the men at the bar sternly warned her. Her own independent streak and jail experience aside, Dorothy seems to have been assigned the part of the naif against whom O'Neill could test a welter of dark sentiments.

O'Neill's final play, *A Moon for the Misbegotten*, was completed in 1943 and details the last days of his alcoholic older brother, James. In this deeply poignant drama, James has a bantering, erotically teasing relationship with Josie Hogan, a woman with whom he ultimately finds redemption, at least of a kind. Josie is a large woman, as was Dorothy. "Her sloping shoulders are broad," he wrote, "her chest deep with large, firm breasts, her waist wide but slender by contrast with her hips and thighs. The same is true of her legs." Most O'Neill biographers believe that O'Neill based the physical characteristics of Josie on Christine Ell, the woman who owned the restaurant over the Provincetown Playhouse, a woman who was larger and more full-breasted than Dorothy. But Christine, although an extremely likable sort, had a reputation for serial infidelity to her husband. James's attraction to Josie comes from a profoundly different direction: her innocence. She isn't sullied; beneath her gruffness, she has a fundamental decency. She offers a respite from the "Broadway tarts" and lost souls among whom he feels more at home even though they feed his drive toward self-destruction. At the end of the play, James realizes some comfort, for the moment, by confessing his darkest secrets to Josie and falling asleep in her arms, a situation not unlike the one alluded to by Dorothy about her nights with O'Neill in the winter of 1917–1918. Dorothy herself believed, and wanted others to assume, that such was the case and that she had been one of the models, or inspirations, for the tough but virginal Josie Hogan.

Yet O'Neill's life was about to change abruptly in the new year, and there would no longer be room for Dorothy in it. He was fast falling in love with a different woman, whom he would marry that spring, Agnes Boulton, a beautiful widow (and, many said, a dead ringer for Louise Bryant) who had left her two-year-old daughter with her family in Connecticut when she went off to New York to see if she could earn a living writing fiction. Ever on the lookout for cheaper rents and roommates with whom to split expenses, Dorothy shared an apartment on Waverly Place with Agnes for a month or so, and an odd ménage it was as she witnessed the growing attachment between the two, could see the depth of Agnes's feelings, probably sensed Agnes's distrust of her, and realized that the time of her intimacy with O'Neill was drawing to a premature close.

A shocking event that month led to a decisive break with O'Neill and his circle. On the night of January 22, 1918, Dorothy was having dinner at a restaurant on Prince Street with O'Neill's painter friend Charles Demuth and a few others, possibly the painter Edward Fisk, the writer Robert Parker, and O'Neill's anarchist crony Terry Carlin. Accounts of what happened that evening by contemporaries and later chroniclers differ on innumerable points, including who else was present to witness the tragedy that followed.

A word about the modernist painter Charles Demuth: Demuth was gay, a fact of which his friends were well aware, and O'Neill's comfort with that aspect of Demuth's life suggests that the playwright didn't share any of Americans' virulent homophobia in the 1920s. Indeed, the character of Charles Marsden in his 1927 play Strange Interlude is generally taken to be a composite of Demuth and another gay painter of their acquaintance, Marsden Hartley. We can certainly assume that Dorothy's tolerance extended along the same healthy lines in her Village days. But Demuth, a painter of precisionist landscapes and elegant still lifes, had something else in common with O'Neill and Dorothy about which he was more discreet: an appetite, far more dangerous than theirs, for the underbelly of New York City life. An aesthete who lived with his widowed mother in Lancaster, Pennsylvania, when he wasn't visiting in New York, he regularly risked arrest frequenting the city's gay bathhouses, approached sailors on the waterfront for oral sex, and occasionally was badly beaten by the rough trade he sought out. When in Manhattan, he liked joining O'Neill and friends at the Golden Swan.

After dinner, the party went on to the Golden Swan to meet up with Louis Holladay, an intellectual comrade and drinking buddy of O'Neill's from their school days who had just returned after a long period on the West Coast doing his best to stay clean and sober. He had come back excitedly to reconnect with his fiancée, Louise Norton, whom he assumed had been waiting for him.

Holladay did show up and was warmly greeted, but he was in terrible shape, having just learned that Louise had broken their engagement and taken a lover, the composer Edgard Varèse, in his absence. He brandished a small vial. Asked by O'Neill what it contained, he said "heroin," indicating he had already used it plentifully. He proceeded to place some more of the white powder on his fingertip and sniff it. Demuth indulged as well. O'Neill, who for all his drinking took a different view of hard drugs, was enraged. "You fool!" he bellowed at Holladay, who was looking worse by the minute. O'Neill stormed out.

Some time later, the group—Holladay, Dorothy, Demuth, and whatever other friends were actually present—moved on to Romany Marie's on Christopher Street for some of her Turkish coffee. Marie's Romanian accent, account of her tribal ancestry, and gypsy attire might have been an affectation like so much else in the Village scene, but her coffee was notoriously good. They wrongly thought Holladay might be calming down.

What happened next at Romany Marie's is clear enough. Holladay couldn't control his despair and didn't stop with the vial. Suddenly his pallor grew worse and his breathing became seriously labored. In a matter of minutes, it was clear that he was dying. The tearoom emptied quickly once the other patrons realized what was happening, with only Dorothy, Charles Demuth, and the aghast Romany Marie left to cope with the situation. Dorothy reportedly cradled Holladay in her arms as he breathed his last. When the authorities and Holladay's sister, Polly, who ran a Village restaurant herself, arrived, everyone lied to the police and said that, as far as they could tell, the deceased appeared to have had a heart attack. Polly testified to his poor cardiac condition. It was several hours before the body was taken to the coroner's, and a thoroughly shaken Dorothy was left to dispose of the heroin. In some accounts, she met Max Bodenheim on the street, who had heard the news, and gave it to him to take care of. Demuth staggered back to the Brevoort, his hotel off Washington Square. When she went to tell O'Neill and Agnes the news, she found O'Neill retreating into himself, already on his way to a drunken stupor.

It was time to effect a change. As William Miller put it, somewhat fancifully, in the first full-length biography of Day, published in 1982, "She had had enough of causes, of 'characters,' of bad free verse, drunkenness, and casual sex." It was time, at least for the moment, to look for a day job and grasp at bringing some structure back to her life. Witnessing O'Neill's heartlessness toward a friend in distress produced a shock as painful and traumatic as Holladay's death itself.

For a brief time, Dorothy returned to Union Square and the political press. Following the shutting down of *The Masses*, Max and Crystal Eastman and Floyd Dell had determined to start another monthly very much in the spirit of their first venture but clever enough to elude the censors. Largely under Crystal's guidance, *The Liberator* was a vigorous combination of political commentary, reportage, original art, and book criticism, but in arguing for a negotiated peace in Europe, the editors could claim to be simply following a strict Wilsonian line. Dorothy had started working there on a very part-time basis in December but now hoped for a real job. As she had been given so much responsibility for the last issues of *The Masses*, she expected, or at least hoped, to be taken seriously in the magazine's offices on Union Square East. In reality, she found herself relegated during her few months there to tending to the mail and keeping the place tidy. The Eastmans did print two of her articles, though.

One, appearing in the first issue in March 1918 (the cover daringly announced "John Reed's Story of the Bolsheviki Revolution" with a drawing of a Russian peasant scattering seeds of goodwill), was a reprint of her November review of Sherwood Anderson's novel *Marching Men*. Possibly the Eastmans felt that Anderson deserved more attention now that they had a new venue in which to provide that, or they might have worried that too few people had seen the final issue of *The Masses*. The other piece, published the following month, was a fictionalized account of an unidentified young woman found with darned stockings and a yellowing chemise, "poorly but neatly clad . . . with eighteen cents in her pocket," washed up on a beach, which she titled "A Coney Island Picture." Dorothy's four-paragraph sketch, probably based on a newspaper report of a real suicide, has the terse pathos of a drawing by John Sloan or Robert Minor.

In April, Dorothy eagerly left the magazine and Manhattan, eager to steer her life in an entirely new direction. She was ready to begin the nursing program at Kings County Hospital. She packed her few belongings and moved to Brooklyn. Only a few weeks into the program, however, she needed to take time off—to answer a subpoena. Politics was not so easily put behind her.

For all practical purposes, *The Masses* was long dead and buried. The post office had seen to it that the magazine had been kept from enough subscribers to drive it out of business in 1917. The Eastmans and Dell were focused on *The Liberator*. But the government wasn't done with them. Charged with conspiracy to obstruct enlistment because of several editorials and articles in *The Masses*, Eastman, Dell, Art Young, business manager Merrill Rogers, the artist Henry Glintenkamp, and the poet and contributor Josephine Bell, who had never even met any of her codefendants, were quickly indicted. The prosecution called several reluctant witnesses, including Dorothy, to testify against their former colleagues. (One can only imagine her family's reaction: both of her older brothers had enlisted in the navy when war was declared.) Thus began a trial that was, in Floyd Dell's apt words, "a scene out of *Alice in Wonderland* rewritten by Dostoevsky."

Dorothy Day had a front-row seat for the spectacle. A Liberty Bond rally was being held outside the courthouse with a band periodically striking up the national anthem, at which time Merrill Rogers would jump to his feet, bringing the proceedings to an awkward and hilarious halt until the judge insisted that patriotic displays had their limits. Dell arrived late one day with the head-turning Edna St. Vincent Millay on his arm; she recited poetry to him during the intervals to calm him down. Art Young made a show of trying to keep awake when he was not ostentatiously sketching the jury. Yet the stakes were high, and the levity of some of the defendants masked a real anxiety on their part about having to serve jail time. Popular opinion was obviously unsympathetic to socialists and pacifists, the prosecution was hot to get the verdict it desired, and the jury men were under considerable public pressure to "do their duty" in wartime. The president and the attorney general were known to want a conviction.

One thing the defendants had going for them was the expertise of Morris Hillquit, one of the city's great lawyers and the darling of *The Call*'s editorial board—"a scholar and a gentleman," in Dorothy's estimation. Hillquit was known for particularly able summations to the jury. Other advantages were the broad-mindedness of Judge Augustus Hand (the federal judge who in

1934 would strike down the obscenity charge against James Joyce's *Ulysses*), the overall vagueness of the charges—*The Masses* had never explicitly urged men to refuse to serve—and, most critically, the staunch belief in the First Amendment of one juror who was probably a socialist himself. Dorothy wasn't the only member of the magazine's staff called on behalf of the prosecution. Hillquit adeptly prepped her, John Sloan's wife (a fund-raiser for the magazine), and others, and their testimony on the stand did nothing to advance the prosecution's case that an antidraft conspiracy had taken place in the offices on Union Square. If anything, the image that came across of their journalistic enterprise was of a contentious group of people who could agree on very little and were more likely to be fighting among themselves than organizing a concerted effort to subvert the Selective Service.

The result was a mistrial. One holdout let his fellow jurors know that they could sit there until doomsday before he would change his mind. That failure didn't stop the district attorney's office from making a second attempt in October, an effort that was even less successful in what were the closing days of the war. Dorothy shared the joy of her friends and colleagues at the triumph of justice, but she also learned something interesting that spring about the radical left: a number of people let it be known that they were angry at Eastman and Dell for their patriotic speeches on the stand and ploys to make the magazine seem less incendiary than it was meant to be. They wanted martyrs for the cause. The individual fate of the men who would have to go to jail and suffer indignity and privation mattered less to them than advancement of that cause. Dorothy, who knew firsthand what it meant to be at the mercy of vindictive prison guards, took the opposite view.

Kings County Hospital was a free hospital for the underserved. It was exactly what Dorothy was looking for. Della, then eighteen, convinced Grace Day to allow her to join Dorothy in the probationers' class, and Grace, grateful that both girls were employed in a respectable job and that they would be nearby, even assisted in making the pink uniforms and the voluminous aprons that the hospital required of its novice female staff. Uniforms and textbooks were paid for by the probationers in the first three months, but after that time, the hospital supplied them with clothing and a ten-dollar-a-month salary. About half of every probationer's class dropped out of the program before the end of the three-month trial period, finding the strain and poverty of their position too much. Dorothy and Della stayed the course.

The first patient Dorothy remembered assisting with was a ninety-four-year-old Canadian woman who refused to be bathed, insisting that she had bathed the day before and didn't need it. "Can't you see we want to take care of you because we love you?" one nurse offered. "Love be damned," the woman snapped. "I want my wig." Embarrassed to be losing her hair, she was mollified when the nurses found a cap for her.

The hours at the hospital were barbarically long. The young women worked from 7:00 a.m. to 7:00 p.m., with a half day free on Sunday and one half day during the week. Two hours each afternoon were given over to classroom instruction. With the war raging and so many nurses having left the hospital for the International Red Cross, the shortage of help was a serious problem, with a single nurse taking responsibility for as many as fifty patients. As a city hospital, Kings County admitted only the most seriously ill New Yorkers, and the probationers found themselves confronting an awesome amount of physical labor, helping men and women into and out of bed, emptying bedpans, walking patients down the hall, and feeding the completely disabled. "We had to change each bed every day," Dorothy later recalled, "bathe all our patients, rub them down with alcohol, dress bed sores, give out medicine, attend demonstrations of procedures, and generally assist in the irrigations and injections, tappings for spinal and lung fluid, and all the other treatments for patients in the medical and receiving wards." Women of less stamina and commitment than Dorothy and Della found the regimen unbearable. Their supervisors were taskmasters: mattresses were wiped down on both sides with a carbolic solution, sheets were folded and tucked in a certain way, not a speck of dust was to be found on any surface.

The catastrophic influenza epidemic had hit earlier in the year, making a difficult situation both perilous and more arduous. Patients were younger; their prognosis more dire. It was heartbreaking to watch men and women, some her own age, soaked in sweat, wheezing for air, their whole lives ahead of them, expire in panic and despair. During the worst periods of the outbreak, time off for the doctors and female staff was almost nonexistent. When the armistice was finally announced, the nurses in Brooklyn were scarcely aware of it. "We were far from Times Square, where the crowds of New York and the countries around are wont to celebrate," Dorothy would remember. "We were too utterly exhausted with the care of the sick and dying to dissipate our energies in rejoicing."

One friend Dorothy made in this period who was a sustaining influence was a Miss Adams, a probationer from Canada several years her senior and a woman of exceptional vigor. She had been the first to recognize the need of the angry Canadian patient to be treated with dignity, her need for a wig more important than a bath or any nurse's well-intended condescension. Miss Adams wasn't a lapsed Catholic, like so many people one met in New York who had been raised in the Church but had fallen away; she was a devout, practicing but not proselytizing Catholic. Dorothy now had someone with whom she could go to morning Mass at a nearby church if she chose, though that act of devotion required rising even earlier than normal. Miss Adams seemed to find it no hardship. There was also a chapel on the hospital grounds, which Dorothy noted was packed even at the start of a weekday. The men and women in those pews weren't people who would have understood Eugene O'Neill's need to flee the embrace of Catholicism, let alone belittle the faith he had been born into; they were believers, people whose lives were grounded in, made larger by, their faith.

"One day, I told myself as I knelt there," Dorothy wrote, "I would have to stop to think, to question my own position." The troubling questions were the obvious ones: Why are we here? What does a life without transcendence, without any hope of a higher purpose, mean? How is it possible that we are alone in the universe? What is the point of all our struggles? That day wasn't just yet, not exactly, but it was coming as questions about life's meaning or futility had been troubling Dorothy throughout her adult life and even before adulthood. Suffering and service provided a context in which such questioning began to seem more vital than ever before.

As the months rolled by, Dorothy came to decide that the highly systematic life she was living at Kings County Hospital was a good thing. Those riotous nights in Greenwich Village seemed a distant memory and not always a pleasant one. Organization and self-discipline did not come easily to her at her age, but community discipline meant that one's life fell into "efficient, orderly lines." That level of efficiency and order allowed one to accomplish more than seemed humanly possible, "disregarding fatigue, both physical and mental."

Perhaps, but not always. There was one woman, "bearded . . . with no breasts," about whom the other nurses spoke furtively and disdainfully. She had a ferocious temper, threw things at the nurses, and was constantly, it seemed almost purposely, soiling herself and intentionally aiming to dirty the nurses' uniforms. Dorothy admitted that she had to grit her teeth and hold her breath while bathing her. One afternoon, after a long hard several hours at work, "the perverse patient" threw her bedpan onto the floor, splattering Dorothy's shoes and stockings. Stunned, Dorothy ran to the washroom and burst into uncontrollable tears. In her memoirs, she recalled the assistant superintendent's tender remarks to her when she went back to her post about the hardships they were all enduring but also about the great responsibilities nursing entailed and the awesome dignity of their profession, what Dorothy was later to term "the sacrament of duty."

Not all of the more difficult people she had to deal with were cranky older patients. Some were fellow nurses who couldn't have cared less about "the sacrament of duty." Della reported to her sister a terrible scene she had witnessed when a young woman died just as the night shift was leaving, forcing the newly arrived morning-shift nurses to tend to the body before they started their rounds, which meant that their day's shift would be extended. On the other side of the screens, they were belligerent in their disrespect to the corpse—complaining that the woman could have waited to die until it was more convenient for them, bitterly commenting on her wetting the bed before she expired, slapping her as they turned her over—all of which everyone on the ward could hear, including her weeping husband, "just a young boy."

In *The Eleventh Virgin*, Dorothy's protagonist meets a good-looking kitchen worker at the hospital who is about to become an orderly for whom she feels an immediate and overpowering sexual attraction. Part of the attraction initially focuses on his broken nose. On line for breakfast one morning, she tells him that he reminds her of a photograph of a bust she had seen of Amenemhat III, a Middle Kingdom pharaoh, whose sculpted nose was similarly angled. "Who the hell is he?" he barks at her. Then he apologizes and asks if she wants her eggs scrambled or poached. A complicated romance ensues.

The truth behind Dorothy's real-life meeting with Lionel Moise (pronounced *Mo-ees*) is something she always preferred to keep shrouded in mystery. The most that can be determined about the start of their relationship is that he was a newspaperman, not a thirty-year-old orderly, and that Dorothy probably met him on one of her weekday or Sunday evenings off when she went back into Manhattan to socialize with old friends. He wrote for the *New York Tribune*, having completed a brief stint in the army that ended with the armistice. He didn't have much use for doctrinaire little publications such as *The Call* or *The Masses*, and his politics were what one might call flexible. (He tended to support labor over management and had a soft spot in his heart for the Wobblies, but in 1920 he accepted a job as publicity director for General John Pershing's campaign for the Republican presidential nomination.) The immediate and overpowering sexual attraction that Dorothy's character feels was very much based on reality, and the object of her desire indicated a similar enthusiasm.

Even if she knew that Lionel Moise didn't look like the type who had a reliable history with women, Dorothy felt no urge to rein in her feelings. The man was robust, amorous, immensely confident, highly opinionated, loaded with colorful stories of his roustabout life (more far-ranging than O'Neill's), some of them even true, and he liked the fact that the pretty young nurse from Brooklyn was so obviously smitten. He also liked the fact that he could tell her to her face that he had no interest in marriage and never would and still she didn't run in the other direction.

After several months of grinding labor, forced celibacy, and unresolved thoughts about religion and vocation, Dorothy found herself preparing to take a large risk without concern for consequences. Nothing Della could say meant anything. Work at the hospital had become painful, and the past was the past: Mike Gold and the artist Maurice Becker, among so many others she knew, had decamped to Mexico to avoid the draft, and politics was something she wanted to put out of her mind. There was an element of free fall in even acknowledging to a man like Lionel Moise so blatantly her attraction, and that felt right, desirable, necessary. Birth control, suffrage, socialism, the sick and the dying, Miss Adams's piety: she didn't want to think about any of that. Turning twenty-one in November, Dorothy was ready—eager—to lose herself in a reckless passion. She was ready to enter into a relationship that would leave her, once again, unmoored.

FIVE

❧ ARDOR ❧

TALL AND BROAD-SHOULDERED, BLOND, JEWISH, THIRTY YEARS OLD, devastatingly well featured, with nothing of Mike Gold's kindness or Eugene O'Neill's ambivalence, Lionel Moise was everything Dorothy was looking for in the autumn of 1918. In her novel, she contrived to be near the attractive man employed by the hospital whenever possible, stopping by the kitchen at odd moments for something more to eat and, once he had commenced his duties as an orderly, helping him get a rowdy patient back into bed. Then it is sneaking out of their rooms and meeting after dark on the hospital grounds or making out at the back of the kitchen, with the Dorothy character indicating her readiness, if a time and a place could be found, to go further. Those pages of *The Eleventh Virgin* have a romantic throb. In prosaic reality, a subway ride to Manhattan brought Dorothy to her lover's apartment.

Lionel Moise came with a perfect package of a life story. He was a wanderer and a journalist, at home in city hall or in waterfront saloons. The year before he came to New York, he had been a newspaperman for the *Kansas City Star*, one of the best papers in the country. (By the end of his life, his journalistic résumé would be formidable, with stints at the *Boston Record*, the *Milwaukee Sentinel-News*, the *San Francisco Examiner*, the *Salt Lake City Tribune*, the *New Orleans Times-Picayune*, two Chicago papers, two New York City papers, and two Los Angeles papers.) It was a peripatetic path he had already committed himself to, exhibiting the sort of restlessness that precluded a stable home life or secure reputation in any one city, but his talent was such that he had no trouble finding a job as a journalist when he felt it was time to move on and see another part of the country. He had a "massive mind," the poet Kenneth Rexroth wrote in his memoir of writers he had known, and a "hard-boiled magnanimity" that impressed many of the young men who came into his orbit.

One eighteen-year-old he impressed was a cub reporter on the *Star*, Ernest Hemingway. Just out of high school and in Kansas City for only a few months before leaving to join the ambulance corps in Europe, Hemingway was struck—awestruck, according to some associates—by everything about the man. He had a facility with language, enormous vitality, and a go-to-hell manner with anybody who questioned him. He was extraordinarily well-read. He tended to keep his distance from the other reporters unless he was three sheets to the wind, he could manage to get anyone to talk to him if he needed the interview, and he was comfortable with all kinds of people, having worked (he said) as a deckhand on a freighter, a lumberjack, and a cameraman for a film company in South America. Women made no secret of their interest. It was rumored around the *Kansas City Star* office that the expensive car he drove was a gift from a female admirer, of whom there were many. Like most of his relationships with women, that union ended badly. The woman reportedly stabbed him in a fight, which he didn't take to kindly, and she ended up unconscious with a broken jaw in the back of the roadster.

In his defense, Lionel would have said he never led anyone on. He could be funny and tender, but he could be unnervingly honest. The women who went for him had to like uninhibited sex as much as he did, they had to accept masculine dominance, and they were expected never to bring up the topic of marriage or babies. He wanted his women to be independent of those middle-class needs—and subservient to his.

Dorothy gave her notice at the end of the year and had to endure the ire of her supervisors at losing one of their better nurses. Lionel had agreed that she could move into his West 14th Street apartment. "Let your conscience be your guide," he told her, kissing her hard, when she broached the subject. Grace Day had taken ill, and, as Della was planning to continue her nursing work, Dorothy had no choice but first to go home to take care of her for a week, but as soon as she could get away, she was in Lionel's flat and his bed. She had acknowledged to her mother that she was "terribly in love" with a man she knew didn't love her and was going to move in with him. She didn't care about the future, about propriety. She wanted him. After recovering from her initial shock and dismay, Grace tried to take the news in stride. Understanding her eldest daughter and trying to influence her down a safer and more conventional path was something she had given up on long ago. The dialogue from that moment in *The Eleventh Virgin* has the ring of verisimilitude: "Why do you ask me what to do? You know you'll only do what you think best for yourself and pay no attention to me, anyway. I can't say anything that I know isn't absolutely futile." The real-life mother, the fictional mother—they were right. "The life of the flesh called to me . . . the satisfied flesh has its own law," Dorothy wrote of that period in *The Long Loneliness.*

The intellectual side of Lionel Moise only added to his attractiveness for Dorothy. He quoted Shakespeare, Nietzsche, and Wilde. He could talk about Camille Corot and Édouard Manet. Together they read *The Possessed,* and it was thrilling to her that they could share a passion for Dostoevsky's great novel about politics and religion, the destructive allure of Nihilism, the search for meaning, and the ethics of suicide. The God-haunted Kirilov, desperate to believe, and the aimless, amoral Stavrogin were exactly the kind of people Dorothy loved to read about. (Lionel insisted that the character he most identified with was Stavrogin.)

Lionel had no interest in Dorothy's opinions, though, or desire to see her form her own tastes, something she as readily accepted as their strict gender roles in the kitchen or the bedroom. His literary gods—Victor Hugo, Rudyard Kipling, Mark Twain, Theodore Dreiser, Knut Hamsun—had to be her literary gods as well, and he let her know he didn't want to see her reading any more of her beloved Joseph Conrad. She agreed, suspecting that she wasn't likely to keep that promise indefinitely. Writers alien to his concept of realism weren't to have a place on his bookshelves, let alone be admired by anyone he slept with. At a later point in their relationship, when they were living in Chicago, he watched Dorothy seated on the elevated subway next to him absorbed in James Joyce's *A Portrait of the Artist as a Young Man.* He quietly fumed before finally grabbing the book and tossing it out the open window of the train.

Dorothy and Lionel did have one interest in common—the thrill of life south of 14th Street. Some of his articles in the *Tribune* dealt with Village life. With Malcolm Cowley and Peggy Baird, now engaged and living in an apartment at 16 Christopher Street, they were "companions in revelry," in Cowley's words. The four of them loved late nights, animated conversation, liquor-fueled parties. A born raconteur, Lionel could play the part of the tough veteran of the newsroom and had known his share of back-alley brawls, but he also wrote poetry, and Cowley seems to have fallen under his spell for a time. Cowley had reason to be grateful. When he came down with influenza during the height of the epidemic, Lionel stopped by to check on him, took one look at his condition, gathered him up in his arms, found a taxi, and then carried him from the cab into St. Vincent's Hospital on Seventh Avenue, probably saving his life.

Like everyone they knew, Lionel was a fan of the Provincetown Playhouse, but it wasn't enough for him to be simply a member of the audience. In February 1919, he appeared onstage there in *The Squealer*, a play about the Molly Maguires in the 1870s doing battle with the mine owners in which he played the turncoat of the title, and in April he was cast for a part in Eugene O'Neill's *The Rope*. (Whether he actually appeared in the production or not is a subject of confusion, as two separate sources reprint programs with a different actor named in that role. The preponderance of the evidence suggests he did.) But if he was contemplating making a career change, rather than simply having some fun in the evening, the reviews of his performance were not the kind to encourage him to leave his day job, although one review did allude to his good looks.

On a daily basis, Lionel's demands on his girlfriend could be relentless. He had a steady salary they could comfortably live on, so Dorothy was told she wasn't to look for a job nor was she to write *anything* until he was ready to instruct her on how to improve her style, which he found sloppy. The novel that she had started a year earlier (presumably *The Eleventh Virgin*) went nowhere, probably for that very reason, even though she had accepted a one-hundred-dollar advance from a publisher, which was spent "riotously." She was the bedmate and housewife, in charge of the shopping and the laundry and seeing that he was well-fed and the apartment kept clean. Lionel was also obsessively jealous. If they dined out with her old friends and he felt she was paying too much attention to any of the male company, his reactions could be frightening. It is hard to believe he would have accepted her protestations that her relationship with Eugene O'Neill had been chaste, and he jibed O'Neill about that. One night Dorothy didn't go home after an especially unpleasant scene in public but stayed with the Cowleys for two days. When she finally returned, she and Lionel made love. Immediately afterward, he told her to clear out.

To those who knew Dorothy as an intelligent, strong-willed woman, her self-abnegating love for Lionel Moise—many would have called it a pathology—was distressing and disorienting. To those who knew her later in life as a devout and increasingly pious Catholic, her willingness to lose herself in satisfying the demands of an egomaniacal man could have been especially confusing, though most friends, acquaintances, and colleagues who knew her after the 1920s had no inkling of the details of a relationship she was loath to discuss.

At this stage in her life, Dorothy was still fighting the faint but insistent religious impulses that kept impelling her at odd moments to church, to attempts at prayer, to the New Testament. Losing herself in sex and obedience to a passionate if abusive lover was one sure way to do that. Yet it was also a way to see what it felt like to *surrender*, or at least diminish—intentionally, consciously, dramatically—all sense of self as the modern world defined and applauded it, committing one's life, even irrationally, to something other than one's ego, comfort, and ambition. Dostoevsky's characters, passionate and unpredictable, had made an impression that would never abate. The example of Thomas De Quincey, indifferent to common sense and polite society, was still alive in her mind.

Della, Peggy, and other friends hoped that Dorothy would now strike out in a new direction, but she made it clear that she wanted Lionel to take her back. She was ready to abase herself to be taken back into his arms. She got word to him that she could be found every evening at a Village restaurant they had been frequenting lately, and if he wanted to see her, he should stop by. She was apologetic for anything she had done to anger him. Night after night, she waited until closing time. Finally he showed up and sat down at her table. He took the book she was reading, Max Beerbohm's *Zuleika Dobson*, and commented on the fact that it was inscribed by a male friend. Nonetheless, he invited her back. Peggy Baird—now Peggy Cowley—was aghast. "You're a fool," she told her.

By that time, Dorothy was in the grip of an obsession she could scarcely control. Her pregnancy that summer, then, should hardly have been a surprise. Was it intentional, part of a desperate hope that it would make a difference to Lionel? Was it accidental? A woman who knew enough about contraception from reporting on Margaret Sanger's work, a resident of a part of town who would have known where to purchase condoms under the counter, might be considered someone able to avoid an unwanted pregnancy, but nothing about Dorothy's state of mind in the summer of 1919 suggests the stability to think clearly. It is entirely possible that Lionel was opposed to the use of condoms, insisting that the women he slept with had to take responsibility for what they did in bed. There was, understandably, no topic—ever—about which Dorothy Day would be less forthcoming than that one. Not the pregnancy nor what followed.

Dorothy knew this was nothing about which she could talk to her mother—her father's reaction would have been an icy silence or a judgmental fury—and she did not, apparently, confide at first in Della. The one person Dorothy felt she could confide in was Peggy. She was of the view that, come what may, Dorothy should have and keep the baby. Having recently found out that she was infertile, perhaps as a result of a venereal infection she had contracted just before her marriage, Peggy even felt a certain measure of envy toward Dorothy. What she didn't want to hear was talk of an abortion. But that was the direction of Dorothy's thoughts. When Dorothy finally found the courage to talk to Lionel about the situation, he was blunt. He loved her, in his way, he told her, but he had been clear about babies and family from the start. In fact, he informed her that he had recently been offered a job on the city desk at the *Chicago Evening Post* and that this might be the right moment for a break. He was packed and gone in no time.

Dorothy followed Lionel to Chicago. She returned to New York a few months later, then the following year went back to Chicago for a longer period, though it isn't clear if they ever lived together in the Windy City. She was pregnant when she first arrived and had to find work to support herself before it became too apparent that she was expecting, and then she concluded that time was against her: if she was going to terminate the pregnancy, it would have to be, for so many reasons, including her own health, sooner rather than later. The abortion probably took place within her first weeks in Chicago. In *The Eleventh Virgin*, Dorothy wrote about her protagonist seeing a woman on the Upper East Side of Manhattan for a procedure that sounds grimly unpleasant. The truth was so much worse that she felt the need to disguise for the novel the actual facts as much as possible.

Given the man Dorothy approached about performing the abortion, it is reasonable to assume that she had solicited names from left-wing contacts in the city. She had neither the time, money, nor social position to seek out a sympathetic practitioner with a higher-class clientele in a clean office in a good part of town or even a female doctor who might have the right résumé. The person she went to—"fat, dirty, and furtive," as she remembered him— was Ben Reitman. Reitman was a figure (more a character) in the field of radical politics. A former lover of Emma Goldman, he had suffered for the cause, having been horrifically assaulted in San Diego when he was attacked by a mob of vigilantes, and he did yeoman's work with the prison and hobo population of Chicago. The problem was that, at almost three hundred pounds, he was himself a less-than-hygienic person, and there were some who wondered if he had actually graduated from medical school. His medical practice catered almost exclusively to prostitutes and women with venereal disease. Promiscuous, bisexual, and self-aggrandizing, he had three things to recommend him: availability, cheap rates, and experience in performing many abortions.

Dorothy's memories of the procedure were bitter. Reitman came to her apartment. He was quick and insensitive, she felt; he left her bleeding on the table, and she had to be helped down by the daughters of her landlord. Several months spent in Lionel Moise's bed had led to that.

Needing the company of her mother and sister and a few sympathetic friends, accepting for the moment that Lionel meant it when he said he was too busy with his new job to see much of her, Dorothy returned to New York. What followed was a period of drift and torment as she recovered from complications from Reitman's poor handling of the abortion and realized that she had no clue about what she wanted to do with her life. Drift turned to despair.

In search of a place to stay, Dorothy approached a friend she had made through the Provincetown Playhouse, Sue Light. She and her husband, an actor and director at the theater, lived at 86 Greenwich Avenue. The Lights talked their Irish landlord into renting Dorothy a room in his family's first-floor apartment. Far away from Lionel, they hoped, she might be able to calm down. Coming home from shopping one afternoon, Sue was met by the landlord's young son who nervously told her that he thought he smelled gas coming from Dorothy's room. Quickly entering the room, they found Dorothy unconscious, the gas hose disconnected from the heater, and dragged her upstairs to the Lights' apartment, where she woke within a few minutes and drank some tea. Dorothy refused to lie down or see a doctor, as Sue urged, or discuss what had happened. Sue Light was never certain whether she had witnessed an embarrassing accident or a suicide attempt. Malcolm and Peggy Cowley held the latter view.

Even more troubling, a second suicide attempt using laudanum followed not long after, Dorothy once confided to an acquaintance. Recovering her equilibrium, facing the world again, was a process that took months. She did eventually force herself to make a decision. It was time to stop being crazy, she told herself and her family. It was time to act like other American girls her age and find someone to provide for her, someone who could offer her a stable, well-ordered life. She probably had that somebody already in mind.

The man was Berkeley Greene Tobey, one of Floyd Dell's close friends. Seventeen years older than Dorothy, sweet but somewhat scattered, he and Dorothy had crossed paths during her first years in New York. Recently divorced for the second time, he lived in comfort in a large apartment on Washington Square, but his dilettante's heart was with the political and literary ferment all around him. A Liberal Club regular, he had worked as a business manager for a socialist magazine, *The New Review*, and bankrolled *The Masses* when finances turned particularly grim there. He and his second wife acted in a play with the Provincetown Players. He knew Theodore Dreiser and Upton Sinclair, with whom he had shared a jail cell one night after their arrest at an anarchist camp in Delaware. Tobey loved the good life, and he loved smart women, especially younger women, but in a less possessive, more casual way than Lionel Moise. Reports on how many marriages he enjoyed in the course of his eighty-odd years vary, but the numbers range from six to eight. "Another strange character," Malcolm Cowley thought.

Bookish, well-off, affable, wine-loving, left-leaning in his politics: he made his attraction known, he seemed a plausible rebound choice to Dorothy, and without much ado the two were married in Greenwich, Connecticut, on February 19, 1921. It is doubtful that any family members were invited. Grace and Della were surely uneasy. Dorothy's marriage was an act, thoughtless and abrupt, about which she would feel great shame for the rest of her life. One can't say, though, that Berkeley Tobey was in any way harmed by a union entered into freely, if precipitously, on both sides.

The newlyweds didn't remain long in New York. Like many of their countrymen in the postwar period, they went to Europe for several months to take advantage of the spectacular exchange rate and the ebullient spirit, to be enjoyed by Americans with money, of those countries that had finally claimed victory over the decimated Central Powers. In London, Dorothy said, she happily walked for miles and rode the double-decker buses and "explored and thought of De Quincey and Dickens." She went to Dickens' house on Doughty Street and to his grave in the Poets' Corner of Westminster Abbey, to De Quincey's Soho, to St. Paul's Cathedral, the British Museum, and the National Gallery. Tobey wasn't a stingy man, and he liked good hotels and good restaurants. How alien to Dorothy's experience that would have been—and how little it did to make her consider, or even hope, that her feelings for her husband might ripen into something genuine and meaningful. Tobey made use of his considerable connections, and he and Dorothy were introduced to a bohemian crowd in London that included the sculptor Jacob Epstein, the creator of the controversial tomb for Oscar Wilde in Paris's Père Lachaise cemetery. That year Epstein was embroiled in an even worse scandal as critics attacked his newest work, *Christ Risen*, both because a Jew had dared to sculpt the Messiah and because the face looked suspiciously like Woodrow Wilson's.

Then it was on to Paris, which made a less favorable impression on Dorothy. Unfriendly people and a lot of drinking were more vivid memories for her than the cafés, the Louvre, or the Eiffel Tower. There her thoughts, she said, turned to her reading of Honoré de Balzac and Guy de Maupassant, and—something Tobey could boast about back in New York—they met Marcel Duchamp, whose *Nude Descending a Staircase* had been the *succès de scandale* of the Armory Show in 1913. Everyone was talking about Dadaism, the new anarchist art movement of which Duchamp was a leading figure, Pablo Picasso's abandonment of Cubism, and the reopening of Serge Diaghilev's Ballets Russes for its first season since the war. That was Berkeley Tobey's milieu but not Dorothy's.

It wasn't until the Tobeys moved on to Italy that Dorothy found a place of real contentment. No record exists of her first impressions of the Eternal City, St. Peter's, or any of the other great Catholic houses of worship or religious art collections around her, which is unfortunate, nor do we know much of her time in Naples other than that she liked to wander the streets on her own and attended the outdoor opera. On Capri, the fabled island on the south side of the Bay of Naples, she told friends later that she knew bliss. No Grand Tour sightseeing, no museums, no cosmopolitan parties—only the sun, the beach, the limestone cliffs, the stunning views of the Tyrrhenian Sea, the food, her delight at observing the locals—and a project. "The six months I spent in Capri," she wrote, "meant that forever after, the smell of Italian cooking, the sound of buzzing flies, the loud strong voices of my Italian neighbors, the taste of spaghetti and polenta and the sour red wine brought me back to the months I spent beside the Mediterranean." And brought her to memories of her project. Once settled into her rented rooms, Dorothy decided to finish the novel she had set aside during her time with Lionel.

Capri was known for its writers' colony and its hospitality to British and continental gay men and lesbians; Norman Douglas's 1917 novel *South Wind* had described it as a place that provided a "sudden strong stimulus" for those buttoned-up souls who needed it, driving one's thoughts "headlong, out of their grooves." D. H. Lawrence had been in Capri the year before, though he left in a disagreeable mood, calling the place "a stewpot of semi-literate cats," and Maxim Gorky was to arrive the next year on Vladimir Lenin's orders, hoping to recover his broken health.

F. Scott and Zelda Fitzgerald spent time on the island. (Fitzgerald was horrified at the number of homosexuals he encountered.) Dorothy might have been there without her husband, or he might have stayed for a while to see her properly accommodated before he traveled elsewhere in Italy. She had less time for him now. She was working a good part of the day. A large part of the novel, *The Eleventh Virgin*, was revised and freshly written in Capri. She had been driven "headlong," out of her old grooves.

It was an auspicious moment to bring to fruition what was, in effect, a bildungsroman. Autobiographical coming-of-age novels were in vogue. What models, if any, Dorothy had in mind when she embarked on her own wasn't something she ever commented on. Given how avidly she kept up with contemporary fiction, she might have been familiar with any number of successful recent examples from Somerset Maugham's *Of Human Bondage* and Sherwood Anderson's *Winesburg, Ohio* to D. H. Lawrence's *Sons and Lovers* and H. G. Wells's *Kipps*. Lawrence and Wells were especially appreciated writers among her friends in New York. She could have read Floyd Dell's foray into the genre, *Moon-Calf*, which had been published only a few months earlier, and she had in fact read Arnold Bennett's popular *Clayhanger*. She knew from adolescence Jack London's *Martin Eden*.

The spirit of Jack London's autobiographical novel hovers faintly above *The Eleventh Virgin*. A restless man, Martin Eden wants more out of life than the situation into which he was born promises him. Preoccupied with sex and social class and meaningful choices, he can never be satisfied with what satisfies those around him. Dorothy's protagonist, if more middle-class than London's sailor-hero, is of a similar age and temperament. "June Henreddy" even reads *Martin Eden* as a teenager and grapples with the same books Eden does in an effort at self-improvement. The significant difference between London's novel and hers would be in her choice of ending. London had written a tragedy; Dorothy Day was writing in a more hopeful vein. Her "coming of age" was still in progress.

Like many first-time novelists, Dorothy made use of the experience of her twenty-three years, changing names, borrowing snippets of conversation, and tailoring real-life events for her purpose. Certain characters can be clearly identified and would have been recognized by their models: her mother, her sister, her brothers, Peggy Baird Cowley, Rayna Simons, Floyd Dell, Margaret Sanger's sister. Others, such as Mike Gold, were used as part of a composite. "Dick Wemys" was Lionel Moise to the life, though enough about his résumé was sufficiently altered that no one who actually knew Lionel would necessarily conclude he was the person being described.

The story, such as it is, follows the rough outlines of its author's life—a childhood full of questions and youthful doubts; college; work for publications that sound a good deal like *The Call* and *The Masses*; her arrest in Washington; nursing; and finally a tempestuous affair with a man who, after leaving her to seek an abortionist on her own, has no more use for her. The title presumably alludes to the parable of the ten virgins in the New Testament, a story about those who are and those who aren't prepared for the day of reckoning.

By the time it was fully formed and completed to Dorothy's satisfaction, the novel ended in an indeterminate way, with June hopeful that she may someday win Dick Wemys back. In the book's epilogue, she wonders if the much-vaunted liberated woman was just wearing "a modernity gown, a new trapping" to appeal to a certain kind of man. More important than the novel's underlying confusion of values, though, was its static and disjointed quality as a narrative, something Dorothy struggled with for some months. *The Far Side of Paradise* it wasn't.

By the end of 1921, the Tobeys were back in Manhattan and took up residence at the New Yorker Hotel, but they were not to be "the Tobeys" for long. Dorothy admitted to herself (what she had known all along) and to her husband, friends, and family that the marriage had been a great mistake. Given that Tobey had a minimum of three more weddings ahead of him over the next twenty years, it is hard to imagine him as surprised or heartbroken. In any event, the union was quickly ended. She left her wedding ring on the bureau one morning and walked out. With an abortion and a divorce on her conscience, Dorothy determined to work on editing her novel and do what she did best at that juncture of her life: seek out Lionel Moise again.

Chicago in 1922 was no cultural or political backwater. H. L. Mencken insisted that the metropolis on Lake Michigan had produced more important writers than New York, and both Harriet Monroe's famous *Poetry* magazine and Margaret Anderson's *The Little Review* had been launched there. The millionaire Jake Loeb ran a salon that was the intellectual equivalent of Mabel Dodge's in Manhattan. Political radicals, of whom there were plenty, gathered at the Dill Pickle Club and made outdoor speeches at Bughouse Square, and small avant-garde theaters performed Shaw, John Millington Synge, Frank Wedekind, and O'Neill. A friend, probably Max Bodenheim, who was living in Chicago at the moment, took Dorothy to a party at Loeb's where she met Sergei Prokofiev, who was in town for the premiere of his opera *The Love for Three Oranges* at the Auditorium Theatre. The party must have involved singing by the guests as the Russian composer joked to the young American that she had a good ear but a terrible voice.

Dorothy had little money, but she did have the stamina and faith to assume that she would land on her feet. Certainly, finding housing in a poor neighborhood wasn't hard. She took a room in what she described as a "slum" on Ontario Street and began a succession of odd jobs to keep the wolf from the door. They included stints as a clerk at Montgomery Ward's department store, a public library checkout girl, a restaurant cashier, a night-shift clerk at a print shop, and an artist's model. She looked up Rayna Simons, now a committed Marxist, who was glad to see her. Her real mission, though, was to see if Lionel would take her back, and there she enjoyed what appears to be only intermittent success.

Lionel was never one to say no to a romp or to female companionship for a night on the town, but an ongoing relationship was of no more interest to him now—and perhaps even less—than it had been in New York. He was having an epic amount of sex these days, Kenneth Rexroth suggested, with even the call girls he romanced fighting over "the beautiful, beloved body of Lionel Moise." Dorothy did her best to cope with that reality, eventually dating other men and trying desperately to achieve some perspective on her life, but it was not easy keeping depression at bay or stopping herself from showing up on Lionel's doorstep, offering to iron his shirts.

A complicating factor was that Dorothy had become friends with another of Lionel's recent castoffs. Mae Cramer, thirty years old, was part of Chicago's bohemian crowd. She had overcome a drug addiction that had led to her arrest on a shoplifting charge, and suffered the futile hope that all women associated with Lionel had, that she would be the exception who would tame him. When he made clear to her that she was in error, Mae took a handful of bichloride of mercury tablets and ended up in the county hospital. Upon her release, with nowhere else to go, she took refuge at an all-male IWW rooming house where she knew the men would give her sanctuary for the night. She called Dorothy and asked her to bring her some food and fresh clothing, which Dorothy did. She decided to spend the night with her friend, who was in an understandably delicate state.

The Chicago police were in the midst of yet another period of harassment of radical groups in the summer of 1922, and that evening happened to be the night of a raid on the rooming house. Dorothy and Mae were caught up in the sweep. The presence of two women in a male boardinghouse, Dorothy wrote, "meant only one thing to the men who arrested us" and what followed, she said, was "as ugly an experience as I ever hope to pass through." Forced to get out of bed and dress in front of the leering detectives, the women were hustled downstairs and made to stand in the street like criminals until the paddy wagon arrived. They were told that they would be booked on a morals charge.

Terrible as her first jail experience in 1917 had been, this time on the wrong side of the law was even more lacerating and humiliating. Brought down to the cells at the police station, where fifteen or so prostitutes had been caught in a vice raid, Dorothy and Mae were manhandled by the police who arrested them, verbally abused by the guards, relieved of their possessions, and locked up with no one paying attention to their protestations of innocence. The toilets were on full view, and the women shared one wash basin. They were brought to court for their arraignment the next day, where a reporter friend recognized Dorothy, heard her story, and set off to find a lawyer and arrange bail. When the time came, though, Dorothy decided she wasn't going to take advantage of her personal connections and abandon Mae.

Dorothy spent the next few days in the city jail, where she witnessed some agonizing scenes: a drug addict banging her head with great violence against the walls of her cell, ignored by the guards and howling in torment, and a constant stream of abuse directed at the women. She also endured a strip search and an aggressive, degrading body cavity examination for hidden drugs. Dorothy was released the next week through the efforts of an old friend from New York who had seen her being taken from court to the paddy wagon headed for the city jail. That friend was Charles Phillips, the Columbia student from the Anti-Militarism League, who was now living in Chicago and knew a sympathetic judge who could intercede on behalf of the two women. As she had given a fake name when she was arrested, no one who knew her would have to know that she had been charged with prostitution, to her great relief. Phillips, a Marxist who had, like so many others, fled to Mexico to avoid the draft (where he helped to found the Mexican Communist Party), teased Dorothy that he only seemed to run into her in the oddest contexts.

Dorothy was sufficiently appreciative to go back to her manuscript and give Phillips a cameo appearance in The Eleventh Virgin. Phillips also probably tried to talk her out of her pursuit of Lionel Moise. Certain that the discolorations he saw on her face were old bruises, he was afraid that that relationship had passed any healthy bounds. Rayna Simons was equally worried and vociferous in denouncing Lionel's power over her friend. Time spent with the prostitutes, and being treated as one herself, left a kind of mark, too.

What most struck Dorothy about her jail mates, aside from their roughness of manner and language, was their vulnerability and resilience, their concern for the well-being of one another and capacity for empathy. Assuming Dorothy was a newcomer to their trade, they had taken her under their wing. To read about Sonia Marmeladov in Crime and Punishment or Marija Berczynskas in The Jungle was one thing; experiencing the reality was another. It was an event in her life, highly traumatic at the time, that she later decided she would not want to have been spared. (One wonders if that topic wasn't another source of Dorothy's lifelong appreciation of Eugene

O'Neill. His 1914 monologue *The Web* presents the most incisive summary ever written of what a prostitute is up against, even if she wants to change, and *Anna Christie*, his 1921 breakthrough play, is similarly understanding. Compassion on the subject was as rare in American drama as it was in social and political life.)

Once she was out of jail and he heard about what had happened, Lionel decided to be helpful. His own days at the *Evening Post* were numbered, as Mae Cramer and a second young woman he had dumped, a seventeen-year-old who had also taken an overdose, had sold their stories to the Hearst papers, bad publicity his employers did not want. He was soon to move on to the *Milwaukee Sentinel-News*. But he did want to see Dorothy in better shape. Having instructed her in the value of reportorial terseness, he got her a job with the City News Bureau, a local version of the Associated Press that covered the police and courthouse beat, an ideal position for someone with a social conscience and a curiosity about the often derailed wheels of justice. She probably encountered some of her former fellow prisoners there again. She also met the reporters Ben Hecht and Charles MacArthur at the courts, the two men only a few years away from great success with their newsroom drama *The Front Page*.

Entrée to the inner precincts of Chicago journalism led in turn to a close friendship with Llewellyn Jones, the savvy literary editor at the *Evening Post*, and Samuel Putnam, Lionel's most brilliant colleague at the paper. Putnam was the *Post*'s erudite art critic and book reviewer. As well-read in modern literature as anyone else in Chicago and conversant with European artists most Chicagoans didn't want to know anything about, he liked to refer to himself as Chicago's—America's?—only Dadaist-Marxist. Dorothy visited his apartment, where his large personal library caught her eye. She must have felt at ease with him as the two talked freely about her religious confusion, and he obligingly lent her some books by Joris-Karl Huysmans. Putnam wasn't pointing her toward the infamous À *Rebours* (*Against Nature*), which she had already read, that fin-de-siècle testament to self-absorption, a decadent's homage to Charles Baudelaire, Paul Verlaine, and the dark philosophy of Arthur Schopenhauer. He gave her the later, dense, almost plotless novels that dealt with the author's renunciation of his previous outlook and embrace of the Catholic Church. Though popular in Europe, they were books Dorothy had never heard of and launched into reading right away.

En Route, *The Cathedral*, and *The Oblate* made a stunning impression, and Dorothy's gratitude to Putnam never diminished. Written soon after *Là-bas*, Huysmans's exploration of Satanism, the occult, and the rites of black magic, *En Route* is just what its title implies, a story of a journey, in this case the journey of a skeptic and misanthrope toward faith. That faith is, by the novel's end, at best tentative. The protagonist, Durtal—very clearly Huysmans himself—is uncertain that he will be able to sustain his need for a mystical union with God, especially as the allure of faith and the allure of art, of Gothic beauty and Catholic ritual, have become hopelessly entwined in his mind. In *The Cathedral*, Durtal is obsessed with the majesty of Chartres and the need to find a spiritual mentor who will understand just what he is looking for—mystery and transcendence, not anything resembling conventional piety. Finally, in *The Oblate*, Durtal becomes a lay resident of a Benedictine monastery, though his life there is not easy or peaceful. Twentieth-century society has no place for someone like him, and anticlerical France has no love for the Benedictines. Yet he is ready to leave behind his doubts, reject the modern world of hyperrationality and arid pleasure, and accept that suffering is integral to a belief in Christ.

The painstaking—even bizarre and self-torturing—quality of Durtal's search, Huysmans's fixation with some of the more macabre aspects of medieval Catholicism, his frustration over his alienation from God and the inadequacy of a life without faith: these were all topics of great interest to Dorothy, though she was by no means eager to replicate Durtal's experience. Neither, on the other hand, was she inclined to reject its meaningfulness or sincerity.

Dorothy observed the young people around her in Chicago who had been brought up as members of a church and could see the advantages. Her roommate when she moved to a different building on the North Side, a French Canadian milliner who worked out of their apartment, was a practicing Catholic, as was the daughter of her landlord. If they didn't seem especially devout, they at least believed in something. Later that year, a friend "in her disorderly life" from a Catholic background, Mary Gordon, observing and respecting her fascination with Catholic ritual, gave Dorothy a rosary, the first she had ever owned.

By degrees, to the relief of everyone around her, Dorothy was letting go of her attachment to Lionel. Della had given up nursing and, possibly at the urging of her mother, come west to be near her sister, a closeness that helped to ease her pain. Dorothy edited her novel once more, preserving its fantasy ending of a possible reconciliation with her lover, and sent the manuscript on its rounds to various publishers. She would have learned about this time that she wasn't the only person from her circle of friends who had been trapped and scarred by an obsessive love. Back in New York, the widowed Mary Heaton Vorse had made the mistake of a third marriage. The political cartoonist Robert Minor was respected by everyone in left-wing politics for his brilliant, original drawings; in his private life, he was no less self-centered than Lionel Moise. Even as Vorse was recovering from a miscarriage, he announced that he was leaving her for another woman and heading to Chicago, to which the offices of *The Liberator* had relocated. (The Eastmans had passed the editorship of the magazine to Mike Gold and the black novelist and poet Claude McKay in 1921, a disastrous mismatch that had lasted only several months. Then Minor had taken over.) Out of work at the moment, Dorothy heard that he was looking for a secretary and, as Floyd Dell was willing to vouch for her, Minor took her on.

Robert Minor's politics had become only more emphatic since the old days. He was now a member of the newly formed Communist Party USA, which had bought a controlling interest in the magazine. Membership in the Communist Party was of no more interest to Dorothy (then or ever) than membership in any other party. She had never even registered as a Socialist. Despite the fact that she must have resented his callous treatment of her friend, she worked at *The Liberator*'s offices on North State Street for several weeks, handling correspondence and editing copy, commenting later that her boss had moments approaching paranoia in his belief that his every movement was being watched by the government. It was pleasing to her to see that Minor welcomed Mike Gold's contributions to the paper, despite the bad blood that Gold, crankier and more doctrinaire by the day, seemed always to be leaving in his wake now. The October 1923 issue printed a poem he had written about the death of John Reed in Moscow and a short story about the racism of a white nurse in a hospital ward treating a dying African American patient.

Dorothy also wrote one article herself for *The Liberator*, a book review in the November issue. It was a cleverly done account, in the form of an open letter to the author, of Floyd Dell's new novel, *Janet March*. The book was a hymn to the New Woman, the postwar female who had an appetite for life, felt guilt-free about sex, and wanted to make her own way in the world. Dorothy voiced her approval of the novel, the character, and the values Dell extolled. Did she even recognize that Janet March was everything her own protagonist, June Henreddy, pining for Dick Wemys and marriage and babies, was not?

As 1923 drew to a close, winter on the Great Lakes made moving elsewhere, preferably to a warmer climate, seem desirable. Lionel was gone, and finally Dorothy accepted that he could not be a part of her life any longer. Chicago had never felt like home, at least not since the family had left in 1916, and Dorothy thought briefly of returning to New York. She wrote to Margaret Sanger, wondering if she might serve as the American Birth Control League's publicity director, but there were no funds to take her on, Sanger replied. Instead, with her novel taken at last by the small New York publishing house of Albert and Charles Boni (the contract, it might be noted, very disadvantageous to the author), she hoped to make a career out of writing. She wanted a fresh start, to leave behind the scenes of past traumas, and her sister was ready to join her in that endeavor. She made a brief trip east to see her mother and the Boni brothers and then headed for the Gulf of Mexico. The new year saw Dorothy, Della, and their friend Mary Gordon established in a new home in the French Quarter of New Orleans.

SIX

❧ CONTENTMENT ❧

N EW ORLEANS WAS "SURELY THE MOST CIVILIZED SPOT IN AMER-
ica," Sherwood Anderson wrote to his brother in 1924, comparing
the "hard fist" of Chicago, which he knew all too well, to the "open hand"
of the city on the Gulf. New Orleans, he felt, offered the charm of Creole
culture, a leisurely pace of life, and a picturesque setting in which to write
and bask in the sun. Dorothy was less interested in culture or leisure, though
the picturesque was on her mind—as was forgetting the immediate past and
pushing herself to get on with her own writing.

From the two rooms she, Della, and Mary rented on St. Peter Street in
the Vieux Carré, within walking distance of Jackson Square and the French
market on the Mississippi River, she worked on her new novel, corresponded
with the Bonis about her constantly shifting publication date, and solicited
blurbs for her dust jacket from Eugene O'Neill, Floyd Dell, Mary Heaton
Vorse, and Llewellyn Jones. She told Jones early in the new year that she
was having, on the whole, a "lovely time" with Della and Mary, though the
three of them were living at the moment largely on shrimp, rice, oranges,
and bananas. Mary had a wonderful sense of humor and exhibited a "huge
appetite for a 'good time.'" It was the right place for anyone in search of a
good time. There were "lots of pretty boys around," she noted excitedly. She
was drinking "a little but not too much" and was in general "being godly
and righteous according to my lights." Presumably Jones, now a confidante,
knew what that meant.

The job Dorothy found was a far cry from her work for *The Call* or *The
Masses*. Editor Marshall Bullard at the *New Orleans Item*, whom she must
have approached with the same tidal wave of enthusiasm she had used
on Chester Wright in New York, managed the oldest afternoon paper in
the South, and her Yankee background was of no matter to him. What he

wanted was a young woman who could write and was willing to take on some juicy assignments from a feminine angle in a city that boasted a busy night life and had as little regard for the Volstead Act as most American metropolises did. Needing an income right away, Dorothy had no trouble presenting herself as the person he was looking for.

Her most extensive work for the *Item* was a six-serial feature on the city's "free" dance halls. To get her stories, she had to go undercover, a frolicsome prospect, spending some time as one of the employees, called "taxi dancers." She and another woman—the sociable Mary?—talked their way into the office of the manager of the Arcadia, told him they had heard on the street that he needed more girls, and were ready to work. They were fresh-faced and willowy, they didn't look inhibited, and they were pretty much hired on the spot.

Between dances with inebriated or amorous partners, Dorothy spent as much time as possible in the dressing room, where she was told never to leave her bag, as thievery was rampant, and where she could chat up her fellow dancers to get their stories and hear about the city's two other principal dance halls. The twenty-five or thirty girls who worked at the Arcadia, Danceland, and Roseland ranged in age from sixteen to forty, and they knew what they were there for. The customers often numbered as many as three hundred—locals (single and married), traveling salesmen, sailors on leave. The last could be particularly assertive. The men were admitted for free to the dance hall, where a jazz band played nonstop, but were required to buy "dance tickets" when, from their perch on the surrounding balcony, they spotted a desirable partner on the floor below. For ten cents per dance (prices varied as did the length of the dance), they could select any available woman they wanted; the women usually made only four or five cents per dance.

Whatever other arrangements were made for after-hours meetings, the management regarded as none of its business. Given the amount of drinking taking place—many of the men brought flasks to share surreptitiously with the girls—and the amount of marijuana on hand, assignations were a given. ("Drink, Dope Flood Halls" was the headline of one of Dorothy's articles.) Sometimes the customers were just gangs of boys, "none of whom looked to be over seventeen," who had gotten drunk beforehand to work up their nerve, came in to dance for as long as they could stay upright, did their best with fumbling adolescent "advances toward intimacy," and then staggered out en masse.

Though the *Item*'s reporter took pains to comment on how little the dancers made and mentioned at least one girl who needed to work at night to supplement her meager income as a salesclerk, the purpose of the series wasn't to serve as a antivice-crusading exposé. Everyone understood that the New Orleans police knew perfectly well what went on at the dance halls and couldn't have cared less so long as the payoffs were timely. The Crescent City's prosperity was linked to its reputation as a hot town. Rather, as with the many such newspapers, Bullard wanted a racy, circulation-boosting account of sin that didn't end up sounding approving but likewise wasn't indignant or moralistic. He wanted his readers titillated. He got exactly the tone he wanted. He also got a complaint: an area naval commander protested Dorothy's characterization of his sailors as the type who would frequent tawdry dance halls and be anything other than gentlemanly. Dorothy heard as well from some of her disgruntled former tea-dance colleagues who had read the articles. She was accosted one night in a bar and, when a glass was thrown her way, ended up with a black eye.

Another of Dorothy's articles homed in on her father's milieu, the local racetrack, where she was allowed to evince a plausible measure of indignation. Her thrust was how hard the management of the Fair Grounds made it for women to place bets, given the inconvenient separate entrance to the betting area, and the off-putting condition of the women's restrooms and the no-smoking regulations, which most women at the track particularly resented. Dorothy was also sent to report on the cabaret scene, to interview the prizefighter Jack Dempsey, and to get an exclusive with the aging Eleonora Duse, the famous actress, who was briefly visiting New Orleans but declined to see her. It was Mrs. Byrne of the birth control movement all over again, the reporter shut out at the doorstep. This time, though, she made an article out of her futile attempts to get into Duse's hotel suite. "Even Sleuth Tactics Fail to Break Actress' Privacy" took up as many columns of print as an actual interview might have. By now Dorothy had honed her reportorial style, its blunt clarity and deadpan humor.

Dorothy stayed in New Orleans not quite five months before returning to New York. Della, who had had a harder time finding work, had left after several weeks at her parents' urging. Once spring arrived, Mary headed back to Chicago. For Dorothy, on her own, there didn't seem to be much point in staying. None of the men she had met made a change of plans seem worthwhile, the intellectual stimulation of New York wasn't to be found in New Orleans, and she was concerned that the Boni brothers hadn't expressed any enthusiasm for an early draft of the second novel, entitled *Moon*, she had sent on to them. John Day told Della to let her sister know that he was willing to pay for her return to New York and "honest womanhood," if she chose, and he would even give her money to find a room in some respectable boardinghouse, "provided any would have [her]." As Dorothy told Llewellyn Jones, "Thank God, I've never had to take advantage of my father's kindly offers." When she needed to borrow money, she preferred to appeal to friends such as Jones.

Dorothy's memories of her brief time in New Orleans were always warm, and she would return several times for very different reasons later in life. Among her most significant memories were those she did not share yet with friends or family and involved moments she would never have spoken about to anyone at the *Item*. Taking the rosary beads Mary had given her, she would sit in a pew at St. Louis Cathedral on Jackson Square, just a short walk from her apartment, to read a booklet she'd purchased in the church shop about how to pray the rosary. In the weeks that followed, she attended Mass and other services, finding herself particularly moved by the Benediction of the Sacred Heart, by the sight of the gold monstrance and the raising of the Host, the elevating sound of "O Salutaris Hostia" and "Tantum Ergo," the smell of the incense and the devotional concentration of the people around her. Indeed, in later years, Dorothy credited the time she spent under the imposing barrel-vaulted ceiling of St. Louis, one of the oldest cathedrals in the South, as the real start of her conversion. Yet when she considered approaching a priest or a nun for guidance, she hesitated for fear that they might read into her questions "some expectation that was not there."

It should also be noted that anyone wanting to reflect on the spiritual and the eternal here would need to look away from the grandiose bronze statue on the square, smack in front of the cathedral. There President Andrew Jackson sits astride his rearing horse, the embodiment of American power—of arrogant, worldly success. It is impossible to contemplate the cathedral from any distance without simultaneously contemplating the famous war hero. He was, in fact, honored at a celebration in the cathedral in 1840, as was President Zachary Taylor several years later after the United States' defeat of the Mexicans in that notorious land grab. The proximity of such a powerful political symbol to that Catholic house of worship is not something Dorothy Day at twenty-seven would have failed to perceive. Nor was it just Manifest Destiny, the Trail of Tears, and a general relish for expansionist warfare that represented to her mind the dark side of the United States as she had studied her country's history. It was politics itself, all political aspiration and ambition, that she was coming to question.

Well-intentioned as socialist agitation or progressive political protest might be in her worldview, Dorothy's heart was no longer entirely with those who devoted themselves to social causes. Mary Gordon was returning to Chicago to become a member of the Communist Party. Mike Gold, Charles Phillips, Maurice Becker, Rayna Simons, Rose Pastor Stokes, Elizabeth Gurley Flynn, Samuel Putnam, and many other friends and professional acquaintances she had known and admired had found a home there or would eventually. Did commitment to a movement, to reformist or even revolutionary politics, have the capacity to move her as mysteriously as the experience of the rituals at St. Louis but whose meaning she wasn't ready to explore any further? She was at that moment doubtful.

Dorothy stayed in New Orleans for her first and only Mardi Gras but not for Palm Sunday or Easter. Having decided to accept a check from her father, after all, she headed north. Back in Manhattan, before finding work and a place of her own, Dorothy roomed with the Cowleys, just back from two years in Europe and living now in an apartment at 33 Bank Street.

Post-Lionel, post–New Orleans, the Cowleys' houseguest seemed to them somewhat tempered in her drinking but more libidinous than ever, almost as if she wanted to air a contempt for physical pleasure. The Cowleys, of course, were the last people in the world to be prudish about the urges of the flesh, but to their eye a lack of joy characterized Dorothy's erotic antics. Malcolm Cowley recalled watching Dorothy seduce a friend of his from Harvard, the poet John Wheelwright, in his own living room. Wheelwright was gay but, like some gay men of that era who brooded about society's prejudices, was open to the possibility of broadening experience. Dorothy evidently provided him with a transitory broadening experience.

It was a time of distinct tension, though, on another level. Happy as she was to reconnect with Peggy Cowley and Sue Light, glad as she was to be able to visit her mother once again, Dorothy was caught in the state of mind normal to any author awaiting a response to her book. She had hoped that her return to New York would signal the start of a promising literary career. That was not to be.

When it appeared in bookstores that spring, *The Eleventh Virgin* was spared the usual fate of most first novels—no reviews at all, a thundering and mortifying silence—but the notices it did receive might have made its author wish for less attention. Cowley was one of the few book reviewers to try to find something good to say about the work of his wife's best friend, but even his was faint praise. (Peggy herself did not think the novel was very good.) In the *New-York Evening Post*, he called it an authentic portrait of Greenwich Village life in its heyday.

The *New York Times*, on the other hand, declared it a tiresomely "adolescent" novel, incoherent in its plot and unimpressive in its prose. The *Detroit Free Press* reported on it as a book with "not much to get excited about," despite the promising endorsement that the review quoted, from Floyd Dell, who called the novel "a moving story of today," full of "riotous and glamorous incident." The *Pittsburgh Press* thought *The Eleventh Virgin* had its vivid moments but that ultimately the author had "woven her story weakly" and offered "little enlightenment" on the question she was posing: How is the young woman of 1924 different from the young woman of her mother's era? The *Indianapolis Star* warned readers that it was the kind of book to leave a "bad taste," while the *St. Louis Star and Times* judged it a rambling novel of flat characters and undeveloped ideas. The *Hartford Courant* suggested that the author had a "slender but definite literary gift" but had expended it on a task "not worth the doing."

The *New Republic* wouldn't give Dorothy even the compliment of a "slender" literary gift. There she was credited with having devised a compelling plot sunk by a lack of realism and a "total inability to write a single line of good, compelling English." Worse came from the *Oakland Tribune*, which ripped the novel apart as the unconvincing story "of a female moron who is inordinately proud of the fact that she remains a virgin after reaching the age of reason." The novel was "not honestly written," the reviewer insisted, branding it as cheaply trying to cash in on a trend and "as true as a plug dime." Her few favorable reviews were brief notices in the *Honolulu Star-Advertiser* and the *Houston Post* along with a puff piece, largely plot summary, in the *Chicago Tribune*, thanks to Llewellyn Jones.

Interestingly, the abortion scene was not the occasion for any particular outrage or discomfort among the book's reviewers. Eugene O'Neill and Theodore Dreiser had written plays about the topic in the 1910s, but they were not widely known. More recently, Floyd Dell's *Janet March*, F. Scott Fitzgerald's *The Beautiful and Damned*, and John Dos Passos's *Manhattan Transfer*, all novels brought out by mainstream publishers, included scenes in which characters ended, or contemplated ending, their pregnancies, though none was as detailed as the description in Dorothy's novel. That year Dreiser was at work on *An American Tragedy*, which in 1925 would become the most famous story of its time, in which a young man urges his girlfriend to have an abortion. Censorship of the issue was fading fast. Had Dorothy or her publishers counted on shock value to give her novel wider attention, the strategy failed. After an initial spurt, *The Eleventh Virgin* sold few copies and went quickly out of print.

Dorothy's family was just as happy the book went nowhere. It was nearly the last straw in her relationship with her father, who now found it difficult to hold a civil conversation with his daughter on the rare occasions they found themselves in the same room, but even Dorothy's two older brothers took umbrage at her airing the family's dirty laundry in public. Friends weren't overly encouraging, either.

Hollywood, to the young author's surprise, took a different view of the book. Stories about bold young women were the rage, and Warner Bros. optioned the novel for a staggering $5,000. (Like most such deals, then and now, the option went nowhere. Changing the title, then changing the plot, various screenwriters worked with the material for several months before the project was finally shelved. Dorothy was in good company, though. That same month Warner Bros. optioned Edith Wharton's *The Age of Innocence* and Willa Cather's *A Lost Lady*.) After paying the government and then the Boni brothers their egregious cut, Dorothy still had more money in hand— almost $2,500—than she had ever had in her life. Peggy Cowley, best of friends, stepped in. She didn't want to see Dorothy fritter away this windfall, something she was perfectly capable of doing, and urged her to buy a house. Whatever the future might bring, she would at least have a place of her own, the stability she always claimed she was looking for. Later in the summer, they went house hunting—or, more accurately, bungalow hunting (Peggy's husband called it shack hunting)—on Staten Island, where, for the manageable sum of $1,200, leaving her enough to live on for several months, Dorothy found a place she liked.

In the meantime, Dorothy reestablished herself in Greenwich Village, taking an apartment with Della. In the mid- and late 1920s, when Dorothy spent considerable time there, the West Village was a highly literary neighborhood. With the Cowleys frequently at the hub of the literary wheel, the number of emerging authors who socialized with one another was considerable, most famously e. e. cummings, Edmund Wilson, Edna St. Vincent Millay, Marianne Moore, Katherine Anne Porter, Elinor Wylie, Josephine Herbst, John Dos Passos, and Hart Crane. Dorothy met Dos Passos at several parties—they had a friend in common in Mary Heaton Vorse—and Crane came over from Brooklyn Heights regularly.

Hart Crane's worst bouts with alcoholism weren't something Dorothy would have seen, as he reserved his truly horrific displays for his intimates, though she surely heard from Peggy Cowley about his active gay sex life. Like Charles Demuth, he was frequently on the prowl for rough trade. Nor was Crane remotely famous yet. *The Bridge*, one of the classics of twentieth-century modernist poetry, was some years in the future—as was Peggy's affair with him after her marriage to Malcolm had foundered. At the age of thirty-two, in 1932, he committed suicide by jumping overboard from a ship in the Caribbean, not long after ending his involvement with Peggy.

Dos Passos, on the other hand, was clearly someone who would not burn out. His was a name that was going to mean something on an international level. *One Man's Initiation: 1917* and *Three Soldiers* had already been published to good notices, and when Dorothy met him, he was soon to enjoy his biggest success with his urban epic, *Manhattan Transfer*, just the kind of vibrant New York novel Dorothy would have liked to write herself. This wasn't the world of artists manqué in tearooms, would-be poets and dreamers, the Village as the "citadel of amateurs," as John Reed had once characterized their turf. This was a world of prodigious talent. Malcolm Cowley was on his way to becoming a literary critic of note, and the Cowleys' good friend who lived nearby, the linguist and critic Kenneth Burke, was as intellectual (dauntingly so) as anyone Dorothy had ever met. Allen Tate and Caroline Gordon, a tempestuous couple from the South new to the Village, were both in New York at the beginning of long careers, he as a poet and his future wife as a novelist. What they all had in common was summed up by Tate: "We were young, we were poor, and we were ambitious." And most stirring of all was the example of Dorothy's old friend, Eugene O'Neill. A

Pulitzer Prize for *Beyond the Horizon* in 1920 had led to one more adventurous play after another.

A natural result of this close proximity to so many fiercely talented, productive people was that Dorothy felt a renewed determination about her
own potential and future. She wanted to make her mark as a novelist, to be
known for artistic accomplishments of which she could be proud. Despite
the soul-flattening reviews of *The Eleventh Virgin*, she continued, with admirable persistence—for more than fifteen years, in fact—to write fiction.

The easy familiarity of the Cowley circle could sometimes be emotionally
fraught. Dorothy and Peggy liked to stop by Caroline Gordon's apartment on
Morton Street—and Caroline genuinely enjoyed their company—but when
Mrs. Gordon was visiting from the South to spend time with Caroline's new-
born, Caroline worried that "wild people" such as Dorothy and Peggy were
rather a trial to a southern lady. Dorothy had recently cut her hair extremely
short in a "pineapple bob" after having bleached it in New Orleans: not a style
common in the better circles of Chattanooga. Worse, she and Peggy smoked
up a storm. Caroline was pleased that her mother had "borne [them] amicably."
Another potential complication was Malcolm Cowley's growing and scarcely
hidden interest in Della. When Peggy had imbibed too much at a party, Mal-
com would ask a friend who was leaving to take her home while he stayed on
to socialize (and later disappear with) Dorothy's sister, a young woman whom
more than a few men found attractive and personable. An on-again/off-again
affair between the two continued for almost three years until Della finally met
the man she wanted to marry. Always protective of Della, Dorothy never commented on the entanglement, but it made for awkward moments.

To her surprise and delight, Dorothy was developing a new romantic
interest of her own, far healthier than her relationship with Lionel. That
one, too, began by way of the Cowley connection. Dorothy may have found
Malcolm's friend Kenneth Burke intellectually intimidating, but she felt no
such hesitation about his wife, Lily. Theirs was a fortuitous friendship. She
had an attractive brother.

Lily Burke was a Batterham of the Batterhams of Asheville, North Carolina. Her parents were from England and remained fastidious Anglophiles all
their days, never bothering to become US citizens. In 1929, the family would

make a brief appearance in a novel by the son of an Asheville neighbor who became famous. In *Look Homeward, Angel*, Thomas Wolfe gave the Batterhams a cameo. There were nine of them: the parents, six girls, and one boy, William Forster, known always by his middle name, pronounced without the *r*. Dorothy had met Lily back in 1919, when she and Kenneth Burke, newly married, moved to the city and began socializing with the Cowleys. Renewing an old acquaintance in 1924, Dorothy and Lily now became intimate friends. It was a sisterly tie that would endure for almost forty years. Lily was bright, sociable, politically liberal, and very fond of her only brother. Forster had been Wolfe's brother's roommate at Georgia Tech, where he majored in biology. He had also studied at the University of Virginia. A serious student, he might have positioned himself for an academic job but never made an effort in that direction or any direction that suggested a career plan. His passions were fishing and gardening.

Though drafted in 1917, Forster had been unable to serve in World War I, having been ravaged by influenza, and he settled in New York, it seems, for no particular reason other than to be close to his sister. Lily introduced Forster to Dorothy, who had actually seen him once before. Forster had performed in a play at the Provincetown Playhouse (at this point, one asks, who didn't?). It was a play she had seen, O'Neill's *Moon of the Caribbees*, but the actor playing the small part of the seaman Olson evidently hadn't made an impression at the time.

He did make an impression in 1924. In falling in love with Forster Batterham—thirty years old, tall, lean, with a southern drawl and a receding hairline but still moderately good-looking—Dorothy was radically revising the contours of her romantic life. The brash men who wanted to upend society (e.g., Mike Gold), the men who believed in their own genius who wanted to make a mark in the world (e.g., Eugene O'Neill), the men who were fierce, controlling, and passionate (e.g., Lionel Moise)—Forster Batterham wasn't like any of them. He was the antithesis of those men. He was quiet and easygoing, when he wasn't thwarted in any way. He was gentle and quirky and seriously color-blind. His inability to color-coordinate his clothes was a source of real amusement to his friends. He believed in holding down a job to pay the bills (he was working in a Manhattan machine shop when Dorothy met him), not in forging an identity based on the work one did. He emphatically lacked ambition. Malcolm Cowley was of the view that his highest aspiration was to catch as many fish as possible. Sue Light found him acerbic and saw Dorothy's interest in him as more maternal than romantic, but Dorothy felt otherwise. Forster was someone around whom she could relax, feel safe for once, and imagine a lifetime of closeness. After all she had been through, he represented healing. Of no small importance, she felt as sexually comfortable with him as she had with any man she had known. He was an attentive lover.

"I have been passing through some years of fret and strife . . . even weeks of sadness and despair," Dorothy wrote in a journal she started early in 1925. But now, with Forster, she felt her life was enveloped with "quiet beauty and happiness." She was tired of dramatic men.

The bungalow on Staten Island played its part. The house she had bought was on the western end of Staten Island on Raritan Bay, a tin-roofed fisherman's shack twenty by eighty feet, with room for a flower and vegetable garden and meadows all around. There was no heat or hot water, but there was a wood stove she could fill with driftwood. From her porch, she could watch the gannets and gulls, the oyster boats and schooners, and hear the surf coming in. She lined the walls inside with the remains of horseshoe and spider crabs, starfish, and the shell of a sea turtle. Dorothy had taken her twelve-year-old brother in as well. John, Jr., had become a handful to his parents, and when they had moved to Florida that year, he had indicated he'd be just as happy not to join them, so the Days had passed him on to the care of his older sister. Grace might have felt some trepidation about that; her husband was glad to have the last child in the house off his hands.

It was impossible to stay at the bungalow through the winter months, so Dorothy and John would decamp to a monthly rental in the Village at the end of every year, waiting until spring arrived to return. But the minute she could be back in her own home, she was there, the city far behind her, its manic pace for the moment forgotten. Forster got on well with John, leading Dorothy to feel she had achieved a kind of perfection. For a long time, the beach brought out the best in her and in her lover. A photograph from the period shows Dorothy, Forster, and John reclining by their rowboat in their bathing suits, the sun in their eyes: three people fully at ease with one another and with the world.

They soon had plenty of company in the warm weather. The Cowleys bought their own place a short bicycle ride away, which had the added advantage of hot running water and Peggy's open invitation for Dorothy to soak in her tub. Mike Gold's brother bought a place for his family, which brought Mike back into her social life on occasion. Their neighbors—Pierre the bootlegger; Lefty, a hard-drinking beachcomber fisherman; the Russian Jewish émigrés; Mrs. Mario, who rented out rooms; and Mr. Harding ("a big polar bear with his white head"), who did yoga on the beach—were different from city people, less obsessed with money and advancement.

Reading the essays of William James on the beach her first summer on Staten Island led Dorothy to his *The Varieties of Religious Experience*. In that book, Dorothy took note of James's remarks on the subject of poverty and the need to rethink contemporary ideas about drive and acquisition. "We despise anyone who elects to be poor in order to simplify and save his inner life," the philosopher of pragmatism declaimed. "The liberation from material attachments, the unbribed soul" had become alien concepts in modern America. Her neighbors, many of them, felt like unbribed souls. Forster was an unbribed soul.

Dorothy and Forster quickly developed a routine that worked for both of them. During the week Forster was in Manhattan at his job, joining Dorothy and John on Friday night for the weekend, while Dorothy sat at her desk during the week, looking down to the beach and attempting to turn out as many pages as possible to make a living as a freelance writer. In her spare time, she was reading and rereading Dickens and Balzac in the hope of making the modus operandi of those two authors hers. Surely success lay in producing volume, in never stopping, in voraciously chronicling one's time and bombarding editors with articles and material for serialization. It is hard to know exactly what Dorothy published in that period, as she kept few records or copies of the originals, but it appears that her articles on gardening for the *Staten Island Advance* were among her few regular publications (and a meager source of income that would have been), though some of her fiction made it into various newspapers. She wrote a children's book, which seems not to have found a publisher, and never gave up hope of writing a second novel.

Even the friends who didn't take to Forster could see that there was a compatibility between the lovers. When Forster was back from work, they spent hours in their small rowboat in the bay in search of fish for dinner or just lying back in each other's arms, listening to the lapping waves. They could devote half the day at low tide to hunting for clams and mussels along the shore. Forster didn't have complaints about Dorothy's indifferent house-keeping and piles of books, and she enjoyed his eagerly offered instruction about botany and marine life. Forster wasn't the insatiable reader that Dorothy was, but at least his taste was sound by her notions (D. H. Lawrence, Aldous Huxley), and he devoured newspapers to keep abreast of world events. The day always started with tea and toast and his poring over the *Times*, railing about some new social injustice, some tale of municipal corruption or another example of the stupidity of the Calvin Coolidge administration, an indignation Dorothy found endearing.

Forster also introduced Dorothy to a cultural experience she had never had before and took to immediately: the opera. Together they would listen to broadcasts on the radio or, sometimes in company with Lily, attend a matinee at the Metropolitan Opera House on 39th Street and Broadway, taking places high up in standing room or splurging for balcony seats. It was an art form that Dorothy discovered served multiple purposes for her, aesthetic and restorative. Her tastes didn't run to bel canto crowd-pleasers. Once she had heard the Ring cycle, she became an ardent fan of Richard Wagner, and the intensity of *Parsifal* and *Tristan und Isolde* was a source of great pleasure. In later life, Dorothy shocked more buttoned-up Catholic friends by her relish for Richard Strauss's *Salome*.

Troubles in the relationship manifested themselves early on, too, which Dorothy could only hope would be assuaged over time or simply reasoned away. Some issues were small: Dorothy had no money but, rather like her father, spent it freely when she had it. At all times, Forster was frugal to the point of being cheap. Forster could be moody and didn't share Dorothy's love of socializing, at least not to the extent that she enjoyed it, which seemed to him excessive. He'd often slip away from parties at the bungalow to walk on the beach. More problematic was his horror of commitment. Freedom meant everything to him. In taking up with Dorothy, he hoped he was becoming involved with a woman who shared his sense of independence from conventional norms. The classic believer in the modern idea of the companionate marriage, he had every reason to assume that Dorothy, given her past, was like-minded on the subject. Two compatible adults, he felt, had no need for the state to provide a license and a contract, let alone a church to bless their union; their love, attraction, intellectual compatibility, and faith in each other should be sufficient to last a lifetime. And if marriage made him more than a little wary, he certainly wasn't interested in the commitment that fatherhood would entail.

Dorothy, on the contrary, was very interested in motherhood and seemed to think she could bring Forster around to share that feeling. It was one of many grave mistakes she made in choosing Forster as the man she wanted to spend the rest of her life with. When she became pregnant early in the summer of 1925, he was anything but pleased. He wasn't brutal in his response in the fashion of Lionel Moise, but he made it known that that was not what he had bargained for. Dorothy had seriously misread her lover. Forster wanted protection; he wasn't the man to protect Dorothy or support her in a situation that called for more than he was prepared to give or capable of giving.

Coupled with his anxieties about becoming a father and what that might entail, Forster was never able to make peace with Dorothy's curiosity about religion. He was not merely someone who didn't believe; he was someone who didn't understand why intelligent people would trouble themselves about the subject at all. Religion made him angry. It wasn't enough that Dorothy wasn't a member of any faith, attended Mass on the island very irregularly, kept her rosary beads out of sight, and didn't often discuss her reading and questioning with him. He sensed that this aspect of Dorothy's inner life, inchoate as it might be at the moment, was going to force a divide between them in the future. It grew to be a source of tension, and he refused to be hypocritical on the subject. He wouldn't pretend he thought otherwise.

In the third month of her pregnancy, Dorothy, Della, and John, Jr., decided to visit their mother in Florida. Dorothy needed a break from Forster, though she pined for him as soon as they were apart, and she was eager to see her mother. The Days had moved to south Florida when John had tired of his newspaper work and had amassed enough capital to become an investor in the new Hialeah Race Track. It was the life he had always dreamed of, his picture on the front page of the sporting section of the *Miami Daily News* in an expensive suit. As "presiding steward" of the track, he spent his days with other worldly middle-aged men whose most significant pleasures were horseflesh, betting, and Prohibition-defying cocktails. He traveled a fair amount, to Havana and other racing sites, and Grace and he were starting more and more to lead very separate lives. Grace rightly suspected that he had more than business on his mind when he was away from her.

Dorothy had decided not to tell anyone in her family about her pregnancy just yet, though Della guessed the truth when she saw her changing into her bathing suit. Thrilled for her sister, she agreed to keep the secret. In all, it was a restful break with warmer waters to swim in than New York afforded, though the humidity that made Grace think she had made a mistake in moving to Florida was equally a trial for Dorothy. Her love letters to Forster during their time apart were optimistic, sexually playful, and completely honest. "My desire for you is a painful rather than a pleasant emotion," she wrote. "It is a ravishing hunger that makes me want you more than anything in the world and makes me feel as though I could barely exist until I saw you again." Her sincerest wish was that, as her pregnancy advanced—as what they had created together could be seen as a product of their deep love—Forster would reciprocate and imagine a happy, if less independent, future with a wife and child.

On her train ride back to New York at the end of September, Dorothy's father met her at Union Station in Washington, DC, where he was staying at the time, for a quick visit, which she appreciated, given the early hour the train pulled in. She was grateful, too, for the money he slipped her. At unpredictable intervals, assuming that the demands on his time and emotions were not too great, John Day was willing to be the caring father. Like everyone in the family, he had to have wondered how in the world she got by. He agreed to send her a monthly stipend to continue taking care of John, Jr. A successful freelance writing career rarely yields much money, and sporadic success in that line of work leaves bills unpaid and the future uncertain. Horace Liveright and other publishers Dorothy had recently approached with the novel she had been working on for more than a year, entitled *Joan Barleycorn*, had found the book disjointed and gave her little in the way of encouragement. If this child she was carrying was to be raised on her income alone, she had reason to worry.

The cold-water flat Dorothy, Forster, Della, and John took for the winter was a reflection of their dire financial straits. It was above a saloon on West Street with a view, and smell, of the Hudson River docks. If Dorothy was right about her due date—she was guessing late February or early March—they would have to stay there for only a few weeks once the child was born before returning to Staten Island, where they would at least have running water, quiet, the vegetable garden, and clean air. Forster didn't seem to feel any special urgency about finding a better job to pay for the expenses that lay ahead, and the mother-to-be kept her anxieties about the possibility of a miscarriage, given her gynecological problems following the abortion, to herself. Between her visits to the free maternity clinic at Bellevue Hospital on the other side of Manhattan, she just kept writing.

Dorothy did have one publishing coup in 1926 that was cause for hope, something that she could boast of to her parents and friends. *What Price Love?*, the title of which was an allusion to the recent Maxwell Anderson play *What Price Glory?*, was a brisk novella serialized in the *Chicago Herald Examiner* with photographs of local actresses playing up the flapper angle of the story. The plot of that effort, which was more successful than her novels because it relied more heavily on dialogue than description (the latter was Dorothy's Achilles' heel as a fiction writer), concerned two young sisters on their own in the modern city, Tamar and Ruth. Tamar's philosophy was that of F. Scott Fitzgerald's "fast girls": "It stands to reason," she tells her more timid sibling, "if you don't let men ever kiss you, you are going to place too much importance on those same kisses." Interestingly, Dorothy had given the character of the more "advanced" and socially rebellious of the two sisters the very name she had decided she would give to her child if it were a girl: Tamara or Tamar—Hebrew for "palm tree."

It was a girl.

On the evening before her due date, Dorothy was relaxing in the bathtub with a book, a habit of long standing. She was approaching the end of an Agatha Christie novel when she felt her first contractions. With so few pages to go, she was determined to finish the book, which she did, but that didn't leave all that much time to rouse Della, dress, take her bag, and look for a taxi to get her uptown.

En route, to distract her sister and the nervous cabbie, Della chatted away, between puffs on the cigarette they were sharing, keeping up a running commentary on past cab rides they had taken on their way to wild parties back in Chicago. At the hospital, an orderly with a strong odor of whiskey on his breath took Dorothy to her room, where a nurse she described as large-hipped with marceled hair prattled on and on about Douglas Fairbanks, her favorite movie star, and doctors came and went. No one seemed overly concerned with the expectant mother until the shooting pains started and then came more regularly. She slept when the pain subsided before the actual labor began. She woke with her mind flooded with thoughts that might have occurred earlier to a more practical person: She had no crib or cradle at home. Was the clothes basket Della had bought going to be sufficient? How long were they going to have to manage in that awful apartment? Did she even have any idea how to raise a baby?

In the early hours of the morning on March 4, 1926, Tamar Teresa was born. Mother and child remained in the hospital for four days, and with each day Dorothy felt greater astonishment at this transforming development in her life, at the beauty of her baby, at the sense of fulfillment and unconditional love she was experiencing. The abortion could be atoned for. A new start was possible. Where Forster was while all that was happening and when, or if, he came to the hospital to see his daughter, Dorothy never said.

SEVEN

❦ CALLED TO GOD ❦

WILLIAM JAMES'S *THE VARIETIES OF RELIGIOUS EXPERIENCE* WAS precisely the right book for Dorothy to have stumbled on during this period of exploration and doubt. James wasn't writing as a theologian, anthropologist, or historian of religions but as a philosopher and psychologist interested in the psychology of religion, and the scion of the brilliant James family wasn't in the business of proselytizing or denigrating. Though the book dates from 1903, when James, a Harvard professor, finished delivering the text as the Gifford Lectures at the University of Edinburgh, he might as well have been speaking as Dorothy's contemporary.

The idea that faith belonged to another era, that its societal origins were rooted in premodern superstition, that its personal origins could be located in a flight from fear and insecurity, was widespread in Europe and the United States in the 1920s, not least among the people Dorothy knew and loved. Approaching the subject from a radically different angle, James asked his readers to make an effort to clear away preconceptions, whether favorable or critical, and to consider the connections between faith and strength of mind, the notion of faith as a critique of modern life, the varied meanings of saintliness and the "mystery of self-surrender," the long and provocative history of mysticism, and the usefulness of an unfanatical asceticism. He wrote as well about the plausibility of human concepts of God evolving over time, and the unseen as an aspect of reality no less potent than the seen.

James's project was an attempt to evaluate the religious life, not by its presumed origins or corruptions but by its purest results, and—while never quite making clear what, if any, faith he practiced—he insisted, though he was indeed a scientist, that it was "absolutely alien" to his purpose to discredit the religious side of life. Uninterested in considering dogmas or institutions, he sought to explore the meaning of what he termed "personal religion" or "religious consciousness." In reading *The Varieties of Religious Experience* on the beach and in her bungalow on Staten Island, Dorothy had encountered a modern intellectual of unassailable credentials, a writer of enormous refinement, who was in effect trying to clarify just what it was she had been held in thrall by when she walked into St. Joseph's Church in Greenwich Village or St. Louis Cathedral in New Orleans or when she handled with such eagerness and uncertainty the rosary beads Mary Gordon had given her.

What those sensations expressed, James believed, was an intuitive awareness of what he called "prayerful consciousness." His contention was that prayer was "the very soul and essence of religion," that it was a process, active and ongoing, the surest means by which human beings found a path to communion with a power that was mysterious and greater than themselves. This led not only to a heightened awareness, but to an inner strength and more deeply felt compassion. Arguments to prove the existence of God were absurd, worse than futile, James asserted; prayer was the gateway to belief and its benefits. There are passages in James's book that do not suggest an unbiased view of Catholicism and its rituals, but many more that resonated with a woman considering what a commitment to faith might mean.

Other aspects of James's inquiry spoke with an especially keen directness to Dorothy. His skepticism about progress as the West now defined it, which put forth comfort and success as the highest values any sensible person should aspire to, was an outlook she already shared. His belief that a faith that wasn't hard won was worth rather little and his insistence that those who had known pain and depression were precisely those who could be most open to the religious experience—not because they needed "healing" or a crutch, not because religion would be a salve for their damaged souls (though that, too, might well be the case), but rather because they were more cognizant than other people of the potential power of the "irrational" and the unseen and the productive, redemptive capacities of suffering— these were startling new perspectives. His allusions to St. John of the Cross and the "dark night of the soul" and to Teresa of Ávila and the "orison of union," though the author's view of the latter saint was not entirely uncritical, prompted Dorothy to want to know more about those great mystics.

Considering that Dorothy's life between the ages of twenty and thirty was marked by an intensity of experience, much of it dark or culminating in darkness, and considering that in later years she, and many of her admirers, wished to pretend that those facts were otherwise, the last point merits reiterating. As James's best biographer, Robert D. Richardson, wrote in *William James: In the Maelstrom of American Modernism*, "With [the chapter entitled] 'The Sick Soul,' James's Gifford Lectures reached their full power and conviction, and his work here joins that of Bunyan and Tolstoy . . . as a major testimonial to the darkness of mind that *precedes, complicates, and ultimately leads* [italics added]—sometimes—to the change commonly called conversion." It was a testimonial Dorothy Day needed to hear.

Still, reading and intellectual speculation were only going to take Dorothy so far in resolving her uncertainties. Well aware of the fact, she was equally clear about one other point and ready to act on it: she did not want her daughter to flounder through her early years as she had. She wanted Tamar to be baptized into the Catholic Church.

One day she plunged into those bracing waters simply by approaching a sixty-year-old nun she saw passing by on the street in Staten Island. Sister Aloysia Mary Mulhern of the Sisters of Charity was from St. James by-the-Sea, a rural annex of Manhattan's New York Foundling Hospital not far from Dorothy's bungalow, and she wasn't the type to be easily rattled. So here was a woman who was not a Catholic and had a child out of wedlock by a man who was not a Catholic, but she wanted her month-old infant to be a Catholic. Sister was more than ready for some conversation.

After meeting at length with Dorothy in private, Sister Aloysia conferred with a local priest who often came to say Mass at the foundling hospital, Father Joseph V. Hyland of Our Lady Help of Christians Church in the Tottenville section of Staten Island. They agreed that it made sense first to see that the mother in question received some instruction and fully understood what it was she was bringing her daughter to, that she grasped the fundamentals of the faith. Thus began the nun's visits to the bungalow. Sister Aloysia always rapped loudly on the door to give notice of her presence, allowing Forster enough time to exit out the back door in his inevitable stew; she didn't want to be there if "he"—the never-to-be-named infidel—was going to be present to scoff or disrupt. She gave Dorothy a catechism to study, a raft of saccharine brochures, and easy-reading lives of saints. How meaningful these texts were to someone who had been immersed in William James, was grappling with Johannes Jørgensen's dense biography of St. Francis of Assisi, pored over (not for the first time) the New Testament, and regularly recited for inspiration *The Imitation of Christ*, is open to question.

One aspect of Sister Aloysia's approach that did help her pupil was that she didn't minimize what Dorothy was up against. She knew, better than Dorothy did, that a loving mother's conversion had to follow her child's in due time; it was right and inevitable if her concern for her daughter's spiritual grounding was sincere. She understood, too, that a break with an atheist lover was nothing she could urge upon anyone, but conveyed the sense that Dorothy would eventually find her way, troubled though she often seemed. "There was a hard row to hoe ahead of us, was her attitude," Dorothy later observed, but her teacher was patient. "She would hang on to that long, formidable-looking rosary of hers, hang on to it like an anchor. . . . All we had to do was depend on prayer."

The baptism of Tamar Teresa Day took place in July 1927 at Our Lady Help of Christians. Having organized a party to celebrate the occasion with friends and Catholic neighbors, Dorothy was happy that Forster had agreed to attend, as he had refused to be present for the baptism itself. He was at heart an affectionate father. He may have hated the idea of fatherhood, but he doted on his own child. He even fished for lobsters to see that their guests were well fed, but when everyone arrived he became silent and finally stormed off. He stayed away for several days.

Money was another, ongoing source of tension. Dorothy's writing brought in pitifully little, and the jobs she took to augment that income—showing houses for a realtor on Staten Island, minding toddlers at a progressive school a few miles up the beach—never seemed to last very long. She also found work back in Manhattan as a publicist and fund-raiser for the All-America Anti-Imperialist League, an organization founded in Chicago in 1925 that had relocated to New York in 1927, now headed by her Communist friend Charles Phillips. Attacked by the US State Department as a tool of the Soviet Union, the League did in fact operate under the auspices of the Comintern, though its employees (like Dorothy) did not have to be Party members. They simply had to agree that US and European commercial expansion and military intervention in Latin America and the Caribbean needed to be publicized, attacked, and curbed. Dorothy felt strongly about that cause and shared left-wing outrage at President Coolidge's decision to send troops to Nicaragua to put down the Sandinistas.

Phillips's exuberant company brought back pleasant memories of their time together when he had been at Columbia University, lambasting Woodrow Wilson and the hollow claims that had led the United States into the Great War and of his rescuing her from the rough hands of the Chicago police. That most committed Communist always had a soft spot for Dorothy. Other friends and acquaintances she made at the time—such as the left-wing novelist Charles Yale Harrison and Fred Ellis, a cartoonist for the *Daily Worker*—wondered how the young woman managed to reconcile her religious stirrings with her political affiliations. She's never going to make a good Communist, Ellis predicted.

As the League's Union Square offices were only a few doors away from the offices of *The New Masses*—Mike Gold's revamping of the old *Masses*, a periodical now with a direct Communist link rather than a socialist slant—Dorothy also had a chance to reconnect with friends she hadn't seen in a while, including Gold, Mary Heaton Vorse, and Hugo Gellert. She kept her job and enjoyed her associations with these friends, though not without some misgivings. The Communist Party cared about the welfare of the poor but was unequivocal in its opposition to religion, and everyone at the League or *The New Masses* was a confirmed atheist. She asked the elderly Spanish priest at the small church that she attended during the winter months in Manhattan, Our Lady of Guadalupe on West 14th Street, about this troubling dichotomy. Father Zachary Saint-Martin's counsel was reassuring. Keep your job, he told her. You have a child to support. That must be your priority, and if your faith is strong enough, there is no need to worry about anything else.

It was good advice, tenderly expressed. Indeed, the first priests Dorothy came into closest contact with in the period immediately before her baptism and throughout the first year or two after her conversion—Father Saint-Martin; Father Hyland, and a second priest she would meet soon after on Staten Island, Father James McKenna; as well as Monsignor (later Cardinal) James Francis McIntyre, at the Chancery Canonical Office in Manhattan—were men of sense and compassion. That great good fortune made a difference: how much worse her trials would have been had she interacted with priests whose counsel was marked by rigidity and prejudice.

For one thing, Hyland urged her not to give up on Forster. It was her duty to try to hold her family together, he reminded her. A father/daughter relationship was a sacred bond, too. Dorothy couldn't be faulted on that count, though. She did all that it was possible to do to assuage her lover's concerns. His resentment was unappeasable. He wore it like an open wound. Dorothy's vow that she would never urge conversion on him, wouldn't ever bring up the topic of religion, wouldn't keep religious images and texts anywhere on view in the house if they bothered him that much, did nothing to change his outlook.

Her means of retreat when things were bad in this period was her pleasure reading, in bed, in the yard, on the beach—not religious texts, but the kind of books that had thrilled and sustained her since adolescence: great novels. Her journals from that period record her consumption of a fantastic amount of prose, including a rereading of *War and Peace*, an immersion in Nathaniel Hawthorne, E. M. Forster's new book, *A Passage to India*, and a reading of the first volume of what would become Sigrid Undset's sizable trilogy, *Kristin Lavransdatter*. The Norwegian Undset was a figure of particular interest to Dorothy, much in the news in the late 1920s (she won the Nobel Prize for Literature in 1928); the daughter of atheists and a Catholic convert herself, she had written in *The Bridal Wreath* about the conflict between a young woman's religious inclinations and strongly sensual nature. Given that her lover wasn't much of a reader, the sight of Dorothy lost in Tolstoy and Undset, ignoring him, no doubt only aggravated tensions in the bungalow.

Forster's mood wasn't improved either by the trying political events of the day. The arrest, trial, and conviction of the anarchist immigrants Nicola Sacco and Bartolomeo Vanzetti on trumped-up charges of robbery and murder had occupied their supporters for the better part of the decade. In 1927, despite the attention drawn to the racial prejudice of the presiding judge, the men's appeals had been denied and a date for their execution was set. Protests engulfed the nation. Della Day had inevitably become more politicized living in Greenwich Village amid the Cowleys and men such as John Dos Passos and Mike Gold's crowd. She had also become good friends with a neighbor, Katherine Anne Porter, who was an activist at heart. That August, she was one of many New Yorkers, including Porter, Dos Passos, Gold, Mary Heaton Vorse, Edna St. Vincent Millay, Susan Glaspell, and

Dorothy Parker, who traveled to Massachusetts, where they picketed and—as intended—were arrested for their acts of civil disobedience on Boston Common. An anarchist at heart, Forster felt strongly about the subject and, when news of the execution finally came through on the radio, he climbed into their bed and turned his face to the wall. It was a "day of grief," Dorothy wrote. He could barely bring himself to speak or eat for days. Of course, he hadn't been motivated to join his sister-in-law to picket in Boston, either. His innate passivity at times infuriated Dorothy.

Dorothy experienced health issues throughout 1927 that she attributed to thyroid problems, but the clinic doctors she consulted insisted her fatigue and weight loss was more likely a by-product of the stress she was under. There was ample cause for stress. Her feelings for Forster could fluctuate wildly between rage and devotion, disdain and passionate need. Her feelings about following through on her instruction with Sister Aloysia fluctuated as she debated within herself if her passion for God was as deep as she hoped and was going to prove lasting. For that matter, Sister Aloysia was a taskmaster. She often treated Dorothy like one of her elementary school students, expecting her to follow the time-honored rote system of Catholic religious education: state the question posed by the Baltimore Catechism and provide the answer word for word. When Dorothy faltered—did she understand the difference between actual and sanctifying grace?, for instance—Sister Aloysia would chide her that she wasn't as smart as she seemed to think she was, that she had taught fourth graders who had mastered their catechism faster than Dorothy. (Sister also upbraided Dorothy for her sloppy housekeeping.) Finally Dorothy was pronounced ready to be baptized into the Church when she herself felt ready.

A final, fierce argument between Dorothy and Forster during Christmas week brought her to that moment. She asked him to leave and not come back. She would have the locks changed if that was necessary. Enough was enough. Four days after Christmas, on December 29, 1927, Dorothy Day was baptized by Father Hyland at Our Lady Help of Christians. "I do love you more than anything in the world," she wrote to Forster shortly afterward, "but I cannot help my religious sense, which tortures me unless I do as I believe right." Religious conversion was a lonely experience, she concluded.

A lack of joy immediately after such a momentous step, the absence of any sense of exuberant resolution, is apparently not an uncommon experience. Only a year before, for instance, in February 1926, the British writer Graham Greene, at the age of twenty-two, had made his first confession and had been baptized and received into the Catholic Church. "I remember very clearly my emotion as I walked away from the Cathedral," he wrote in his memoirs in 1971. There had been, he admitted, "no joy in it at all, only a somber apprehension." That might describe Dorothy's state of mind as well, and exacerbating the problem for her was the stunning absence of support she would encounter in the ensuing weeks and months.

Forster wasn't the only one who saw Dorothy's baptism as a sad, or at least bizarre, misstep. To so many people who knew her over the last decade, she had now become an unsettlingly inexplicable individual. "It was like a curtain coming down," she told a friend years later. No longer was she Dorothy Day, the quixotic and mercurial young woman with a baby and a future that promised to be as colorful and messy as her past. Now she was Dorothy Day, *a Roman Catholic*. And that designation, among her secular and highly political circle of friends and relatives, defied reason and caused noticeable discomfort. The Cowleys and the Lights, Caroline Gordon, Lily Burke—all wondered if her decision was simply a reaction to a tempestuous past, a means to break with episodes both shameful and pain filled. If so, they could imagine her one day rethinking her melodramatic choice. Charles Yale Harrison expressed the view that Dorothy's decision to join the Church of Rome had more to do with her aesthetic sense and love of Catholic ritual than anything more doctrinal. Her new friend Katherine Anne Porter thought she exhibited signs of an inherently fanatical personality. "Such a strange end for her!" Porter wrote to Della, wondering if her sister would really hold on indefinitely to her "ingenuous convert fanaticism."

Dorothy's brother John, fifteen and awakening to an interest in science and politics, thought his sister was giving in to her usual, annoyingly morbid streak. Della was working for Margaret Sanger and was disheartened by the social policies of the Church her sister was now allied to. Mike Gold was one of her few old friends who could accept that the path of a woman he had once loved might sharply diverge from his own—could be unfathomable to him as an atheist and a Communist—while his affection and respect for her might be undiminished. The same could be said about Mary Heaton Vorse, but the list of those who refrained from judgment, whether spoken or just implied, is not very long.

That isolation took its toll. Dorothy had long since accepted that her family was never going to show any interest in, or understanding of, the subject. Her father and older brothers in particular made her feel freakish. Her mother acted dazed, uncomprehending. But equally off-putting was the number of people who did profess a faith, but only in the most superficial way. The "regular churchgoers" she knew in Manhattan or on Staten Island provided little sustenance, personal or spiritual. Theirs was the outlook summarized by George Eliot in a book long admired by Dorothy, *The Mill on the Floss*, in which the principal family of that story practices a religion that "consisted in revering whatever was customary and respectable," to believe in baptism, the sacraments, and burial in a proper churchyard because one was never "to be taxed with a breach of traditional duty or propriety." Dorothy's idea of religion, from the first, was that its beauty had nothing to do with custom and respectability and everything to do with larger yearnings. Yet there doesn't seem to have been anyone Dorothy knew at this time to talk to, any peer who might understand the complications of her situation and provide support in moments of loneliness or anxiety.

Not surprisingly, skeptical friends voiced what was, from their perspective, a plausible concern: namely, why did Dorothy have to choose Catholicism of all religions, a faith that made unique demands and extravagant claims, a faith that in Protestant America seemed plausible only if one was born into it? The Catholic Church, seen in that light, was nothing a rational, intellectual person of the twentieth century would commit herself to when more moderate, socially acceptable choices—e.g., the Episcopal or Unitarian Churches—might serve the same purpose. But those alternatives would not have served the same purpose; they were profoundly different, in Dorothy's view, less concerned with a mystical essence, more attuned to the rationality of faith and a progressive here-and-now—*lesser in all ways*. In response, she could have echoed Maggie Tulliver, the heroine of that same wonderful George Eliot novel: "I was never satisfied with a *little* of anything."

Faith in God and Christ as the Redeemer, a belief in Transubstantiation and the life to come, the veneration of Mary and the saints, delight in saying the Joyful Mysteries and the Sorrowful Mysteries of the Rosary, a willingness to be guided by a confessor and to accept the role of confession and absolution in a redeemed life, respect for the papacy and a two-thousand-year-old tradition: indeed, it wasn't "a little." It was *everything*.

* * *

In the new year, now that Dorothy and Forster were living apart, it seemed unlikely that they would ever reconcile, though it would really be two or three years before she would definitively give up all hope. She let him know that five dollars a week would take care of his end of the household expenses—she was determined to be as self-supporting as possible—though, as it turned out, she often didn't get even that. Forster just wasn't a driven man of business, and the little shop he opened in Lower Manhattan selling bicycles, train sets, typewriters, and radios barely paid his own rent in the city. He would come out to Staten Island on weekends to do the necessary repairs on the property, work on the ever-erratic plumbing, and see that his common-law wife and baby had fresh fish for dinner. He loved playing with Tamar and walking with her on the beach, but the tension in the air between the adults was constant, even though the weekend would sometimes end with Dorothy and Forster back in bed together.

That spring, finally having broken off her affair with Malcolm Cowley, Della married Franklin Spier, an Orthodox Jewish advertising agent and book consultant to publishers. (Mike Gold was Franklin's best man.) No longer would the Day sisters be sharing winter quarters. Dorothy found her way this time to a building on Hudson Street, between Perry and West 11th Streets, where Katherine Anne Porter, Caroline Gordon, and Allen Tate had also taken rooms. With its dark halls and narrow, uneven staircases, residents called 561 Hudson Street Casa Caligari after the recent Fritz Lang horror film *The Cabinet of Dr. Caligari*. Dumpy though it was, Dorothy enjoyed the camaraderie there.

"Creaking up the stairs," the writer and sometime Village resident Josephine Herbst remarked about the building and its ragtag tenants, "you half expected to see a skeleton wag from the ceiling, but instead a door opened on the second landing to a view of a child strapped to a high chair while it gobbled its bowl of bread and milk. It was Dorothy Day's little daughter, a rare sight, for children were few and far between for our generation. When you came to Katherine Anne's room, the prospect opened surprisingly to a domestic pavilion with gingham curtains at a window, a flowering primrose, a small cookstove with a coffeepot sizzling away, a gray cat on a cushion in a child's rocking chair." The female writer occupants of

Casa Caligari were billed by Malcolm Cowley as the three most talkative women in New York.

At that moment in their friendship, Porter and Day got along rather well. Porter read the novel Dorothy was constantly revising and, though she probably had reservations about its quality (everyone did), offered to help her find a publisher. No one was interested, though.

Some letters indicate that she was able to sell a manuscript, which may or may not have been the same novel, through the Bell Syndicate, a New York–based newspaper service that placed cartoons, fiction, and features with assorted papers around the country. Where, or if, *Joan Barleycorn* ever actually appeared in print is uncertain. No copies have been tracked down. That year Dorothy did publish a much-discussed essay, though, her first article with Mike Gold's monthly.

"Having a Baby" appeared in the June 1928 issue of *The New Masses*, and the author had to have been thrilled by both its publication and by the company she was in. Her name appeared in big black letters on the cover alongside the names of Ezra Pound and John Dos Passos (that by itself, in Village terms, was "making it"). In an issue that included an antigovernment tirade by Pound, a review from a left-wing perspective of the recent theater season by Dos Passos, an excerpt from the novel Gold had been working on that would become *Jews Without Money*, poems by Louis Untermeyer and Village troubadour Alfred Kreymborg, and a blistering attack on e. e. cummings's new play, *Him*, Dorothy described in lively detail the Bellevue free clinic, nurses both hard-bitten and sympathetic, fellow expectant mothers both frightened and brazen, the cab ride to the hospital, the petrified cabbie, the tipsy orderly taking her to her room, the lightning-fierce pain of the contractions, the mercy of ether. She closed with a description of her daughter four days later, "sleeping with the placidity of a Mona Lisa" as the new mother, happy as a human being could be, pondered her flattening stomach and looked out the hospital window at the "restless water" of the East River, the gulls wheeling overhead.

The persona created by the essay's narrator was as authentic a self-portrait as Dorothy ever devised—tart, droll, observant, and ready to embrace a new life with the deepest love. For good measure, she also named the many novels she had read over the last nine months that included a birth scene—all written by men ("the idiots")—and concluded that, of course, not one of them knew what he was talking about.

The most popular and widely reproduced journalistic piece Dorothy produced, "Having a Baby" was a personal essay with something for everyone: just the right amount of sentiment without being treacly, a political edge (the free clinic experience, so different from what rich women would have enjoyed) without being propagandistic, an admirable terseness, a pitch-perfect blend of the serious and the comic. In the contributors' notes at the back of the magazine, Dorothy was warmly identified as "a game young modernist and adventurer." Mike Gold had done right by her.

The following winter, the last before the onset of the Great Depression, Dorothy and Tamar took up residence in a run-down boardinghouse on West 14th Street. It proved to be a more than usually difficult winter. Dorothy came down with a prolonged and devastating attack of the flu, leaving her weak and depressed and wondering nervously what would become of Tamar if something happened to her. Finances were a constant source of dread. She worked for a time for the Fellowship of Reconciliation, a Christian pacifist organization that paid very little, before landing a position at MGM's office in New York as a synopsis writer, a job that paid much better. Reading, or skimming, a novel a day and typing a six-page summary that suggested its possibilities, or lack of possibilities, as a film property brought in as much as twenty-five or thirty dollars a week, and the work could be done from home. Still, surrounded by piles of novels and banging away on her typewriter, Dorothy was unable to meet the overdue taxes on her Staten Island home while paying her bed and board in Manhattan and various childcare expenses, and finally she accepted that she would have to rent out her bungalow, making other arrangements for the summer.

A priest she had met on Staten Island had a suggestion. The Marist Novitiate in Prince's Bay on Staten Island closed each summer, but three priests and three brothers stayed on and needed a cook. The job would provide room and board for her and her daughter for those months. Would Dorothy be interested? Indeed she was. Her host, Father James McKenna, the associate novice master at the novitiate, proved to be a gem—a "gentle, understanding soul" not unlike

Father Zachary Saint-Martin, a friend as well as a mentor, who enjoyed taking Tamar with him on his rounds to see that the novitiate's cows were milked, the chickens fed, and the garden watered. He was amused rather than horrified by Dorothy's summer visitors from Manhattan—Communists, anarchists, men like Mike Gold and his brother. He cheerfully chauffeured them back and forth to the train station. He was a consoling figure when Dorothy slipped into a period of depression or broke down in the kitchen in a fit of tears.

Father McKenna was helpful in another way when he gave Dorothy a copy of *The Spirit of Catholicism* by the German theologian Karl Adam that had recently been translated into English and was much talked about in Catholic circles in the 1920s. Even George Orwell, never known for a sympathetic view of Catholicism, called it a "refreshing" and insightful book. On more than one level, it was a wise gift to pass on to a bookish new convert who still felt she knew rather little about Church dogma and had yet to resolve all her lingering doubts concerning the large step she had taken.

One concern very much on Dorothy's mind was directly addressed by Professor Adam—namely, that religion was the necessary corrective to "the narrow hermitage of self" that characterized modern life with its imprisoning walls of egotism and alienation. A fellowship of faith spared one the desolation of aloneness. He also offered a portrait of the Catholic Church that was very unlike the one-dimensional view she had heard about growing up; rather, his characterization of the Church was of an institution that had been growing and reforming from its earliest days, fully acknowledging that its history was not unstained. That last assertion was the crucial one when talking to nonbelievers, just as it was an aspect of Dorothy's own uneasiness. How could one take seriously an institution that had a history marred by Inquisitors, witch-hunters, anti-Semites, and popes as greedy, libidinous, and unspiritual as the Medici pontiffs? Adam wrote of the Church as an entity that was transformative, never static, perfect when it was most closely attuned to Christ's gospel and flawed when governed by men who ignored or misread that gospel. He asked that more subtlety of thought be brought to any discussion of Catholicism than modern skeptics, eager to demean and stereotype, were wont to do.

Stereotypes obscured a more complex truth. The Inquisition and the impiety of the Renaissance popes *should* be a source of grief to Catholics, Adam asserted. Christ suffered again and again on the Cross through the misguided actions of his own church. And everyone could see that some of its rulings (the suppression of Galileo's teachings was one of his examples) had been "the decisions of a fallible authority," challenged and changed over time for good reason. Catholics, like all people, thought and acted as men and women of their time, and "eminent popes, bishops of great spiritual force, theologians of genius, priests of extraordinary graces and devout layfolk" were never the rule, in any age. None of that meant that the Catholic Church did not serve a crucial spiritual purpose, however, or that in its ideal form it was unworthy to guide its followers. The pope speaking ex cathedra on matters of faith—e.g., on the doctrine of the Immaculate Conception of Mary—was one thing, indeed something to be taken as infallible because it was informed by the Holy Spirit. The pope agreeing to a determination of the Curia *in forma communi* (as in the Galileo prohibition) was quite another.

These were distinctions Dorothy had never pondered before, and *The Spirit of Catholicism* offered Dorothy a sense that there was much more to learn about Catholicism than Sister Aloysia had been able to impart, that she needed to study and reflect more even as she continued to be dutiful about Mass and confession and had been confirmed the year before, with Father Zachary as her sponsor. She was still floundering—there was so much to assimilate, so many paradoxes for an intellectual person to consider, nothing about conversion felt as easy as she had hoped it would be—and only gradually did the anxiety about the choices she had made for herself and her daughter lessen.

Dorothy's professional floundering continued as well, worse than ever, in fact. It was around this time that she set aside her fiction writing to work on a play. Enthusiastic about the final result, she shared with friends her optimism about an imminent breakthrough. In town, Father Zachary would even ask at odd moments about her progress. "Have you sold your play yet?" he would whisper hopefully from his side of the grille after Dorothy's confession. Like all of her major creative efforts, though, the project never brought her the success she craved.

Dorothy destroyed all copies of her unproduced drama at some later date, so we are unlikely ever to know anything about it—its subject matter, its characters, or its quality, all of which would be fascinating to reflect on today. As a purely practical venture, it must be said that the idea of writing a play to make some money wasn't far-fetched at the time. Women in the theater were enjoying a healthy measure of success in the late 1920s. Rachel

Crothers made a good living from her plays, and Susan Glaspell, whom Dorothy knew from the Provincetown Playhouse, would soon win the Pulitzer Prize for Drama. Everyone interested in theater in 1928 was talking about the journalist Sophie Treadwell, whose adventurous *Machinal*, about the electrocution of a woman convicted of murder, became a kind of cult classic. Crothers, Glaspell, and Treadwell were inspiring examples. Dorothy saw the latest O'Neill work on Broadway that year, the Freudian *Strange Interlude*, which included a character based on the gay man with whom Dorothy had shared the horror of Louis Holladay's death, Charles Demuth.

Her play can't have been as lacking in merit as she ultimately came to believe as she passed it along to several people she knew in the theater world who were encouraging, and the script made its way to some film industry people who read it and liked it enough to talk of optioning the story. That teaser went nowhere—Hollywood men were always a lot of talk—but it did lead to a lucrative offer in mid-August 1929. For the first time in her life, a job promised Dorothy a solid financial foundation. The deal: a three-month contract with the Pathé film company in California, recently bought by Joseph P. Kennedy, as a dialogue writer for scripts that might go into production. The salary: a munificent $125 a week.

In early September, Dorothy and Tamar set off, from Pennsylvania Station with Forster there to wish them well. A new friend, an older woman named Lallah Rogers, joined them soon after their arrival, her train ticket paid for by Dorothy. Rogers was a widow whose eighteen-year-old son had recently committed suicide, a tragedy for which Dorothy was a shoulder to lean on, and she needed a change from New York. They probably met through the Casa Caligari crowd, as Rogers knew Katherine Anne Porter. She made an appearance in Dorothy's life for no more than several months and then disappeared from view.

Dorothy wrote regularly to Forster from the West Coast, her letters expressing a jumble of emotions and intentions—some full of hope and affection, others hectoring, many bemoaning the state of their relationship and Tamar's need for a father's presence. She complained bitterly about being doomed to a life of celibacy, now that she had accepted the Church's teaching about sex outside of marriage, and she expressed her dismay about having had to choose between her faith and the man she loved when she wanted both. Forster was more realistic. A choice had been always inevitable.

What was also inevitable was Dorothy's dislike of Hollywood. When she and Tamar arrived, they stayed at the comfortable Hotel Washington on the studio grounds in Culver City. Later she found a small house with Lallah only a mile away and an English nanny to look after Tamar. That munificent salary seemed to bleed into nothing in short order, though. Lallah became sick and had to be hospitalized, and Dorothy paid her bills. The nanny didn't come cheap. There was no Staten Island vegetable garden, no fish to be caught for dinner from the nearby beach. And the work itself was hardly satisfying. The reactions to her plot synopses and critiques of new screenplays were lukewarm, and she felt anything but appreciated by the studio bosses. She was just another New York writer, one among many, who didn't seem to have a feel for the product she was supposed to be promoting. "Life in this place broadens the fanny and narrows the mind," she told Forster.

As she expected, Dorothy's contract with the studio wasn't renewed in December. One after another, each week throughout the fall, after the stock market crash and a buyout by another studio, the writers in her department departed; cutbacks were taking place in every area of the film industry. Dorothy felt no great regret over any of it. Aside from the climate, very little about southern California had appealed to her. She had made no friends, and the work had become both tedious and pointless.

Despite the studio's offer to pay her way back east, Dorothy decided not to return to New York, or not just yet. Manhattan was a setting that provided "occasion for sin," she later admitted, a remark that raises the possibility that she had not been celibate, with Forster or with someone else since her lover's leave-taking. For a thirty-two-year-old woman who had enjoyed sex throughout her twenties, abstinence did not come easily. (Twice since Tamar's birth Dorothy had thought she might be pregnant again.) New York also meant the "uncomfortable situations" attendant on her conversion that she was desperate to avoid. More time away from the old circle of friends who didn't know what to make of her felt desirable. Mexico City seemed a plausible alternative, and Lallah was willing to join her to see what life south of the border, much touted in the US press that year, was like. A hastily made arrangement with George Shuster, the editor of the Catholic magazine *Commonweal*, to contribute a few articles on Catholic life in Mexico meant that she wouldn't have to live entirely on her savings. Della and Mike Gold, both of whom knew the Manhattan philanthropist Otto Kahn, saw that some money came her way from that generous source, too.

In a used Model T that wouldn't go over thirty miles an hour, with an intrepid four-year-old at her side, Dorothy headed south, meeting up with Lallah early in the new year. They rented an apartment together for ten dollars a month in Mexico City—"in a poor neighborhood but a grade above poverty," she told Forster in a letter dated January 4, 1930—with one room for Lallah and two for Tamar and herself and a terrace filled with potted plants and caged birds. She cooked on a small oil stove in her room. The comforts of California were left behind.

Though Mexico had been "discovered" by American writers early in the 1920s, it was in some ways a very odd choice of residence for someone such as Dorothy Day, a recent convert to Catholicism and a woman with a toddler to care for. The anti-Catholic president Plutarco Elías Calles had left office two years earlier, but the effects of his campaign to secularize the state, which had led to a murderous purge of the clergy and a bloody civil war from 1926 to 1928 between Catholic rebels and the government, were as deeply felt as ever. In a grim situation that would persist until 1940, hundreds of priests had been imprisoned, shot, or hounded out of the country, with parochial school education banned. Pope Pius XI had issued an encyclical decrying this state of affairs. The country in the 1930s was experiencing what Graham Greene would call "the fiercest persecution of religion anywhere since the reign of Elizabeth." Though Dorothy wasn't planning on going anywhere near Tabasco or Chiapas, the southernmost provinces bordering Guatemala, where the government's pogrom had been most severe, she was still living in a nation in the throes of a brutal cultural shift. Mass was celebrated in the capital city at those churches that had been allowed to stay open, but an atmosphere of official disapproval was everywhere present.

From the point of a view of someone who wanted to be a respected writer, then, Dorothy's time in Mexico represents a lost opportunity. Despite having a young child to take care of, she was in a perfect position to offer a series of "dispatches from the front" that wouldn't actually have to have been "from the front" (Mexico City, always lax in enforcing the anti-Catholic laws, was far from Tabasco and Chiapas), but still had merit as having been written by someone living among Mexicans. Personal accounts of the anti-Catholic fervor that had so disrupted Mexican life for the last decade would have interested the editors of some mainstream, secular journals. It was the kind of ambitious project she might have pushed through several years earlier, and the material was certainly there all about her. A physical and spiritual landscape that Graham Greene would later examine in *Lawless Roads*, his travel book, and in his remarkable 1940 novel, *The Power and the Glory*, would have allowed Dorothy, as a Catholic journalist, formidable opportunities to make a name for herself. (Evelyn Waugh, another Catholic writer, paid his own visit to Mexico City in the 1930s and completed a polemic about anticlerical Mexico, *Robbery by Law*, a considerably less admirable book than either of Greene's.) But, for one of the few times in her life, Dorothy's nerve failed her. The first articles she sent back to *Commonweal*, pieces that had a political thrust, were rejected. She decided, rather too quickly, that she didn't know enough about politics and couldn't realistically educate herself about the Mexican political situation and its treatment of the Church, and so gave George Shuster over the next three months what he presumably wanted: articles of no real depth, tidbits from "the woman's angle."

One was about a visit to the Shrine of Our Lady of Guadalupe. Another was a general "Letter from Mexico City." A third was an account of the spring fiesta in Santa Anita and the Palm Sunday, Easter Sunday, and Easter Monday Masses she attended in Mexico City. During the latter service, Indian boys hurled handfuls of roses and poppies—a "steady storm of blossoms"—onto the three priests and crowds of worshippers below from apertures in the dome of the church. Tamar's growing piety, a source of pleasure to her mother, was often mentioned in her articles. Dorothy's emphasis in her journalism on the maternal side of her life had not gone unappreciated even in far-flung corners of the world. She had the satisfaction that month of meeting the painter Diego Rivera ("a huge man, hearty and genial," if decidedly anti-Catholic), who lived not far from her neighborhood and who told her about the popularity her essay "Having a Baby" had enjoyed in Europe and the USSR.

In February, Dorothy met up with another New Yorker in Mexico City who provided both companionship for several weeks and a second, short-term source of income. Mary Heaton Vorse had come south looking for an economical setting with few distractions in which to finish a novel she was writing about the recent Gastonia, North Carolina, textile workers' strike. She rented the apartment of an American journalist, Carleton Beals, who lived in Mexico City much of the time but frequently traveled. In the crusading spirit of Upton Sinclair, *Strike!* was a brisk, dramatic account of a particularly vicious episode in US labor relations in which mill owners kept their employees laboring for fifty-five-hour workweeks at subsistence wages and, when the workers finally decided to fight back with the aid of several Communist organizers, crushed the strike with the help of local vigilantes, brought the organizers to trial, and even shot and killed some of the strikers and one of the labor activists, a young woman. Vorse had been on hand to witness all of it and was eager to get her story into print while the horror was fresh in the public mind. When the novel was in its final stages, Dorothy signed on as her dictation secretary.

Earnest as Vorse was about her labor activism and reportage, she was a bit of a character, a warmhearted, quirky woman Dorothy was always charmed by, and she was thrilled to be in Mexico. Every morning, Dorothy remembered, she "twisted herself into some intricate knot on top of a bright orange serape and began the day's work. If anyone dropped in to invite her for a little jaunt to Teotihuacan or Xochimilico, she looked at them haughtily, with upraised eyebrows, looked at the thousands of sheets of yellow paper strewn on the bed all around her, counted her pencils, bounced an apple in one hand, and didn't answer." Later, after going through the morning mail, she'd pour sour cream into her coffee and stir it meditatively, and begin to dictate. It was always the same attire: a handwoven, embroidered coat that Mary had bought in northern Africa, and when the pitch of creation reached a stressful point, the shoes would come off and her toes would wiggle "thoughtfully."

As she dictated, Vorse would "curl her legs under her in a most acrobatic fashion or double up her knees until they were higher than her head and sink her chin and mouth further and further into her African coat." By this time, Dorothy would be barking at her that she was mumbling, which made it impossible to catch every word, and that led to an authorial demand not to be scolded, followed by a break from novel writing to show Dorothy all of her newly purchased dresses and pottery and then—a sudden swerve back to work. "Clad in her negligé, she was on the bed again, one leg propped on the foot of the bed, her arms behind her head dictating."

Vorse's novel ended with great drama and sadness, focusing on the murders and funerals of the strikers. Dorothy loved the book and those chapters in particular, and her admiration for Vorse's passion for social justice, facility with words, and disregard for what anyone else thought of her only increased. Though neither woman knew it at the time, Vorse was one of the first people in Dorothy's circle to have an FBI file started on her in the 1920s. That Vorse wasn't actually a committed Communist—by the early 1930s she was quite critical of the Party—meant nothing to J. Edgar Hoover; she was a radical woman and therefore a menace to society. Dorothy's own file would be started a few years later.

Between her savings from Pathé and the money she made from her own writings and her stenography for Vorse, Dorothy was able to keep her apartment in Mexico City and, for another ten dollars a month, rent a cottage outside the main part of the city in the canal-dotted suburb of Xochimilco. Reachable only by gondola, the one-room stone house had a thatched roof, one window, and a garden of roses, heliotropes, geraniums, and cacti—a heavenly retreat, Dorothy felt, despite the nightly parade of inebriated men outside the window. Katherine Anne Porter showed up there in April, also in search of the right setting for her literary work, and stayed with Dorothy and Tamar for a few days. She had heard that Carleton Beals was going to be out of the city again for some months and so might help her find lodging or even consider renting out his own place as he had for Vorse. She asked him to meet her at Dorothy's, where he did give her some leads about affordable rentals. (Meeting Carleton Beals must have been interesting to someone of Dorothy's background: he was a contrarian of the first order and a fierce critic of US policies toward Latin America, and he had just been released from a Mexican jail to which he had been taken for offending a local politician.)

Porter found Dorothy's cottage charming and even included a few lines in her short story "Flowering Judas" that seem based on the house, but several days of intimacy between the two was more than sufficient. Porter quickly found her own place and, as she was putting the finishing touches on several stories, signed Dorothy on as her dictation secretary.

The Katherine Anne Porter connection is something of a peculiar one in Dorothy's life. Fundamentally, in the long run, the two women didn't like each other. Porter felt more warmly toward Della, whose personality and politics she found agreeable. She could relax around Della in a way she couldn't around Dorothy. Dorothy's conversion was a sore point between them, and the easy familiarity of the Casa Caligari days was gone. Porter hated it when Dorothy kept expressing her hope that Porter, a lapsed Catholic, might herself return to the fold, and when she placed little religious statues around Porter's bed when she stayed overnight, her houseguest was irate. She complained that spring to Caroline Gordon that Dorothy seemed always ready to pick a quarrel with her. That might well have been a case of the pot calling the kettle black: Porter was a prickly personality at all times.

Issues of jealousy could have been a factor between the two women as well. Porter was unable to have children, having had her ovaries removed after a venereal infection, while Dorothy was a joyful mother, loquacious on the topic of the wonders of motherhood, and brought Tamar into every conversation. At the same time, Dorothy's own fiction was going nowhere, while Porter's first book of stories was going to be published that fall, and her literary career—when she could actually get herself to sit down and produce some pages—was headed in the right direction.

Porter also nursed a grudge about Dorothy's borrowing a copy of a short story she had just completed, "The Cracked Looking-Glass." Porter contended that after several days she had to ask Dorothy to return the story; Dorothy then admitted, without seeming in any way apologetic or regretful, that she had lost it. Not having a duplicate, the furious Porter was forced to rewrite the story, more than fifty pages, from scratch.

One evening that April, Porter was sitting in a restaurant back in Mexico City when a young man in an outsized cowboy hat came in, "highly drunk, tottering," looking for Dorothy. The man was twenty-six-year-old Eugene Dove Pressly, and Porter took an instant liking to him. He was good-looking, liked to sunbathe nude and wasn't averse to being photographed while doing so, and held his liquor most of the time, though not on that occasion. They commenced an affair soon after, and he eventually became her fourth husband and the model for a character in her most famous work, *Ship of Fools*. Had Dorothy been interested in Pressly herself? Neither woman ever commented on that possibility, but their relationship became more strained in the weeks that followed.

Much as Dorothy enjoyed the warmth and exotic atmosphere of Mexico, it wasn't the wisest choice of temporary home for a child. Tamar became ill at the end of May. The high fever, the shaking chills, and the abdominal pain meant only one thing: she had contracted malaria. Given the severity of the illness and the limited medical resources nearby, Dorothy realized that they would have to head back to the United States. Porter told Della that she intended to throw a good-bye party at her place during the first week of June before Dorothy and Tamar left to catch a boat home from Veracruz, but Dorothy let her know that she wanted any gathering to be at her own apartment. Porter promptly dropped the subject and didn't even attend or bid her farewell. The estrangement between the two women was complete. Dorothy landed in Florida, where her mother eagerly awaited her arrival, and right away took Tamar to a doctor, who put the child into the hospital for several days. Dorothy took her home a few weeks later, still weak and shaken, to Staten Island.

That fall, Porter's book came out. *Flowering Judas* was published by Horace Liveright in a limited edition, but word of mouth in literary circles was so favorable about the collection of well-crafted stories that she was clearly established, at last, as a writer whose work would be closely followed in the future. Mary Heaton Vorse's novel, another Liveright book, also appeared that autumn, to glowing reviews and strong sales. Mike Gold called it a "burning and imperishable epic." Sinclair Lewis, now a Nobel laureate, praised it in the pages of *The Nation* (urging President Herbert Hoover to read it), and *The New Republic* and *The New Yorker* were similarly enthusiastic. The year 1930 was a productive one for many friends and acquaintances. John Dos Passos brought out *The 42nd Parallel*, the first volume of his great trilogy, while Hart Crane reshaped American poetry with *The Bridge*. Dorothy heard that Caroline Gordon was in the last stages of the Kentucky family saga she had been working on, *Penholly*, to be published a few months later.

Bringing a novel or play to fruition, gaining a foothold in that impressive company: surely, Dorothy felt, she could do the same. Now that Tamar was out of danger, that would be a priority, Dorothy promised herself, in the new year.

EIGHT

⚜ PURPOSE ⚜

A MAN WHO FINDS HIS WAY TO CATHOLICISM, OUT OF THE TANGLE of modern culture and complexity, must think harder than he has ever thought in his life," G. K. Chesterton wrote in *Christendom in Dublin*. That was a statement to which Dorothy could readily assent. There was nothing simple or precipitous about the choice she had made. Chesterton went on to note in that same work that the convert must also "feel all the counter-attractions of Paganism, at least to know how attractive are those attractions." That was another sentence speaking directly to Dorothy's younger self. His conviction, though, that an embrace of Catholicism necessarily led to an immediate and glorious transformation, a renewal in which the convert would find himself "suddenly in the morning of the world"—that had been far from her experience.

For most of 1931 and well into 1932, Dorothy lived with the certainty that she had made the right decision in converting, yet she was left with one large, unanswered question: What, really, did that amount to? She prayed, confessed, attended Mass, read about the saints, and saw to it that Tamar, now of school age, received religious instruction. But daily life involved too much drift, too little actual fulfillment, even or especially on a spiritual level. Struggling to make ends meet, she wrote a gardening column for a small Staten Island paper, the *Staten Island Advance*, and freelanced for Catholic periodicals such as *Commonweal*, *The Sign*, *America*, and *The Tablet* of Brooklyn. Her articles tended to be human interest stories, family centered and sentimental, though she also wrote for *America* about the growing Communist presence in US political life. Her account of a Cooper Union forum at which Earl Browder, the head of the Party in the United States, had spoken made mention of her old friend Malcolm Cowley, now a fellow traveler. The article took a mild jab at Cowley's glib sense of politics. She visited her mother in Florida for long stretches, to Grace's delight (while her father was off who knows where), and amassed pages for the novel she must have feared by now would never be published. "Our Brothers, the Jews" was an article that dealt perceptively with rising anti-Semitism, but *America* rejected it.

At least she and Tamar were not entirely on their own. Dorothy had always been fond of her younger brother, and she liked the young Spanish woman he had married, the daughter of a family she knew from the beach community on Staten Island. John and Tessa, both Communists and soon expecting a child, moved into Dorothy's tenement apartment at 436 East 15th Street at Avenue A to share expenses. As far as their father was concerned, they were a good match—the two of his five children he could most comfortably do without, lost to good sense in their similar but separate ways. Though John was more respectful of his sister's religious nature than his father or two older brothers were, he was often just as puzzled by it. His sister was one of the smartest people he knew. How, he wondered, could she feel any allegiance to an institution that most people, especially his fellow Party members, viewed as reactionary and benighted?

The few friends from the old days Dorothy was still in touch with were Mike Gold and his brother George Granich, who liked stopping by the apartment for coffee and conversation, and Mary Heaton Vorse. It was with the tireless Vorse that Dorothy went to Washington, DC, in December 1932 to cover the national Hunger March, a gathering organized in part by the Communist Party in which three thousand unemployed men lived for two days and two nights on the streets of the capital, waiting for a court order permitting their parade, and then marched down Pennsylvania Avenue to urge congressional action for relief measures. En route to Washington, speeches had been made in several cities along the way, all examples of the right to peaceable assembly, Dorothy noted, that were respected everywhere except by local thugs in Wilmington, Delaware, who smashed the windows of the church the New York contingent had gathered in, and the Wilmington police, who used tear gas and clubs against both the mob and the marchers.

As the marchers approached Washington, the city "was in a state bordering on hysteria," she wrote. Marines from MCB Quantico had been called out, guards surrounded the White House, the Capitol, and other government and public utility buildings, and armed American Legion volunteers stood shoulder to shoulder with the police and National Guard. Mike Gold and Malcolm Cowley were there also to witness the madness of a government that regarded its desperate, hungry, unemployed citizens and their wish to make their plight known as a threat to the nation. "I do not blame the harried police, the firemen, the reserves, even though they cursed and bullied and taunted the marchers as though they were trying to provoke a bloody conflict," Dorothy wrote. Rather, she blamed the yellow press, which characterized any political protest involving the Communist Party in any way as dangerous and un-American. Yet if no other group was stepping forward to organize such a protest, why should these men, who had no resources and no hope, refuse that aid? she asked. Her article for *America* was one of her most incisive pieces of journalism.

Before leaving Washington, Dorothy went to the campus of the Catholic University of America, a few miles from the Capitol. The great Basilica of the National Shrine of the Immaculate Conception on the edge of the campus was still under construction, but the mosaic-tiled crypt with its low vaulted ceiling beneath it was open, and there on December 8—a holy day of obligation, the Feast of the Immaculate Conception—she pondered what she had seen, the triumphantly peaceful display of need and bravery in the streets of the city, and offered up a prayer. Writing an occasional article was not enough. Bearing witness was admirable in its way, but she wanted to play a more active part in alleviating the suffering she saw all around her. Yet she had no sense of how to do that, not in a manner or on a scale that would mean anything. She did not intend to join the Communist Party. She was committed to the Catholic Church. Yet the Church offered no guidance on this question. She asked God to show her the way.

Dorothy returned to New York the following day. After the long bus ride, she was looking forward to relaxing with Tamar and enjoying a quiet dinner, but she found a disheveled middle-aged man waiting to talk to her. Her sister-in-law told her that the man had been by earlier in the week, quite insistent about wanting to see her, and she had told him to return when Dorothy would be back from a trip out of town on the ninth. There he was. John had taken one look at the caller—a Bowery bum, if ever he saw one—and would have told him to go away and not to bother them again, but Tessa had decided otherwise.

The man was Peter Maurin, and he would have returned to East 15th Street no matter what John or anyone else said, though he appreciated Tessa's graciousness. "She had a Spaniard's courtesy," he commented. He had been directed there by George Shuster of *Commonweal*, whose office he had been haunting for days while he peddled his idea of a new Catholic publication of a more radical nature than yet existed. He even suggested that Shuster might want to think about reorganizing his own magazine from the topical and generally liberal Catholic publication that it was into the kind of platform Peter had in mind. Shuster had no intention of entertaining such an outlandish suggestion, but he told Peter that he might like to talk to a talented young woman he knew with a background in journalism, Dorothy Day. In what Dorothy would soon learn was his usual impractical fashion, Peter had forgotten to ask Shuster for her address and, instead of going back to the *Commonweal* offices to get it, had wandered about Union Square that week until he found someone who knew her and could provide the address.

Peter did want to talk to her—and talk and talk and talk—in a heavy, not always decipherable Frenchman's accent. He was, Dorothy later wrote, "a short, broad-shouldered workingman with a high, broad head covered with graying hair. His face was weather-beaten, he had warm gray eyes, and a wide, pleasant mouth. The collar of his shirt was dirty, but he had tried to dress up by wearing a tie and suit which looked as though he had slept in it. (As I found out afterward, indeed he had.)" His pants were stained, and his suit jacket pockets were crammed with books and papers. He looked like so many of the soapbox orators one saw at Union Square and Columbus Circle during the Depression, and indeed that was a practice with which he was familiar.

What Peter wanted to talk about was the Church, Catholicism, the state of the world, the salvation of souls, the extent of the compassion Christ asked of us, the intellectuals he had known in France, Americans' attitudes toward poverty and the impoverished, his plans for a Catholic newspaper, Dorothy's evident potential as a writer and leader, and the need for more discussion and debate about what a Christian life looked like—"clarification of thought" was his favorite phrase—which too many priests seemed ill equipped to provide. He discoursed about the need for a "green revolution," to get back to the soil, to create farming communes for scholars and workers that would be "agronomic universities." He talked about people opening their homes to those who slept on the street, that it was an affront to

God that Christians allowed such suffering in their midst. Education was the foundation of all meaningful change, and Peter said he could tell that Dorothy was not as educated about Church history and papal encyclicals and contemporary intellectual currents as she might be, and he was on hand to be her tutor.

The man was impossible to get rid of. He would come by the next day, having been shown the door the night before when everyone was ready for bed, or a few days later, and sit down and commence conversing exactly where he had left off. He seemed never to have heard of small talk. Some days, Dorothy went about her business, hoping he would not turn up and more or less ignoring him if he did; on other days, he was actually captivating in his enthusiasm and sincerity. He would recite from memory what he called his "Easy Essays," free-verse poems that encapsulated his thought, filled with allusions to the writers and saints he believed in and the political and spiritual values he espoused.

Very little about modern life appealed to Peter, he made clear, not its faith in material success or "progress" as desirable goals, not its devotion to technology and individual freedom, and not its belief that the worship of God was compatible with self-protective, middle-class comfort. The greatest heroes of the Church, he felt, were St. Francis, who had embraced voluntary poverty; St. Vincent de Paul, who had espoused boundless charity as the most noble of the virtues; the monastic St. Benedict, who had believed in the dignity of manual labor; and St. Dominic, the ultimate "clarification of thought" religious figure—not one of them a likely saint for the modern era. As his biographer Marc H. Ellis characterized him, Peter was a vigorous "dissenter against modernity." He was also, Dorothy finally concluded, an Alyosha, a Prince Myshkin, the kind of holy fool she had read about but never encountered in real life.

Dorothy was uncertain at first how much she wanted to do with a Prince Myshkin in the flesh. She was also uncertain exactly what he was asking of her. We didn't understand each other at first, she later observed. His background, as she pieced it together over succeeding weeks, didn't offer all that much clarity.

Peter was twenty years her senior. Born in 1877, the eldest son of twenty-two children, three by his own mother, who died in childbirth in 1884, and nineteen by his father's second, much younger wife, Pierre Joseph Aristide

Maurin grew up in a farming family in the south of France. His father was a deeply religious man, and it was a pious family circle. Peter stayed on the farm until he was fourteen, when he was sent away to school to study with the Christian Brothers. Devout in his faith, he entered a novitiate at sixteen to study for the priesthood but, questioning whether he really had a vocation, never took his final vows. He did, however, work for the next several years at various schools run by the Christian Brothers. He fulfilled his compulsory military service in 1898 and 1899, a duty that was as abhorrent to him as he had imagined it would be. The Dreyfus Affair and Émile Zola's "J'Accuse . . . !" were still burning matters, the anti-Semitism of the French military was undisguised, and the aggressive nationalist spirit a man in uniform was supposed to exemplify was a stance he found hard to accept.

By 1902, now in his midtwenties, Peter was in Paris, where he had attached himself to Le Sillon (The Furrow), a secular movement started by the Catholic political thinker Marc Sangnier, whose aim was to remake France as a Christian republic, ending any conservative Catholic hopes for the restoration of the monarchy and focusing on the need for a better relationship between the Church and labor. Peter attended the group's meetings, joined a study group, walked the streets of Montparnasse distributing its newspaper, made a meager living selling coffee, tea, and cocoa, and spent his evenings reading. Le Sillon was condemned in 1910 by Pope Pius X, who believed that its focus on leveling social differences smacked of socialism. Long before that papal admonishment, though, Peter had left the movement, feeling that it had become less religious and too political in its emphasis for his taste, and left France. In his late twenties, he crossed the Atlantic to make a new life for himself in Canada and eventually the United States.

So much about Peter Maurin's life is shrouded in mystery, and his move across the ocean is a part of the mystery. He was still eligible to be called up for reserve duty, so a desire to avoid that excruciating possibility is a plausible factor in his decision to leave his homeland, but as with everything about this man, one suspects more to the story, more that will never be known.

For two years, Peter lived in Canada, homesteading on the frontier until his partner was killed in a hunting accident. A long period of aimless wandering began as he worked in the wheat fields of Alberta, dug ditches for the Canadian Pacific Railway, and quarried stone in Ottawa. It wasn't until 1911 that he went to the United States to live and to learn English.

He worked in a Pennsylvania coal mine and a Michigan sawmill. He was once arrested for vagrancy. By the early 1920s, he was apparently in Chicago, where he lived a more settled middle-class life as a French teacher, though he gave that up and took to the road again. At the time he met Dorothy he was working off and on at a Catholic boys' camp in upstate New York and frequently taking the train into Manhattan, where he wandered the streets, spent hours at the New York Public Library, joined in the public-square political debates that were so much a part of city life then, and stayed at a fifty-cents-a-night flophouse on the Bowery.

So circumspect was Peter about many details of his personal history that his admirers over the years who tried to ferret out an exact chronology and a full life story usually had a hard time of it and eventually gave up, as did Dorothy. About one stage of his peripatetic life, he was understandably terse, perhaps even feeling that his few words on the topic said enough. Concerning his time in Chicago, he remarked quietly, mournfully, to a few people, "I did not always live as a Catholic should." How many people, including Dorothy, understood the full weight of that sentence is unclear—it is entirely possible that she never knew—but what it meant pertained to something more than a time of attenuated faith. Peter was suffering from syphilis. Untreated, or unsuccessfully treated, that illness would, sixteen years after this first meeting with Dorothy, contribute to his death.

Peter Maurin was a man of startling contradictions. Though many who met him over the years were quick to use the same dismissive phrase—"French peasant"—he was, in fact, astonishingly well read. The Bible, Church history, papal encyclicals, social theory, economics, philosophy, biography, Thomas Carlyle, Marx, Hugo, Nietzsche, Ibsen, Tolstoy, American authors such as Thorstein Veblen, Lincoln Steffens, and Henry Adams: he had a wealth of knowledge at his fingertips that didn't jibe at all with his scruffy appearance and scattershot persona. That was surely one aspect of her new friend's makeup that led Dorothy to take him more seriously than others were apt to at a first encounter.

Not surprisingly, Peter was chockful of recommendations of writers Dorothy had to read: G. K. Chesterton, Hilaire Belloc, Léon Bloy, Charles Péguy, Eric Gill, Christopher Dawson, R. H. Tawney, Arthur Penty, the Dominican Father Vincent McNabb, Karl Adam, Prince Kropotkin, Nikolai Berdyaev,

Jacques Maritain, and Emmanuel Mounier, amid a torrent of other names. All of those were suggestions Dorothy was open to, and a few (e.g., Chesterton, Belloc, Adam, and Prince Kropotkin), she was already acquainted with, but when she seemed pressed for time, Peter was happy to prepare lengthy digests. He had correctly sensed that Dorothy's interests included the religious and the political and, most particularly, their points of overlap.

The Chestertonian style of paradox and relentlessly playful drollness never quite captured Dorothy's imagination. Yet Chesterton's belief that modern urban life had stripped human consciousness in the West of any feeling for the magical or miraculous, that pure reason and individualism had become traps, that capitalism was not going to bring about lasting social justice, and that a commitment to faith in a skeptical age could actually feel daring and adventurous: these were concerns that spoke to Dorothy. Most important, the Sage of Beaconsfield—like Dorothy, a convert—insisted that orthodoxy, properly viewed, was not a constraint but a source of joy. Joy mattered to Chesterton. Joy mattered to Dorothy.

Such reading was selective, though. There were aspects of Chesterton's thought that Dorothy (and Peter) would ultimately choose to ignore: he wasn't a pacifist, having ardently defended the Allied cause in the war, as he would later be a supporter of Francisco Franco's murderous tactics in Spain, and he was an anti-Semite, though a vehement critic of Nazi policies toward the Jews. The same was true of Hilaire Belloc, Chesterton's frequent collaborator and another writer Peter urged on her. It was a thorny issue that would require more attention in the years ahead.

It was really two movements, or (more accurately put) two schools of thought, that Peter was most determined that Dorothy learn more about in those first weeks of their acquaintance: distributism and personalism. Distributism was best known as the great idealistic cause uniting Chesterbelloc, as the pair was labeled (a coinage owed to their friendly antagonist George Bernard Shaw), though books such as Kropotkin's classic *Fields, Factories, and Workshops*, Arthur Penty's *Post-industrialism* and *Toward a Christian Sociology*, and Nikolai Berdyaev's trenchant reflections in *The Bourgeois Mind and Other Essays* were equally crucial texts about which Peter could wax ecstatic for hours.

Distributists upheld the right to private property—they were no more inclined to believe that socialism was the answer to society's ills than they were to think that capitalism as it had evolved would ever be anything other than rapacious—but they wanted to see it distributed more evenly, which meant that the means of production needed to be spread more widely. Monopolies and trusts had to go; medieval-style guilds and local ownership of factories had to be encouraged; mass production phased out; and a return, at least on some level, to a more agrarian way of life made feasible. As Catholics, the distributists took their inspiration from Pope Leo XIII's 1891 encyclical *Rerum novarum*, the first papal address concerned with workers' rights and the plight of the urban poor, and Pope Pius XI's 1931 encyclical *Quadregesimo anno*, a document insisting on the need for a fair living wage for all and warning that totalitarianism and capitalism had the potential to be equivalent evils.

From the distributist perspective, bigger was never better, the more a man was master of his own property and workday the better, and acceptance of individual responsibility for making life more equitable was essential. The welfare state was not the answer. Overcrowded cities necessarily created degradation and an occasion of sin that a simpler, self-sustaining rural life did not. The noted sculptor-author Eric Gill, a figure Maurin admired and as authentic a Luddite as any of his fellow distributists, lived what he preached in a spartan arts and crafts community in Sussex—though more recent biographical research has suggested that occasions of sin (i.e., sex with his daughters and the family dog) were plentiful even in the countryside.

Derided by some as a form of nostalgic medievalism and appreciated by others as a wake-up call to a society in thrall to technology, big government, and uncontrolled urbanization, distributism was a peculiairly British project. Personalism, on the other hand, was very much a French Catholic intellectual enterprise. Less well known on this side of the Atlantic in the 1930s, it was—and still is—less easily definable territory. The difficulty of explicating the works of the theorist Emmanuel Mounier, a prodigy barely out of his twenties, never deterred Peter, though. It was his life's blood. The most comprehensive and radical critique of Western society imaginable, personalism decried almost everything about modern life: the extremes of individualism and collectivism, the political Right and the political Left, capitalism and communism, parliamentary democracy and totalitarianism. Society had reached a pathological crisis point in the fourth decade of the twentieth century, Mounier believed, in which the bourgeois perspective on all aspects of life had demeaned the autonomy and value of the person, left men willing to serve almost any kind of centralized authority—corporate or governmental, Communist, fascist, or Western capitalistic—and created a belief system predicated on the guiding assumption that "material comforts can effect a miracle of happiness."

Mounier's was a call to end the subordination of individual labor to impersonal capital, to decentralize authority, to restore to modern men and women a sense of control over their destinies. It was only in a faith-affirming, personalist context that society might save itself from what was coming, Mounier believed, but that possibility would require a revolution in thought, not an adjustment of an economic system, as the Marxists claimed, or the right leadership from above, as all politicians claimed.

Particularly troubling from the perspective of personalists such as Mounier and his sometime intellectual ally, Jacques Maritain, was that modern man seemed oblivious to the truth of his situation. "If you wish to astonish a Nazi," Mounier wrote, "tell him that he lives under a dictatorship." If you wish to astonish an American, he further suggested, tell him that he is a cog in a system whose aim is economic hegemony across the planet and the triumph of consumerist desire, a desire that, properly stoked, will never be satiated. Those living under fascism, communism, and American capitalism had ceded their personhood to a "collective consciousness," each assuming that his was sounder than the others and had been freely chosen. Peter Maurin was onto something in his relentless conversation on these themes. Those were exactly the issues that mattered to Dorothy Day in 1932.

Nor were Mounier's ideas compelling to Dorothy strictly in the abstract. When he wrote of "the person," he was most explicitly not thinking of men alone. If men were the more active, visibly important figures in every culture, as he saw it that was not how Nature or God had intended it to be. Women had been enveloped in the "fragile curtain" of another false system, "installed in a life of submission" in which they could ignore the universal need for "constant interior development," "delud[ing] themselves by cultivating femininity with a vengeance," circumscribing their own potential by accepting the roles of housewife and mother (unpaid, no less) and a "zeal for the family [that] is a specialty of bourgeois decadence." Mounier's view of family life was particularly biting—he argued for a more communitarian arrangement—just as his view of education was that it was too much about vocational ends (determined by society's needs), conformity, and the spirit of advancement and competition. Both the nuclear family and the modern school "stifled youth before it had a chance to hear the call of life." Each young person had to hear that call on his or her own, find his or her own way to a vocation that had personal meaning. Freedom was the cornerstone of personhood, and the mania for comfort, security, and stability its biggest obstacles. Emmanuel Mounier could have been describing Dorothy's life journey to that exact moment.

Peter Maurin was the classic autodidact, the sort of man who didn't understand why anyone wouldn't drop everything immediately to read every book by an author he was excitedly recommending. That Dorothy had responsibilities and other interests never dawned on him. So determining exactly which writers she explored in the first fevered months of their acquaintance and which she read at her own pace over the next few years is hard, if not impossible, to determine. And some of Peter's passions would have seemed obscure to many literate Americans in the 1930s, though not to French and British intellectuals.

That was certainly the case with Léon Bloy, the onetime atheist poet of the fin de siècle, later a devout Catholic, an adherent of the most extreme voluntary poverty, and an antimodernist of a millenarian bent. The same could be said for Charles Péguy, the poet and polemicist, a romantic and sometimes dogmatic French nationalist who also abandoned his early atheism for an idiosyncratic and conditional attachment to the Catholic Church. Likewise R. H. Tawney and Father Vincent McNabb—known as the "Mahatma Gandhi of Kentish Town"—who wore only handwoven clothes, traveled everywhere on foot, and refused to use a typewriter in composing his anti-industrialist, back-to-the-land treatise, *Nazareth or Social Chaos*. Had Dorothy heard of Tawney or McNabb? Had anyone outside of specialized circles heard of them in the United States? Was anyone listening to the erudite Arthur Penty and his jeremiads about scientists as the new high priests of our age and the dangerous places that the worship of scientific progress, even to the imminent splitting of the atom, might lead us? Perhaps not. But a writer's popularity or obscurity meant nothing to Peter, no more than a writer's accessibility or the fact that a particular French book had not even been translated into English yet. Peter was willing to be the dogged explicator.

What Peter was presenting to Dorothy was an amalgam of potential intellectual influences, all of whom would speak to a woman who, he rightly sensed, didn't believe the golden age simply awaited the end of the Depression or the defeat of fascism or the day when labor and management came to terms. Eventually she would read and ponder all of those writers. He had at first an inflated notion of her power—he told her she could be a modern-day St. Catherine of Siena, pointing the Church in the direction of reform—but also saw more accurately that she was not a person of conventional habits or a conventional turn of mind.

Timing is everything, and Peter was coming into Dorothy's life at precisely the right time. She was certain, she later said, that her prayer at the National Shrine of the Immaculate Conception had been instrumental in this completely unexpected development. God had answered her plea.

Divinely answered pleas are rarely streamlined. Peter could be more than eccentric at times—closer to downright daffy. Once, a few years into their association, Dorothy watched him address a crowd of striking longshoremen. Instead of talking about the issues at hand, he went on for the better part of an hour telling his audience about the French novelist André Gide and Gide's recent disillusioning trip to the Soviet Union. At another time he tried to talk Dorothy into backing him on a troubadour project. Five Catholic minstrels would be employed to travel about, medieval style, from state to state, chanting and singing and praising the Lord, seeking hospitality where they went (they could use a car if someone donated one, Peter supposed). He speculated about the many prostitutes who walked the streets of the Lower East Side, wondering if they couldn't be persuaded to marry some of the indigent men he knew from the Bowery and take up farming in the countryside. One thing Dorothy had to learn quickly in her relationship with Peter was when to nod a lot and let some notion slip quietly away.

The newspaper was not a notion she wanted to slip away. The more she thought about it, the more the thought excited her. She was a journalist at heart, and Peter was convinced that the time was ripe for something different from *America* or *Commonweal*, a less mainstream forum for the ideas the two of them were now joyfully, confusedly, animatedly discussing. And so was born, still extant today—still sold for a penny a copy—*The Catholic Worker*.

While Dorothy's brother was helpful in getting the first eight-page issue going, Dorothy probably wrote most of it herself throughout the spring of 1933, a herculean labor that could be managed only once. When it came time to think about finding a printer and dealing with the realities of cost, Peter suggested that they look for funding from a priest he knew. That contact turned out to be more of Peter's wishful thinking, but Dorothy did manage, by putting off her rent and other bills and enlisting the help of two priests she knew, to scrape together the fifty-seven dollars needed to pay the Paulist Press to print 2,500 copies. She attempted to secure an interview with former governor Al Smith before going to press, but the Happy Warrior, now a plutocrat, declined. She didn't need to look for big names, though, to fill her pages, as she had plenty of good material at hand. She also knew what she wanted for a title, leading to her first disagreement with Peter, who wanted the paper to be called *The Catholic Radical* or, preferably, *The Christian Radical*. Dorothy got her way with an allusion—and an implicit challenge—to the Communist Party's *Daily Worker*.

New journalistic enterprises tend to evolve in noticeable ways from their first, often hesitant or undefined first issues. Remarkably, that wasn't the case with *The Catholic Worker*. Once she had been inspired by Peter and convinced of the rightness of the project, Dorothy had a clear vision of what the paper should do, and that vision was evident from the day it was ready for circulation. The two lengthy above-the-fold articles made clear her principal concerns of the moment.

One was about child labor in the United States and the other about racial discrimination and exploitation. Both showed a keen awareness of current events. The child labor report informed readers that the number of underage employees in the workforce was declining, but not for laudable reasons. Rather, according to the Department of Labor, employers had found, in this fourth year of the Depression, that they could pay desperate adults the same wages they had once paid to adolescents and so no longer had any need for the ill-paid minors. The second article told of the War Department's exploitation of Negro workers in the South, men laboring twelve hours a day, seven days a week, for ten cents an hour, building levees for the Mississippi River and Tributaries Project. The "exposé," even when it was secondhand, would be a feature of *The Catholic Worker* for decades to come.

Other features of the inaugural issue included some of Peter Maurin's

"Easy Essays," an account of the Scottsboro boys' trial, a human interest story about an indigent family, information about impending strikes, and a review of a book about the history of Irish Catholicism. The issue came with a highly calculated dedication as well—to the New York Police Department. "If the police don't want to buy this paper," Dorothy announced on the front page, "we will give it to them."

The launch date and location were strategically chosen: May 1, Union Square. The square was packed with Communists, socialists, and curious on-lookers for the annual celebration of the Russian Revolution. Three young men had been asked, or directed, by their parish priest to help Dorothy sell the paper. As expected, they were looked at questioningly by those who didn't understand why anyone would be hawking a paper with a religious title in Union Square and were approached menacingly by Party members who didn't appreciate the intrusion on their turf. Two of the three helpers decamped in the face of the scoffing, jostling, and aggressive remarks; one, Joe Bennett, stuck around—and stayed with the paper as a writer for the better part of a year. (Tragically, Bennett, whom Dorothy thought the world of and who grew as a reporter with each issue, died of heart trouble just two years later, at the age of twenty-four.) That first day, he and Dorothy returned to East 15th Street with copies left over—presumably they had known they wouldn't be able to sell all 2,500 copies in one day—and Dorothy immediately began mailing them to parishes and colleges all over the country.

That letters to the editor over the next weeks and months came in from as far away as Nova Scotia, Nebraska, and California suggests that those first long-distance recipients of *The Catholic Worker* must have been happy to share the paper, mailing their own copies far and wide. *Commonweal* gave the fledgling paper good press, and parochial schools across the country began to order copies for their libraries. By anyone's standard, it was an overnight success, almost unprecedented among religious publications.

Peter was not happy with that first issue, though, and not only because his name was misspelled as *Maurain* on the masthead. In fact, he was rather surprised to see so much about strikes and wages, employers and employees, stories of injustice, topical matters. It wasn't quite what he'd had in mind. He had been expecting a vehicle for his favorite authors, his concerns, his philosophizing. He was looking for a paper with more devotional material.

He was feeling petulant enough to disappear for a few weeks, but then came back. He didn't have much to say to anyone who asked what his absence was all about beyond the typically Maurin-esque comment "Man proposes. Woman disposes."

Subsequent issues of the paper, which occasionally expanded to twelve pages when time and funds permitted, gave Peter as much space as he wanted for his free-verse essays, alongside heartbreaking articles about evictions and families left on the street, the machinations of the city's notoriously exploitative hotel industry, and the breaking up of Hoovervilles in Manhattan. Readers were offered excerpts from papal statements about their obligations to help the poor, critiques of the National Recovery Administration, calls for boycotts of city department stores—e.g., Ohrbach's and Klein's—for unfair labor practices, and lengthy (not to say, interminable) excerpts from Dorothy's novel in progress. Catholic Charities was an object of attack for accepting funds from the Rockefeller Foundation—a writer for *The Masses* was not about to forget John D. Rockefeller's authorization of murderous violence against the Ludlow, Colorado, miners and their families in 1914— and Dorothy expressed dismay that birth control was being taught in some public-school classes. Her appreciation of Margaret Sanger was now a thing of the past and a source of tension with Della, who remained a firm supporter of the birth control movement.

Anger about the conditions black Americans were subjected to was for some readers an unexpected constant. During its first year, the paper kept its readers abreast of developments in the Scottsboro case, expressed support for the various antilynching bills that had languished in Congress for a decade— legislation that FDR would never see his way clear to support—and reported on new incidents of lynching in the South. Statistics from the Urban League on black unemployment rates were reprinted. Joe Bennett was sent uptown to cover the deplorable conditions at Harlem Hospital, a state of affairs that, *The Catholic Worker* insisted, would not have been tolerated in the city's hospitals for white patients. When Arthur G. Falls, a black doctor in Chicago who had seen the paper, wrote to Dorothy to comment on the masthead, which depicted drawings of two shirtless white laborers, that example of implicit bias changed very quickly. In succeeding issues, one worker was white and one was black. By 1934, Dr. Falls was a correspondent for the paper.

There was, to be sure, a double-edged quality to *The Catholic Worker*'s coverage of racial problems. Dorothy openly worried that the field was being ceded to the Communists, the only white political force in the country speaking out against racism, and in effect urged Catholics to reconsider their prejudices in light of the political implications of that development. Concern for black Americans, then, was as much about advancing the cause of anticommunism as it was about helping to combat racism. At the same time, though, her feelings about bigotry and its real-life victims were genuine. Her indignation was heartfelt. She went to Harlem to meet with Elmer Carter, the editor of *Opportunity*, to talk to him about finding black writers who might want to write about racial issues for the *The Catholic Worker*, and some months later, she reprinted Carter's own editorial from *Opportunity* on blacks and Catholicism. Why, he mused, are there so few black priests? Why are most black Americans drawn to Protestantism rather than the Church of Rome?

Dorothy's own assessment of those problems was that a large share of the blame for the plight of the American Negro had to be placed upon the shoulders of white Catholics. Priests and parishioners alike did not make black people welcome in their churches, were indifferent to discrimination all around them, and thought they were still godly people even when they refused to see black men and women as brothers and sisters in Christ. Hence, whenever there was something positive to report, some small sign of progress being made—a Catholic interracial conference, for instance, or the opening of the first black Catholic high school in Alabama or a bishop (e.g., the crusading John McNicholas of Cincinnati) speaking out against prejudice— Dorothy made sure that such news made it into the paper as well.

More writers were obviously needed to keep up the momentum. Dorothy advertised in the paper, letting any interested parties know that their services would, of course, have to be provided without hope of salary. *The Catholic Worker* was a labor of love.

The first assistance came from a young woman, Dorothy Weston, who had studied at Manhattanville College, Fordham University, and the Columbia School of Journalism. She was a fluent writer and an efficient presence on what would soon become a small but dedicated staff. Her name appeared on the masthead of the second issue, replacing John's. Dorothy's brother had found a job outside the city and departed with Tessa and the baby, wishing his sister well.

Given the left-wing slant of the paper, critics were as quick to respond, and they were as vociferous as Dorothy's supporters. Monsignor James Francis McIntyre, the chancellor of the New York diocese, remembered later that he had had "no end of trouble" with complaints about the first issues of *The Catholic Worker*. Some readers were incredulous that the Church would permit the distribution of such a publication, promoting as it did racial unrest and political discontent. One angry priest suggested that the archdiocese call in the police to shut the newspaper down. McIntyre told a mutual friend at that time that he was sure Dorothy would "sooner or later secure the approbation of the diocese"—implying that she did not have it at the outset—but his was a delicate position. Cardinal Patrick Hayes, the head of the archdiocese, had no intention of condemning a paper focused on social justice, let alone shutting it down, though neither was he comfortable being its public advocate and allegedly considered a reprimand on two occasions. When referring to the passivity and conservatism of American Catholic clergymen, Peter's contributions had a bite the archdiocese did not appreciate.

Dorothy didn't make it any easier for Hayes or McIntyre when *The Catholic Worker* came out strongly in favor of a child welfare bill that the Roosevelt administration had been trying to push through Congress. The Church hierarchy (including all eight New York State bishops) was against this proposed bill, feeling that the federal government's interference in matters pertaining to family life was already too extensive and that sufficient child labor protection guidelines were in place in most states and local communities.

City Hall wasn't enamored of the new publication's positions, either. Mayor Fiorello La Guardia let Dorothy know, through an aide, that he thought her criticisms of Harlem Hospital and the city's facilities for the homeless were excessive and unfair. Dorothy's response was to recount the entire conversation, down to a merciless description of the oily messenger with his city car and polished shoes, in a scathingly sarcastic article entitled "The Mayor Objects." When self-serving politicians go after you, Dorothy told her small but growing staff, you know you are doing something right.

Perhaps the greatest compliment, however inadvertent, came at the end of the year from another Catholic journalist, not exactly a radical himself. "You may think you are newspaper editors," the Jesuit editor of *America* told

Dorothy, "but agitators is what you are." Exactly: agitators in a political sense and agitators in a spiritual sense.

Evidence that this was a moment in American life of great spiritual as well as physical hunger sometimes came from an unlikely source. In January 1934, Dorothy made what was now a rare trip to the theater, but it was an occasion of the kind she was loath to miss, a new play by an old friend. *Days Without End* is probably Eugene O'Neill's least-known work and for good reason. Despite an able cast, it received the most lacerating reviews its author ever experienced, playing at Henry Miller's Theatre in Midtown Manhattan for only a few weeks, never to be revived again. No biographer has ever had a kind word to say about it. None of that was to the point, though, as far as Dorothy was concerned, and she wrote a fairly positive review in the February issue of *The Catholic Worker*.

O'Neill's drama is about a man, John Loving, for whom one faith after another (the hedonism and nihilism of his youth, radical politics, Nietzsche, literature, marital love) has proven inadequate. Still, he fights the call of religion with all the indignation of a confirmed atheist, of the urban American male too sophisticated to believe in what he cannot see. At the end of the play, after a long interior battle spread out over four acts, Loving enters a church, where he feels a "mystical exaltation" while praying for forgiveness for his adultery and for the recovery of his wife from a serious illness. He accepts the truth of Christ's words, "I am the Resurrection and the Life." He is reborn, or returned to the self of his earliest childhood, when he did believe in a higher power.

Interestingly, the Catholic priest in *Days Without End*, uncle and mentor to the protagonist, is named Father Baird, potentially a borrowing of a name—Peggy Baird's—well known to O'Neill and Dorothy from more frolicsome times. Father Baird even quotes from Francis Thompson's "The Hound of Heaven"—"Ah, fondest, blindest, weakest, / I am He Whom thou seekest!"—the poem that O'Neill had recited to Dorothy at the Golden Swan seventeen years earlier.

To his publisher, Bennett Cerf, O'Neill was honest in a way he wasn't with everyone who read the play in manuscript. "It is an attempt," he told Bennett, "to express what I feel are the life-preserving depths of Catholic mysticism—to be fair to a side of life I have dismissed with scorn in other plays." It was not a topic New York theatergoers were remotely interested in or even found stageworthy, and by any standard, *Days Without End* is an inept story, stiffly told. Yet it confirmed Dorothy in her view of O'Neill as a person who could not ignore the inner pain he felt, a man who would always struggle spiritually and never entirely let go of the Catholic ideas of forgiveness and expiation he had imbibed in childhood, and—however great his earthly success—would never know true peace without God. Dorothy eagerly recommended the play to her friends.

The past was evoked in a less pleasant form several weeks later when Malcolm Cowley published *Exile's Return: A Literary Odyssey of the 1920s,* the first of his many chronicles of the Lost Generation and the book that significantly advanced his career as a critic and memoirist. A passing mention of Dorothy, presumably meant as a humorous compliment of sorts—or a jab after Dorothy's slighting reference to Cowley in her *America* piece the year before—made mention of the fact that she had been a favorite at the Hell Hole in the old days because of her ability to drink most of the other patrons under the table. Friends let Cowley know that Dorothy was furious with his bald reference to her wayward days, and, a gentlemanly sort, he eventually felt obliged to offer an apology. In truth, there was nothing to apologize for. He had merely expressed, however glibly, what he knew to be the case, but to a person inventing a new self, reminders of inconvenient realities were rude, unnecessary, presumptuous, and obstructive to her current aims. It was not how she wanted Peter Maurin to view her or how she wanted the young people to think of her who were gravitating to *The Catholic Worker.* The fact that the reminders were coming from the man who had had a long-term affair with her sister only added salt to the wound.

★ HOSPITALITY ★

B Y THE TIME FRANKLIN DELANO ROOSEVELT WAS INAUGURATED AS president, New York City had seen more than a quarter-million evictions and an estimated 20,000 of its citizens were wandering the streets at night looking for a place to sleep. The national Children's Bureau put the number of teenagers nationwide who were on their own, part of the "vast, homeless horde," at a quarter million.

New York City's six-story Municipal Lodging House on East 25th Street was packed every night with people of all ages, its 3,300 beds taken by desperate men, women, and children with the overflow sleeping on benches and floors. Exactly where is the Catholic Church in the midst of this crisis? Dorothy and Peter asked.

Several early issues of *The Catholic Worker* addressed a topic dear to Peter's heart: houses of hospitality. Peter spoke and wrote regularly about the practice in some communities in early Christian times of keeping a space available in one's home for wayfarers who required rest and sustenance. He liked to call it a "Christ room." As different ideas about space and privacy evolved in the West, that tradition of Christian hospitality had died out. It needed to be revived, Peter declared. It would be best, he thought, if bishops and parish priests took the lead for such a revival, but even he knew that was a far-fetched idea. Rectories and episcopal palaces in modern America were not about to open their doors to unwashed strangers.

If individuals and families were no longer inclined to provide a "Christ room," hospitality might need to take a different form in the modern world, Peter suggested. The modern house of hospitality he had in mind would not be like a traditional Progressive-era settlement house, with its social workers and classes and programs for "improvement," or like a city shelter or Salvation Army hostel, which required its overnight guests to vacate the premises during the day. Rather, the two nouns he liked, linked as they were—the one implying *home* and the other implying *unconditional welcome*—were the key to his thinking. The Catholic Worker—now the name of an entire movement, not merely a radical newspaper—could provide an example.

If the doctrine of the Mystical Body of Christ meant anything, Peter asserted, it meant that the stronger members of the body had an obligation to care for the weaker ones. Moreover, it followed that those who worked in the modern house of hospitality, who served the guests, should live with them, as one of them, in voluntary poverty. To enjoy a life of middle-class comfort while working amid the poverty-stricken was to create an unnatural imbalance that did no one any good. Such a gap constantly reminded the poor that they belonged to another category of being, that they were not our brothers and sisters in Christ, and hindered the giver's own spiritual evolution. Voluntary poverty brought into living practice the radical egalitarianism preached by Jesus. The guests might be invited to do the cooking, Peter mused, but should never be treated as anything other than guests.

In a way, Dorothy had been engaged in this kind of welcoming since the moment she had accepted Peter into her life. It wasn't unusual for him to come back from a day out and about in the city having encountered someone he liked who needed a place for the night, and she would make room in her apartment now that John and Tessa were gone and the offices of *The Catholic Worker* had taken over the vacated barbershop on the ground floor of her building. By the end of the year, when money started to come in from the sale of the paper and donations, the Workers rented an eight-dollar-a-month apartment near Tompkins Square, heatless and rat-ridden, for some men Peter had met who had been sleeping in Central Park, and shortly afterward they found another apartment in the area—with six rooms, five of which could be used as bedrooms, with a full working bathroom—for several women who had been laid off and evicted and come to her for help. Dorothy recognized those as a feeble temporary solution to what was only going to be an escalating problem. An actual building was going to be needed to realize Peter's vision. In the winter of 1934–1935, they found a property, affordable but in need of extensive repair, at the corner of Charles and Washington Streets, next to a police station and within two blocks of the Hudson River.

With the rental of the ramshackle eleven-room, four-story building at 144 Charles Street, Peter's concept of a real "house of hospitality" took shape. The women were lodged on one floor, the men on another, with Dorothy and Tamar on another and the kitchen and offices on the ground floor. The aim for the people who might wander in was not job training or rehabilitation; that was a goal far beyond the group's capacities and, in any event, an approach that smacked of condescension toward the "guests"— which was how the people they served were to be referred to, Dorothy explained. Some Workers liked the term "clients," but Dorothy and Peter had to explain that that word implied something very different, less warm, less personal, less "equal." She and Peter intended their house to be open to anyone who was hungry or homeless, anyone who had nowhere else to go and no friends or family to take them in. Some would come by for a meal; others would ask for shelter, and if there were beds available, they were free to stay for as long as they needed and wanted. Such openness meant, necessarily, that some of the least socialized and least socially acceptable individuals would be welcome. Jane Addams at Hull House would not for a minute have put up with some of the people Dorothy and Peter regarded as their guests. But then, Jane Addams and Dorothy Day had different objectives in mind.

To be sure, there were appreciative people by the dozens, and eventually by the hundreds, who came by for a meal or to find some item of clothing to keep them and their children warm from the donated-clothing room the Worker opened once the Charles Street house was ready. There were people who were down on their luck and who hoped one day, when economic circumstances changed, to find their bearings and make a stable life for themselves. That was always to be encouraged, and it did sometimes happen. Those people would all their days remember the Catholic Worker with gratitude.

Others, though, lived in a different world. They were products of a destitution and despair so extreme that they had been irreparably broken by their life experiences. They were society's castoffs, and they were never going to be "right." They were not "reformable," and they were not polite. But what they were entitled to, the Catholic Worker credo insisted, was patience and a roof over their heads and a manner of treatment no different from what would be accorded to anyone else invited into one's home. They were to feel they were in the presence of loving, godly people who looked upon them without condescension or judgment, as equals, as brothers and sisters in Christ. Yet that was to be achieved without proselytizing or even discussing religion with the guests.

Grateful or belligerent, a fair number naturally brought with them not just the odors and unsightliness of life on the street but vermin. And *everyone* at the Catholic Worker fell victim to the occupational hazards of living in a seriously untidy, unhygienic environment.

"We did not need hairshirts around Houses of Hospitality," Dorothy wrote. The lice caused everyone enough discomfort. The bedbugs became impossible to eradicate. No one on Charles Street had cause to romanticize poverty.

Thievery soon became an issue as well. There are three things you have to accept about very poor people who have lived on the street, Dorothy would repeat over the years: they don't smell good, they aren't grateful, and they are apt to steal. She didn't intend those remarks, often made to new Catholic Workers, to be a moral judgment; she meant them as a blunt statement about the nature of poverty and desperation at that abject a level. Not only were visitors told to keep an eye on their jackets and purses, but even some of the food in the kitchen would disappear before mealtime, the cook of the day having sold some of it in the neighborhood for the price of a bottle of cheap wine.

Some observers wondered if the house on Charles Street—and the same would be true for every house the Catholic Worker moved to—had to be quite as bad as it was. More than a few priests who came to visit were disconcerted by what they encountered. Dorothy's brother and sister certainly were. One visitor felt no hesitation in speaking up. Catherine de Hueck was a Russian baroness (or so she said; it made for a great story) who had fled the Soviets and now, like Dorothy, had opened her own Catholic hospitality house in Toronto. She would eventually be forced out of Canada by a Church hierarchy that found her social doctrines too radical and went on to open a similar facility in Harlem. She and Dorothy became friends, though the relationship seems to have been a little more intense on Catherine's part. Highly emotional, compassionate, robust, and fearless, even reckless, Catherine said whatever came into her head. She had no problem voicing her qualms to Dorothy when she first set foot in 144 Charles Street.

The houses Catherine ran had firm rules, even a constitution. (The idea of a Catholic Worker "constitution" defies imagination.) She thought that

Charles Street needed to be swept and mopped and disinfected more than it was, and she saw nothing wrong with asking the guests to do that. Dorothy's insistence that no matter how clean they attempted to keep the rooms, they would revert to a deplorable condition soon enough, given the state of their transient population, fell on deaf ears.

Catherine summarized to a priest who knew both of them the key differences between St. Joseph House, as the Charles Street house was now called, and her Friendship House. She understood that Dorothy believed in organization but only the kind that "must grow freely," that Dorothy did not believe in a training period for her workers (something Catherine emphatically did think necessary), and that Dorothy—the true anarchist, the true personalist—allowed "individuality of personnel to have full sway" in her house and "no uniformity except in fundamentals." She saw Dorothy as being inherently resistant to rules and regulations and of a more left-wing political stance than Catholic radical teaching usually leaned toward. Both women were open to calling the police if a truly violent person could not be dissuaded from inflicting harm, but Dorothy was more willing to cajole and wait and pray and see what developed. If Jane Addams would have had problems with some of the people Dorothy let stay, so, too, did the baroness. Even a friend, ally, and regular visitor, Thomas Barry, agreed that the place was "a madhouse."

Edward Breen was one of the more extreme examples of the madness that had to be dealt with. Writing to Catherine, Dorothy referred to him as "at the moment, my greatest and most miserable worry." Born in Ireland, he had studied with the Jesuits at Clongowes Wood College (possibly at the same time James Joyce was there) and come to America to be a newspaperman. He had enjoyed a successful career, even writing book reviews for George Shuster's *Commonweal*. But by the time Dorothy met him and he showed up without a nickel in his pocket to move into the house on Charles Street, he was well on his way to alcoholic dementia. His cursing was vile, meant to shock; his clothes were always hanging off him in ways approaching indecency; and he was belligerent about not bathing if he didn't want to. His racism and anti-Semitism were a particular problem. Dorothy herself was a "nigger-lover," as he liked to tell her, and he would inform anyone, especially blacks and Jews at the house, that he didn't know why he had to live in a place with so many "niggers and kikes." He was given the job of doorkeeper, but that didn't work out too well. "He sits there like a Cerberus," Dorothy wrote, "and growls and curses at everyone who comes in for a bite to eat or for some clothing." Once, he took a turn at answering the mail and wrote an unacceptably aggressive response, forcing Dorothy to apologize and explain the situation to the outraged correspondent. Thereafter, he was kept away from the mail.

Dorothy's fear was that if she called the police to take her unruly guest to the hospital, he would end up unattended, as most alcoholics were, or abused in a mental ward. What to do? "He, after all, is Christ," she reminded Catherine de Hueck. "'Inasmuch as ye have done it to the least of these,' you know. . . . Can you imagine Christ in a psychopathic ward?" When Mr. Breen's tirades reached a limit no one could stand anymore, one of the men would find him a room in a neighborhood boardinghouse, but he always ended up coming back. He remained at the house until he died in 1939.

In *The Seven Storey Mountain*, his famous autobiography of faith, Thomas Merton wrote about a trip he had taken as an undergraduate at Columbia University to the Bellevue morgue as part of his Contemporary Civilization course. That nightmarish experience had taken place at exactly the same time Dorothy was opening the Charles Street house. At the morgue, Merton had seen "rows and rows of iceboxes containing the blue, swollen corpses of drowned men along with all the other human refuse of the . . . city: the dead that had been picked up in the streets, ruined by raw alcohol. The dead that had been starved and frozen lying where they had tried to sleep in a pile of old newspapers. . . . The dope-fiend dead. The murdered dead. The run-over. The suicides. . . . The dead of venereal disease." They were all waiting to be shipped up the East River for burial in a common grave, like so much garbage.

It was to spare Mr. Breen that kind of death, to acknowledge even—or especially—him as a child of God, lost and difficult as he might be, that the Catholic Worker extended its hospitality.

So who were the young people who shared Dorothy's willingness—even passion at first—for that labor, for getting a monthly paper to press under the most trying conditions and living amid New York's poorest, wearing donated clothing, doing without a salary and the most basic comforts, the remotest sense of security or privacy, or any hope of family approval?

Those who found their way to her doorstep in the first years were a diverse group, some lost themselves and hoping to find an answer, some adventurous, most devout Catholics who felt stirred by Dorothy's efforts in a way they hadn't been by their parish priest. Some were unemployed and without immediate prospects; others were college graduates who could have embarked on a stable career path but were willing to forsake their parents' hopes for a new vision of their future. What they tended to have in common was resilience, a certain quirkiness, and a heightened social conscience, or at the very least an awareness that all was not right with the world they had been born into.

Many were quite young. Stanley Vishnewski, a Lithuanian kid from Brooklyn, had just turned eighteen. The son of an immigrant tailor who didn't understand what in the world his son was doing with that odd group of people who expected him to work for no pay, Stanley told varying stories about his introduction to Dorothy after he saw a copy of the paper and wrote her a fan letter. In one version, he claimed he had seen an old lady carrying a heavy typewriter into the building. (Dorothy wasn't forty at the time.) He had played the gallant and helped her out. He had no particular skills to offer, a fact that didn't change over his four decades at the Worker, but he was a reliable fellow with a wildly irreverent sense of humor, a quality that always endeared people to Dorothy, and he loved playing the tireless newsboy with a stack of the papers under his arm.

Already on hand to welcome Stanley when he came to stay were Big Dan, an ex-policeman; Little Dan, an ex-bookkeeper; and Mary Sheehan, a "sharp-tempered soul," Dorothy said—all, no doubt, Peter Maurin's finds. So was Margaret Polk, a single mother from a mining town in Pennsylvania brought in by Peter. Margaret, who claimed to have visions, had her baby while at the Catholic Worker and for years insisted that her daughter be blessed by every cleric who ever set foot in the house. At the sight of a Roman collar, she ran to get the girl. A Lithuanian like Stanley, she cooked well but was a source of concern as she demanded an occasional night on the town, which, Dorothy feared, would someday lead to a second baby they would all have to take care of.

Julia Porcelli was no older than Stanley Vishnewski when, as a senior at Cathedral High School in Manhattan, she was sent by her school newspaper to cover the Catholic Worker's picketing of the Mexican Consulate during the height of the anticlerical violence in Mexico. There, on a bitterly cold December morning, she met Peter and Dorothy. Taken with Peter Maurin and his teachings even more than she was with Dorothy, she knew that a commitment to their kind of struggle was what she had long been pining for. Peter seemed a true prophet, Julia felt, while Dorothy had an allure more like that of Greta Garbo, mysterious and beautiful in an unconventional way. She moved into St. Joseph House a year after her graduation.

Julia was slight of build but a resourceful, determined soul, Dorothy noted. She could write and type, which made her an asset to the paper, and she was the kind of young woman who, meeting a family of nine children on Charles Street whose father was out of work and whose mother was dying of cancer, took a Saturday job at Woolworth's to earn some money to help them out—and then took her manager at Woolworth's to the city's labor board when she had complaints about unfair practices at the store.

Many of the volunteers, such as Vishnewski and Porcelli, stayed with Dorothy for years, while others merely passed through or continued to live at their own home while helping out. Eileen Corridan was a journalist and the niece of a Jesuit, John Corridan, the labor priest who served as the real-life model for Father Barry in the 1953 film *On the Waterfront*. A difficult personality (both "helpful and obstructive," Dorothy felt), she provided much-needed assistance with the paper beginning in the first months of 1934 and then departed by 1936 to see if she could find a full-time job in journalism.

Ade Bethune, a nineteen-year-old Belgian-born art student at Cooper Union, gave of her services for more than a decade but continued to live with her parents. She put her stamp on the paper when she showed up and suggested to Dorothy that a publication composed entirely of text with the occasional photograph was a bit grim and would benefit from some more lively visuals. She contributed just that with her dark, penetrating, stylized woodcuts of saints and biblical scenes, which began appearing with the March 1934 issue. (One slightly demented New York Franciscan saw Bethune's art as the smoking gun concerning the Workers' evil intent. She was providing a Soviet style of drawing, "Communist caricature," with her modernist imagery, he warned the hierarchy.) Overcoming her extreme shyness, Bethune took her turn hawking the paper on the street, embracing the mentorship of Dorothy and Peter as few other Workers did.

Albert Coddington, who went by the name of "Tom," wanted no part of mentorship. A high school teacher who had recently lost his job and been evicted from his apartment, he arrived in 1934. In addition to needing a place to stay, he might have joined the Catholic Worker as Dorothy Weston's boyfriend, as they were married only several months after his arrival. According to Stanley Vishnewski, he held himself aloof from many of the other Workers and saw editing the paper and philosophizing as his calling, not manning the breadline or helping the guests try on secondhand coats. A devout Catholic, he was one of the more theologically well-versed, politically strident, and opinionated young men to join the group. That would ultimately prove a source of considerable friction.

John Cort was Tom Coddington's intellectual match, though they overlapped for only a short time. A recent Harvard graduate in history and French literature, he had converted to Catholicism in college, had come upon a copy of *The Catholic Worker* in Boston by happenstance, and took pleasure in hawking copies outside area churches. Hearing Dorothy speak in Boston about her house of hospitality was a revelatory experience for him, and so he quit his job to join the community in New York. In an unexpected way, Dorothy had made life at the Catholic Worker sound like fun, he later wrote, not the grisly undertaking some listeners took it to be. Indeed, she seemed to him the sort of person who wanted to find enjoyment in whatever she did, who was motivated by "the duty of delight," a phrase from John Ruskin she liked to quote.

One of the sharpest young men to join the Worker in the thirties, Cort was like the even more acerbic Coddington in that he had at best a grudging respect for Peter Maurin and was unwilling to pay him the deference others did. Indeed, Cort at times liked to tweak Dorothy herself about her own foibles and inconsistencies. One easy target (for anybody who cared about it) was the way she professed a faith in anarchism and independence, but only if her word was law. On that front, this boss-who-pretended-not-to-be-a-boss could give as well as she got, though. Dorothy had a tongue on her, as Stanley had noticed approvingly from the start.

Bill Callahan, the son of a New York State Supreme Court judge, was as serious about his faith and as intellectually impressive as Cort. A pacifist, forceful writer, and expert editor, he had been educated at one of the city's best Catholic schools, Regis High School, and the City University of New York. He was also an able public speaker and later enjoyed taking to the road and going on the radio to talk about the work being done at the paper and the Catholic Worker view of the political issues of the day. The *Pittsburgh Press* referred to him when he was in that city to give a speech in 1937 as "the managing editor of *The Catholic Worker* and the stormy petrel of the Catholic press." Dorothy liked his tart manner enough to give him his own column in 1938, "The Gadfly." Callahan would remain with the Worker until 1940.

Peter did some recruiting on his own when he spoke to younger audiences, though his image at the podium had to have struck most college-age listeners as disconcerting. Rare was the student who could manage even to get past Peter's thick accent, let alone harken to his message about distributism, holy poverty, and Christian personalism, but Gerry Griffin of Marshalltown, Iowa, was one. A born nonconformist, Griffin had never planned to spend his whole life in the Midwest, and having heard Peter talk at Columbia College in Dubuque, right after commencement he found his way to New York, where he would be a mainstay for several years. With Joe Zarrella, he was one of the managers of the house when Dorothy and Peter were away.

Zarrella, a nineteen-year-old son of a barber and lapsed Catholic, had seen someone selling *The Catholic Worker* in Union Square on May Day 1935 and had bought a copy ("The bug bit me, and I was captured," he said). He was an affable, well-built, good-looking Italian, a favorite of Dorothy's, and he idolized her. His friends at the house were always trying to set him up with Julia Porcelli. He eventually married another Catholic Worker, Mary Alice Lautner, who joined them from Indiana. Alice had been given a copy of *The Catholic Worker* by her brother, a priest, with the sage words "This is what you're looking for."

It didn't escape the notice of the women that Dorothy favored the men when looking for editorial leadership on the paper. She was a woman of her era in that regard. But she also harbored some anxiety, potentially even some guilt feelings, about the presence of good-looking young women in a less-than-secure situation. Dorothy Weston, Eileen Corridan, Mary Alice Lautner, and Agnes Bird, a young New Yorker just out of college whose services were initially declined by Dorothy (until, that is, she became aware of Agnes's expert typing skills), were attractive and approachable. Coming to live in a bad neighborhood, or even just working during the day in a building filled with all kinds of unreliable men, they caused Dorothy to worry about their safety and even sometimes their own good judgment. Mary Alice Laut-ner felt "frozen out" of any real responsibility in her first months in New York. It took time for Dorothy to resolve those concerns in her own mind, to trust that the women knew how to look out for themselves. Agnes Bird worked as Dorothy's secretary from 1938 to 1942.

Yet Dorothy was always encouraging when anyone, male or female, showed the least interest in public speaking. She and Peter would try to nudge shy people, such as Ade Bethune, to take a turn at addressing some group that wanted to learn more about the Catholic Worker, but Bethune wanted no part of it at first. Dorothy Weston, on the other hand, was espe-cially adept as a speaker and was encouraged to make the rounds of Com-munion breakfasts and once even to give a speech on a soapbox in Union Square. Not unwisely, Dorothy felt that the best possible advertisement for the movement was her devoted, often charismatic, and decidedly young workforce.

A break from the rigors of journalism and tending to the needs of their iras-cible guests was the lectures and roundtable discussions—the "clarification of thought" events—that Peter had been itching to get started. Especially for the more intellectually and theologically inclined among the group, those events, sometimes occurring three or four nights a week, were the real perquisites of the job. Initially, Peter expected audiences so large and eager to hear him talk that he rented a hall accommodating a few hundred, only to have fifteen people show up. Thereafter, the lectures and discussions of what was dubbed by Dorothy the "Catholic Worker School" were held at the house, first in the office or the backyard at East 15th Street, later in the more commodious Charles Street house. An equally striking example of Peter's impracticality from that period was his opening with a friend, Steve Hergenhan, a Catholic Worker storefront in Harlem that aroused consider-able suspicion and eventually had its windows broken. He appeared on the stage of the Apollo Theater one night to see if he could stir interest but, with the audience naturally expecting a comic monologue, was promptly "given the hook." Not even Julia Porcelli's Saturday-morning sessions of reading to neighborhood children brought the place into the good graces of Harlem's residents.

Those freewheeling evenings covered a range of topics. They might involve talking about G. K. Chesterton's biography of St. Francis of Assisi and the ways in which the Catholic Worker was a Franciscan endeavor or the distributist authors Peter recommended to everyone. They were about the rise of nationalism in the West, racism in the United States, the situation in Mexico, the fascist threat, pacifism, the NRA, Emmanuel Mounier's personalism, Jacques Maritain's philosophy, neo-Thomism, economic theory, modern art and religion, or the evolution of the concept of the Mystical Body of Christ, which was, of course, at the heart of Dorothy's profession of faith. Mercifully, Peter was not the only speaker or discussion leader. The professors he and Dorothy approached from Columbia, Fordham, and New York Universities, historians and sociologists as well as theologians, proved happy to give of their time. They brought interested students and colleagues along with them. Priests across Manhattan heard about the evening talks, whose schedule was always posted in the paper, and stopped by, as did people who lived in the neighborhood. Some volunteers were knowledgeable or brave enough to try their hand at leading a session—one evening, John Cort tackled the papal encyclicals on labor—while the less educated, such as Stanley Vishnewski, sat there rapt, pencil in hand, taking down every word. "Clarification of thought" it was for some; for many others, it was a first introduction to those issues and ideas.

It was no small pleasure after the discussions when Dorothy joined everyone at the dining room table or a nearby watering hole to continue exchanging ideas, even arguing long and hard, while smoking up a storm and downing a late-night libation. The imbibing aspect, however, ended abruptly with an executive order from Dorothy when she decided that a few too many of her treasured circle didn't know when to stop. The last thing she wanted was to have a give-and-take explication of Church doctrine used as a means to exacerbate anyone's drinking problem.

Fairly early on, some rather prominent figures in the Church accepted Peter's invitations, including Father John Ryan, the foremost social reformer among the US clergy and an important Roosevelt ally (known as "the Right Reverend New Dealer") and Father John LaFarge, Jr. The erudite LaFarge, a descendant of Benjamin Franklin and a son of the famous painter John La Farge, was also the most outspoken clergyman in the country on the subjects of racism and anti-Semitism.

Another notable discussion leader—certainly the most meaningful for the Catholic Worker's purposes—was a friend of Peter, Father Virgil Michel from Saint John's Abbey in Collegeville, Minnesota. Michel was a Benedictine theologian and social ethicist, founder of the journal *Orate Fratres* and the Liturgical Press, a translator of Mounier, and a crucial figure in the liturgical reform movement. Though he was too fastidious a man to find the Catholic Worker's standards of organization and cleanliness to his liking—you always had to shake your coat out carefully after a visit—he was a wholehearted supporter of its mission and its founders. He took to Dorothy at once, perceiving her to be "one of those martyr-figures and lay apostles so much needed in extreme times." He felt she was eminently on the right track by merging theology and social work, faith and action in the world. She saw him as the best, most articulate advocate among the clergy she could imagine for what she and Peter were doing. It was a perfect union of kindred spirits.

Indeed, if anyone joined the Catholic Worker in the 1930s and did not understand upon arrival that their cause was every bit as much about their own spiritual development as it was about social progressivism and alleviating poverty, they quickly learned better. There was a reason Dorothy urged all the Workers in the house to attend Mass daily, as she did herself—*urged*, not forced. There was a reason she urged taking time off for prayer and observance of the sacrament of confession and absolution, as she did—again: *urged*, not forced. If Father Michel had one criticism to make about an esteemed speaker such as Father Ryan, it was that his focus on New Deal legislation was too divorced from his Catholicism. Michel regarded social reform as vital—Catholics certainly had to play a role in the crisis of their time— but saw moral reform as a deeper, foundational concern. Between the two, Dorothy stood with Michel rather than with Ryan. Justice in a material, earthly sense was what the Worker was about, Dorothy wanted the people around her to know, but it would not by itself effect the transformation she hoped to see in the United States. The change she was working toward was broader and deeper.

Father Michel preached the gospel of the broad and the deep. Specifically, his leadership in rethinking Catholic liturgy was something that mattered to Dorothy and about which she wanted the young people around her to be knowledgeable and sympathetic. Too many Catholics in her time,

Dorothy could see, adopted an essentially passive approach to their religious life. There was a catechism to be memorized, a parish priest to answer all questions, a Mass to sit through each week. The experience was not active, intimate, robust in any way. Liturgical reform suggested a different approach, and those were ideas, foreshadowing the immense changes of Vatican II, that Michel wanted aired. Celebration of the Mass in Latin appealed to many, but might not a service in the vernacular have more meaning? Couldn't a dialogue Mass, in which the laity spoke up and responded in accepted forms to the priest's words, rather than the voices of the priest and the altar boy being the only ones ever heard in the church, serve a purpose? Learning prayers other than the same half dozen taught by the nuns might touch deeper chords. Compline, the practice of group praying or singing at the end of the day, could be a source of radical rejuvenation.

Not everyone at the Worker was comfortable with the optional "new" prayers and practices Dorothy urged on the group. Saying the rosary and letting the priest do the rest was the approach that some in the house were used to and wanted to stick with. A few Workers thought Dorothy was being even more eccentric than usual with that strange business about liturgical reform and personal involvement. Others, when Mary Sheehan or Margaret Polk came out of the kitchen after dinner and banged a pot up and down the halls announcing Compline, were happy to join in a communal prayer or song. Dorothy had no doubts: vocal, communal, even innovative worship cemented the bonds of a community, made one more eager to work for the common good, and made the presence of a living God all the more real.

Father Paul Hanly Furfey of the sociology department at the Catholic University of America in Washington, DC, a leading figure in his field, was another who agreed to participate in the roundtable discussion evenings whenever he was in New York. He was ecstatic with what he encountered. "It was love at first sight," he asserted about his first impressions of what Dorothy and Peter were attempting: the newspaper, the house, the ambition and level of intellectual and spiritual exchange. Years later, when referring to his 1936 book *Fires on the Earth*, he told Robert Ellsberg, the paper's editor in the late 1970s, "I didn't just write about the Catholic Worker. I absorbed it into my own self. The Catholic Worker viewpoint became my viewpoint. I was converted internally."

American Catholic clergymen of the 1930s are a group none too easily or glibly categorized—ranging from die-hard reactionaries obsessed with orthodoxy and communism to parish priests whose concerns extended no farther than their own parish, to men quietly and admirably tending to the needs of others, to Church reformers and progressive, even radical, social activists with a national following and a determination to change the world. For the priests who were part of the last-named group, the Catholic Worker was a wonder and a source of hope.

With the newspaper so evidently a success, the "clarification of thought" sessions attracting enthusiastic participants, and a house of hospitality functioning at full capacity, Peter Maurin could feel that a significant portion of his message had been acted upon by the woman whose apartment he had invaded two years earlier. Yet he had no intention of letting her forget the other matter about which he felt so passionately—and talked incessantly.

The idea of an "agronomic university," as Peter liked to call it, "captivated the young men around the Catholic Worker that winter of 1935," Dorothy later wrote. "I do not believe the women were so sold on it. I knew I was something less than enthusiastic." Tamar was eight and used to urban living; her mother felt the same: "I loved the life of the city."

Nonetheless, in the spring, the Catholic Worker acquired its first "farming commune," on Staten Island. A single house on only a single acre and not so very far from Manhattan, it wasn't exactly what Peter had in mind, but to Dorothy it seemed a plausible start, "a valid training ground for the larger farm to come." The house had eight bedrooms, a kitchen, and three rooms built around an L that could be used for meetings, and a wraparound porch with a view of Raritan Bay. The rent would be manageable as long as donations continued to come in. For the year in which they held the lease, then, Dorothy became a commuter, dividing her time during the week between the Village and the island.

The part of the project that worked at all worked reasonably well. The vegetables raised in the garden were plentiful enough to feed anyone staying at the farm with a surplus sufficient to bring box loads back to the city, and everyone loved the location by the water for summertime discussion sessions. The drawbacks were what could have been expected, even if one overlooked the frenzied guest from Manhattan who believed he was Vladimir Lenin reborn and insisted on hoeing the soil with his toes and sleeping in the garden at night. Peter's idea had been that a pastoral setting would encourage "scholars to become workers and workers to become scholars," a phrase he used repeatedly. The reality was that few of the "scholars" wanted to take their turn with the planting and sowing and cooking, and tensions sometimes ran high. "Each pictured the commune in terms of his own desires," Dorothy noted. When the landlord declined to renew the lease, the farming idea was abandoned for the moment.

Dorothy probably felt relieved. The success of *The Catholic Worker* was her principal concern at the moment, and an unexpected result of the newspaper's reach, and the word of mouth that accompanied it, was that both Dorothy and Peter became, separately, speakers in great demand. People who had read the paper wanted to hear firsthand about the Catholic Worker. Their audiences at first were students and faculty at Catholic schools, seminarians, and members of Catholic discussion clubs. Most of the time, people didn't know in advance what they were getting with Peter Maurin as a guest lecturer. Stories became the stuff of Catholic Worker legend about hosts calling to ask why their speaker had not shown up at the bus or railway station when the only person there was "some bum" asleep on a bench—Peter, of course. Dorothy's public image was more acceptably genteel. Peter was a vagabond wanderer who never troubled himself about where he would lay his head at night. For Dorothy to go on the road, it was necessary that the host group pay her bus fare and find her lodging in someone's spare room; if a modest honorarium was offered (and eventually it was expected), all the better, as it helped to pay the bills back home.

Leaving Tamar with Della and her family in nearby New Jersey or having her stay with neighbors she trusted, Dorothy entered those waters with some trepidation. She was not a naturally adept speaker. Even more remarkably, given the fact that she gave more than several hundred talks—possibly thousands—throughout her long life, by most accounts she never became a strong or eloquent speaker. (She was more a "homily giver," one of her nieces by marriage remarked.) She claimed never to enjoy the experience, which is even harder to believe. She counted on her presence and the uniqueness of her story to hold her audience, and on those fronts she was secure.

The upper Midwest, especially Wisconsin and Minnesota, proved from the start to be particularly fertile territory. Nina Polcyn was nineteen and a junior at Marquette University in Milwaukee when her parish priest began distributing *The Catholic Worker* after Mass. Enormously impressed by what she read, she brought the paper to the attention of her journalism professor, who urged her to invite the intriguing woman to speak on campus, which she did. Dorothy spent the night with the Polcyns, sufficiently impressing them that they allowed their daughter to spend a summer at St. Joseph House after she graduated. She eventually went back to New York and stayed for several months. (She subsequently became one of Dorothy's closest friends and allies, helped to found a house of hospitality in Milwaukee, and later ran Chicago's principal Catholic bookstore, a job that enabled her to come to Dorothy's financial aid repeatedly over the years.)

The Jesuits at Marquette didn't seem to feel the trepidation their order's colleagues at some eastern colleges felt about the presence on campus of an alleged rabble-rouser and New York radical. Nor did the Benedictine nuns at the College of St. Scholastica in Duluth, a women's college at the time, feel put off by the title of her lecture when she visited: "Experiences of a Communist and a Catholic." The school paper's headline read "Militant Catholic Champions Cause of Laboring Classes."

At the College of Saint Catherine in St. Paul, Abigail Quigley—the future wife of Senator Eugene McCarthy—recalled how freely copies of *The Catholic Worker* were circulated on campus. At Saint John's University in Collegeville, her husband-to-be was immersed in the same progressive atmosphere. Father Michel was one of his teachers and a significant influence on his thinking about faith and society. Michel's students were encouraged to read Mounier, Maritain, Chesterton, and Péguy—all names that surfaced in Eugene McCarthy's speeches of the 1960s—and no one, least of all Michel, worried about the whisperings of dangerous political affiliations. Michel's sudden death in 1938 while still in his forties was a devastating blow for Dorothy.

Even some in the midwestern hierarchy were fans. Bishop Joseph Busch of St. Cloud, a more liberal prelate than many, had stopped in Manhattan to meet Dorothy on his way back to Minnesota from Italy—he told her he had first come across *The Catholic Worker* in Rome!—and said that he would be happy to introduce her to audiences in his diocese. Archbishop Samuel Stritch of Milwaukee and Bishop Hugh Boyle of Pittsburgh felt the same admiration.

Some seeds were planted that bore immediate fruit. Invited to speak at Saint Louis University, Dorothy appeared before not her usual audience of twenty or thirty or forty listeners but a law school auditorium filled with eight hundred students and alumni. One recent graduate, Cyril Echele, was so taken with what he heard that he wrote to Dorothy asking for a list of subscribers to the paper in St. Louis so that he might look into beginning a branch of the Catholic Worker there. He did exactly that, and when a Worker from New York, Herb Welsh, moved to St. Louis, the two men opened a house of hospitality in that city.

In many ways, for a long time Dorothy fared much better in midwestern venues than she did closer to home. Eastern parish priests, teachers, school administrators, and mothers superior were skittish about the signals from their episcopal leadership, not exactly ringing endorsements. When several students at St. John's University in Brooklyn (now Queens) were caught distributing *The Catholic Worker* on campus, they were reprimanded; the Vincentian priests did not want a Communist paper spread among their student body. Later discovered selling it on the subway, the unrepentant young men incurred the wrath of their dean. Sister Peter Claver, an early admirer of Dorothy's work and purportedly the first nun to contribute a dollar to *The Catholic Worker*, was told by her mother superior that she was not to see that woman of dubious political views and affiliations until further instructed. Fordham University's Jesuit president, Robert Gannon, was a rock-ribbed Republican whose students knew better than to bring the paper onto campus, despite the approval of a few of their professors. The Catholic Worker's stance on any number of issues—capitalism, pacifism, racial integration— was, at best, distasteful to Gannon. A noted Jesuit professor of ethics at the school, Ignatius Cox, could at times adopt what Dorothy described as a "threatening" stance.

All of that Dorothy faced with equanimity, and when Father McIntyre suggested that a priest as editorial adviser for the paper might temper some of the criticism, she was more than amenable to the suggestion. She knew who she wanted. A Paulist, Father Joseph McSorley of the Church of St. Paul the Apostle at 59th Street and Ninth Avenue, was happy to assume the role. An unflappable type, he was already her spiritual adviser and had been a bemused fan of the newspaper from the beginning.

The challenges of getting the word out were daunting and the long bus rides and lectures, coupled with the management of the house, took a toll on Dorothy's health and stamina. She began to suffer from migraines, which would continue to be a problem for many years. She also suffered from guilt about leaving Tamar; a child of ten or twelve needed to see her single mother more, not less. Those were issues that Dorothy knew would require more attention in the days ahead. Decisions, choices, would have to be made. For the moment, she tried to put those concerns out of her mind.

The excitement that the newspaper was generating had been for her a surprise and a cause for elation. By the end of 1933, circulation reached a remarkable 25,000; it was at 40,000 a year later and at 110,000 by the middle of 1935. One of Peter Maurin's cherished projects was well under way. A need was being answered.

TEN

❧ CHALLENGE ❧

Jesus's observation in Matthew 19:24, in which we are told that it is easier for a camel to pass through the eye of the needle than for a rich man to find his way into heaven, might well be taken more as metaphor than literal truth (most Americans certainly hope it is a metaphorical statement), but the sentiment behind it is one that Dorothy had come to believe. She had always been unwilling to brush aside biblical admonitions about wealth too quickly or too easily, though in the midst of an economic crisis an emphasis on doing without struck many of her countrymen as bizarre.

Faint glimmerings of that line of thought had not gone entirely unstated in earlier American religious contexts. In 1849, Archbishop John Hughes had delivered to his New York City parishioners one of his most important homilies from the pulpit of St. Patrick's Cathedral. He spoke on the theme of earthly success as potentially at odds with the deepest spirituality. He was addressing men and women who had been told, as Americans who had come of age under Andrew Jackson and James K. Polk, that it was their manifest destiny to prosper—to use all, to take all, to feel pride in their dominance—and to grow rich by the fruit of their ambition and acquisitive labor. Hughes speculated that any individual's attainment of his or her desires to their fullest extent might actually be better taken as a sign of God's disfavor, that some conscious inhibition of one's material success might be essential to a meaningful communion with the Creator. Quakers, Mennonites, Isaac Hecker's Paulist Fathers, and others, of course, had always shared that concern.

Yet postwar America had not been in a self-denying mood, even in a religious context. *The Man Nobody Knows* by Bruce Barton topped bestseller nonfiction lists in the 1920s precisely by catering to a commerce-affirming culture. Barton's Jesus is not the lamb of God, compassionate and all-forgiving, but an equivalent of the modern-day American businessman, a strong-minded entrepreneur with a big idea who defied an empire and built a worldwide organization from the ground up. Revivals across the heartland and in major cities were about what faith could do for the faithful right now, what one could *get*—healing, problems solved, a better life—out of testifying for Jesus. With her gaudy Angelus Temple in Los Angeles and mastery of modern media techniques, the evangelist Aimee Semple McPherson was pure Hollywood; Cecil B. DeMille couldn't have done better. Catholic prelates such as Boston's Cardinal William O'Connell lived like potentates in the 1930s, and far too many priests for Dorothy's liking enjoyed a protected existence in comfortable rectories. Charles Coughlin, the reactionary Michigan radio priest, was busy building a broadcasting and public relations empire that was as much about politics and xenophobia as religion.

A second aspect of Dorothy's thinking, heightened by contact with Peter, had to do with the role of the laity in public life. An active, independent lay apostolate, of the kind promoted by the French Catholic intellectuals who dominated Maurin's Great Books List, was a less familiar notion in the United States. Organizations such as the Knights of Columbus and the Catholic War Veterans had been founded by laymen, and philanthropic agencies such as Catholic Charities were combined efforts of the clergy and the laity. Watchdog groups—the Hollywood-monitoring Legion of Decency was the most famous—tended to be ecclesiastical in origin. Nonetheless, in all ways that counted, the laity was expected to follow the lead of its pastors and bishops. Catholic Americans, still a part of a sociological ghetto, were told that their principal concern was for their own salvation and spiritual well-being, for their family, neighborhood, and parish. The Catholic Worker represented a different, far less constrained order of being.

Finally, Peter's inspiration and Dorothy's own political history underscored obligations to the poor that, while originating in the midst of an economic collapse, were not connected merely to the Depression itself. No matter how much some people wanted to pretend otherwise, the injunction to do right by "the least of these," who will always be with us, as equivalent to doing right by God Himself, laid bare a conflict with a culture that believed in making a distinction between the "deserving poor"—working-class and middle-class victims of the Crash, laboring men and women unfairly thrown down into the abyss of poverty—and the poor who did not deserve help. An ethos that stressed the virtues of rugged individualism, no-holds-barred competition in the marketplace and, most disturbingly, success as a sign of God's favor had no use for the "undeserving poor," the alcoholics and the misfits, the lazy and the lost and the unappreciative. The poorhouses that occupied land on the fringes of many midsize American cities had never been intended to embody Christlike compassion; they were meant to degrade their inhabitants who had failed to realize the promise of America. That was an approach Dorothy wanted no part of. It was an affront to the entire concept of the Mystical Body of Christ. You joined the Catholic Worker only if you believed that there was no such thing as an undeserving poor person, no such concept as wasted charity or misplaced love.

The Charles Street arrangement didn't last long. Only eleven months after moving in, the landlord informed Dorothy that the bank was foreclosing on him. The building was sold and torn down the following year. That situation led to a mad scramble to find new lodgings.

After a prolonged negotiation with a woman who owned two buildings in Little Italy, the Worker found a new home at 115 Mott Street, except that it wasn't at first exactly *on* Mott Street. Gertrude Burke owned an apartment building that faced the street, but she also owned a much older, more run-down building tucked away behind it, past a small courtyard, that did not extend all the way to the street behind it. There were twenty rooms in the oddly positioned rear building, which could easily house the offices of the paper, the Workers who would be living there, and the estimated twenty guests who would be coming with them. Several months later, there were sixty people staying in the house, but by then Mrs. Burke was renting the Worker rooms in the building on the street. Eventually, as the original tenants moved out, Dorothy took over both buildings and the storefront. The city, however, had demanded a cleanup and renovation before the Workers were allowed to move in.

Mott Street was a neighborhood of tenements, small factories, bakeries, livery stables, laundries, and fish markets, Dorothy later remembered, and it can only be surmised what the inhabitants thought of the new occupants, their style of life, and the troubled souls they brought with them. Dorothy herself was a curiosity. "When I first saw her," a woman who had been a little girl in the neighborhood remarked years later, "I thought she was a foreigner. . . . She looked like somebody just off the boat. At that time, in my neighborhood, the Italian women all dressed very modern, so she stood out like a sore thumb . . . tall, with no makeup, and stunning eyes. Beautiful!" She also impressed the neighborhood women by attending Mass every day, but when anyone suggested, alluding to her piety and concern for the poor, that she might be a saint, she shut that talk down pretty quickly with a terse "Bullshit!" It would be a few years before Dorothy purged her conversation of the blue language she had cultivated among her male colleagues at *The Call.*

Conditions, even post-renovation, were scarcely better than they had been on Charles Street, though at least heat and electricity were no longer an issue. There was a serious rat problem in the basement, the smell of urine from a back alley was overpowering, and the windows didn't fit properly, a torment on wintry days. To John Cort, the place resembled "a stage set worthy of O'Casey and Gorky." Not even the murals of the Holy Family that Ade Bethune painted on the dining room wall made it look less grim. It was inexplicable to many of the Workers that they weren't closed down by the Board of Health immediately. "We violated practically every health rule in the book," Joe Zarrella recalled. "No hot water. Primitive cooking facilities. One toilet for the whole floor. No heat except for open fireplaces and a few kerosense heaters. Most of the time we dressed up to go to bed. No place to take a bath or anything like that." The mattresses would periodically be taken up to the roof and washed with kerosene, the iron bed frames and springs blowtorched, and the bedbugs would come pouring out. But they were back soon enough. The Board of Health did come by, and efforts were made to placate the civic authorities, but they never lasted long. Rather little of this situation made the pages of *The Catholic Worker,* of course, where a modified upbeat tone was the usual order of the day.

Some aspects of living in a house of hospitality were easier to get used to than others for the middle-class men and women who had enlisted in the cause. There were plenty of faucets in the building but no bathtubs, so that meant a trip to the city's public baths for a good wash, hardly the most pleasant of settings, or to a willing friend's apartment if you knew someone who lived not too many subway stops away. It was surprising, John Cort thought, how quickly you could get used to the idea of a weekly, rather than a daily, shower. In that regard the hot New York summers were much worse than winters.

Harder to deal with were the guests who didn't even see the point of a weekly, or even a monthly, shower. Or making their beds or helping with the housework, if they were long-term residents, or lifting a finger to do anything. Peter and Dorothy didn't believe in badgering; personalist philosophy dictated that a good example, rather than an order, was the appropriate response. Yet "you could throw good examples at some people and watch it bounce off like peanuts off a tank," Cort noted. With the number of "good example" people vastly outnumbered by the "bad example" guests, Cort in some frustration took matters into his own hands one day. Sick of watching Tex, an out-of-work seaman with whom he shared a room, sleep twelve hours a day and then expect to be fed without any effort to help, he posted rules when Dorothy was away: everyone in the house had to be up by 9:00 a.m., had to make his or her own bed, and had to contribute to the housecleaning. When Dorothy returned, she sided with the indignant guests and the posting came down. The Abbess, as the Workers sometimes called her, had spoken.

There were at least three dimensions to the work that had to be completed on a daily basis at the house: the morning shift to serve all those who were waiting outside for coffee, the midday dining shift for the day crowd, and the feeding of the full-time residents, whose number kept fluctuating. Peter and Dorothy took their turns at setting up and cleaning up.

The morning labor involved serving coffee and bread for as long as the supplies lasted. Mott Street allowed for a breadline in a way that Charles Street, a building on a street corner next to a police station, had not. Not everyone in the neighborhood was thrilled with the practice. As many as four hundred men lined up every day at 5:00 a.m., in good weather and bad. Feeding that number could entail 125 loaves of bread and vats of coffee. Later in the day, when fewer people were at the door, a lunch of soup, bread, and coffee would be served to as many people as the dining room would accommodate—or, again, until supplies ran out. Then the guest-residents, a population of anywhere from twenty to fifty (with several homeless people staying for years), and the Workers themselves had to be fed throughout the day.

Food bills could run to $1,500 a month. Everybody had to take a turn shopping for the day-old bread, the vegetables that area merchants thought too old to sell, the cheap cuts of meat that could be found on occasion, the culinary donations one begged for. A Catholic Worker soon learned that there was no disgrace in begging—in the form of polite and repeated requests—for help. That was how the money was raised in the first place. At an irregular pace, checks came in the mail, and the paper paid for itself now. The idea of applying for funding from a foundation, the government, or the archdiocese was anathema to Dorothy. Again, personalism pointed in another direction. When funds ran low, as they often did, Dorothy asked everyone to pray that much harder. The house was named after St. Joseph. St. Joseph was expected to come through.

The Mott Street house was also, obviously, a less-than-ideal place in which to raise a daughter, and that was not a problem easily resolved. Tamar's aunts—Della, Tessa, and Tessa's sister, Tina—doted on the girl and talked among themselves about the difficulties of her situation, about which they knew they could do little. They could only shake their heads at Dorothy's motherly delinquencies, and they weren't the only ones to do so. Even when she was home, Dorothy could be forgetful of the child and a child's needs for attention, privacy, and security. She could forget that the sight of so much poverty and suffering was harder for a young person to assimilate than an adult. When overcrowding became an issue in the house, she rented an apartment for herself and Tamar for several months on nearby Bayard Street, but she began to accept so many speaking engagements that it didn't seem to make much difference. Back on Mott Street, Tamar's possessions—her beloved seashell collection, her microscope—regularly disappeared in the house with no locks on the doors. An unhinged young woman in her twenties who fantasized that Dorothy was her mother would, in fits of jealousy, steal Tamar's toys and clothes. The only times of calm and closeness were to be found when they went to Florida to visit Grace, who delighted in seeing her granddaughter, and Dorothy and Tamar could stroll along the beach and feel the intimacy they had known before the days of the Catholic Worker.

Accurately assessing the situation, people in the area were inclined to take Tamar under their wing. The Johnsons were an older couple who had once needed the help of the Catholic Worker and now lived in their own apartment in the front building on Mott Street. Their spare bedroom was always available for an overnight guest, and Tamar was fed better there than she ever was with Dorothy. Her mother worried that she was being spoiled by the comforts of the Johnson home. In the same sense, Dorothy proved an equally erratic monitor of her daughter's education. A boarding school, the Academy of St. Dorothy on Staten Island, where Tamar was reasonably content; then a parochial school down the street, to keep her closer to home; then another boarding school, Oak Knoll in New Jersey, where she was thoroughly miserable; then back to St. Dorothy's—the constant moving from one school to another did nothing to provide more stability in Tamar's life or advance her education. As a leader of a religious movement, Dorothy Day had more confidence than she often acknowledged. As a mother, she was all too often flailing.

No matter what was happening with the paper or on the lecture circuit, Peter would not let anyone forget about his goal of a large rural retreat, his "agronomic university." The greater the distress the Workers faced in the city, the more plausible the project sounded to some of them. People needed rest and a change of setting. Nature was restorative, nature was God's handiwork uncorrupted by urban blight, nature offered a means for a man or woman to reconnect with the earth and to see the world anew. The distributists had plenty to say on that subject.

In the spring of 1936, a property was found in Easton, Pennsylvania, seventy miles from Manhattan, with a wonderful view of the Delaware River. It was on sale for $1,250. A *Catholic Worker* subscriber of some means, a schoolteacher from Baltimore, had pledged $1,000 toward the purchase, though her offer came at first with some serious strings attached. She was enthralled with the idea of a religious farming commune and wanted a small house built for her on three acres of the property where she could live and pray on her summer vacations. She expected the residents of Mott Street to build it, noting that it sounded as if Dorothy had for too long been encouraging the indolence and indigence of those Bowery men by not forcing them to work. The money came through, but the patroness, once Dorothy made clear the nature of the enterprise and the reality of the rough-and-tumble guests the farm would house, did not join them for long. Dorothy recognized that the woman's values were clearly at odds with Worker philosophy, but at that point, a check was a check.

What the Catholic Worker now owned was eight acres of woods, twenty acres of cleared land—hilly and rocky but usable—a large barn, and a seven-bedroom house, sans electricity and running water, that was in serious need of repair. Automobile parts, broken glass, and mounds of other detritus had to be carted off before the tomatoes, asparagus, rhubarb, sweet corn, potatoes, watermelon, and other fruit and vegetables could be planted. At least the Workers gave the place a name everyone liked: Maryfarm.

The impracticality of the venture, which never became self-sustaining, must have seemed overwhelming even at the time. Only after signing the deed did they discover that there was no water on the property. The spring they had drunk from when they first went out to inspect the land belonged to a neighboring farm, a fact about which no one had thought to inquire. For months, until their own well was dug, cisterns had to be used to catch rainwater. Two readers in Kansas read about the project and sent money to buy a cow, not that anyone from Mott Street knew a thing about what to look for in purchasing a cow or how to tend to it. The horse they bought for plowing died of old age and had to be replaced in the first year. The produce they were able to grow? At first, only piles of lettuce. "As farmers, we were, perhaps, ridiculous," Dorothy freely acknowledged. *Perhaps?* Still, she described the first summer at Maryfarm as joyous. About twenty-five men and women moved in, intending to stay full-time, with dozens more coming on weekends and during the summer—single men, single women, poor families of different races and faiths—and the discussion sessions were as lively as ever. There was a sense of adventure. During school vacations, Tamar would be there watering the flowers and vegetables, helping take care of any babies in the house. Expectant mothers, married or (more often) not, were never turned away from the farm or the house in the city. John Filligar, the only farm-savvy Worker, managed the tractor and taught Tamar about planting and farm animals.

The problems that would bedevil the farm, leading to its closing eleven years later, were also evident from the start. The winter was brutal, no matter how many blankets one piled on, and most residents fled back to the city until spring arrived. Farmwork without expertise or hired hands turned out to be more daunting than anyone had anticipated. Money was a never-ending source of contention. Those who helped put out the paper and run the house in the city complained that the farm was an unreasonable drain on the Worker's finances; those committed to running the farm complained that they were never given the support they needed. Seeds, tools, farm machinery, wood for building, more livestock (the goats and pigs they wanted), basic supplies—everything cost money. Far too many people showed up who had no intention of picking up a hoe or watering a vine or washing a dish, and the truculent nature of many of the residents was no less a problem in Easton than it was in New York. Some Workers exhausted themselves running back and forth between the two.

Not surprisingly, Maryfarm quickly acquired its own Mr. Breen. More than a few people, when under the influence, took their unhappiness out on the newly plastered walls, the farm tools, and the gardens. At one point, it was discovered that a handsome, clean-cut young man staying with them was using the farm as a place to hide the stolen goods that funded his heroin habit. He had to be taken back to New York by John Cort for detox treatment, "shaking like a leaf in a windstorm." Once word spread that Dorothy had opened a kind of retreat in the countryside, pastors started sending their alcoholic priests to Easton to dry out. They often came with full flasks.

In 1933, not long after Dorothy met Peter, Father Vincent McNabb, the British Dominican, had published *Nazareth or Social Chaos*, his critique of urbanization and argument for the contemplative, self-sustaining rural life as the solution to the world's spiritual and economic malaise. It was, in many ways, the ultimate distributist tract. Dorothy and Peter read it then; it was a topic at more than one roundtable discussion. Easton was, at least in Peter's mind, going to be the realization of McNabb's ideal. Dorothy, one assumes, had some doubts.

When tensions grew, there was one escape for Dorothy that others, excepting Peter and Bill Callahan, who had taken to public speaking with a vengeance, did not have. Her travel schedule suddenly became formidable, staggering. In an eighteen-month period beginning in 1936, she spoke at colleges, convents, seminaries, churches, town halls, union halls, and Catholic women's clubs in Vermont, Massachusetts, New Jersey, Pennsylvania, Ohio, Indiana, Illinois, North Dakota, Minnesota, Wisconsin, Tennessee, Arkansas, Alabama, Florida, Missouri, Kansas, and California. Most of the time, she traveled by bus; on the occasions when she took one of the used cars donated by a supporter, it was considered proof of the miraculous when she returned in one piece, given her abysmal driving skills. Whenever possible, she would call on the bishop of the diocese she was in. The farther the destination from New York, the more talks she would try to schedule in the days or weeks she might be there. Topics ranged from the origins of the Catholic Worker to life in the Bowery, voluntary poverty, the right to strike and unionize, the darkening world situation, and the challenges facing modern Catholicism in a time of economic stress and embattled faith.

Welcome as she was in many venues, there were others where her presence made people nervous. Concern over her radical reputation even applied to old friends. Passing through Memphis on a speaking tour in support of tenant farmers in 1937, Dorothy got in touch with Caroline Gordon and Allen Tate, who a few years earlier had left New York and returned to the South they were so attached to. Caroline was honest about her reluctance to have Dorothy stay with her. The charge that she had entertained a Communist would be ruinous to her already shaky standing among her conservative Tennessee neighbors. Dorothy reassured Caroline that she was not a member of the Party, and an invitation was, in the end, extended. Dorothy, Caroline, and Allen spent two days together, putting any awkwardness behind them and reminiscing about Greenwich Village. "I think Dorothy began praying for [my conversion] at that time, observing my parlous spiritual condition," Caroline later commented about a conversion that would indeed take place ten years later.

Dorothy's visits were sometimes focused on the houses of hospitality that were opening in different cities. Each house wanted her to pass judgment (hopefully, praise) on their labors and offer guidance, a request that was both gratifying and irritating in that she didn't want to be seen as the director of some sort of national organization with a uniform approach to corporal works of mercy. Personalism demanded personal initiative, an appetite for trial and error, individuals not looking to others to provide centralized authority.

In reality, though, when the need for leadership and advice was dire, as was frequently the case in the early days of Boston's Catholic Worker, where the house was challenged by in-fighting and by Cardinal O'Connell's on-again, off-again support, Dorothy was ready to play her part. She conferred with Father Furfey about the problems there, as he knew most of the principals firsthand, and she even offered to meet with the cardinal, a cagey man who set up an appointment with her but, when she came to Boston and showed up at the episcopal residence, claimed to be too busy to meet her.

As often as not in this period, though, her crisscrossing of the country was connected to imminent or ongoing labor disputes. Peter beseeched her, gently but insistently, to devote less time and energy to the unionization and wage battles that were being fought all over the United States. "Strikes don't strike me," he liked to quip. But strikes *did* strike Dorothy. She relished being on the scene to interview those in the trenches for her columns, to provide moral support and, as she stressed to skeptical bishops, to show that the Communists weren't the only ones who cared about the downtrodden. Sometimes it seemed to her that the Church hierarchy was actually more interested in fighting "godless communism" than in addressing poverty and unfair labor conditions; it was a useful tactic, then, to pretend that focusing on the latter was really about subduing the former.

In those heady if exhausting days between 1936 and 1938, Dorothy aligned the Worker with the striking seamen in New York City in their prolonged fight against their corrupt union as they worked to establish their own association (which would become the National Maritime Union), teamed up with Mary Heaton Vorse to study conditions in the steel mills and coal mines of Pennsylvania, and interviewed both John L. Lewis at his union's headquarters in Washington, DC, and Governor Frank Murphy, a Catholic and the most labor-sympathetic governor in the country, at the state capitol in Michigan. After visiting the Gordons in Memphis, she went to Arkansas to meet with a hundred black tenant farmers who had been evicted from their land for attempting to join the Southern Tenant Farmers Union. Dumbstruck by the poverty in the tent colony she saw, where many of the children and adults were dressed in flour sacks, she immediately sent a telegram to Eleanor Roosevelt, describing the scene. At the first lady's request, the governor of Arkansas made his own inspection but announced that all he had seen was a community of lazy blacks being stirred up by "some Catholic woman" from out of state.

Pittsburgh was probably the city Dorothy visited most often in the 1930s. In what was then the United States' leading and most contentious industrial center, she was thrilled to meet Father Charles Owen Rice. Rice was one of the most committed "labor priests" in the country, and it was exciting to learn more about the Catholic Radical Alliance and the St. Joseph House he and Fathers Carl Hensler and Barry O'Toole had established there. The Alliance had been founded, the priests wrote, because it was high time in the United

States for a "changed and reformed social order that will be Christian and just in every sense of the word." She was especially taken with the zeal of the priests who had walked the picket lines with striking Heinz workers fighting for a union and had opened their house of hospitality in the midst of Pittsburgh's multiracial Hill District. Rice was energetic, sarcastic, and impervious to criticism, a steamroller of plans and ideas, and he was probably the cleric with whom Dorothy had the most in common. That admiration was mutual.

En route to Flint, Michigan, to cover the much-publicized 1937 autoworkers' strike against General Motors, Dorothy accepted the invitation of Archbishop John McNicholas of Cincinnati to spend a day with several midwestern bishops and talk about the work for which she was now acquiring a considerable reputation or at least stirring episcopal curiosity. McNicholas was the sort of prelate she could respect unequivocally: he didn't see the struggle for unionization as un-American, his sympathies were with the men in Flint, and he sent checks periodically in answer to the Catholic Worker's increasingly desperate appeals. She went on her way with the Cincinnati archbishop's warm encouragement.

Once in Flint, Dorothy met with strike leaders, including Congress of Industrial Organizations (CIO) director John Brophy, a Catholic, to whom she made an impassioned plea to be sure that his men continued to maintain the Gandhian technique of the sit-down strike, which the Flint labor action had originated in the United States. One night she was helped through a basement window to spend the evening in one of the plants occupied by the strikers. She was recognized as the kind of reporter, of whom there were too few, who would dispute the accounts in the mainstream press that the strikers were a destructive, Moscow-led mob. Inside, she attended a strike meeting in the factory where she heard Josephine Herbst, a Communist acquaintance from her Village days, deliver a passionate call for solidarity, and watched eager college students in a basement office work with the publicity men to ready the strikers' press releases. It was a bracing experience, as Dorothy later recounted it, an event that showcased the integrity of the labor movement. The Flint strike and its method of organization also pointed out, she wrote when she arrived home, the need for Catholic college students to volunteer as "apostles of labor . . . taking advantage as the Communist does of the opportunities each strike offers to reach the masses, to learn from them and to teach them."

From Michigan, it was on to Chicago that spring, where the visiting New Yorker caused a stir by accepting the hospitality of a priest in a black neighborhood. The decision about her lodging rubbed some people the wrong way twice over: first, that a woman was going to be an overnight guest in a rectory and, second, that a white woman was making herself at home in a black part of town. Such criticism meant little to Dorothy. She had arrived to write about an imminent steelworkers' strike and to see what Dr. Falls's newly opened house of hospitality on Taylor Street was all about, and she was going to do just that.

Twenty-year-old John Cogley, a future editor of *Commonweal* and, in the 1960s, the religion editor of the *New York Times*, was involved with the house and always remembered their first meeting. "Dorothy Day was then about forty and a strikingly attractive woman," he observed, "not conventionally beautiful perhaps, but handsome and evenly featured." She knew the impact she could have on young men like Cogley. Taking him out to dinner with a friend of his, Tom Sullivan, who would later come to work on Mott Street, she regaled the two with stories about Eugene O'Neill, John Reed, Emma Goldman, and her old Chicago college friend, Rayna Simons, who had joined the Communist Party, had lived in China, where she had supported Sun Yat-sen's Kuomintang, and had died in Moscow in 1927 while studying revolutionary tactics at the Lenin Institute. What daring people this woman knew, what a wealth of impressions she had to share, this lean, chain-smoking raconteur from Gotham—who wore a beret and rolled her own cigarettes, no less—fresh from the front lines in Flint. Who could resist her?

(Tom Sullivan would have been just the type to appeal to Dorothy as well. He and Cogley had been invited to dinner at a Chicago rectory one night as the guests of a priest they were friendly with. Another priest at the table, no fan of Dorothy Day, remarked, "I'd rather be seen going into a brothel than into a Catholic Worker House." Sullivan's retort was typical: "Well, we should all go where we feel most comfortable.")

It was apparent that Miss Day knew her own mind and wasn't much interested in diplomacy or consensus decision-making. Dr. Falls's arrangement, which involved less social work and more time spent with discussion groups, was not to her liking. Without consulting the Taylor Street group, she found a ramshackle apartment, paid a few months' rent on it, and then asked Cogley and another friend of his, Paul Byrne, a Loyola University sophomore, to move in and run it as a true house of hospitality after she returned to New York. That was more important than attending college, she maintained. Byrne's middle-class parents were highly distressed by the proposal, but Cogley had been on his own in the midst of the Depression for some time, and both men—religious at heart, idealistic, socially conscious—agreed that she was a hard woman to argue with. Listening to her carefully enough, you ended up believing in what she believed in.

On the day of her departure, Cogley and Byrne took Dorothy to the bus station. "At the last minute," Cogley recalled, "she gave us the key to the new place she had rented and a brief set of instructions. Immediately after the bus left the station, we were to go to the site of the Republic Steel Co. strike and join the massive picket line there. She had heard there might be violence. It was possible we would be caught up in it. 'Just think,' she said cheerfully, 'you might get killed and the Church would have its first labor martyrs.'"

They were not among the ten protestors murdered when the police fired into the crowd, but neither did the new house Dorothy envisioned work out as planned. For once, an area church was doing work that rendered a house of hospitality in that neighborhood superfluous. Yet meeting Dorothy and pondering her ideas about voluntary poverty had changed Cogley's life, as it would so many people of his age and outlook. A year later, he was in New York and became a part of the family on Mott Street for several months.

In some of her talks, Dorothy sought to make clear that she did not regard unionization as a panacea for all of America's ills, least of all its spiritual ills. If working men and women were solely concerned with better wages for themselves and not with larger ideas about community, societal change, and our God-ordained obligations to one another, the labor struggle would mean nothing in the long run. Speaking to the student body at the University of San Francisco on Armistice Day 1937, she made just that point, reiterated many times in *The Catholic Worker*. On that same whirlwind trip to California, which took her from the northern part of the state to Los Angeles and San Diego, she stopped at San Quentin to visit Tom Mooney, who had spent the last twenty-two years incarcerated there for a deadly anarchist bombing he had not committed. Often on her mind was the New Testament injunction to visit those unfortunates locked away in prison. That was yet another act of mercy too many religious figures failed to attend to, in her view. She had been behind bars, and she knew what the presence of a priest or bishop would mean.

Attention in print continued to come from myriad directions. Dorothy made good copy. In the daily press, that attention was largely, but far from unanimously, positive in the mid- and late 1930s. When the *Democrat and Chronicle* of Rochester, New York, identified the Catholic Worker to its readership as "a group that has worked among Communists and Negroes in various parts of the country," the editors might have thought they were being coy, but their snide intent was clear enough. A significant number of newspapers went out of their way when the founder of the Catholic Worker was coming to town to identify Dorothy as an "ex-Communist" or a "former worker for the Communist Party who had joined the Catholic Church."

That many people thought she had once been a card-carrying member of the Party taking orders from the Kremlin didn't seem to distress Dorothy, and she never went out of her way to dispute that claim in print. Any fine line between sympathy with, and actual membership in, the Party didn't interest her. There was, after all, a strategic angle to be played by not refuting those statements: how much more compelling is the guest speaker who once prayed to the false god, now brought safely to Rome. In that case, she was playing the part of the reformed temperance speaker who knows the evils of which she speaks. To be fair, Dorothy sometimes gave critics reason to wonder about her current affiliations, as when she made statements such as one delivered before a Detroit audience in the fall of 1937, saying, "I believe the aims of Communism are Christian aims, but the means they take to achieve their objectives are opposed to religion." It was not exactly the condemnation of Marxism-Leninism the bishops were looking for. More reporters than not, though, wrote respectfully about her and the Worker mission. That would change as a world war loomed.

In 1937, H. A. Reinhold, a German priest in flight from the Hitler regime with whom Dorothy had been in correspondence and whose reports from Hamburg she had published, visited New York. Like Father Michel, Reinhold was an advocate of liturgical reform and, unlike most priests in Germany, unstoppably vocal in warning his superiors that any compromise with Nazism was a calamitous mistake. He had been detained by the Gestapo for statements against the Führer. Several months after his visit, he wrote in the prestigious British journal *Blackfriars* about 115 Mott Street, its wide-ranging influence, and its disparate guests. With Reinhold, Dorothy couldn't have asked for a more sympathetic publicist. Describing the filth and decay of the building and the neighborhood in almost lurid detail, Reinhold nevertheless applauded a remarkable community in which young Christians "fight the hardened bourgeois mentality and the capitalistic deafness of a number of their co-religionists." Truly, "this was a dangerous movement," he declared—one that represented a threat to unbridled capitalism, to communism, and to Christians who merely gave lip service to their faith.

Reinhold was amazed that, in a country of Catholics so tightly controlled by their clergy, a lay movement had become as important as Day's, but "the bold and naïve simplicity which is its distinguishing mark," was part of what made the Catholic Worker the force for change it was evidently becoming. That and its unusual founders: a woman whose "vocation is the raw poverty of a modern slum without protection" and a Frenchman who took Jesus at his word more literally than anyone else the writer had ever met.

Dissenting voices were heard, of course. Bishop John Noll of Fort Wayne, Indiana, was convinced that Dorothy was a Communist, at least in spirit, and he wasn't the only bishop who thought that. Many priests and laymen felt that a Catholic organization (run by a woman, no less) had no business sticking its nose into political matters, in particular those that concerned the economic balance of US commerce. The strictures of one critic stung a bit: the Jesuit priest John LaFarge had been a roundtable discussion leader and an early admirer of Dorothy's work, praising her for her compassion, her vow of poverty, and her racial values. (Though no one knew it at the time, he had been personally tapped by Pope Pius XI to prepare an encyclical on anti-Semitism, a document suppressed after the pope's death and the existence of which was not made known until the 1970s.) Yet reading about her speeches concerning strikes, unions, and pacifism, LaFarge felt impelled to write a series of articles in *America* taking her to task for crossing a line. In the realm of charity, no one could fault the Catholic Worker, he agreed; but when it attempted to articulate a program of higher, scripture-validated, Church-supported values, it needed a deeper intellectual grounding than the organization could boast. Again: the Church knows best; the laity should know its place.

The tide was about to turn against Dorothy on other issues, though, with more serious ramifications. A coup in Spain in 1936 had initially seemed like an event of less-than-international consequence. In fact, it was to have profound meaning far beyond Madrid and Barcelona and point to ways in which the Catholic Worker—the movement, the paper, and its founder— would find itself at odds with the people who should have been among its closest allies.

ELEVEN

❧ PRELUDE ❧

Approval of *The Catholic Worker* in Catholic circles, lay and ecclesiastical, as well as in the columns of Catholic publications, came to a grinding halt over one of the most divisive issues of the day: the Spanish Civil War. As the events of that foreign conflict unfolded, the skepticism of many parish priests about their younger parishioners hawking a newspaper put out by that troublesome woman was confirmed in their minds by Dorothy Day's blunt refusal to fall into line with the Vatican's thinking about that conflict.

What was happening in Spain, in addition to the ideological fault lines that were now made painfully visible across Europe, was also a harbinger of more unease to follow, a prelude to a certain kind of alienation. From that point on, there would be few, if any, occasions when Dorothy would be willing to acquiesce to received opinion about explicitly political and military issues. Like Emmanuel Mounier, she believed that Western civilization was reaching a pathological crisis point in her time.

The forced abdication of King Alfonso XIII in 1931 and the formation of the Second Spanish Republic had brought about some needed democratic reforms in Spain but had also led, through the republic's various iterations and factionalizing, to an increasingly left-wing drift, a curb on the long-entrenched power of the Church, and the government's announced intention to end parochial school education. A growing anticlericalism eventually included mob attacks on churches and convents. When Francisco Franco and other right-wing generals, nominally Catholics, initiated a coup in 1936, a two-year civil war of unexpected ferocity began.

By any reasonable standard, there was no "right side" in the conflict, as writers covering Spain, including George Orwell, John Dos Passos, and even Ernest Hemingway, knew, for a Catholic, there were only two abhorrent sides. The supporters of the government, termed Loyalists or Republicans, brutalized the civilian opposition, murdered priests, monks, and nuns by the thousands, desecrated Catholic cemeteries, and allowed the growing number of violent Stalinists in their ranks to purge the anti-Stalinists. The Falangists under Franco, termed Nationalists, with their Moroccan mercenaries, were no less heinous in their tactics: summary executions, torture squads, the mass rape and public humiliation of Loyalist women, the slaughter of laborers and intellectuals. The support given to the Loyalists by international volunteer groups, such as the Abraham Lincoln Brigade, was misguided, as Dorothy read the situation, no less than the Vatican's backing of Franco because of his anticommunism and alleged concern for the welfare of the Church.

The Catholic Worker was in good company among Catholics in refusing to praise General Franco as a defender of civilization and Christianity. Jacques Maritain, Emmanuel Mounier, Eric Gill, Virgil Michel, Paul Hanly Furfey, and the French novelists François Mauriac and Georges Bernanos (the author of the novel The Diary of a Country Priest, a work Dorothy much admired) were all in agreement that neutrality was the only proper stance in relation to the awful alternatives presented by the Spanish Civil War. (Maritain, Mauriac, and Bernanos initially supported Franco but withdrew that support when they learned about Nationalist atrocities. In Mallorca, the horror-struck Bernanos witnesssed a series of mass murders supported by the local Church authorities, a "disgusting spectacle," he wrote.) Yet even had she stood alone, Dorothy Day would not have found it in her to express approval in any form of a man whose intention had always been to establish a military dictatorship secured in power by terror, certainly not after the Luftwaffe's bombing of the Basque town of Guernica. She knew what she saw: a false Catholic and anti-Semite, only another version of his appalling allies, Adolf Hitler and Benito Mussolini.

The Church hierarchy on both sides of the Atlantic took a very different view and was more than willing to overlook Franco's fascism, especially after the USSR came more openly to the aid of the Loyalists. George Shuster lost his job at Commonweal when circulation declined over his magazine's stance on neutrality. Parochial schools by the dozens canceled their orders of The Catholic Worker. Convent, seminary, and Catholic college invitations to speak dwindled to a trickle for a time, and some New England bishops discouraged their clergy from visiting any houses of hospitality. Furious letters arrived at the Worker, accusing Dorothy of everything from dangerous naïveté to playing the role of "a wolf in sheep's clothing, serving your Red [master] Joseph Stalin."

An especially high-powered critic was Father Charles Coughlin, the self-aggrandizing "radio priest" who operated out of a Detroit suburb. In the summer of 1937, he assailed *The Catholic Worker* in his own paper, *Social Justice*, which was sold in many churches after Mass. His editorial position was echoed by Patrick Scanlon in his equally reactionary Catholic paper, *The Tablet*, published in Brooklyn. Bishop Michael Gallagher of Detroit, Coughlin's mentor, was on his side in the attack. Gallagher had been angry enough over the *The Catholic Worker*'s initial refusal to endorse Franco to wonder aloud whether Dorothy Day and her paper were not out-and-out Communist tools merely "camouflaged with Catholic paint." The criticism of men such as Coughlin, Scanlan, and Gallagher meant little on Mott Street, of course. Their tone and narrowness revealed them for what they were.

One episcopal attack meant a great deal, however, and cut to the bone. Archbishop McNicholas had impressed Dorothy with his pro-labor politics, his support for civil rights for black Americans, and admiration for the Catholic Worker. He was nonetheless a believer in Franco's mission and had become increasingly displeased with the editorial positions of *The Catholic Worker* and *Commonweal* concerning Spain. In response to Dorothy's request to go to Cincinnati to smooth over any disagreement, his chancellor sent a letter on his behalf in September 1938 that had the force of a blast. The archbishop wasn't in a mood to meet her. After the usual appreciative nod at the corporal works of mercy Dorothy had initiated in New York, Monsignor Matthias Heyker pressed his point: "His Grace is not interested in any attempt you make to formulate principles or to state norms for the moral conduct of the people. The Most Reverend Archbishop knows that this will prove to be your undoing, because no one in your group is qualified for this work. The Church does not expect you to do it, and she will probably have to condemn you for attempting to do it."

Heyker continued his criticism through four paragraphs. The Catholic Church had the Vicar of Christ and more than enough bishops and theologians to guide the faithful on moral questions and to articulate the rightness of Vatican policy, and it was not Dorothy Day's place to involve herself in such matters. Much as the archbishop respected the holy poverty of the Catholic Worker, "he is very much opposed to your publication, or any publication, conducted by lay persons, assuming a role for which it is utterly unqualified. I am sure His Grace hopes that he will not have the painful duty of condemning your publication for the Archdiocese of Cincinnati [as he had banned *Commonweal*]."

Greater clarity Dorothy couldn't have asked for, though there must have been some slight satisfaction mixed with anguish in that acknowledgment that *The Catholic Worker* was at least taken seriously, even as a threat. Circulation had reached an astonishing peak of 190,000 that spring with its five-year anniversary issue. No one could pretend she wasn't by now a figure of influence.

If Dorothy's refusal to side with the Church and Franco made her innumerable Catholic enemies, her refusal to at least acknowledge that the Loyalists had more justice on their side stirred just as much anger from the Left. She would have joined creditable company had she at least given lip service to the anti-Franco, democratically elected faction in the conflict. Eleanor Roosevelt, Reinhold Niebuhr, John Dewey, John Steinbeck, Upton Sinclair, W. E. B. Du Bois, André Malraux, W. H. Auden, and Jawaharlal Nehru all did so. That she adamantly refused to do. "We were torn apart from both sides," Joe Zarrella remembered. Even Mike Gold, normally so willing to forgive Dorothy anything, was for the moment alienated from her.

Attacked from without, Dorothy was probably not surprised, either, by the attacks and questioning from within that materialized in those years before the Second World War, criticisms of her leadership that had nothing to do with Spain. That she wasn't seen as anyone's idea of an ideal leader, she knew. Plenty of the young people working on the paper or stirring the soup in the kitchen were ready to tell her that she was away too much, that she was too disorganized, that she refused to delegate authority, and that her anarchistic approach to house rules and expectations made life hell for any sane people living at 115 Mott Street or in Easton. When she was there, according even to some Workers who loved her, she was a frustrating paradox, a dictator who didn't believe in centralized authority, and when she was gone, it was every man and woman for himself or herself. This was no way to run a house of hospitality, as Catherine de Hueck kept insisting, and she had reason to know. Dorothy was also a woman of moods, and when she was tired, she was snappish. When contradicted, she was steely. Stanley Vishnewski liked to set newcomers at ease by remarking, "Oh, once you get to know her, she's just like any other crabby old lady."

Yet none of that was what bothered Tom Coddington and the woman he married a few months after coming to the Catholic Worker, Dorothy Weston, who had been the paper's crackerjack first coeditor. They had come to see the daily corporal acts of mercy as ultimately futile and even absurd. The drain on funds and energy was colossal, and the ingratitude and rudeness of many of the guests was unacceptable. The white men on the breadlines, largely Irish and thoroughly racist, wouldn't let black men get into line with them, and there was nothing anyone inside the house could do about it. The turnover of young people who were willing to help was worrisome. For every Stanley Vishnewski, Joe Zarrella, or Julia Porcelli who appeared to be in for the long haul, there were dozens of others who stayed only a few weeks or a few months.

What Tom Coddington and Dorothy Weston wanted was a transfer of power and focus. Tom wanted the thrust of the Catholic Worker, staffed if necessary by salaried professionals, to be more propagandistic, to use the paper and the public forums to advance a political agenda that would be about more than charity and personalism, with the breadlines relegated to a secondary consideration or eliminated. The political action group he had founded as a concurrent offshoot of the Catholic Worker, known as the Campions (named after Edmond Campion, a Jesuit martyr to Queen Elizabeth's Reformation torturers), was a better model, he insisted. Dorothy Weston wanted to take charge of the paper and even offered to "buy" Dorothy out, whatever that was supposed to mean in the context of a not-for-profit, barely-break-even publication. Peter Maurin was aghast. If that came to pass, he told Dorothy, he would have to leave and she should depart with him. Those young people had missed the whole point. Father Virgil Michel tried to mediate the argument, but Tom and Dorothy finally had to go, and some bitterness was felt on all sides.

Other departures, or driftings away, were more amicable. John Cort left on better terms, but there had never been any question that the future of someone so concerned with labor activism did not lie exclusively with the Catholic Worker, and he became a major force in the development of the Association of Catholic Trade Unionists. He also felt it was time to go, as he began to show the first signs of tuberculosis, another occupational hazard at the Worker. Other Workers left to marry, often partners they met on Mott Street (romantic backstairs involvements were not unheard of at the Worker), and to raise families. It was felt by some at the time that Dorothy was uncomfortable with the idea of married couples remaining on the job. As she knew from painful personal experience, commitment to the Catholic Worker placed unique demands on family life.

For the brave and the curious, though, 115 Mott Street continued to be a mecca. Priests, nuns, and theology professors came by, as did reporters and sociologists and ever more college students who had heard about the "clarification of thought" sessions. Frank Sheed and Maisie Ward of the Sheed & Ward publishing house, British Catholics who had relocated to New York, visited; Maisie became a friend and admirer and wrote some generous checks over the years. A fair number of minor celebrities made an appearance in Little Italy. Prince Hubertus zu Löwenstein-Wertheim-Freudenberg, a German aristocrat in flight from the Hitler regime and an ardent Catholic, was one. Antoine Allard, the Catholic scion of one of Europe's major banking families, was another. Jacques Maritain paid a second visit in 1936 on a trip to New York. Hilaire Belloc was an especially welcome guest.

In 1937 and into the first months of 1938, Belloc, the French-born British distributist writer, was on a lecture tour in the United States, which included a brief tenure as a visiting professor of history at Fordham University. Harry McNeil, a Fordham University professor who had arranged some of the Catholic Worker's discussion evenings, brought him downtown. As a fan of his wildly eccentric travelogue, *The Path to Rome*, Dorothy was thrilled to have Belloc spend part of a day with her to see what the Catholic Worker was all about. (His intellectual ally, G. K. Chesterton, had died the year before.) She and John Cort went out to dinner with McNeil and Belloc afterward. Her respect for him would never diminish—Belloc was a "Johnsonian figure," an expansive intellect, in her mind—and she was presumably excited about her daughter and son-in-law's decision to name her eighth grandchild, born in 1957, Hilaire Hennessy.

The matter of Dorothy's occasionally selective awareness rears its head again, though, when considering her feelings about Belloc. Devout Catholic, anti-Communist, anti-capitalist, favorite of Pius XI—Belloc was all that. But was Dorothy aware that he was also a defender of Franco at his most brutal? A man who refused to see any wrong in Mussolini and his "rescue" of the Abyssinians from barbarism? It is impossible to believe that she was ignorant of those facts. She had to have been familiar as well with his distasteful 1922 book, *The Jews*. Was she aware that he was in touch with Father Coughlin during his stay in the United States and was planning to write for Couglin's odious magazine *Social Justice*? Possibly not.

What everyone who came to Mott Street could see was how many of New York's poorest were being selflessly served each day and how financially precarious a situation the Worker was in. The urgent appeals in the paper (with headlines such as "We're Broke Again") were not yielding the results they once had, nor were Dorothy's speaking honoraria bringing in much. Two books she hastily wrote within the same twelve-month period were an effort, in part, to cope with the ever-looming financial disaster in the hope that some royalties might be forthcoming.

The Preservation of the Faith Press published *From Union Square to Rome* in 1938. It took the form of an answer to her brother John's questions about the direction her life had taken. Dedicated to John, it was a conversion memoir meant to clarify—for her brother or for any agnostic or Communist (both of which John was)—the feeling and the reasoning behind her turn to God and the Church of Rome and the mission of the Catholic Worker. Though she later felt the title was a mistake, implying a too-emphatic break of her life into discrete halves, the book did make an effort to explain to her brother that, indeed, she had been a "Communist in sympathy" for many years, approving of the Party's interest in an economic revolution, but that she had always felt that its program lacked the deeper dimension that only the gift of faith and the compassion of Christ could provide. Concern for the poor had brought her to left-wing politics. Concern for the poor had also brought her to a belief in God and the call of the New Testament and, ultimately, to Mott Street. The Communist and the Catholic were led by not-dissimilar impulses, she wanted John to know, but at the same time they were very different.

From Union Square to Rome is an autobiographical sketch. It recounts in crisp prose and a terse summary fashion a questioning adolescence, a sense of having always been "haunted by God" even before she quite knew what that meant, the readings—Thomas De Quincey, Fyodor Dostoevsky, Jack London, and Upton Sinclair—that had pushed her to think beyond the worldview of their parents. Rayna Simons, now implicitly acknowledged as a key influence, was given a chapter of her own, and subsequent chapters narrated Dorothy's recollections of her college days in Urbana, writing for *The Call* and *The Masses* in New York, and her time in Chicago, New Orleans, and Mexico—minus the gritty details of Lionel Moise and the abortion, her tempestuous relations with Forster, and any other emotional and sexual entanglements she had experienced. (How much John knew of any of the pre-Forster parts of his sister's life is not clear.) The birth of Tamar is given a central place in describing her increasing readiness to embrace the supernatural. "Even the most hardened, the most irreverent, is awed by the stupendous fact of creation," Dorothy wrote. "No matter how cynically or casually the worldly may treat the birth of a child, it remains spiritually and physically a tremendous event." She went further: "I pity the woman who does not feel the fear, the awe, and the joy of bringing a child into the world."

Finally, what John saw as morbidity, Dorothy characterized as abundance; what John and other critics took to be cannibalism—the partaking of the body and blood of Christ in the Mass—Dorothy offered as evidence of Christ's love, a mystical completion; what John saw as divine failure in permitting a world of so much evil, Dorothy saw as a drama of free will with the hope of redemption. Any response the book elicited from John—or Della or Grace—is, unfortunately, nothing Dorothy ever commented on.

Several months later, in the late summer of 1939, Sheed & Ward published *House of Hospitality*, following its serialization in *The Catholic Worker*, with a lively dust jacket design by Ade Bethune. It was a very different kind of book from the more personal, poignant memoir. Rambling, repetitive, slapdash in its prose, never clear in its chronology, *House of Hospitality* has the feel of a patchwork for a good reason: it was based on notes Dorothy had taken while on the road and drafts of her printed articles. It told of the opening and the running of the Charles Street and Mott Street houses, described many of the more memorable guests, aimed to give some sense of what it took to produce a paper such as *The Catholic Worker*, and recounted her endless travels. It was also an occasion to provide quick sketches of those indefatigable men and women who were devoting their lives to the cause in New York and, across the country, those who were in the forefront of the labor movement, especially among the liberal clergy. Nor was the author reluctant to use the book to name names in a critical spirit. The sheriffs, mayors, and company executives who treated striking workers like subversives, disdained the rule of law, and were only too ready to give the order to inflict as much physical harm on legitimate protestors as they could get away with were explicitly and angrily identified. The book's most compelling pages deal with the violence and abuse the labor movement in the 1930s was subjected to. As a record of a society that had lost its moral center, *House of Hospitality* has a place in US social history.

The publication of the two books didn't bring in much money or any great sense of elation, though. "The year has been hard," Dorothy confided to her diary at the end of 1939. Speaking engagements in eleven states (all those hours on buses!), answering what she estimated to be more than a thousand letters, more threats from the Board of Health about conditions on Mott Street, complaints about fights and out-of-control alcoholism at Maryfarm, impatient creditors, and "what care I can give a thirteen-year-old child"—all that had left her "worn down," in desperate need of a few weeks' rest, prey throughout that year to depression and migraine headaches. Tamar's restlessness with her mother's long periods on the road was becoming an issue.

There had been two losses to deal with as well, one temporary and one not. For the better part of a year, Peter Maurin simply disappeared. He was starting to become more scattered than usual. Eventually, he tired of his wanderings and found his way back to New York. His absence, though, had left Dorothy feeling unmoored, and his growing pessimism about the ways in which his dream for the Catholic Worker had not played out exactly as he intended was nothing Dorothy could assuage. Even an idealist like Peter could see that Maryfarm was not a distributist Catholic utopia. Father Mc-Nabb or Eric Gill would have fled in horror.

Her father's death was a different kind of blow. John Day died in Manhattan at age seventy; he had been working as an inspector for the New York State racing commission, staying when he was in town at the Empire Hotel on Broadway. He and Grace lived separate lives, he had grown only more racist and anti-Semitic over time, and he never evinced any desire for a reconciliation with the three of his children—Dorothy, Della, and John—whose character and values he disapproved of. Oddly enough, he carried a pocket Bible with him on his travels all his days. He requested that he be cremated without any religious observance and that his ashes be scattered over the Hialeah Race Track in Miami, where he had spent his happiest times. To think tenderly of John Day, as Dorothy did at that time, required an extraordinary faith and capacity for forgiveness.

A rock-solid faith was needed for what was coming on the spiritual, political, and humanitarian fronts. The economic crisis showed no signs of abating and had even worsened after a recession in 1937 that had sent unemployment numbers skyrocketing, and a conservative backlash against Roosevelt at the polls in 1938 had brought New Deal reform legislation to a halt. The specter of a Nazi Europe, a Francoist Spain, and a Japanese-controlled Pacific began to look like realities that would have to be borne.

Then, too, it was particularly dispiriting to see how many Catholics in Europe and the United States embraced, to one degree or another, the anti-Semitism that educated people had hoped was dying out in civilized countries but had, in fact, merely taken different and varied forms. Father Coughlin was only the most famous purveyor of religious bigotry in the United States, and he wasn't quite the fringe figure optimists claimed, or wanted to think he was, at the time. The offensive Prayer for the Jews—"the perfidious Jews"—was still a part of Good Friday services in many Catholic churches. Jew-baiting Catholic publications such as The Tablet had an enthusiastic following, and parish priests regularly counseled young people to restrict their contact with Jewish peers. Some opinion polls in the late 1930s suggested that more than 50 percent of Americans believed that European Jews were not entirely blameless for the Nazi persecution visited upon them. Street violence against Jews in New York, Boston, and other cities spiked dramatically in 1939 and continued to be a problem well into the early 1940s. Some audiences Dorothy spoke to in the heartland angrily let her know that they thought that her sympathetic remarks about the plight of the Jews were credulous, annoying, and misguided.

Karl Adam, the eminent German professor of theology, was a grave disappointment in this regard. In international theological circles, he was as well known as Coughlin was in the US media and as admired by such literary Catholics as G. K. Chesterton and Hilaire Belloc, who also aired anti-Semitic opinions. But he had a very special meaning for Dorothy. *The Spirit of Catholicism* was a text that had deeply impressed her in the days following her conversion, when she was still trying to sort through the finer points of her attachment to this Church about which she knew rather little, and she had recommended that generous, articulate book to many friends and potential converts over the years.

Yet, in 1939, a full year after Kristallnacht and not long after the invasion of Poland, Professor Adam gave a lecture to an audience of a thousand German Catholics in Aachen, urging the men and women of his faith to come to terms with National Socialism, understand that Nazi ideology was not necessarily incompatible with Catholicism, and focus on the positive elements of the new order, such as Hitler's drive to create a "blood unity" among Aryans. It was a theme he had been toying with for several years. Some priests expressed dismay at Adam's nationalist interpretation of Catholic theology, his support for conscripting seminarians into the Wehrmacht if the need arose, and his refusal to condemn Nazi brutality outright, especially toward the Jews. The Gestapo indicated that it would be pleased to interrogate any critics of Adam's speech it could find.

Dorothy never commented publicly on Professor Adam's woefully misguided thinking but, considering how much his books had meant to her—how sensible and persuasive a spokesman for the Church this man had been—her disillusionment can only have been profound. It is, indeed, a fault that could be firmly laid at the doorstep of both Dorothy Day and Peter Maurin that, although not anti-Semitic themselves by any stretch of the imagination, they had been far too reluctant to criticize those prominent, widely respected Catholic men such as Adam, Chesterton, and Belloc who were. Coughlin was an easy target and a fair one in the eyes of every rational person; Adam, Chesterton, and Belloc, less so. (Interestingly, more than twenty years later, the aging German theologian was invited to be an observer at the councils of Vatican II.)

Yet that was a subject about which there was reason to be continually, relentlessly, disillusioned. Voices were heard arguing that the worst days of Vatican-supported anti-Semitism lay in the past. That view conveniently ignored the fact that, despite his admirable public statements against anti-Semitism, Pope Pius XI was silent in 1938 when Mussolini's government announced its new racial laws, barring Jewish children from public schools and calling on Catholics to avoid any association with a polluted race, as he had been the year before when the Synod of Polish Bishops had adopted a resolution urging the separation of Jewish and Christian students in Polish schools. In Warsaw, Cardinal August Hlond had called for the boycotting of Jewish businesses. The only aspect of the new laws in Italy that disturbed the pontiff sufficiently to provoke a serious protest was the clause that treated converts to Catholicism as still Jewish and invalidated their marriage to Catholics. The questionable accommodations that Pius XI's successor, Pius XII, was busy making with the government of Nazi Germany throughout the decade are too well documented to require comment.

Dorothy's response in the spring of 1939 had been to join with a group of like-minded American Catholics in the formation of the Committee of Catholics to Fight Anti-Semitism. Fordham University philosophy professor Emmanuel Chapman, a convert from Judaism who had been brought to the faith by Jacques Maritain, served as head of the group. Word of mouth was initially quite strong, and a Midtown office was opened. Former *Commonweal* editor George Shuster, Harry McNeil, Father H. A. Reinhold, Catherine de Hueck, the archbishop of Newark, and several priests with a national reputation (John Ryan, John LaFarge, and Paul Hanly Furfey) were glad to lend their names, and the organization's membership soon included a significant number of priests, nuns, writers, and even a handful of celebrities such as the boxer Gene Tunney. The Hollywood censor Joseph Breen signed on, bringing with him the film stars Don Ameche and Irene Dunne. Catholic Workers, ex–Catholic Workers, and allies such as John Cort, Bill Callahan, and Julie Kernan were on board. Within several weeks, nine local chapters had opened from Boston to the West Coast, and its eight-page publication, *The Voice*, was enjoying a six-figure print run. Anti-Semitism, *The Voice* told its readers, was both un-American and un-Christian, a form of hatred beneath any true Catholic.

Or was it? All did not go well for long with the anti-Coughlinites. By the end of the summer, a name change was thought advisable: The Committee of Catholics to Fight Anti-Semitism was rebranded as the Committee of Catholics for Human Rights, and the articles in its publication, now called *The Voice for Human Rights*, broadened from a concern for Jewish suffering to more "universal" issues, including discrimination against Catholics. The far-left leanings of some of its members, including Dorothy, and the aspersions the group had cast on Father Coughlin had rubbed too many people the wrong way. (*The Voice for Human Rights*, one reader fulminated to the president of Fordham, "shows evidence of the guiding hand of Dorothy Day," as blistering a criticism in that woman's mind as she could make.) Harry Mc-Neil was told by his dean at Fordham that he should not expect his customary raise if he continued his affiliation with the group. The poor man bowed to economic necessity. With membership and contributions dwindling fast, the Committee closed up shop a year after its founding, to be reopened more innocuously later in the war.

Not that Dorothy—or Peter—was ready to retreat into silence on this topic. In the November 1939 issue of the *The Catholic Worker*, she reprinted her favorable review, which had appeared the month before in *The Jewish Daily Forward*, of Jacques Maritain's critique of European anti-Semitism, *A Christian Looks at the Jewish Question*. Maritain singled out Polish Catholics as having a particularly lamentable record on the subject. Three months earlier, in *The Catholic Worker*, Peter had published a plea for the US government to open its borders to more Jewish refugees fleeing Nazi terror, and in the January 1940 issue he attempted to dismantle the reigning stereotype about Jewish financiers by naming the many eighteenth- and nineteenth-century Christians who had been the real architects of modern banking and rapacious capitalism.

Professor Chapman, Dorothy's friend and the group's leader, paid the highest price for his involvement with the Committee. He was let go from his teaching position at Fordham at the end of the school year in 1942, the university's president, Robert Gannon, agreeing with several indignant letter writers that "his activities on behalf of Jews in America [had become] a source of annoyance and embarrassment."

If Dorothy found herself at odds with the temper of her times in her concern for persecuted Jews, that situation was nothing compared to what followed. To be a pacifist on the eve of a world war initiated by two murderously aggressive empires was, ultimately, to alienate almost everyone.

No one should have been surprised about *The Catholic Worker*'s position on the subject. During the early days of the Spanish Civil War, Dorothy had made her views abundantly clear. "*The Catholic Worker* is sincerely a pacifist paper," she had emphatically declared in the November 1936 issue. Bill Callahan had represented the paper at a National Catholic Press Association convention that same year and proudly "stepped into a hornet's nest of criticism" when he announced that *The Catholic Worker* would never support a man of violence such as Franco, Catholic or otherwise. Even before that, the paper had condemned Mussolini's invasion of Ethiopia, to the displeasure of many Italian American readers, and given favorable review space to any new books about pacifism that came their way. No, absolutely not: there were no circumstances, she maintained, in which the use of violence—least of all, the taking of life—was ever to be seen as morally acceptable, and the bishops could say what they wanted about St. Thomas Aquinas and the Church's long-held, finely tuned "just war" theory. Furthermore, she took it for granted that everyone who saw himself or herself as part of the Catholic Worker family agreed with that stance. The Fifth Commandment is not an ambiguous one.

Dorothy knew she was moving onto tenuous ground with that issue. Many in the Church hierarchy—most vocally, John McNicholas of Cincinnati—expressed their opposition when Congress proposed the first peacetime conscription act in the nation's history in 1940, but the isolationist mood that had dominated the country's thinking about involvement in foreign wars and preparedness for its own defense had been lessening by degrees for the better part of a year. Lend-Lease, against which Dorothy had spoken out, and a pro-British press were bringing Americans around. The bill called for a lottery, which would lead to the induction into the military for a one-year period of up to 900,000 men between the ages of twenty-one and thirty-six. To the Catholic Worker, the handwriting was on the wall. "To fight war," Dorothy insisted, "we must fight conscription."

In July 1940, Dorothy went to Washington, DC, to appear before the House Committee on Military Affairs. She took with her the draft-age Joe Zarrella and Monsignor Barry O'Toole, the Pittsburgh labor priest, now a Catholic University philosophy professor whose views aligned with hers and whose erudite pacifist essays she had been publishing. They spoke against the bill, alongside representatives of several women's peace groups and various religious denominations. She told Bill Gauchat, the founder of the Cleveland Catholic Worker, that she felt they had been "listened [to] with great respect" and thought that the hearings had been an opportunity "to put over some personalist propaganda" in the corridors of power. The bill's proponents, however, had found more prestigious backers. Among those speaking up for conscription were the World War I hero General John J. "Black Jack"

Pershing, Harvard University president James Conant, and Roosevelt's new secretary of war, Henry Stimson. The Republican nominee for the presidency that year, Wendell Willkie, was known to be on board as well.

Though it took some weeks of acrimonious debate, it wasn't really surprising that the Selective Training and Service Act, also known as the Burke-Wadsworth Act, passed the House by a vote of 263 to 149 and the Senate by a vote of 58 to 31. About the only encouraging aspect of the effort to defeat the legislation was an inclusion in the bill of a statement that the rights of conscientious objectors would be respected if they were connected to a recognized religious body. That was cold comfort to Catholic men, however, as the Church hierarchy was in the main by no means sympathetic to conscientious objection. The recently installed archbishop of the New York diocese, Francis Spellman, had the year before been named by Pope Pius XII to be the Church's US military vicar. No support was going to come from that quarter, obviously. Dorothy's appearance before Congress was not entirely without impact, however. J. Edgar Hoover's FBI agents in charge of keeping watch on subversives began their file on Dorothy a few weeks after her testimony to Congress. She was one to investigate, Hoover was certain.

Quite apart from the government's legislative action, a debate had opened on the extent to which Catholic Workers around the country had to agree to follow Dorothy's lead on the pacifist question, and it soon turned acrimonious. The Detroit, Cleveland, and Boston houses agreed with her stand, more or less; the Chicago, Seattle, and Los Angeles houses emphatically did not, while those at the Milwaukee and Pittsburgh houses found themselves divided but leaning toward the government's position on preparedness. Catholic Workers at the Buffalo and St. Louis houses had managed to maintain peace by banning any discussion of the topic, whether in print or among themselves. At the St. Francis House of Hospitality in Seattle, the New York *Catholic Worker* was no longer given out or offered for sale; the Chicago *Catholic Worker*, published by Ed Marciniak and John Cogley (who had since left Mott Street to return to his hometown), which didn't insist on pushing a party line on pacifism, was sold instead. In Los Angeles, bundles of the New York *Catholic Worker* were discarded upon arrival. When she heard about it, Dorothy was furious.

It was in this raw climate that Dorothy issued what Catholic Worker Tom Sullivan called her one "encyclical"—or, as another Worker termed it, her *diktat*. In a letter sent to all thirty houses of hospitality, she wrote that she was well aware that not all those who considered themselves Catholic Workers "stand with us on this issue." She could tolerate differences of opinion, unfortunate as it was that she had not been able to convince those who disagreed of the rightness of her view. But if her newspaper was going to be suppressed by anyone, "it would be necessary for those persons to disassociate themselves from the movement."

Everyone had to play a part in publicizing Dorothy's values about war and peace; whoever didn't had to go.

Father Reinhold, the peripatetic German émigré Dorothy held in high regard who worked now at the Seattle house, wrote at once to express his anger and dismay. The Catholic Worker stands for far more than pacifism and anticonscription, he argued, and to employ "a dictator's methods, lay down party lines, purge dissenters" was a grave misstep. Plenty of subscribers to the paper agreed. Circulation began to decline precipitously, dropping in a one-year period from 120,000 to 75,000. One reader, an admirer and newly ordained priest in Louisiana, suggested that she would be seen as sharing Father Coughlin's insensitivity to the Jews; the Nazis had to be stopped. Surely, Father Jerome Drolet wrote, Dorothy must be aware that "a pagan brute force" was threatening the end of civilized life in the West and the extinction of Jewry. If there were ever a cause to fight for, this was it.

Good friends such as Catherine de Hueck, Frank Sheed, and Maisie Ward tried to persuade Dorothy to modify her stand. Frank and Maisie, as Britons whose homeland was under attack, thought she was being rigid in her spirituality and willfully blind to the real-world consequences. In essence: Who was she to act as if she knew better than the pope and the bishops that her view was necessarily the only one in line with scripture? Frank wrote Dorothy, "Surely it is at least questionable that you should weaken the whole Catholic Worker movement by insistence upon your own personal view as against views that you can hardly deny the right of your fellow Catholics in the movement to hold." Maisie told Catherine de Hueck that she would love to debate her erring friend in a public forum on the subject.

John Cogley and Tom Sullivan worried that their future with the movement in Chicago was in jeopardy. If war against Nazi Germany were declared, they were pretty sure what they would do. Nina Polcyn was at the moment uncertain about where she stood on the matter, but she knew that many of her male peers at the Milwaukee house would not refuse to fight. Father Charles Owen Rice, a fan of Dorothy's to the point of adulation, wrote to her from Pittsburgh, "I hope you do not feel we have all let you down," but, for once, he could not follow her lead. Father Carl Hensler, the other founder of the Catholic Radical Alliance in Pittsburgh, agreed. That ended for the moment the once warm relationship with the two priests. Father John Ryan, "the Right Reverend New Dealer," dismissed the Catholic Worker viewpoint in print as too absurd to "deserve formal discussion." Wilfrid Parsons, the Jesuit editor of *America*, insisted in an article in *Commonweal* that "there is nothing in the teaching of the Catholic Church which states that the citizen is exempt from the obligation of bearing arms in a war . . . regardless of whether it is just or unjust."

Even Peter Maurin thought Dorothy might be less strident, less single-minded, on this subject. "Men are not ready to listen," he told her. Jacques Maritain had already spoken up for the concept of a just war. Bill Callahan, Stanley Vishnewski, and Joe Zarrella were among the Old Guard prepared to stand by Dorothy unequivocally.

The Church's teachings concerning the definition of a "just war" were, in the minds of many, not without merit. It had long been argued that both the Old Testament and the New Testament acknowledged that there were times when violence was preferable to injustice and therefore acceptable to God. In such an instance, the cause had to be moral, not for profit or revenge; the taking of life had to be authorized by a recognized civil authority; all other means of peaceful resolution had to have been tried and exhausted; a probability of success had to be evident; and an openness to renewing efforts for peace had to be present at all times in the midst of the violence. Dorothy understood that reasoning. She also knew how rampantly and injudiciously it had been applied in the past, how many prelates had blessed departing troops they should have been imploring not to fight.

Most upsetting to many of her readers, Dorothy pointed to the Allied statesmen who had forced the punitive Treaty of Versailles down Germany's throat in 1919 as the real cause of the world crisis they faced. This retributive act had been followed by decades of indifference, no concerted international economic effort to help impoverished Germans or to rein in Nazism before it was too late, and a drift toward war that was hardly surprising in a hypernationalist time. Pray for Poland, pray for England, pray for France, pray even for Germany, she urged. "If this seems like madman's advice, we can only say again that Christians must be fools for Christ's sake." A front-page broadside in *The Catholic Worker* the month Poland was invaded, entitled "We Are to Blame for New War in Europe," was incendiary rhetoric, and she meant it to be. Worst of all, post-Guernica, Dorothy feared that any new war would show little or no regard—on the part of either side—for the once-recognized distinction between combatants and civilians. Warsaw and Coventry, Rotterdam and Dresden, Hiroshima and Nagasaki would prove at least that concern to be well founded.

TWELVE

❧ WAR ❧

A s Nazi armies fanned out across Europe, emigration for those who could find their way across the Atlantic increased rapidly throughout 1940 and into the first weeks of 1941. Dorothy made the acquaintance of some notable Catholic refugees soon after they landed in New York. One was the Nobel Laureate Sigrid Undset. A longtime critic of National Socialism, she had lost a son in action and fled Norway, knowing she would be a particular target for the Gestapo. Mutual friends arranged a dinner in Brooklyn one night with John LaFarge, which gave Dorothy an opportunity to offer her condolences and express her enthusiasm for *Kristin Lavransdatter*. Undset impressed her as a woman "of great health and vigor," as knowledgeable about American as Scandinavian literature. She, in turn, told Dorothy how much she admired *From Union Square to Rome*, a book she had even lectured about in her homeland. She returned to Europe as soon after the liberation of her country as possible.

Others had no intention of returning to Europe. Hélène Iswolsky, just escaped from Vichy France, was introduced to Dorothy by a cosmopolitan friend of the Catholic Worker, Julie Kernan, who held a job in publishing, served as Raïssa Maritain's English translator, and knew a good many writers. The warm feeling between the two women was mutual and immediate and would last a lifetime.

Iswolsky's background was utterly unlike that of anyone else who became an intimate member of Dorothy's circle. The daughter of the last tsarist ambassador to Paris before the Bolshevik Revolution had ended her privileged existence and plunged the family into exile and genteel poverty, she was a convert to Catholicism from the Russian Orthodox Church and a serious literary and religious intellectual. Making a catch-as-catch-can living as a writer in France in the 1920s and '30s, she had spent time in the company of Rainer Maria Rilke, Igor Stravinsky, Erik Satie, Sergei Prokofiev, and the painters Raoul Dufy and André Derain and was on close terms with the most famous Russian exile, Alexander Kerensky, the late tsar's successor until Lenin's arrival on the scene, who was also living in New York then. Hélène's friendship with Jacques Maritain and Nikolai Berdyaev in Europe was something Dorothy and Peter were eager to hear about, she agreed with the Catholic Worker concerning Franco, and her credentials were even more firmly established by the fact that she knew Emmanuel Mounier and had written for his journal, *Esprit*.

Theirs was an unlikely friendship in terms of class and background. To someone whose coming out as a debutante had taken place amid Romanov splendor, 115 Mott Street was at first encounter "an unusual, strange, and frightening world," Iswolsky recalled. She wasn't used to the sights and smells of men and women soaked in alcohol, unbathed for weeks at a time, covered with sores, picking at their lice, talking to themselves and sometimes rudely to Dorothy. She nonetheless sensed what she felt was the nobility of the house, a spiritual grounding she could admire. Impressed as she was with the Catholic Worker, though, she was in no position to join the community, as she was responsible for the care of her invalid widowed mother, but she wanted to stay in touch with Dorothy. A love of Dostoevsky and Tolstoy was another natural bond between the Russian and the Russophile, but Iswolsky introduced Dorothy to another Russian writer, Vladimir Solovyov, who would be almost as important to her as the authors of *Crime and Punishment* and *War and Peace*.

Their shared adoration of Tolstoy was also the source of one of the most pointed snubs of Dorothy's life. Iswolsky wanted her new friend to meet the great novelist's daughter and favorite child, Alexandra, who had left Russia years before and was living not far from New York City at the time. Evidently, Countess Tolstoy had heard of the Catholic Worker and Dorothy's Communist sympathies and was none too pleased with the prospect of a spontaneous visit. With the two women getting no farther than her doorstep in Nyack, she glared at Dorothy and then said to Iswolsky, "Hélène, you have fallen into bad company," and that ended that.

Sigrid Undset and Hélène Iswolsky were reminders for Dorothy of a need she had always known and that required tending. It was what Dorothy felt when she was around Mary Heaton Vorse, Katherine Anne Porter, Caroline

Gordon, Maisie Ward, or Nina Polcyn: namely, that proximity to other intellectual women had always been a sustaining, even if not always openly acknowledged, element of her life.

Burdened to the breaking point as Dorothy was with practical concerns and a schedule that would have crushed a person of less stamina, there was such pleasure to be had in conversations, relaxed or robust, with other smart women about religion, books, and politics. She had felt that with Rayna Simons in Urbana and would feel it when she became better acquainted with the wraithlike Raïssa Maritain, Jacques Maritain's highly literary wife, after the Maritains left Europe during the war and settled for the duration in the United States. The intensity of Raïssa, she said, even reminded her of Rayna. Dorothy would feel a similar appreciation when Judith Gregory, a Radcliffe graduate, showed up some years later to help edit the paper while she worked on her dissertation on Simone Weil.

In an ideal world, Tamar, her own daughter, should have been part of that company as she grew up. Problems that had been percolating for years were coming to a boil, though, and Dorothy's failings as a mother—painfully evident and discussed now by many who knew her—were yielding predictable results. Tamar wasn't becoming the confident, articulate individual people assumed the daughter of Dorothy Day would be. If anything, she was uncertain, torturously shy, easily intimidated by her mother, and burdened by the thought that she could never measure up to her mother's expectations. Dorothy knew what people said. At the same time, Ade Bethune thought that Dorothy spoiled Tamar when they were together, while acknowledging that tendency as the natural reaction of any guilt-ridden parent who was away too much of the time.

By the time she was in her midteens, Tamar had been placed in yet another boarding school, this time a French-speaking academy run by nuns in Montreal that stressed cooking, spinning, and weaving as much as academics. Girls bathed in cotton shifts in the interests of modesty, and they were strictly segregated from the sight of any boys. Though she received daily postcards, Tamar saw her mother only on holidays and rare occasions. For a girl who didn't make friends easily and whose French was close to nonexistent, the experience had to have been awkward, at best.

* * *

Once the conflict in Europe stretched from Oslo to Kiev, once the Nazis occupied Athens and most of North Africa, the drive to keep the United States
out of the war became all the more urgent for those who looked askance at
that prospect, and the tone of some issues of *The Catholic Worker* took on
an edgy, strident quality. But war was approaching. The nation was all too
obviously gearing up for a wartime economy. This was a source of concern
at the Catholic Worker on more than one front. The thought that desperate economic conditions might finally be alleviated because men would
be put to work building weapons of destruction was heartbreaking in itself.
The aftereffects of that development, the way in which it would change the
United States forever, worried Dorothy even more. A country once thoroughly militarized does not readily abandon that stance.

Moreover, she suspected, big government would be here to stay, and in
Dorothy's mind the encroachment of the state was always something about
which to be wary. In the late 1930s, she had applauded some aspects of Roosevelt's New Deal and questioned others. She joined progressives in signing a
petition for a constitutional amendment guaranteeing a minimum wage and
a forty-hour workweek, though she had opposed the establishment of Social
Security. She was not alone in worrying that too many programs, too much
bureaucracy, too many promises from on high, inevitably led to a backlash
when those promises could not be fulfilled, as the 1938 midterm elections
sweeping a conservative Republican majority into Congress had attested.

An even more fundamental problem, Dorothy believed, was that the
American people were being conditioned to embrace an entirely new
outlook, one that left them feeling overly reliant on government—"Holy
Mother State," as she termed it—and less concerned with personal initiative
and their responsibility for other members of their community. In a society in which the government would—purportedly—always take care of its
neediest citizens, individuals would no longer feel the necessity to become
personally involved in looking out for their neighbors or even their own
family members. The doctrine of the Mystical Body of Christ demanded that
every believer think about the less fortunate and actually *do something* to
help, and that *something* was not to feel complacent because one paid one's
taxes and could assume that a federal or state agency would step in and al-
leviate every problem. That approach too often did not resolve the problem
and always widened the gap between the secure and the needy. Moreover,

assenting to big government curtailed everyone's personal freedom. Dorothy was a student of Belloc's *The Servile State*.

In the months before and immediately after Pearl Harbor, Dorothy traveled more than ever, frenetically so. There was a message to be delivered to anyone who would listen—a message about the need to resist the temper of the times, not to lose sight of Christ's teachings in a climate that made forbearance and forgiveness seem irrelevant. There was also more to escape in New York than ever before. St. Joseph House was responsible for more than fifty full-time residents now, some as troublesome as anyone who had lived there before, and 1,500 people were coming by to be fed each day. The scramble for food, clothing, and funds had become overwhelming. Joe Zarrella and Gerry Griffin made it a practice to shield Dorothy as much as possible from the reality that they came closer to having to shut their doors more often than she knew. As two of her biggest admirers—Zarrella as someone completely and adorably smitten; Griffin in a more curmudgeonly fashion—they accurately sensed that there was only so much the increasingly exhausted woman could cope with.

No amount of resourcefulness seemed to help. When it was decided that the overflow of women from Mott Street was too great, Dorothy took to wandering the streets looking for rental prospects. She found what looked like a possibility, grim but affordable, at 104 Bayard Street, not many blocks away. She was able to secure twelve decrepit apartments, all for a total of $48 a month. Julia Porcelli agreed to run things there, but within two months the city condemned the deteriorating property and everyone had to tramp back to Mott Street, where conditions were now becoming dangerously overcrowded.

Inner sustenance for the overworked founder of the Catholic Worker came from an unexpected direction in the early 1940s, one that was not pleasing to everyone in the movement and was deeply distressing to Tamar but that her mother found a life-changing experience. Dorothy became committed to the idea of the retreat—or, rather, a specific form of retreat that had been developed by a French Canadian Jesuit, Onesimus Lacouture.

Religious retreats for Catholics were on the rise in early-twentieth-century America, encouraged by Pius XI's 1929 encyclical *Mens nostra*, commending the practice of spiritual exercises for both clergy and the laity.

A retreat meant time spent away from worldly concerns and generally involved a day, a weekend, or a weeklong period of prayer and reflection, silence and fasting, study of the Bible, discussions, and spiritual exercises led by priests trained in different styles of retreat. Dorothy had participated in a rather rudimentary one at a convent in Manhattan in 1933, not long after the first issue of *The Catholic Worker* had come out, but she had gone alone and left not feeling refreshed or uplifted.

Her friends Maisie Ward and Sister Peter Claver were strong adherents of the practice, and through Sister Peter Claver, Dorothy met an older Josephite priest in Baltimore, Pacifique Roy, a disciple of Lacouture. He came to Mott Street to see the house, greet the residents and Workers, help with needed carpentry (his specialty), and talk the night away. Dorothy was impressed by all that he had to say. She and a few others attended some of his Lacouture-inspired retreats in Maryland. "It was as though we were listening to the gospel for the first time," she wrote later in her memoir *The Long Loneliness*. "We saw all things new. There was a freshness about everything as though we were in love, as indeed we were." She wanted everyone affiliated with the Catholic Worker to have this experience, and she felt as well that she had at hand, in Easton, the perfect setting for large-scale religious retreats.

Many around her argued that the Easton community should be called the disaster it was and shut down. Maryfarm had brought into the countryside the usual range of Catholic Worker humanity—the earnest, the desperate, the annoying, the questing, the scholars who weren't going to be turned into workers, and the workers who weren't going to work. "At the very least, it is an interesting experiment," Father Paul Hanly Furfey wrote in 1936, when the negotiations for its purchase were under way. But of course there were plenty of reasons it would not be a success, and only an early supporter of the Catholic Worker as ardent as Furfey could think otherwise. (He changed his mind completely after a visit or two, calling it Peter Maurin's worst idea.) A failed "farming commune" Maryfarm might be, but as a "retreat center," it might justify its existence. For a while, later in the 1940s, Dorothy referred to it by that term.

On the basis of her limited experience in Baltimore, Dorothy felt an unrestrained optimism about all that a proper retreat could accomplish. She wrote in a bizarrely hopeful vein to Gerry Griffin that year, "I am completely sold on this retreat business. I think it will settle all problems, bind up all wounds, strengthen us, enlighten us, and in other words make us happy." In the late summer of 1940, as the acrimony about the pacifism "encyclical" was at its peak, she asked—or, more accurately, directed—Catholic Workers from across the country to join her at Maryfarm for a retreat that would be led by Father Paul Hanly Furfey. Seventy-five people showed up, and Father Roy was on hand to speak as well. That Labor Day weekend retreat, though, didn't make a pacifist of anyone who wasn't one already.

James O'Gara from the Chicago house thought the whole experience was "a disappointment, in the sense that the pacifist position wasn't really thrashed out." Father Furfey raised the issue in one session, while Arthur Sheehan from the Boston house was entrusted by Dorothy with a presentation on the rationale behind pacifism. But there wasn't any give-and-take to speak of. Silent dissent was expressed by people such as John Cogley, who sat there all too obviously unconvinced. Everyone in attendance probably realized that there wasn't much point to any discussion; Dorothy had already articulated the Catholic Worker's position on the subject and had intended for the retreat to be an opportunity for resisters to change their minds, not a forum for debate. The mistake had been the implied promise of a specific, more worldly focus—i.e., the Catholic Worker's response to the coming war—and that was not a mistake Dorothy would make again. In the future, retreats would be about the gospels, spiritual growth, and the unique demands of a religious life.

The next year, the retreat wasn't led by Furfey and it wasn't held at Maryfarm and it had little to do with pacifism and more with the call to a more exacting view of one's commitment to the faith. More than a hundred Workers attended. Father Roy had recommended a younger, more vibrant colleague from Pittsburgh, Father John Hugo, to be Dorothy's retreat master. Dorothy met him on one of her trips through western Pennsylvania and agreed with Roy that he was an apt choice. He led the 1941 retreat on the grounds of a Catholic school in Oakmont, Pennsylvania.

Off-putting as he was to some people, controversial as he was to become, the thirty-year-old Hugo was exactly the person Dorothy was looking for at that moment of her life. The initial euphoria of the Catholic Worker experience was wearing off, and the demands of the situation she had created were wearing her down. The inspirational Father Virgil Michel was dead, Peter had provided all the guidance and support that he could, and she was almost sickened by what she saw when she considered the state of American Catholicism—namely, priests and their parishioners who purported to love Christ but lived their faith in a perfunctory way, happy consumers and dutiful patriots, always asking too little of themselves.

Hugo asked a great deal. And he was honest and probing in a way too few priests Dorothy had ever met were. His reading of the New Testament was specific and uncompromising. His devotion to St. Francis of Assisi, St. John of the Cross, and St. Ignatius of Loyola was exemplary. It was necessary that we understand what we have all embarked on, he reminded his retreatants. Christianity was a supernatural religion, a calling to love and sacrifice in a way that secular society could simply no longer fathom. Spiritual perfection, he maintained, shouldn't be the goal of priests, nuns, and saints alone, but something every follower of Christ should aspire to.

As such, a life called to holiness meant that any deep attachment to things of this world had to be severed, not because worldly pleasures were inherently evil (some were and some weren't) but because they distracted from the highest, holiest pleasure. Suffering was not merely to be accepted, then, but embraced. Christ asks us to share his pain on the Cross. Christ demands, literally, that we give all that we have, that we love our enemies, that we turn the other cheek. Hence pacifism was more than justified; it had to be a central tenet of faith for any true believer. Vengeance was never acceptable, only boundless compassion and abnegation of the self. A Hugo retreat was about the profound *radicalism* of the Gospels.

Father Hugo could be stirring and elevated in his language, but he could also be concrete in his examples. Cigarettes were a perfect example. In an era when smoking was ubiquitous, Hugo pressed the point that someone who claimed to be a follower of Christ should be able to give up this habit or craving—and not only *should be able to* but *should want to*. After more than twenty-five years as a joyful nicotine addict, Dorothy determined at the moment to quit and did—more or less.

Reaction to this approach to faith was predictably mixed. Many Catholic Workers found Hugo's strictures excessive, his passion agitating, his tone grim. He was a Jansenist, Jim O'Gara felt. Ade Bethune, among others, agreed. The reference to the Jansenists, participants in the complex French theological movement of the seventeenth century, denoted only one thing by the twentieth century: an unseemly renunciation of even the most innocent pleasures. *Jansenist* was a shorthand word; it implied an unhealthy outlook on the natural world, one not acceptable to any sensible modern person. It would always be the easiest handle with which to criticize John Hugo.

Nina Polcyn found the experience difficult but delighted in observing Dorothy's fervor and copious note-taking. Stanley Vishnewski's criticism was more typical of Stanley. He joked that the austere message of the Hugo retreats made one "envy the pagans and the unbaptized." Tamar would have been a very atypical American adolescent had she not agreed with Stanley, and of course the situation was much worse for her: Stanley could shake his head, crack a joke, and choose not to attend if he felt that strongly (if he could deal with Dorothy's disapproval), while Tamar had no choice but to do her mother's bidding. Her resentment at sitting through the retreats year after year and watching her mother's piety take on a new dimension became ferocious.

Some who attended took what they found meaningful and ignored the rest. Julian Pleasants of the South Bend, Indiana, Catholic Worker was there for the 1941 retreat. He remembered that Dorothy "didn't say that we were out of the movement if we didn't go, but she said [attendance] was essential," that one was apt to fall by the wayside if an effort was not made. Enough said. Yet Pleasants didn't worry about the renunciations and commented that what he got out of the experience was the absolute necessity of daily meditation, not a bad thing, he concluded. Dorothy Gauchat of the Cleveland Catholic Worker felt that Hugo's message was not a blanket one of endless self-denial—Catholic Workers denied themselves plenty simply by being Catholic Workers—but had more to do with the *extent* to which satisfying one's desire for comfort and security informed one's life and created a distance from God.

For Dorothy, the Hugo retreats, of which she attended several over the years, facilitated what can only be called a second conversion. She felt more clarity about her faith, felt more deeply imbued with its richness and mystery, than she ever had. The rightness of Hugo's emphasis, which was not about sin and damnation, not about institutional authority or blind obedience, but about an unbounded love and potential that made all other concerns peripheral, seemed exactly right to her. She was disheartened when, in December 1942, Hugo's superiors withdrew permission for him to lead retreats, forcing her to find other priests to take his place, but by then his influence had taken hold.

The attack on Pearl Harbor rocked the Catholic Worker. The pages of Dorothy's FBI file, opened on December 26, 1940, began to accumulate. In April 1941, J. Edgar Hoover had recommended "that this individual be considered for custodial detention in the event of a national emergency." Some early reports came into the Bureau from field agents suggesting that Dorothy was actually a Russian. Six months later, agents went to the Chancery offices in New York to interview Father McIntyre. He acknowledged that *The Catholic Worker* had been a troublesome publication, eliciting complaints far and wide, but he was willing to vouch for Dorothy's sincerity and the fact, of which he was quite sure, that she was not a Communist or a threat to national security.

Others, less well informed, thought differently. After war with Japan and Germany was declared, letters from people in various parts of the country who merely glanced at *The Catholic Worker* and did not like its tone and editorial policies arrived on Hoover's desk, urging that the editors be investigated for treason. Particularly disturbing to those critics were the many articles in support of conscientious objectors. Ultimately, Hoover decided that he would not place Dorothy in Group 1, the category calling for imminent internment, but in Group 2, the Bureau's designation for "individuals believed to be [only] somewhat dangerous but whose activities should be restricted."

One irritating problem for the director was that his agents kept coming back to report that they couldn't find any concrete evidence of subversive activity on the part of Day or anyone else at the Worker. Before the end of the war, Hoover had his men interview dozens of priests and a few bishops in cities where houses of hospitality had been opened, search the grounds of Maryfarm, and examine the Catholic Worker's bank accounts. He pressed the assistant attorney general to determine if the sedition laws were flexible enough to prosecute those treasonous Catholics, but the answer that came back was not the one he was looking for.

Government officials weren't the only ones unhappy with the wartime politics and propaganda of the Catholic Worker. The costs of the Worker's stand on the war *from within* were painful to contemplate. The paper's circulation dwindled to 50,000 by 1942, less than half what it had been in June 1940. The Baltimore, Chicago, Milwaukee, and San Francisco houses were among the first to close; sixteen of the thirty-two houses in operation in 1941 folded within a year. (By 1945, only ten would be left in operation.) Many of the men who worked in them had gone to war or jail or to serve in the military as designated noncombatants, and there was no one willing to take their places. Dorothy listed the closings in one mournful column of the paper: Akron, Baltimore, Burlington, Chicago, Los Angeles, Milwaukee, Minneapolis, New Haven, Philadelphia, Rutland, Sacramento, San Francisco, Toledo, Troy, Washington, DC, and Worcester. Several farming communes across the country, though, were still functioning, she noted with pride, and the New York house and Maryfarm were digging in.

Other houses hung on under less than auspicious circumstances, looked at suspiciously now by police and clergy. A priest at the diocesan offices in Rochester, New York, told the FBI agents who inquired that the Catholic Workers in his city were "tolerated by Bishop [Kearney] but [were] not welcome guests because of their connection to Dorothy Day and Peter Maurin." When subscriptions to *The Catholic Worker* in the area dried up, Theresa Weider, one of the tough-minded founders of the Rochester house, took it upon herself to stand outside different churches each Sunday and hand it out. Inspired by Dorothy's example, some women felt that they did not need the approbation of episcopal authorities.

Dorothy openly admitted that her stand on pacifism had, in effect, split the movement. Exactly, friends like Maisie Ward told her, and that consequence could easily have been avoided. Patriotism was not at odds with faith, Maisie believed. Dorothy was far from convinced about that.

Some of the house closings were more irksome than others to Dorothy, depending on the attachment she felt to the principals. Her beloved friend Nina Polcyn, the young woman counted on as a mainstay of the Worker in the Midwest, wrote sheepishly early in 1942 to let her know that she didn't think the Milwaukee house would last much longer. The men had gone off to war, and the staff was down to her and one other woman, neither of whom felt safe being alone in the house at night without male colleagues. The need for the house was not what it had been before the war. Dorothy's response was testy. "I do not believe there are no poor in Milwaukee [who need attention]," she wrote back in an angry telegram. She felt Polcyn was giving up without enough of a fight, and relations between the two cooled, but only for a very brief time, ending when Polcyn came east for the summer to help out.

New faces replaced old in New York as some of the men went off to war, others to jail, and others to conscientious objector camps. Joe Zarrella and Gerry Griffin were among the newly departed, Joe to a camp for conscientious objectors and Gerry to the army to drive an ambulance in the Middle East. Thirty-two-year-old Arthur Sheehan, an ex-seminarian exempt from the draft because of his status as a recovering tuberculosis patient, came down from Boston, where he had been working at the house of hospitality there, to join the New York house. He already knew Peter Maurin well from his travels in New England. Jack Thornton and David Mason joined him from Philadelphia as things were winding down there, though Thornton left by 1943 to join the army as a noncombatant.

Sheehan and Mason were two of the most committed, reliable men Dorothy had ever worked with, and she felt comfortable leaving both the house and the paper in their hands when she was away. Forty-four years old at the time of Pearl Harbor, Mason was so close to the upper age limit for the draft that he assumed he was safe in ignoring the notices from his draft board, but the government thought otherwise and one day agents showed up at St. Joseph House to cart him off to jail while he was in the middle of cooking the evening meal. Asking his age and taking one look at his gray hair, the judge at his trial dismissed the case and told him to go back to what he had been doing.

Not everyone who came by to help in the early 1940s did so voluntarily or stayed long. The poet Robert Lowell, a recent convert to Catholicism living in New York at the time, working part-time for Sheed & Ward—and a conscientious objector who would soon go to prison for his stand—sent his wife, Jean Stafford, downtown. She was not happy. In a letter to the writer Peter Taylor, she described her impressions of the Catholic Worker experience: "I had to walk seven blocks through the kind of slums you do not believe exist when you see them in movies, in an atmosphere that was nearly asphyxiating. The Worker office was full of the kind of camaraderie which frightens me to death and I was immediately put at a long table between a Negro and a Chinese to fold paper, a tiring and filthy job. The second time, it was about the same except that Mott Street seemed even more depressing and that time I typed. After I described the place to [Lowell], he immediately wanted to go down and live there." Her husband's religious beliefs, which she did not share, struck Stafford as pure fanaticism, and she was relieved when a priest he liked told him that his calling was his work as an intellectual. "Henceforth," she concluded, "I do not have to go to the Worker but instead I have to go to work in a friendship house in Harlem under a Baroness de something." It is doubtful that Stafford lasted much longer under Catherine de Hueck's direction, though her place was a good deal tidier.

The war was the major topic of the day, but other issues occupied Dorothy's attention and that of her writers and filled the pages of *The Catholic Worker*. In particular, race in America continued to be a theme of the paper's reporting, and space was regularly allotted to coverage of incidents of brutality and discrimination, not all of them in the South. Marie Conti, who helped manage the Detroit house (one of the best run in the country, Dorothy felt), wrote at length about a white protest in 1942 aimed at keeping black families out of the Sojourner Truth Housing Project in Detroit. Most of the protestors, a loud and determined group, acknowledged to Conti that they were Catholics but became enraged, almost to the point of violence, when she informed them that their church did not support segregation. They had certainly never heard their own priests utter a word about integration, nor did they think the Church as they knew it could have any business telling them they had to accept black people as equals. Conti and her kind were troublemakers, and the idea was preposterous.

The Odell Waller case was publicized in *The Catholic Worker* on several occasions. A Virginia sharecropper, Waller had shot his white landlord and been sentenced to death, though the crime involved some ambiguities and, of course, Waller hadn't been tried by a jury of his peers, meaning black men or poor whites; he had been tried by a jury of middle-class white men who could pay the poll tax and were therefore eligible to serve on juries. Waller's case had been taken up by the NAACP and garnered support from people such as Eleanor Roosevelt, John Dewey, and Pearl Buck. Dorothy printed a letter she had sent to President Roosevelt, urging clemency, and asked readers of the paper to do the same, but the effort was futile; Waller died in the electric chair in 1942. The paper also published a call—heeded by almost no one— for Catholic colleges to open their doors to black students and printed three sonnets about race by Claude McKay, the Harlem Renaissance writer and ex-Communist with whom Dorothy had become friends after his conversion to Catholicism in 1944. Indeed, it could be said that in the years before the civil rights movement gained momentum in the 1950s, *The Catholic Worker* was one of the most vocal white publications decrying the immorality of racial prejudice. Dorothy wasn't averse, either, to raising the obvious question that many black people asked but few white people cared to consider: Why should black men submit to conscription and agree to fight for a society that in some parts of the country treated them no better than Germany treated its Jews?

In a similar vein, Dorothy deplored the internment of the Nisei. If she had had doubts about Franklin Roosevelt all along, that confirmed her most negative view of the president and his administration. On a trip to California in 1942, she visited the camps (or came as close to the fence as the guards would allow) where Japanese American families were being detained and spoke to several residents. "I saw a bit of Germany on the West Coast," she wrote bluntly in a front-page account of her trip. Again, a variation on the same question about race and justice arose: What was the point of claiming that a democratic nation was waging a virtuous war against fascism when the virtuous defenders of democracy carted many of their own citizens off to barbed-wire enclosures in the desert because of their ancestry? Those were issues about which Dorothy felt a simmering rage.

Not that racism didn't rear its ugly head on Mott Street. An unmarried Japanese American woman, Kichi Harada, had been living a comfortable middle-class life in Manhattan but, the victim of prejudice, had lost her job and home and, in desperation, had come to live amid the squalor of the house, often doing the cooking. After Pearl Harbor, many of the residents made life even more painful for her, spewing racial epithets and insisting that "the Jap" had to be watched or she'd poison everyone. When anything untoward happened in front of Dorothy, she could exhibit what she called a "righteous rage" and set the offender straight, but Harada could be protected only so far. There was also the guest with a pro-Nazi German boyfriend who liked to hang a swastika above her bed and was not the most amiable companion for the outraged Jewish woman she shared a room with. Julia Porcelli did her best to keep the peace.

* * *

During the war, Arthur Sheehan came into his own at the New York house and in a sense on the national Catholic stage as well. Remembered principally as Peter Maurin's biographer, he is a person who has never quite been given his due in chronicles of the Catholic Worker. Yet Dorothy knew his merits and encouraged him to make productive use of them.

Back in 1935, the Catholic Worker had initiated a program of support for pacifists when Bill Callahan founded Pax, an organization modeled on the British group of the same name. It aimed to promote Catholic teachings about peace and raise the level of public discourse. He pushed things a little too far when a monthly Pax column in *The Catholic Worker* explicitly urged men to resist registration for the draft that was about to be instituted. Father McIntyre let Dorothy know that a line had been crossed, possibly a legal as well as a doctrinal one, and she agreed to "stand corrected." Sheehan was more diplomatic than Callahan, and after Callahan's departure, he reorganized Pax under a new name, the Association of Catholic Conscientious Objectors. Under the auspices of that group, he and his associates answered hundreds of requests for information from men who were considering applying for status as COs. During the war, he visited the Danbury, Connecticut, prison to work with the parole board and arranged for Catholic prisoners there to be released to do alternative service in hospitals in New Haven, Boston, and Baltimore.

Dorothy and Arthur Sheehan understood the need to put a human face onto the conscientious objector debate. Even many priests derided COs as cowards. Toward that end, the editors solicited personal narratives by men who were in jail or in a recently opened internment camp in New Hampshire, where the winter cold was excruciating and malnutrition approached a critical level before the camp was closed down in 1943. Catholic Worker Dwight Larrowe provided a running commentary on conditions at the camp, and the writer J. F. Powers (famous later for the Catholic novel *Morte d'Urban*) told of his experience in jail in Minnesota. Ammon Hennacy, a sometime Catholic Worker in the Midwest, wrote lengthy accounts of his year in the Atlanta penitentiary, where he was imprisoned and brutalized for refusing to fight in World War I. Hennacy, whose life would become more intertwined with Dorothy's after he moved to New York in the 1950s, was a modern-day Thoreau—meaning exactly the kind of rebellious soul that would infuriate the flag-waving public. Giving Hennacy space in the paper cemented the image of *The Catholic Worker* in the minds of many as an un-American publication, as did the article "Feed the Axis" in the November 1942 issue, calling on the Allies to do something for the starving children of Germany, Italy, and Japan.

Dorothy's own feistiness grew as the war continued. Her January 1943 editorial about female conscription, an idea under consideration in Washington, elicited a particularly sharp reader response. Under no circumstances would she cooperate with the system, she wrote, even to the extent of filling out the Selective Service forms. If it came to that, she hoped other women would follow her example of civil disobedience. As always, few people were willing to criticize the government in wartime. When Bishop Gerald Shaughnessy of Seattle addressed a Knights of Columbus gathering and spoke out against the Allied bombing of urban centers filled with civilians, Arthur Sheehan rushed the text of his remarks into print, titling it "Western Bishop Pleads for Morality in War."

With the death during the war of Father Barry O'Toole, Dorothy's partner at the congressional hearings, *The Catholic Worker* lost a high-profile clergyman willing to go on record on behalf of conscientious objectors. That made all the more important the voices of those who did speak up. Under Dorothy's influence, Father Ryan had changed his mind on the subject and wrote about pacifism, while Father Hugo became a prolific contributor to the paper. His "Catholics Can Be Conscientious Objectors" in the March 1943 issue answered those of his clerical peers who doubted the theological basis for a refusal to serve, and his "The Immorality of Conscription" in the November 1944 issue was an exhaustive treatment of the subject. Both were reprinted by the Worker as pamphlets to distribute around the country.

It would be inaccurate to say that the case for pacifism was entirely absent from public discourse in the United States before the mid-twentieth century. From the time of the great eighteenth-century Quaker abolitionist Anthony Benezet, voices had been heard urging resistance to all armed conflict. But they were few in number, largely ignored, and often scorned even by their own churches. Dorothy Day never referred to Benezet in her writings, but she and Arthur Sheehan were placing themselves in that hallowed lineage—a line that extends from Benezet to William Ladd (the founder of the American Peace Society in 1828) to Henry David Thoreau to World War I–era resisters such as Ben Salmon (a martyr she praised in her columns)—when they refused to be silent about the injustice of forcing men against their conscience to take up arms.

Resistance to the Vietnam War twenty years later made Dorothy Day a countercultural hero; resistance to World War II made her, for many Americans, a pariah.

The FBI continued to be zealous in its surveillance. In April 1943, Dorothy spoke at Harvard, making her usual case for the pacifist cause and the right to conscientious objection. She told her student audience, many of whom were preparing to enter the armed services after graduation, that she had received letters from more than a few servicemen who said they wished they had heeded her counsel before swearing an oath and putting on their uniform. The confidential informant planted in the audience informed the Bureau that he would do all he could to find out the identities of those who had written such letters.

That spring, the Philadelphia house of hospitality shut down. Only two men were left to staff it, and with so many seamen finding jobs in the dockyards, the number of homeless needing a place to sleep or be fed had dropped precipitously. Before it closed, though, FBI agents cornered Paul Toner, who ran the house, and got an earful. Either Toner was not a fan of Dorothy (something she never suspected) or he was intimidated by the agents and told them what he thought they wanted to hear. He had spent a summer in Easton before opening the house in Philadelphia, he said, and there had met the founder of the Catholic Worker, whom he characterized as "a very emotional and inflexible woman who took the destitute and the downtrodden as well as dope fiends and drunkards from the city" to the farm. He brought up her common-law marriage to a former anarchist and her illegitimate daughter. Dorothy Day was theologically unsound, Toner was at pains to tell his interlocutors, and would have been better off if she had spent time in a novitiate, grounding herself more sensibly in Church doctrine before starting the Catholic Worker. One imagines that was not regarded at the Bureau as vital information.

Another person with his own FBI file came by that year to see what 115 Mott Street was all about, though his situation had nothing to do with pacifism and everything to do with the fact that he was sleeping with a Danish beauty whom Hoover thought (erroneously, as it turned out) might be a German spy. Lieutenant John F. Kennedy, his older brother, Joseph, and several friends in uniform paid a visit. The sons of Ambassador Kennedy might have been slumming, they might have been there at their pious mother's behest, or they might have been genuinely intrigued by what they had heard about Dorothy Day and her mission—in any event, they were treated as all visitors were and given a tour, and later Dorothy and the young men went out to dinner at an all-night restaurant on Canal Street. There is no record, though, of the sixth-wealthiest family in the nation ever having written a check for the Catholic Worker, and twenty years later Dorothy was decidedly not a fan of the first Catholic president of the United States.

Much of 1943 that wasn't consumed by the usual activities and problems, with editing the paper and lecturing, involved projects that never came to fruition. Dorothy had hoped to found a retreat home that would be used specifically for alcoholic priests. The number of men who suffered from the problem was considerable, but she received little encouragement from the Church officials she spoke to. She was also working on the book about Peter Maurin that she had long wanted to write. Peter was not doing well. He often seemed unfocused and was sometimes unable to travel on his own, which gave the project a particular urgency, but it was proving much harder than she imagined to tell the story of the life of the inspiration behind the Catholic Worker.

Finally, everything broke. Dorothy felt she couldn't go on. She wondered if it was time to leave The Catholic Worker in the hands of others who were younger and more able and abruptly wrote a "farewell column." She needed at least a year away, she felt. Grace had moved back north from Florida, in declining health, and Dorothy wanted to spend time with her; she wanted to reconnect with her siblings, if possible; she wanted to see Tamar more often. She needed time to rest, read, meditate, pray without interruption. She wanted nothing more to do with the vast correspondence she had to attend to each week. She didn't want to hear any more about money, bad food, bedbugs, and squabbles. She left the paper in Arthur Sheehan's capable hands, instructing him to take her name off the masthead.

As she expected, the high quality of The Catholic Worker was maintained during her absence—but it was an absence that was considerably shorter than anticipated. Dorothy went first for a few weeks to the Grail, a center for training women for the lay apostolate in Illinois, and then settled into rooms in a Dominican convent on Long Island. After five months, she accepted that a reclusive life was not for her, and, though still far from refreshed, she returned to Mott Street.

The bulk of Dorothy's diaries from 1942 to 1944 were probably among the papers she destroyed in the late 1950s or early 1960s at a moment when she decided to sift through and expurgate some of her personal archive. That gap, one of many, coincides with a time of enervating self-doubt and fatigue as she began to think of herself as a profound failure, both as a leader and as a mother. An especially pressing worry concerned her daughter. Men were beginning to pay inappropriate attention to a girl of her age. Dwight Larrowe, the CO who later became a Trappist monk, made his interest clear when she was as young as fifteen. He wasn't the only one. The realization that Tamar was no longer a child, that she was an attractive teenager who lived unchaperoned in an unstable environment, might well have been the reason Dorothy chose to send her to school in Canada for the academic year 1941–1942.

In a chiding letter written during the summer after Tamar left Montreal, Dorothy scolded her daughter for helping out so little at Maryfarm, not even tending to her own garden, and spending her days sitting about with David Hennessy, a resident of the farm who was thirteen years her senior. "This protest on my part has nothing to do with Dave," she added. "As far as I know him, he is perfectly all right"—a statement that involved some disingenuousness—"but my protest is the way you are wasting your time and devoting yourself exclusively to him." To Gerry Griffin overseas, she wrote more truthfully a few months later about her daughter's interest. "Do pray she gets over it, for he drinks, and he certainly doesn't like work, and he boasts of being a dreamer, not a worker." A sixteen-year-old's crush on an attentive and unreliable twenty-nine-year-old man did not bode well, Dorothy was sure.

At the end of that summer, at the invitation of Ade Bethune's mother, Tamar went to stay with Ade and her family, who were now living in Rhode Island. The plan, thoroughly agreeable to Tamar, was that she spend a year studying in Newport in Ade's art apprenticeship program. A warm and humorous person who understood teenagers far better than Dorothy did, Ade would also tutor her in other more academic areas. The elder Bethunes were a delightful couple who enjoyed her company. Tamar's own respite from the

Catholic Worker came to an end several months later when Dorothy decided it was time to look to the future.

"The career I think you should be fitting yourself for is farming," she wrote to Tamar that summer of 1943, "whether on one of the farming communes or on a farm where you are working and earning a salary." With strict instructions, she passed on the course catalogue and admissions forms to an agricultural school in Farmingdale, Long Island. She had asked for Ade's advice, but *The Catholic Worker*'s admired artist told her just what she didn't want to hear: that her daughter needed time, that she needed high school, that she was scarcely literate in some ways. Her formal education had been too scattered. Pressing her into a vocational school would be a mistake.

That counsel was not well received. "I know you are happy at Ade's," Dorothy acknowledged in another letter to Tamar, "but you cannot be a child all your life, and I disagree with her idea that high school will help you." High school hadn't done much for her or her three brothers, she maintained. In the end, in the manner of all such nervous, controlling parents, she told her daughter, *but the decision is yours*—in effect, stay a dependent with the Bethunes for another year, if you want, while wasting your time in high school in Rhode Island or New York, or prepare for the "career" I think you should have. Tamar, of course, went off to Farmingdale, where, not coincidentally, Dorothy was living during her retreat. Knowing that Tamar and David Hennessy were in constant correspondence, Dorothy made Tamar promise that she wouldn't even consider marriage until she turned eighteen. Forster didn't want to be involved one way or the other.

Looked at in a certain light, though the age difference was troubling, David Hennessy might have seemed a plausible life partner for Tamar. The only boy of eight children of working-class parents, he had dropped out of high school, but he wasn't unintelligent or anti-intellectual. In fact, the writers who mattered to Peter and Dorothy were of great interest to him, especially Chesterton and Belloc. He was a practicing Catholic, he wasn't opposed to living at Easton, and he had a medical deferment as a result of an accidental gunshot wound he had suffered to the side of his head and his ear a few years earlier. Yet none of that was enough to assuage Dorothy's fears. She probably knew that David was as disdainful of the retreats as her daughter was. She might have known that he could be comically sarcastic about her behind her back. She surely didn't know, as no one else did at the time, that he had been in love with a close male friend before he met Tamar. The world was not a kind place to a closeted gay man in the 1940s.

At odd moments, Dorothy worried that she was being a Mrs. Jellyby, alluding to the absurd mother in *Bleak House* who is more concerned with her charitable efforts on behalf of an obscure African tribe than she is to her own needy, neglected daughter at home. A few people familiar with the situation would have thought the analogy fit. The difference between Dorothy and Charles Dickens' character, though, was that Mrs. Jellyby had no intention of going to Africa and actually making a difference in anyone's life; she enjoyed her long-distance philanthropy and, in her flibbertigibbet way, scarcely noticed her daughter's unhappiness. Dorothy was aware that her daughter was suffering and knew that her own efforts in the life she had chosen with the Catholic Worker had cost them both dearly. She was active in the world as a moral force, as a pacifist, as a Catholic. Christ's hardest command, his most heart-stopping statement at odds with twentieth-century life—that those committed to his way *must* put family second (or cast family off entirely), that a commitment made to the Cross must be total—was not an animating force in the life of the ludicrous Mrs. Jellyby. It was, in large measure, in Dorothy's. There was no middle ground.

Tamar finished her course of study at Farmingdale, where she became particularly interested in and knowledgeable about organic farming (which became a lifelong passion) and dutifully waited until shortly before her eighteenth birthday to inform her mother that she was going to do what she had actually intended all along: she was going to marry David Hennessy.

There was precious little Dorothy could say at that point.

On April 19, 1944, Tamar and David were wed before a small Catholic Worker gathering at St. Bernard's, a church in Easton, and a priest who seemed distressed by the age difference of the bride and groom. Aunt Tessa's mother provided the bride with a hand-stitched and -embroidered wedding dress. A neighbor loaned them his car to get there. Peter, unsteady on his feet, walked her down the aisle. John Filligar cooked a wedding breakfast, and David Mason came from the city with a traditional Italian wedding cake from a Mott Street bakery. Wedding presents included farm animals; the cottage the newlyweds were going to inhabit on the property would have its own livestock, garden, and orchard. David named their new home "Cobbett Cottage," after William Cobbett, the radical nineteenth-century British political essayist, gardening authority, grammarian, forefather of the distributists, and body snatcher (he was responsible for transporting Thomas Paine's body from New Rochelle to England, where he thought it should be buried and more properly honored). Cobbett was an eccentric after David Hennessy's heart.

Dorothy was torn by conflicting emotions, pleased that her daughter seemed so happy and was going to embrace a rural life in Easton and nervous about her new son-in-law's prospects in life. To Gerry Griffin, her most trusted confidant at the moment, she worried that he seemed too gruff and unstable. "He may grow into a Mr. Breen," she wrote in prescient despair. Yet she put a good face on the matter. One would never guess from the chatty tone devoted to her daughter's marriage on the front page of *The Catholic Worker* that Dorothy felt anything other than the normal joy of the mother of the bride. As a journalist, she could be blisteringly honest about public issues, poverty, race, pacifism, and faith. Closer to home, she could prevaricate with the best of them.

As the war drew into its final year, Dorothy did her best to reawaken her old energy and balance. She could travel now freed of guilt about Tamar, home with a husband and pregnant within four months of the wedding, and she visited ten cities in the Midwest between mid-1944 and mid-1945, staying for a week in Chicago. She arranged for two weeklong retreats in 1944. Her reading was as eclectic as ever: Cardinal John Henry Newman's sermons, Arthur Koestler, *The Old Curiosity Shop*, Maisie Ward's book on G. K. Chesterton, Raïssa Maritain's memoirs. In February 1945, she attended a reception for the Maritains at the New School for Social Research; now that France had been liberated, the French philosopher was going to the Vatican as his country's ambassador. Dorothy gave him copies of *The Catholic Worker* to give to the pope. Several weeks later, she saw an exhibition of paintings by a friend of the Maritains, Georges Rouault, at the Museum of Modern Art, a body of work in which, Maritain wrote, "all usual canons of beauty are shattered." Rouault became one of Dorothy's favorite artists as well.

Two months later, Tamar had the first of her nine children, Becky, and it was possible for Dorothy to hope that she might be wrong about the future of her daughter's marriage. David Hennessy was in a rare ingratiating period. He had offered to bring his mother-in-law's manuscript to the attention of an editor he knew, though—probably not a surprise to its author—her biography of Peter was judged too discursive and not remotely publishable in its present form. She put it aside for the moment. Her son-in-law's interest in William Cobbett had also inspired her to read him more widely, and those unusual essays were something they could happily talk about together. Cobbett was a type Dorothy had always thrilled to, a nonconformist who gave fresh meaning to the term. "He was against the system," she wrote in her March column, "but his indignation was large, general, and generous."

At times, the intrusion of politics into her world never seemed to stop. Though the Catholic Worker had long since been taken off the list of potential subversive organizations and the war against Japan was only several weeks from its conclusion, FBI agents came to 115 Mott Street again at the end of June. There they met with a priest who worked at various neighborhood parishes and at Maryfarm, helped out at the house a good deal, and regularly contributed to the paper, especially during the war years. They wanted to know where they could find a man he knew, a young anarchist named Clifton Bennett, who had not reported to his draft office. Father Clarence Duffy—Irish-born, alcoholic, and never a pushover—did know Bennett but declined to say anything concerning his whereabouts. In their report, the agents characterized the priest as adamant on that score but friendly and accommodating in general.

Then they met Dorothy. She was in the house that afternoon and happened to come in while the agents were with Father Duffy. Friendly and accommodating she was not. They reported that she "abruptly broke into the conversation in a very belligerent and hostile manner," berating them and criticizing the Selective Training and Service Act. They characterized themselves in their report as forbearing and scrupulously polite while they informed her that they were not interested in her views on the law and were there to see Father Duffy on a specific matter. She had had enough. She wanted them out and on their way. In particular, it seems they wanted the director to know that they had been spoken to disrespectfully. Dorothy wouldn't have challenged their assessment. I have met many a man from the FBI, she wrote in *The Catholic Worker* the next month, "but none so stupid . . . as these two."

Respect, disrespect. What did they matter now?

A month later, the war in the Pacific was over, but not until two atomic bombs had been exploded, the first on Hiroshima on August 6 and the second on Nagasaki on August 9. They were the fulfillment of every fear Dorothy had voiced concerning the war. One expected moral obscenities from the Nazi high command and the Imperial Japanese military government, but not from the Allies. The use of napalm and the practice of obliteration bombing over enemy cities using incendiary cluster bombs—on Tokyo, Berlin, Hamburg, Cologne, and, most famously, Dresden—resulting cumulatively in hundreds of thousands of civilian deaths (which in the view of many military historians did little to bring the war to a speedier end) had been horrific enough to contemplate, but a single bomb that could reduce a metropolis and its inhabitants to ash suggested a frightening new world in the making, providing humankind with a godlike power to destroy the planet while distancing itself more than ever from God.

Dorothy's scorn for the new president was withering. "Mr. Truman was jubilant," she wrote in the September issue. "President Truman. True man; what a strange name, come to think of it. We refer to Jesus Christ as true God and true man. Truman is a true man of his time in that he was jubilant. He was not a son of God, a brother of Christ, brother of the Japanese, jubilating as he did." About the bodies of women and children vaporized and scattered to the four winds: "Perhaps we will breathe their dust in our nostrils, feel them in the fog of New York, feel them in the rain on the hills of Easton." Nor was she at ease with the hierarchy of the Catholic Church in the United States, which did not issue the forceful condemnation of the use of the atomic bombs that she hoped for.

Twenty-seven years earlier, supporting President Wilson's decision to go to war against Germany, Cardinal James Gibbons of Baltimore, the dean of the US episcopacy, had reminded Catholics that "the primary duty of a citizen is loyalty to country. This loyalty is exhibited by an absolute and unreserved obedience to his country." That kind of thinking, Dorothy believed, justified Hiroshima and Dresden no less than it justified Dachau and the Warsaw ghetto and Stalingrad. The Worker's neighbors threw confetti and danced in the streets, but VJ Day brought scant joy to 115 Mott Street.

THIRTEEN

❧ BURDENS ❧

THE YEAR THE WAR ENDED, DOROTHY TURNED FORTY-EIGHT. HER hair was fast turning white, she looked older than her years, and she wore only the frumpy dresses she could find in her size in the clothing donation room at St. Joseph House. Yet she was still an arresting presence. She had a height and a chiseled jaw that commanded attention; a voice that, when she chose, could hold a room; an unaffected laugh and a probing stare; Modigliani eyes, as Garry Wills would write after her death.

She had a grandchild to exult in, a new generation to welcome as the older generation was passing away. Grace Day expired of a heart condition in October 1945, at the age of seventy-seven, with her daughters at her side, and, one by one, longtime members of the community died. In *The Catholic Worker* in 1946, Dorothy wrote about the deaths of Kichi Harada, their much-abused house cook, and Mary Sheehan, one of the first women to join the community. She speculated about those whose safety she had fretted over throughout the war—Joe Zarrella, Gerry Griffin, Tom Sullivan—and waited to see who would be returning to New York and who would be moving on to a new life. The late 1940s was the period in which the Catholic Worker would need to regroup as its numbers and influence appeared to be on the wane.

She speculated about her brother Donald as well. Grace had died without knowing how things stood with her oldest child, who had ultimately followed a path that the family found as strange as Dorothy's. As a correspondent for the *New York World* in Europe, he had married a Russian woman and come to share her views about the evils of Communist totalitarianism. When Finland was invaded by the USSR, he refused to return to New York as his editors demanded but instead joined the Finnish army and stayed to fight. In 1944, Donald and his wife left Finland for Germany, where he made broadcasts for the Nazis, tinged with more than a little anti-Semitism, in support of their war against the Soviets. His aim was for the United States to realize that it had more to fear from a Soviet victory than a Nazi victory. Consequently, after the fall of Nazi Germany, he was imprisoned by the US military authorities, and it was unclear if he would ever be allowed back into the United States.

The war had unsettled so many things. The immediate neighborhood was becoming a severe trial. Bad as things had been during the Depression, shopkeepers on Mott Street hadn't needed to gate their doors and windows at night, and there was a feeling then that everyone was in the same precarious boat. By 1946, Dorothy told her readers, the shops around her did need the protection of metal gates. Windows were being smashed at night. Looting was on the rise. The vandalism and thefts weren't random, either. It was the stores owned by Chinese and Jewish merchants that were being targeted. Due to a nearby subway expansion and extensive drilling underground, the street was also inundated with rats, far beyond the usual number residents lived with. Marge Hughes, who had joined the Worker in 1940 and now served as Dorothy's secretary, was cutting bread one day in the kitchen when one ran right over her hand. Troops of them would scamper up the staircase past anyone sitting on a step. The building was not a safe space for children anymore, though as many homeless families with little ones were seeking shelter there as during the worst of the Depression.

The ground was shifting intellectually and philosophically as well. The secular writers Peter had pressed upon Dorothy had seen their day. Hilaire Belloc and the distributists were relics in the postwar world where the Labour Party's welfare state and all that it implied quickly became the dominant force in Great Britain (not that *The Catholic Worker* ever stopped writing about them), and middle-class Americans were eagerly looking forward to the benefits of a recharged economy. Father John Ryan, the New Deal's most forceful advocate among the Catholic clergy, had died a few months after the father of the New Deal. With the onset of the Cold War and with the Depression now a part of history, pacifism, voluntary poverty, and the spirit of St. Francis of Assisi began to seem as remote to American life as the concerns of the abolitionists or the suffragettes. That was a troublesome reality for Dorothy Day and the Catholic Worker to come to terms with.

Just as seriously, but in a different way, Emmanuel Mounier—the guiding light of personalism, a hero to both Peter and Dorothy in the 1930s—was now a questionable source of unadulterated inspiration. The war had changed both him and his journal, *Esprit*. Christian charity could be misplaced, he argued when advocating swift retributive justice against collaborators, and his hatred of capitalism and fear of US expansionism were such that now he was willing to overlook or make excuses for Stalinist thuggery in Eastern Europe. In 1932, Mounier had insisted that the evils of East and West must be rejected alike; in the late 1940s, Soviet control of Czechoslovakia could be justified in the pages of *Esprit* by the United States' support of the fascist Franco. None of that represented the Catholic Worker's outlook. (The extent to which Dorothy was really aware of these unsettling developments in France is an open question, though. Her usually well-informed friend Hélène Iswolsky was not or pretended not to be. She wrote an obituary of Mounier in *Commonweal* in 1950 that was entirely laudatory.) The new voices out of Europe were not optimistic and personalist; they were war-weary and existentialist.

More immediately, there was cause for concern about Peter Maurin. For a long time, it had been clear that something was wrong. He was losing weight, losing focus, not finishing sentences. At times he acted irrationally. Two weeks before his sixty-fifth birthday in 1942, amid all the bitter, heated attention at the Catholic Worker concerning conscription, Peter had gone downtown to the Selective Service office and registered for the draft. He was following the letter of the law in doing so; all men up to the age of sixty-five had been instructed to register, though that cutoff point was seen as a formality. The likelihood of anyone over the age of fifty ever being called into service was slim to nonexistent. Many men in their sixties ignored the law. No one would have noticed had Peter not done so. No one else who was going to turn sixty-five in a matter of days thought twice about it. It is possible that he was making a statement about Dorothy's disapproval of the very act of registering, but there is nonetheless an inexplicable dimension to that choice. Dorothy never discussed in print that upsetting situation, that bizarre capitulation to secular authority.

By 1946, Peter couldn't be trusted to go places by himself. Once, he disappeared for four days and had no clear recollection of where he had been. Luckily, most of the time, he had Arthur Sheehan by his side. Arthur was the son he had never had, and the mutual respect and affection of the two men was the envy of many in the house, including Dorothy. In his heyday, Peter had Sheehan with him on many of his travels, helping him to find audiences and places to stay, taking notes on his talks, basking in the praise his mentor enjoyed and encouraging him in every way. Sheehan left the Catholic Worker in 1947 to marry and take a job with CARE, a nonsectarian international relief organization, though by that time Peter was having trouble remembering his protégé's name. His memory was fading fast. Alzheimer's, vascular dementia, the corrosive effects of syphilis on the brain: whatever the real cause, it was heartbreaking for Dorothy and those close to Peter to watch, and a new generation of Workers was coming to the house who would never really know Peter's importance to the movement. By the time Sheehan left, Peter had to be reminded to eat and helped to dress himself properly. Some of the new young people in the house treated him simply as a senile old man of no consequence. All that time, he was aware of what was happening to him. Having relinquished everything in a life committed to holy poverty and sacrifice for others, he was now being asked, as Dorothy chose to express it, to give up the very last things he possessed: his mobility, his speech, his mind.

The immediate postwar years were just as difficult for Tamar. She later told her daughter that she knew within weeks of her marriage that she had made a terrible mistake. By the time she was twenty-one, she was pregnant with her third child by a husband who had not found his way to a steady income. That year—1947—she and David took the children to West Virginia, purchasing a derelict farmhouse with no electricity. David had been eager to create some distance between Easton and his mother-in-law, but the choice wasn't promising.

They were surrounded by other dirt-poor farmers, most of them illiterate, who didn't know what to make of the Hennessys. Putting enough food on the table was a constant problem. The heating in the uninsulated house came from a woodstove and a kerosene heater, which meant that the kitchen floor couldn't be washed in the winter for fear of the water freezing. Dorothy gave them a fifteen-year-old car that had been donated to the Catholic Worker years before, and Forster kicked in $250. David worked at a nearby tomato-canning factory for sixty cents an hour and hired himself out as a day laborer while trying in a desultory way to keep up a mail-order Catholic book business he had started at Maryfarm. Tamar, an excellent weaver thanks to her year with the nuns in Montreal, wove rugs to sell and raised chickens for eggs to market in town. Dorothy and Stanley Vishnewski would come for a visit every several weeks, Granny bringing D. H. Lawrence novels for Tamar and shoes for the children that usually didn't fit.

Maryfarm in Easton came to a long-anticipated, ignominious end during this period as well. The property had become divided into two warring zones, a lower-farm area where Dorothy and the Catholic Workers stayed and where the Hennessys lived before departing for West Virginia, and an upper-farm area occupied by three families and several single men. A middle-aged lawyer who did pro bono work for various Catholic institutions and alcoholic priests, Guy Tobler, had moved in toward the end of the war and proved to be a near-psychotic presence. Little by little, in insidious ways, he gained psychological control of the residents of the upper farm.

To her horror, Dorothy learned that he had formed a kind of cult involving sexual humiliation of the women, corporal punishment for anyone who disobeyed him, genuflection before him as their spiritual master, and rejection of Dorothy as Satanic. Tobler was so aggressive in his dealings with Dorothy that she feared for her safety, and nothing she said or did could extricate the families from his power. She deeded the upper farm to two of the families who lived there, disassociating the Worker from them entirely, and then began the long-drawn-out process of trying to sell the rest of the land and be done with it. In 1947, she bought property in Newburgh, two hours north of New York City. Also called Maryfarm, it would be less a farming commune, she insisted, and more a retreat center.

The demise of the Easton Maryfarm was a practical matter, a pragmatic necessity, but it was also a development weighted with symbolism, an admission of significant failure. Other signs were discouraging. The circulation of the paper was stagnant at 60,000, one half of its prewar average, and turmoil reigned at some of the houses, nowhere worse than in Boston. Disagreements among the fractious Workers there led to their decision to dismiss their leader, Jane Marra, a woman Dorothy had known as the steadying influence in the house. The archdiocese of Boston then withdrew its support, and Dorothy felt obligated to do the same. She instructed the Workers to hand over any money left in their account to the archbishop and cease using the "Catholic Worker" name. Such was her authority with them that they did as they were told. In her column in *The Catholic Worker*, Dorothy officially announced the closing of the Boston house.

Yet—and there was always a *yet* with the Catholic Worker—there was still an inspirational element to the community, especially the New York community, that could not be discounted, a ripple effect of the corporal works of mercy. The Catholic novelist Harry Sylvester thought enough of the heartfelt work that took place on Mott Street to dedicate his 1947 novel, *Moon Gaffney*, to Dorothy, John Cort, and "all good Catholic radicals."

That same year, Helen Caldwell Day, a devout African American Catholic convert in training to be a nurse, was urged by her priest in Memphis to pay a visit. She went to New York to meet Dorothy and Peter, though by that time Peter's ability to hold a coherent conversation was quite limited. What most struck Helen at that first encounter, though, was the roughness and chaos of the house and the almost unnatural forbearance of those who tended to the guests: "I didn't understand how they could take the abuse and curses of those men and women who benefited from their hospitality, who ate their food and wore their clothes and slept in the beds and gave nothing in return, not even a 'thank you.'" The whole experience seemed too arduous—almost pointless. Having grown up in poverty in the rural South, Helen found the idea of voluntary poverty disconcerting. She was impressed, however, by the complete absence of racial prejudice among the young people of the Catholic Worker community, unique in her experience, and decided to spend a year working there. Four years later, she opened the Blessed Martin de Porres House of Hospitality in Memphis.

In moments of despair, Dorothy had often asked Peter if he never became discouraged. His outlook was that their work should have nothing to do with notions of "success" or "failure," or with anything measurable, or lasting, in ways that they could determine or count on. They were about sowing seeds, planting, both literally and figuratively, and that was all God expected of them, he assured her. That was all God expected of anyone. The intention, the effort, and the love were what mattered.

Those sowers, those planters—the ones who weren't themselves drinkers or unhinged or hopelessly quarrelsome—were her salvation. Joe Zarrella didn't return from the war, as he and his wife moved back to Indiana to raise a family and become labor activists, and that was a loss. Gerry Griffin did, however, after driving an ambulance in the army. He was both a great help and a trial. Dorothy could tease him, he was someone who loved Dostoevsky's novels and the opera as much as she did, and he was a respected confidant. She had written to him with frankness during the war about her personal woes, her loneliness and religious musings, the books she was reading, and the fights at the house she was mediating.

Yet Griffin was even more sarcastic than Dorothy was, and he didn't hide his prejudices. He was misogynistic and anticlerical—he was no fan of the retreats—and all too often exhibited what she called a "fiendish pride." His return didn't work out. By 1947, it was time to part company. "I should be used to men failing me," she wrote in a good-bye letter to him. "I've had to bring up a child alone, and I've certainly seen more than my share of the gross and selfish in men. I've had many men love me but few protect me. As a matter of fact, the love I've had has been hate, too. It's better to have that purgatory here than later. I've wanted human love too much."

Griffin was replaced by some stalwarts. Tom Sullivan and Dorothy had met back in Chicago before the war, he had served in World War II, and he now came to New York to become part of the community there. He was a roll-up-his-sleeves kind of guy, in the office or on the farm, a good writer, and someone who knew how to adapt to Dorothy's moods. He would remain with her for almost ten years. Jack English, who had spent a large part of the war in a Romanian prisoner of war camp, had started with the Catholic Worker in Cleveland and soon after arriving in New York became someone dear to Dorothy's heart. He was a prayerful and compassionate man, an able editor for the paper, but a damaged soul whose lifelong struggle with alcoholism was wrenching to observe.

The paper acquired a major intellectual with Bob Ludlow, the son of a Pennsylvania coal miner, who had first heard, and been moved by, Dorothy and Peter when they had both spoken when he was a student at St. Thomas College in Scranton in 1937. A conscientious objector during the war, an individual of great intensity, he came to Mott Street in 1947 and quickly assumed a dominant place on the staff. He also led the way in the attention *The Catholic Worker* gave to Mahatma Gandhi. Ludlow wrote about the Gandhian concept of *satyagraha*, a spiritual resistance to abuses of power, as knowledgeably and passionately as he wrote about the *Summa Theologica* of St. Thomas Aquinas, the papal encyclicals, or Cardinal Newman's evolutionary view of

Church teachings (i.e., the Church makes mistakes that it invariably corrects over time—e.g., its teachings on Galileo or slavery, its current ambiguity about pacifism). The respect for a Hindu like Gandhi irritated some readers who believed that the paper's concerns should be strictly Roman Catholic, but Ludlow's take on that was simple: they should read my columns more carefully and know better. If Dorothy felt at times that his prose was too high-flown for the paper's usual audience, she knew she had in Ludlow a theoretician, which the movement needed, someone who could be a kind of successor to Peter Maurin, articulating the bedrock values the Catholic Worker stood for.

A woman finally assumed a major role with the paper with the arrival of Irene Naughton, who joined Bob Ludlow, Tom Sullivan, and Jack English on the masthead. Irish, red-haired, resilient, given to ebullient laughter, she was "one of the brightest writers we ever had on the paper," Dorothy felt. Irene had both a spirit and a prose style Dorothy liked. Arrested with another (male) Catholic Worker and hauled off to jail for picketing outside the Palisades Amusement Park in New Jersey—black families were allowed into the park but not permitted to use the swimming pool—she was undaunted by the brutality of the cops and wrote about her experience in a lengthy article. She wasn't above helping with the farmwork or cleaning up some vomit-covered older woman who dragged herself back to Mott Street after a binge. She liked to write about economics, unemployment, corruption in unions, and topics usually left to the men, and she did it with some bite. "The common man in America is no more free than that schizophrenic in Ward's Island is Napoleon, but it makes them both happy to think so" was her conclusion about the greatest obstacle to social change—complacency—in the postwar world. With people such as Ludlow, Sullivan, English, and Irene Naughton at the helm, Dorothy felt that the paper was in excellent hands.

The first presidential election since the death of Roosevelt took place in 1948 and, from the Catholic Worker perspective, illustrated everything that was going wrong in America. The major-party candidates—President Harry S. Truman and New York governor Thomas E. Dewey—were equally abhorrent to Dorothy, both committed to an arms race, a peacetime draft, and containing the demands of labor. Southern racists were emboldened to run their own Dixiecrat candidate, Strom Thurmond of South Carolina, while the Progressive, Henry Wallace, the only true supporter of civil rights and an easing of tensions with the Soviet Union, was heckled and pelted with eggs on the campaign trail.

In May, Dorothy sent a letter to the editor of *Commonweal*, which C. G. Pauling printed despite his displeasure with it, that encapsulated everything that angered her about the current political climate. "Things Worth Fighting For?"—its intended emphasis was on the question mark—took note of US oil companies rushing to Saudi Arabia to secure concessions that would keep the United States well supplied with oil for decades, while the American workers there had to agree to respect the Islamic weekly calendar and work on the Christian Sabbath. It took note of the recent fierce election in Italy, the results of which the West had cheered—the Catholic, capitalist, conservative Christian Democrats had defeated the secular, pro-Soviet Popular Front—questioning the legitimacy of a victory that entailed armed force at the polls. Dorothy was particularly severe about how the GI Bill was seducing young men into joining the military even before they were drafted, filling them with "a warm glow of self-love" while giving them "intensive training in how to escape death, how to kill." All of this was taking place, she asserted, while we were paying less attention than ever to the fact that injustice and inequality were rife on our own shores. "We are losing the battle at home, without the Russians lifting a finger," she maintained.

Compassion and solidarity with our fellow man was being forgotten in an environment rigidly focused on dualities. "Greater love hath no man than this, that he lay down his life for his brothers," Dorothy quoted from John 15:13, adding just what too many Americans, she felt, did not want to hear—"and the Russians are our brothers, the Negro is our brother, the Japanese are our brothers, the Germans, the Mexicans, the Filipinos, the Jews, the Arabs."

What was most astonishing about the publication of this letter was the fact that *Commonweal*'s editor felt obliged to respond in print in the same issue in stinging terms. He began with a compliment: the views expressed were no surprise because "[Dorothy Day's] contemporaries have learned to expect from her no compromise, no acceptance of hate, no deviation from what she considers the demands of absolute justice and charity." Pauling then took strong issue with her characterization of the reasons men go to war. "That passage," he chided, "reflects an automatism, a determinism unworthy of her thinking and style; it could have been written by one who knew nothing of the human heart and who denied the soul. It could not have been written by Charles Péguy; perhaps it should not have been written by Dorothy Day."

That the editor of a major Catholic publication had no problem with a permanent draft and the sight of an entire generation of young men donning uniforms and preparing for a war with the Soviet Union suggested to Dorothy just how effective American propaganda had been and how uncommitted the Church was to pacifism. This is not to suggest that she was naive about the heinous leadership of Joseph Stalin or indifferent to the suppression of religion in Eastern Europe. But it was maddening that a nation that had produced Tolstoy and Chekhov, Tchaikovsky and Berdyaev was being caricatured in broad strokes as a barbarian culture alien in every way to the "free world," a "free" world in which Great Britain and France had still not granted their colonies independence and the United States was intent on becoming an imperial power with a lock on Saudi oil. "If we could achieve a better understanding of Russia," she remarked to Hélène Iswolsky, "a great love, what a tremendous contribution to peace that would be." Iswolsky couldn't have agreed more. She was teaching Russian literature at Fordham University (a position that did not survive the worsening Cold War climate in the 1950s) and enthusiastically offered to teach a course on the major Russian writers at the Newburgh farm, an offer Dorothy was pleased to accept then and several more times over the years.

In addition to the usual names, Iswolsky talked in her seminar about one writer who captured her friend's heart, the Russian mystic, poet, intellectual, and confidant of Fyodor Dostoevsky, Vladimir Solovyov. Outspoken in his opposition to anti-Semitism and capital punishment (in tsarist Russia, of all places) and almost exiled to Siberia for urging that the assassins of Tsar Alexander II be shown mercy, he was a fresh voice in Russian spirituality even in a country known for its original thinkers. Dorothy was particularly taken with his book *The Meaning of Love*. Like Iswolsky, Solovyov was a believer in an ecumenical approach to Christianity who hoped one day to see a reconciliation between the Russian Orthodox and Roman Catholic churches, a cause of great interest to Dorothy as well.

Erudite and sociable, Iswolsky was an intellectual mainstay in Dorothy's life in this period. Back in the city, she occasionally took Dorothy to the

Byzantine liturgy at St. Michael's, a Russian Orthodox church on Mulberry Street, and proudly introduced her to one of her mentors in exile in New York, the irascible Alexander Kerensky.

Kerensky was a has-been of history, and there were some who thought the same of Dorothy, who were prepared to relegate the Catholic Worker to a footnote in US and religious history. With understandable pique, Dorothy felt defensive about that perspective whenever she encountered it or thought she encountered it. John Cogley published a reminiscent essay about Mott Street, "Storefront Catholicism," in *America* in the summer of 1948, which she took to be a statement that the glory days of the Catholic Worker had passed. (In fairness, Cogley's article does not read that way today.) The newspaper's circulation was certainly not on the rise, though, and better-paying speaking engagements had dropped off. In the eyes of her critics, she was becoming, as her granddaughter wrote in her family memoir, the "batty aunt" of the American Catholic Church.

Ironically, if Dorothy was at the moment, from any quarter, being dismissed as a figure from another era, she was still someone notable people wanted to meet. That fall, Evelyn Waugh was in New York for a week as he began an extended lecture tour. The cream of the city's Catholic society showed up at the Plaza Hotel or invited him to their Park Avenue apartments. Introductions were provided by way of an impeccable source, Clare Boothe Luce, the Catholic wife of Henry Luce, the editor in chief of *Time* and *Life*. But Waugh had also been instructed by his friend and spiritual adviser back home, Father Martin D'Arcy, "to [go to] the slums," as he explained to his wife, "to see Dorothy Day, an autocratic ascetic who wants all of us to be poor, and her young men who are poor have a paper called 'Catholic Worker' and a soup kitchen." Arrangements were made for a luncheon he would host for her and any Catholic Workers she wanted to bring with her, a group that included Stanley Vishnewski and Tom Sullivan.

"Perhaps to tease, perhaps with misplaced benevolence," Waugh's biographer Martin Stannard, wrote, "he invited her to the best restaurant in town." When Dorothy heard where he had made reservations, she begged off, apologizing for her "class consciousness"—"Chambord's is as formidable to me as 115 Mott Street is to you"—and convinced Waugh to compromise with a simple Italian restaurant on Mulberry Street. He was game. In the Luces' chauffeur-driven Cadillac, the author of *Brideshead Revisited*, a devoted Tory, went to Little Italy for a tour of the house and a close-up look at "the radicals." He wouldn't compromise on the fact that lunch had to include cocktails and wine, and they stayed at Angelo's talking until four in the afternoon.

Stannard continued: "Waugh encountered in Mrs. [sic] Day a personality as tough and autocratic as his own, yet infinitely less selfish—a disarming combination. Confronted by this genuine ascetic whose entire working life was devoted to practical charity, he discovered a more sympathetic version of [a close friend's] argument: that the aims of Christianity and capitalism were fundamentally opposed. It was not an idea he cared to ponder for long, but he retreated to the Plaza somewhat chastened." Waugh did, however, send a check when he returned to England, and at a later date he instructed Frank Sheed to send Dorothy the royalties he was owed for an essay.

The "batty aunt" still had some fight in her, and a fight could be simultaneously frustrating and rejuvenating. In December 1948, the 240 grave diggers of Calvary Cemetery in Queens, members of the Local 293 of the International Food, Tobacco, and Agricultural Workers Union, went out on strike against their employers, the trustees of St. Patrick's Cathedral, who included, of course, Cardinal Spellman. A smaller group from another cemetery went out on strike in sympathy. The men worked hard, a six-day week for $59.40 a week, and their principal demand was to work a five-day week for the same salary with overtime a part of their new contract. A six-day week, if Saturday was now considered overtime and the archdiocese insisted that working on Saturday was essential because of the number of graves that had to be opened—would cost the archdiocese $77.25 per man. The trustees, who did not initially involve the cardinal, said that was out of the question. As their paychecks stopped, some of the men came to the Catholic Worker looking for counsel, support, and, for the more financially strapped, food. Catholic Workers took food directly to the homes of some of the most desperate men, who were worried about feeding their children, joined their picket line, and attended their strike relief committee meetings.

Once he was involved, Spellman not only refused to meet with the striking grave diggers—he did meet once with some of the wives, who described it as a very frustrating session—but implied that their union was under Communist influence, which made everything about their actions illegitimate. He made it clear that there was nothing to negotiate, and if the men did not return to work by the end of January, he would break the strike. He told the press that he would have no problem doing that. A month later, with more than a thousand coffins piled up at the cemetery under tarpaulins, that was just what it came to. The cardinal called in seminarians from Yonkers, a few of whom were sons of the men out on strike, and told them to cross the picket lines and dig the graves. He was on hand to be photographed as that took place. Within days, the nervous men returned to work with little to show for their efforts: a five-dollar-a-week raise with the six-day schedule still in place and a new union affiliation, the American Federation of Labor (AFL), as the cardinal had insisted that each man take an oath that he was not a Communist and would have nothing more to do with the International Food, Tobacco, and Agricultural Workers Union. Reading about it in the paper, the angry Ernest Hemingway sent Spellman a snippy letter.

In her own letter to Cardinal Spellman before the strike ended, Dorothy beseeched him to remember that the strikers were asking not only for increased wages and improved working conditions but for "their dignity as men, their dignity as workers, and the right to have a union of their own, and a right to talk over their grievances." She also pointed out that the wage increase they were asking for was not large and that the men had not accepted the help offered to them by the representatives of the Communist Party of America. She ladled out the praise, hoping that as "the outstanding Cardinal of the Church in America, a diplomat, a confidant and advisor of Pope and President . . . a Prince of the Church, and a great man in the eyes of the world," he would consider their appeal and at least agree to speak with them. "I do beg you so with all my heart to go to them . . . as a father to his children," she wrote. There was no response, ever.

We can be sure there was a response from those in the archdiocese who heard about the letter or who followed the Catholic Worker's position in the paper: on certain topics, this woman, this ex-Communist, was not, many Catholics felt, a sufficiently dutiful daughter of the Church.

Legend has it that Dorothy herself joined in the picketing of the cathedral or the Chancery offices. In fact, the three Catholic Workers marching with signs in their hands were the intrepid Irene Naughton; Mike Kovalak, the son of a coal miner and a somewhat unstable ex-Benedictine who had been with Dorothy for several years (often exhorting her to help him gain readmission to the seminary); and Helen Adler, a recent college graduate and newcomer to the movement. The trio notified a priest in the cathedral beforehand of their intentions; he told them to follow their conscience on the matter, and they then went into the cathedral to pray. It was not the most dramatic of episodes, but a statement was made. If the cardinal was bothered by anything, it wasn't three protestors; it was Dorothy's tart words in print in the April issue of the paper in which she summarized her view of the situation. The cardinal himself had suffered "a loss in dignity" in the debacle, she wrote. He had the sense to say nothing, though. Julia Porcelli, always one to look on the positive side, considered the cardinal's forbearance a sign of his wisdom and character. Others thought he was being merely crafty. No prelate wanted to go on record now as an opponent of the Catholic Worker, however disapproving he might be behind the scenes.

Dorothy's letter and editorial were in a sense about more than one strike and one prelate. They were an expression of disappointment with the state of Catholicism in America. Where in the United States was there a cardinal like Great Britain's Henry Manning in the nineteenth century, whose heart—and voice—were known by all to be with the working class and who had argued that if there were such a thing as a just war, surely there was such a thing as a just strike? The midwestern Depression-era bishops, such as John McNicholas and Hugh Boyle, who had been early supporters of the Catholic Worker, were nearing the end of their days (both died in 1950). They were a different and altogether too-rare breed.

For a good part of that year, Dorothy found herself in a discontented state of mind, with her anger spiraling out in many directions: at her daughter's worsening situation, at the problems at the house (at one point there wasn't even money for coffee), at the values of postwar America, at the sheer obstinacy of the Church hierarchy.

The sorrow and guilt Dorothy felt about her daughter's situation was never so much as hinted at when she wrote in her columns about the Hennessys and their life on the farm. The Hennessys' existence might have been a Laura Ingalls Wilder tale, full of challenge and triumph, as far as the readers of The Catholic Worker knew. The truth burst forth in a startling letter, though, that Dorothy wrote after one of her less pleasant visits to West Virginia. She took out her frustrations on Tamar when her daughter told her that she couldn't stand her desolate farm life any longer and wanted to find a place to live on Staten Island. What followed were pages of ire and recrimination. Staten Island was out of the question, she told Tamar, as the rents were nothing the Hennessys could afford and she had no money to help them. There wasn't even room for them in the house on Mott Street. Dorothy had asked about the possibility of work for David at various bookstores in Manhattan, but no one was hiring, and she doubted he would be able to keep the job if he had one. In effect, she was saying: you have made your bed, now lie in it.

Then Dorothy launched into a severe critique of her daughter's character flaws: "No matter what one does for you, you are not grateful. . . . You have been helped ever since your marriage. You have had the fruits of my toil"— and the only results had been scenes and self-pity.

"A few people may have fed you the idea that you were abused and neglected [as a child]," but, her mother charged, Tamar's life with the Worker had been full of contacts with people and privileges for which she should feel some gratitude and obviously didn't. She was tired of complaints and criticism and temper tantrums when she was visiting in West Virginia. More startlingly, she accused her daughter of not encouraging and loving her husband enough. She closed by saying that she wouldn't write again until Tamar made up her mind "to make the best of things, do [her] share in the marriage, and quit complaining." It was a missive her daughter saved all her life and that marked the lowest point in a troubled relationship.

Unrest at home, unrest on the national scene: *The Catholic Worker* continued to document incidents of racial violence and discrimination, from the case of the Groveland Four (a repeat of the Scottsboro boys' travesty of justice) to the fact that most Catholic parishes were making no effort whatsoever to integrate their congregations. Yet, to Dorothy's dismay, no matter how outspoken her journalism, nothing seemed to change. The articles that the paper printed in 1949, such as David Mason's "Jesus Christ or Jim Crow?," could have been published in 1933.

Foreign policy presented an equally dire picture. In 1949, the nation was unnerved by the explosion of an atomic bomb by the Soviets and the victory of the Communists under Mao Zedong in taking control of China, a development rife with recriminations in Congress and from the press about who was responsible for the "loss" of China, as if the impoverished and badly governed nation under Chiang Kai-shek had been something the West could consider a safe part of its sphere of influence, something that actually could be "lost" to the enemy. The Vatican responded with a decree excommunicating all Catholics who belonged to the Communist Party. Congressman Richard Nixon promised to expose the "Red spies" who were infiltrating the United States. Loyal Americans were supposed to be reassured that Nixon and J. Edgar Hoover were on the case.

The silencing that year of Father Clarence Duffy, who had been aligned with the Catholic Worker off and on for more than a decade, was not unconnected to the fear the Church had of seeming to be out of step with the times in that regard. Duffy's outlook was akin to that of the post–World War II French "worker priests" who had abandoned their rectories and lived among the proletariat, taking jobs in factories by their side. He believed that to be a left-wing, rough-and-tumble political priest rather than a parish priest was not a bad thing. In New York and Boston, he took to the podium regularly, even when Communists shared the platform. He was "not coming out in favor of bingo," as Dorothy put it, but lacing into big business, strike-breakers, and segregationists.

Yes, Father Duffy was a truculent personality, Dorothy freely admitted, a person almost impossible to get along with. He drove everyone at the Catholic Worker mad. He thought the Catholic Worker was too timid and conservative. Not surprisingly, his superiors wanted him off the public speaking platform. The image of a priest having an egg thrown at him by a heckler or assaulted by a mob attempting to rip off his Roman collar, which did happen, was nothing any prelate wanted to see in the morning paper. Dorothy wrote two lengthy articles for *The Catholic Worker* supportive of Duffy and reflecting on the tension between conscience and obedience, which every Catholic must feel. It required a balancing act. A priest, of course, had even less leeway than a Catholic Worker when it came to challenging hierarchical authority.

It was a bad year, on the whole, the dismal end to a painful decade, and it involved still more pain with the death of Peter Maurin.

On May 15, 1949, Peter died at the Newburgh farm. He had been looked after with great care and affection toward the end, especially by Tom Sullivan and Mike Kovalak. Theresa Weider of the Rochester house had taken him in for a winter, and he had been kept warm and well-fed. Tamar, who knew all of Peter's quirks and faults and still loved him as the one grandfatherly figure in her life, went with David to visit him in Newburgh whenever she could. John Filligar would shave him, and Father John Faley—a formidable personality and another recovering alcoholic priest from the city who was staying on the farm that year—saw to it that he regularly received Communion. He finally became incontinent and unable to speak. "He had not smiled for months [before the end]," Dorothy later wrote. "There had only been a look of endurance, even of pain, on his face."

When the end came, he was surrounded by several people praying for him and attempting to make him comfortable. He began coughing, tried to lift his head from his pillow, fell back, and began breathing heavily. Then it was over. He was tenderly dressed in a suit from the clothing donation room and laid out for the night, surrounded by flowers, in the conference room where he had led so many "clarification of thought" evenings, and then taken down to New York.

The news reached Dorothy at an already emotional moment. She heard about Peter's death while she was staying with Bill and Dorothy Gauchat at the Cleveland Catholic Worker farm, on her way back from attending the funeral in Missouri of Larry Heaney, one of the Workers she—and everyone—most admired. Heaney had worked at the Milwaukee house, spent time at Maryfarm, refused to serve in the war, and with his wife and six very young children started the Holy Family Farm in rural Missouri. If ever there was a Worker who lived Peter Maurin's doctrine of forsaking all personal comfort so as to better help the needy, he was it. John Cogley wasn't the only person willing to call Heaney the one true saint in their midst. He had contracted pneumonia and died of a lung abcess at the age of thirty-six.

When Dorothy arrived back home, she was bowed by sorrow but moved by Peter's appearance and the loving services. He looked "like granite, strong, contemplative, set for eternity," she said. His agony belonged to the past. Several priests were present in the house through the day, leading mourners in saying the rosary, and several more attended the funeral down the street at the Church of the Transfiguration. His pallbearers were Arthur Sheehan, Bob Ludlow, David Mason, John Filligar, Marge Hughes's husband, Joe, and Hazen Ordway, a young man devoted to Peter who had served jail time during the war as a conscientious objector. Julia Porcelli, Ade Bethune, and Stanley Vishnewski, three people who had known him for almost all of his time at the Catholic Worker, were there amid a huge crowd from Mott Street, Newburgh, the neighborhood, and Worker houses in other cities. Peter was buried in St. John Cemetery in Queens, in a plot provided by a Dominican priest who knew him, Father Pierre Conway, who offered up his own space in the Conway family plot.

It might have been a surprise to some people that Peter Maurin was better known than they realized and more widely respected. The *New York Times* acknowledged his death, as did a brief notice in *Time*, perhaps through Clare Boothe Luce's influence. The Vatican newspaper, *L'Osservatore Romano*, also made mention of his passing.

Peter's death meant rather less to the young people on Mott Street or in Newburgh who hadn't known him in his prime. Dorothy's insistent statements that he was the one responsible for any good the Catholic Worker had done in the world were always taken with a grain of salt. It was obvious to everyone that Peter never would have managed to keep a newspaper or a house of hospitality going, that he was too scattered, too given to wanderlust. Yet Dorothy was right in demanding that primacy be given to inspiration. Without Peter, it never would have occurred to her to attempt to start a newspaper, open a house of hospitality, become a spokesperson for a new path in life.

While Peter was alive, Dorothy and those who believed unequivocally in Peter's greatness—Sheehan, Sullivan, Porcelli, Bethune, Ordway, Marge Hughes—felt that they were privileged to live in the presence of a latter-day St. Francis of Assisi. Peter could be irritating, exhausting, and confusing, but he was a perpetual reminder that their mission was not at its heart about politics, labor, or even the alleviating of suffering; rather, it was about joy in poverty, renunciation, love for all humanity, the example of the saints, and an unreserved commitment to God. The Catholic Worker was, in its essence, a Franciscan movement. With her Prince Myshkin gone, that burden of reminder fell exclusively on Dorothy's beleaguered shoulders.

Dorothy's final arrest, protesting with striking farm workers in California, 1973.

Courtesy of Bob Fitch Photography Archives, Department of Special Collections, Stanford University Library

Dorothy and her sister, Della, c. 1910.

Dorothy and her brothers, Donald and Sam, c. 1899.

Dorothy reading at home, c. 1912.

Dorothy (*center*) in 1917, holding a copy of *The Call* opposing the U.S. involvement in World War I.

Dorothy and Forster Batterham on Staten Island.

Dorothy reading to Tamar, c. 1930.

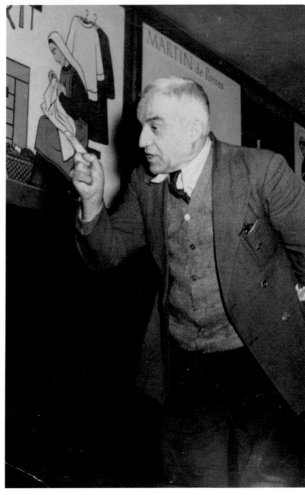

Peter Maurin, the French vagabond-intellectual whom Dorothy credited with founding *The Catholic Worker*.

Readers of *The Catholic Worker* in Union Square in the 1930s.

Ade Bethune's woodcut illustrations of the Works of Mercy for *The Catholic Worker*.

With anti-Semitism on the rise in 1939, *The Catholic Worker* was at pains to remind its readers of the bonds that linked Judaism and Christianity.

Outside the *Catholic Worker* office on Mott Street: John Cort, left; and Julia Porcelli and Stanley Vishnewski on the right.

Ammon Hennacy protesting the nuclear arms race, c. 1957.

Cold War protest: Dorothy and other Catholic Workers arrested for refusing to participate in nuclear air-raid drills.

Dorothy on the balcony of Saint Joseph House on Chrystie Street. *Photograph by Robert Lax, courtesy of the Robert Lax Literary Trust*

At work in the offices of *The Catholic Worker*, reading copy, in the 1960s.

Dorothy with her grandchildren
in Vermont in the 1960s.

Dorothy in Red Square
on her trip to the Soviet
Union in 1972.

Dorothy walking in the woods at Tivoli
in the 1970s. *Courtesy of Bob Fitch Photography
Archives, Department of Special Collections, Stanford
University Library*

away at 223 Chrystie Street, just south of Houston Street. It was a five-story brick building—as was the case at Mott Street, two buildings that had been made into one—with a ground floor that could house the business office, a kitchen, and a dining room accommodating fifty people at a time. The second floor had room for the editorial offices and the large open hall where the rosary could be said every noon and Compline every evening and the Friday-night discussion sessions could be held. There was a paved courtyard in the back, three upper floors for bedrooms for those who lived in the house (about forty people at this time), and a New Orleans–style balustrade across the front porch. A statue of St. Joseph was placed on the porch as soon as the moving was complete. With oil heat and more bathrooms than they were used to, Dorothy was afraid they would all be spoiled, she told Ammon Hennacy. The neighbors on Chrystie Street weren't as tolerant as the neighbors on Mott Street had become at the sight of the men and women who lined up every morning or banged on the doors at night in a stupor, but eventually a truce was established. In May, they settled in with the usual disparate, troubled crowd, including a black Caribbean family who couldn't find housing for themselves and their eight children, who ranged in age from six months to eighteen years.

At the same time, Dorothy was in the midst of what proved to be a protracted effort to sell the Newburgh farm. It was too far from the city, it wasn't attracting the number of retreatants she had hoped it would, and the noise of planes landing and taking off from the nearby Stewart Air Force Base was getting worse. She looked hopefully, once again, to her beloved Staten Island.

The farm she found after not too much hunting and purchased for $16,000 was twenty-two acres that came with a ten-room farmhouse, a barn, a pond, and plenty of room for a garden. Dorothy was determined that every effort should be made to ensure that it wouldn't degenerate into the madness that had plagued Maryfarm. On balance, then—strenuous and nerve-wracking as buying and selling property and moving everyone about could be—the Catholic Workers could feel by the end of 1950 that they had found not one but two safe harbors. For the moment. But, then, everything was "for the moment" with the Worker.

In October, the first Mass was said at the Peter Maurin Farm. Dorothy couldn't wait to organize regular Sunday retreats there, indifferent to the fact that the number of young people from Manhattan willing to come over on those occasions had dwindled to a very few. They didn't want to be chided for their barhopping, their sexual urges, their failure to fast. The retreat was more an expression of Dorothy's need, not theirs. Still and all, she felt a sense of accomplishment. The Worker's coffers might have been emptied, but St. Joseph would come to its aid and the future didn't necessarily look grim.

It was an ominous year, though, for civil liberties in America. Herb Block, the brilliant *Washington Post* cartoonist, coined the word "McCarthyism," drawing it as a label on a barrel of tar after the Wisconsin senator made headlines with his notorious concoction of charges about 205 Communists in the State Department. The Internal Security Act of 1950, also known as the McCarran Act, was passed over President Truman's veto, mandating an array of restrictions on US members of the Communist Party, including foreign travel, and the New York State Legislature passed the Feinberg Law, later upheld by the Supreme Court, permitting the firing from teaching jobs of members or allies of the Communist Party. College campuses across the country began to tailor their lists of acceptable outside speakers to the temper of the times. The threat to academic freedom was of particular concern to *The Catholic Worker*'s editorialists. Once universities restricted the content of speech, there would be no forum for the loyal opposition, but conformity of opinion was exactly what the government wanted, Dorothy felt.

Those who insisted that the Catholic Worker's outlook on the world situation was, as always, absurdly naive felt that they had plenty of evidence to support their anxieties. North Korea's invasion of South Korea in the summer of 1950 and the Chinese invasion of Tibet brought back memories of a Nazi juggernaut that had not been stopped in time. When Governor Dewey of New York argued for mobilization and the registering of all seventeen-year-olds, male and female, he wasn't considered an alarmist, any more than New York City mayor Vincent Impellitteri was when he pledged before the Senate Armed Services Committee that the 6 million residents of his city were ready to stand by their posts and would not evacuate in the event of a nuclear strike. Had His Honor been in favor of evacuation, where those millions were to go remained anyone's guess.

To argue that that entire way of thinking was wrong came at a price. To suggest that the United States' interest in South Korea was more tied to its investments there than to any real concern for the country's people, especially its poor people, was "to run the risk of being accused of using Communist propaganda," Dorothy acknowledged in a letter to the editor of *Commonweal* in December, responding to an article in that magazine about the need for national defense. But she had heard enough. She had heard enough about us versus them, about "the free world" and preserving our "way of life" at any cost and about national defense. "I would say that our way of life, as we are living it, is not worth saving," she wrote in one of those clipped sentences designed to provoke her audience. The United States as an armed fortress, as the arms supplier to the world, as a nation that could live with the idea that a nuclear war was winnable, as a society that allowed racial segregation and thought that the Beatitudes were just pleasing rhetoric: there was no reason to think that this was a prize worth killing and dying for. John Cogley, now an editor at *Commonweal*, strongly disagreed but printed the letter.

The problem with expressing such thoughts was not so much that the generally liberal readers of *Commonweal* would be shocked but that the image of the American Catholic Church would be tainted in the eyes of the Vatican, more conservative Catholics, and Protestant Americans. A few months later, Dorothy heard from the archdiocese. The end of Cardinal Spellman's patience had evidently been reached. His chancellor, Monsignor Edward Gaffney, asked Dorothy to come to his office, where she was presented with a simple ultimatum: the paper would have to change its name or cease publication. Too many people were assuming that it was a newspaper approved by the Church hierarchy, that the more extreme opinions expressed in its pages were those of the Church, and that mistaken perception could not be allowed to stand.

Gaffney's demand caused considerable consternation downtown. Michael Harrington, a young man new to the house and the paper, urged her to dig in her heels. Jack English suggested adding a box to the first page of the paper reading "Published Without Ecclesiastical Approval." The letter Dorothy ended up writing to the Chancery pleased no one on the staff. Everyone found the tone obsequious. Bob Ludlow and Irene Naughton thought it humiliating.

"First of all, I wish to assure you of our love and respectful obedience to the Church," Dorothy wrote, "and of our gratitude to this Archdiocese, which has so often and so generously defended us from many who attack us." She noted that although the title of the paper had been the same for eighteen years, she would be glad to receive criticism or even disciplinary caution for any future theological errors. She pointed out that *The Catholic War Veteran* made use of the same religious adjective, but no one assumed that the views expressed in that publication were those of the archdiocese. She feared that the enemies of the Church would find ammunition in any change in the status of the paper, as such a development would be perceived by everyone as censure. She promised to be "less dogmatic, more persuasive, less irritating, more winning" in the future. Dorothy knew what she was doing. Monsignor Gaffney did not respond. The matter ended there, the awkward subject never to be raised again.

Dorothy's relations with the hierarchy in general were in an odd state. For some prelates, she was now persona non grata; Charles Buddy, the bishop of San Diego, forbade nuns in his diocese to attend her lectures. For others, she was more ambiguous. Whenever she was in Los Angeles, as she was in 1950, she would always visit Archbishop McIntyre—the monsignor who had been her contact with the archdiocese in New York back in the 1930s— and he was invariably gracious, warmly encouraging her in her work. She quite liked him. At the same time, he was equally discouraging to anyone who attempted to do the same in his own archdiocese. He'd ask her about Father Clarence Duffy as if he were an old, admired friend of his, yet he'd reprimand the Catholic activists who worked to overturn California's miscegenation law, and he had no use for Dorothy's friend the progressive Father H. A. Reinhold. Dorothy never knew what to make of those inconsistencies, and it is hard to believe that the archbishop was entirely sincere in his regard for Dorothy. He was a political man, in any case.

Approval from men and women of stature in the world was never something Dorothy took for granted, and it offset the mixed messages received from the Church. When the psychiatrist Karl Stern published his remarkable memoir, *The Pillar of Fire*, in 1951, he singled out Dorothy Day and Jacques Maritain as the two people who had meant the most to him as he had grappled with an inner spiritual struggle that had taken him from a German Jewish childhood in pre-Nazi Germany to a life as a Canadian émigré, renowned Freudian analyst, and convert to Catholicism. Stern had met Dorothy in Montreal when she visited Tamar in school there in 1941, and after the war he visited St. Joseph House on trips to the United States and came away convinced that her work among the poor was a mark of deep holiness. He was also aware that Dorothy took to heart the hierarchy's lack of support and urged her to ignore any insensitivity on the part of the bishops ("most of them have always been like that") and know that among the simple priests and nuns he knew in Québec, she and Peter were revered figures.

In turn, Dorothy was supportive of Stern when he faced the inevitable backlash for writing about his abandonment of the faith of his fathers. "You must suffer terribly over the controversy among the Jews," Dorothy wrote to him. "I do feel for you. But thank God you wrote it. You had to. You were inspired, I know. It is a beautiful book of calm and peace. Everyone I know is reading it." She was there for him, too, when his son committed suicide (she went immediately to Montreal) and in dark moments when he felt his faith weakening, just as he was for her when she needed someone she trusted to let her write freely about her own weaknesses and fear of failure. Theirs was a correspondence between loving confidants and intellectual equals.

Likewise, though on a less intimate level, when Jacques Maritain came to Mott Street again in 1950, Dorothy basked in the glow of his good opinion of her. She liked to attend Hélène Iswolsky's Manhattan salon, which Iswolsky called the Third Hour, where she was welcomed by fellow discussion participants such as Alexander Kerensky and W. H. Auden. The poets Allen Ginsberg, Ned O'Gorman, and William Everson, who became Brother Antoninus when he joined the Dominicans in 1951, were admirers. When she stayed with Caroline Gordon and Allen Tate on a trip to Minnesota, where Tate was teaching, she knew she was in the company of two people who had come to feel an enormous respect for her. That stopover was in the midst of a trip that was probably a record even for Dorothy—from Maine to North Dakota, twenty-seven cities in two months, she proudly noted in her column.

Asked once by a new arrival about the turnover of Catholic Workers at the house and the paper, Dorothy commented, "This is a school. No one's meant to stay here forever." Some people remained for months, others for years, but except for Stanley Vishnewski, no one spent an entire lifetime at the

Catholic Worker. The positive side of that fact was that fresh faces, and the idealism and energy that came with them, were needed from time to time, and, as it happened, they always did turn up. Some came from very unlikely families. Paulina Sturm was the daughter of Alice Roosevelt Longworth, a granddaughter of Teddy Roosevelt, and a recent convert in her twenties.

In 1951, a young man from the Midwest volunteered his services at 223 Chrystie Street. Twenty-three years old, Michael Harrington had grown up in St. Louis, the city that had the distinction during the Depression of being home to the largest Hooverville in the country, though his own background was comfortably middle class. Jesuit educated, he was a graduate of the College of the Holy Cross in Worcester, Massachusetts, where G. K. Chesterton was regarded as a demigod, and a Yale Law School dropout with an MA in English from the University of Chicago. He had literary ambitions, newfound left-wing political beliefs, and a sometimes wavering but at the moment steady faith. He liked what he had heard about Dorothy Day. "All I knew of the Catholic Worker when I walked into its House of Hospitality was that it was as far Left as you could get within the Church," he later commented. For two years, it was a good fit.

Harrington was an asset to the paper from the day he arrived. He was a voracious reader, a quick writer, and someone Ludlow, Naughton, and Sullivan could work with. He could write a political column or review a book by Hannah Arendt, Martin Buber, Karl Stern, or the French philosopher Gabriel Marcel with equal facility, and he was as interested in literature as religion and politics, ably reviewing Ralph Ellison's *Invisible Man*, a new book of poetry by Dylan Thomas, and an edition of the letters of Sherwood Anderson. He was also a perfect "click" with Dorothy, as everyone at the house noticed: good-looking, bookish, conversationally glib, skilled at public speaking, and polite in the way of a well-brought-up parochial schoolboy but never fawning. His values were right, too: anti-Franco, anti–birth control, personalist, and, while he was at the Worker, dutiful in his churchgoing. Dorothy could take his ribbing, sometimes. He liked to ask her when she converted the world to organic farming communes on the Worker model, how she planned to deal with the billions of people on the planet who'd starve to death.

Beneath the irreverence was a deep admiration. Having floundered for some time after college, Harrington was proud to be associated with a woman willing to take the stage at Carnegie Hall with I. F. Stone and other left-wing radicals at a peace congress to attack the Internal Security Act and the police state that the United States was becoming. Here was a mentor willing to speak up for Elizabeth Gurley Flynn when she was arrested under the Alien Registration Act, also known as the Smith Act, targeting undesirable "subversives." She had the force of character to write to President Dwight D. Eisenhower and Cardinal Spellman urging clemency for Ethel and Julius Rosenberg and to address a Communion breakfast of hundreds of Gimbel's employees at a Midtown hotel when she knew beforehand the skepticism and impatience she'd be met with. That particular breakfast was followed by a vintage Dorothy Day moment. She left the Biltmore Hotel to attend Mass at a nearby church. To her astonishment, immediately after Communion, the organist launched into the national anthem. The congregation stood and sang. Dorothy knelt.

When Ammon Hennacy finally arrived in New York, after he and Dorothy had engaged in a long, affectionate correspondence, he roomed with Michael Harrington, an experience that proved to be Harrington's sorest trial at the Worker. Hennacy loved to rag the young socialist he shared quarters with. He himself had long since abandoned his faith in any political organization, and he would needle Harrington, now committed to the Party, with stories he knew of socialists. "When I'd first wake up," Harrington recalled, "I wouldn't open my eyes. I'd first listen to see if he was around because I knew he'd be waiting, just waiting. He would say, 'I knew a socialist in Ohio in 1911 who became a white slaver. I knew a socialist who used to beat blacks.' I mean, he knew every horror story about socialists." He also loved to taunt his roommate about his sensitivity to the bedbugs, an infestation Hennacy claimed had no effect on a hardened old-timer, a real man, like himself.

At bottom, their relationship was a case of two monumental egos sharing the same space, physically and figuratively, both vying for Dorothy's approval, though they had more in common than either would acknowledge, including their ambivalent feelings about Catholicism. Yet there was a key difference concerning the Church: one was coming and the other was going. By the end of 1952, Harrington admitted to Dorothy that he could no longer attend Mass in good conscience. Heaven, Hell, Purgatory—it all seemed too implausible. Hennacy, on the other hand, entered the Church that year, with Dorothy serving as his godmother and Bob Ludlow as his godfather. She had given him a copy of Karl Adam's *The Spirit of Catholicism*, always a persuasive text. Possibly, the godparents were among the few people optimistic enough to think his commitment would last; most observers suspected that it originated in the new convert's romantic interest in Dorothy. Sometime later, Hennacy admitted, "If she had operated the Mormon Worker, I would have become a Mormon."

Yet if Ammon Hennacy's faith in God or the Church was not to be counted on—he was a better Tolstoyan or Gandhian than Catholic, and he did, in fact, leave the Church in the 1960s—his belief in the mission of the Worker was durable, as was his respect for Dorothy. When he was in New York, he both wrote for the paper and regarded himself as its premier newsboy, establishing a posted schedule should anyone want to join him and see how it was done by an expert—a specified time, one day each week, on Wall Street, at Times Square, in front of St. Patrick's Cathedral, on Fordham Road in the Bronx outside the gates of Fordham University, in front of a church on Lexington Avenue whose conservative pastor he loved to bait. He also set a new standard for fasting as a form of protest, feats of endurance that he wasn't shy about advertising, and was as devoted a placard-wielding picketer as could be found on the sidewalks of Manhattan, especially in front of the IRS. Taxes dutifully paid meant a well-funded Pentagon.

Though aware of all of Hennacy's faults, Dorothy had a soft spot for the man, and when others in the house complained about the overbearing ego they had to live with, how Hennacy consumed all the oxygen in every room he occupied, she would answer that he had given up everything in life for his beliefs—he never had any money, possessions, home, or stable family life—and should be left in peace with his huge ego. It was all he had. She knew perfectly well how difficult that ego was to put up with as she struggled to help him edit the several hundred pages of his exuberant but rambling life story, eventually published by the Libertarian Press as *The Autobiography of a Catholic Anarchist*.

Life for the Hennessys continued to be a trial. They gave up on West Virginia, relocated for a time to a suburb of Baltimore, where David found a job for several months, and then moved north to the new Peter Maurin Farm, living in the barn on the grounds for six months before finding their own cottage nearby. Frank Sheed helped out by giving David a job in the mail room at Sheed & Ward; later, he worked as a grave digger and a night watchman, always hoping to keep his mail-order book business going. To anyone who knew them, the prospects for success with the marriage or for David's long-term employment looked equally grim.

In July 1951, Tamar gave birth to her fifth child, Mary, joining Becky, Eric, Susie, and Nicky. The birth of a baby almost always signaled a thaw in relations between mother and daughter, as Tamar needed Dorothy's support and Dorothy was willing to suspend her usual criticisms of her daughter's housekeeping and complaints about her husband. Those complaints about David seemed, even to her, more than justified now. Her son-in-law, she told Jack English, had become a surly man who took no pleasure in his children or home life, while her daughter was becoming "more womanly, more gentle, and grave under it all." There was so much to pray for these days—that Tamar and the children might find their way to some kind of stability, that David might find his way free of the demons that were consuming him, that Ammon Hennacy would be true to the faith he said he was willing to embrace.

There was reason for Dorothy to ponder more rigorously her own path in life and its impact on those around her as she had decided to write a second memoir. As with every book she published, the gap between her intention and the final product was considerable. "When writing in haste for the *Worker*, one gets away with murder," she told Bill Gauchat, explaining why she wouldn't be visiting him at the Worker's Ohio farm that summer as planned. Writing for a New York trade publishing house ("a big bourgeois firm") and an exacting editor was another matter entirely, and a rewrite of her whole manuscript was required. Months were consumed with that task.

Finally, in January 1952, *The Long Loneliness* was published by Harper & Bros. It is the book Dorothy Day is best known for, and it might have brought more people to the Catholic Worker in the next two decades of her life than anything else. Its reach in the long run was vast.

Dorothy had touched on her personal story in *From Union Square to Rome* thirteen years earlier. *The Long Loneliness* provided considerably more anecdotal detail and the same quiet, but more carefully crafted, prose. The fact that the Peter Maurin biography, which she was still working on from time to time, was an unpublishable mess (and would always remain so) suggests either that Dorothy found it easier to write about herself or that her editor had in fact provided useful counsel about shaping and pruning the new manuscript. The memoir still had an unevenness to its flow in parts, as if some of what was included was there because it struck the author simply as what she best remembered and felt like writing about at the time, yet the portrait from childhood through Peter's death and the move to Chrystie Street was vividly textured and, as she intended, inspirational. There was less squeamishness than in her columns about sharing what she had seen over the years: little girls in big cities forced into prostitution by their desperate parents, children in southern shacks competing with dogs for food scraps. Dorothy was also able in the course of the narrative to name and comment on the dozens of Catholic Workers who had helped her bring Peter's vision to life, in New York and elsewhere. Emotional debts were paid with this book as well.

With a brooding cover illustration by Fritz Eichenberg depicting a shattered Mary on the ground near the Cross consoled by an angel and a title phrase describing our time on Earth borrowed from Mary Ward, a seventeenth-century English nun, *The Long Loneliness* aimed to be more than an exercise in autobiography and Catholic Worker history. It raised, implicitly, some of the same questions Dorothy's columns and lectures always had: How much of Christ's message were Christians really willing to accept? How much were they willing to believe with Dostoevsky's Father Zosima in *The Brothers Karamazov* that love is a "harsh and dreadful thing" and, in the end, is all that we will be judged by? If we had cared enough about the poor all along, would we be worrying today about communism and conscience, social unrest, and war?

Dorothy wanted good reviews for the book, and, if nowhere else, there was going to be a glowing one in *The Catholic Worker*. She told Tom Sullivan to assign the task to Michael Harrington. He produced what Sullivan called a "love letter . . . a valentine," extolling the memoir in extravagant terms. The cautious editor talked his friend out of having it printed as written, pointing out that when he looked back on it, he was sure to be embarrassed by its gushing contents. He urged him to submit a review that was largely a respectful plot summary. Harrington had no objections, but Dorothy was nonplussed when it came out. *That*—that piddling review—was supposed to sell books? Sullivan explained the inappropriateness of the original, a reviewer praising his own boss to the high heavens. "You wouldn't want to have that printed in the paper, would you?" Sullivan asked. "And why not?" Dorothy snapped. The review in *America*, tepid at best, was nothing to please her, either.

There was even more reason to be unhappy when Dorothy read Father H. A. Reinhold's review in *Commonweal*, which called the book "a bit weary, disenchanted, repetitious, and rather too meditative." The onetime ally she hadn't seen since the time of the war and their bitter disagreement over pacifism didn't hold back: "The picture is painted by a faint hand and the colors are wan with sadness." He also made reference to the fixation on poverty of the Catholic Worker as "exasperatingly morbid."

On the other hand, Reinhold compared the author to Mahatma Gandhi and noted that she had to be credited with having "opened the portals of the Catholic heart for America to see the Church in a new light." The two old friends made up when he paid a visit to St. Joseph House soon after, and in a later column Dorothy was moved to conclude that Reinhold was a "truly great man." No one who wore the Roman collar had been more outspoken and prescient in warning of the threat the Nazis posed to religion, more devoted to the cause of liturgical reform, more concerned with the Church's adopting a vigorous program of social action.

The secular press was more enthusiastic about *The Long Loneliness*. Day's memoir "would probably horrify anyone who believes the Church should be supported only because it encourages a convenient and tractable orthodoxy," the *Chicago Tribune* critic wrote, praising the book's boldness and honesty. Favorable reviews in the *New York Times* and *Newsweek* were heartening and led the editors of *The New Yorker* to commission one of the magazine's famous two-part profiles on the founder of the Catholic Worker. Yet none of that translated into the kind of sales Dorothy was hoping for. In its first month, the book sold 7,000 copies, and another 2,500 went during the course of the year, adding $2,500 in royalties to the $1,000 Harper & Bros. had given as an advance. Dorothy gave $500 to Tamar and used the rest to pay off several pressing bills.

The *New Yorker* profile, however, meant exposure to an entirely different and much wider audience than Dorothy had ever known before. The writer assigned to the task was Dwight Macdonald, a new staffer well known in

left-wing circles who had once edited *Partisan Review* and his own publication, *Politics*. According to Michael Harrington, some ethical lines were
crossed in seeing the articles into print that the *New Yorker* editors would
have seethed over had they known. Macdonald let Dorothy read his copy
before he submitted it, making what changes she wanted, which included
striking Malcolm Cowley's irritating reference to her drinking habits in the
1920s. "Like so many people," Harrington remembered, "Dwight fell in love
with Dorothy."

Macdonald's opening line, something to cause everyone at the Chancery to sit up, said it all: "Many people think Dorothy Day is a saint and
will someday be canonized." Amid the usual *New Yorker* ads for expensive
Buicks, blended Scotch whiskey, Broadway musicals, French perfume, and
Cartier jewelry, he told the story of Dorothy, Peter, the development of the
Worker, and the varied responses, secular and ecclesiastical, that their actions and outlook evoked. He was at pains to observe that the woman was
not a glibly charismatic figure. "Upon first meeting her," he wrote, "most
people who are familiar with her career are surprised to find, that far from
being dynamic, she is quiet and almost diffident . . . her platform manner is
retiring and hesitant, and she makes not even a stab at rhetorical effect." Yet
she had become a personage. Not long before, Macdonald noted, Mary Heaton Vorse, the labor reporter, had been visiting a patient in a small Catholic
hospital in Indiana, and when the nursing sisters there had learned that she
knew the founder of the Catholic Worker, "they crowded excitedly around
her, eager to hear more about this woman they all knew and admired by
reputation."

Macdonald's profile raised the subject of the Worker's involvement with
labor struggles in the 1930s, which had first brought Dorothy into a contentious relationship with the more conservative elements of secular and
religious society, but acknowledged the shift that had taken place. Dorothy
freely admitted that her enthusiasm for unionization had diminished over
time as she no longer saw most of the leadership behind that cause as genuinely radical, committed to "building a new society within the shell of the
old," in a phrase Peter had often used.

Macdonald also took pains to emphasize the spiritual as much as the
socially progressive aspect of Dorothy's life, lest any of his readers wanted to
see her simply as a more ambitious Mother Jones or Frances Perkins. "For

all her brushes with authority," he noted, "Miss Day is a Catholic first and a radical second." That was something even the young people at the house sometimes forgot. When she remarked, more than once, that if *ordered* to do so by the archdiocese, she would cease publishing the paper, she meant it. To understand Dorothy Day, one had to understand the importance of the Catholic Church to all that she believed in and hoped to accomplish. Macdonald got that right.

Dorothy was on the road when the article came out but heard from friends everywhere what a glowing portrait Macdonald had drawn of her. The imprimatur of *The New Yorker* didn't mean much in some communities, of course. Arriving in the Pacific Northwest, she discovered that a prominent woman in Washington State's Republican Party had circulated a pamphlet definitively "proving" that Dorothy Day was a Communist, a smear campaign that resulted in the cancellation of most of her lecture invitations in the Seattle area. In an election year, she generally did her best to steer clear of politics. To his consternation, Tom Sullivan had to be forcefully reminded that *The Catholic Worker* did not endorse candidates and his editorial backing Adlai Stevenson over Dwight Eisenhower had to go. He could canvass for votes on the street on his own time if he wished, but he had to accept that in terms of party politics, the paper would take no stand. Dorothy was astonished that she had to explain this so often: changes of leadership in the White House had nothing to do with the kind of changes that she and Peter Maurin had envisioned and fought for.

By the 1950s, perspectives on Dorothy Day covered a wide spectrum. To some, she was a frighteningly ascetic woman, obsessed with travel on a shoe-string budget, convinced that fasting and greater self-sacrifice would solve most inner conflicts. Her state of health worried many of her friends. In 1948, she had been hospitalized for an operation, the nature of which was never discussed in her letters or diaries but was probably gynecological, and the first stirrings of arthritis were making themselves felt. Headaches and dental issues were a constant problem, and every winter the flu took its toll. In 1954, she had another surgery for what she feared was uterine or rectal cancer but was a polyp and prolapsis ("painful and agonizing for weeks," she told Jack English). Vacations, of the kind she had once taken to Florida to see her mother, were a thing of the past. To some people, then, on first meeting, she looked bone-tired. Yet to others, she was a figure of remarkable stamina, someone whose energy energized others.

To the members of her family and even some of the Catholic Workers, she appeared a woman of increasingly rigid piety. She refused to hear a critical word about the Lacouture retreats and in 1955 became a Benedictine oblate, or lay adherent to that order's monastic tradition, at the St. Procopius Abbey in Lisle, Illinois. She applauded Pope Pius XII's canonization of the reactionary, antimodernist Pope Pius X in 1954. She considered attending Mass twice a day if time allowed (which it did not). To others, however—even if her robust conversational cursing had gone the way of cigarettes and alcohol—she was an intriguing and formidable personality whose company people vied for. The writer Dan Wakefield, a student at Columbia University in the mid-1950s, found her "quietly imposing" and was impressed by the intellectual caliber of many of the young people around her. By now, no one who met her hadn't heard of her in one context or another and perhaps came with expectations of their own.

The young people Dorothy was surrounded by had heard enough of her Greenwich Village past to gossip about it ceaselessly among themselves. The titillating rumors added to her glamour, a paradoxical attribute for a woman with a widening waistline who dressed in secondhand clothes, and glamour was a quality in desperately short supply on Chrystie Street. In 1953, Eugene O'Neill died, and of course everyone wanted to know if she had been lovers with the most famous playwright of modern times, though no one was imprudent enough to ask point-blank. Hart Crane one could ask about because he was gay, and there was a thrill in pondering that link: it was like knowing your great-grandmother had been intimate friends with Lord Byron or Percy Bysshe Shelley. (Lionel Moise had died in 1952, but his would have been a name unknown to any of the young people at St. Joseph House.) When Agnes Boulton published her memoir of her marriage to O'Neill, *Part of a Long Story*, a few years later, evoking in the pages about Dorothy the image of a sensuous and knowing paramour of the writer, Dorothy might have been irked but her protégés were thrilled. It is also hard to believe that everyone who knew about "Told in Context," the short essay she then wrote concerning her time with O'Neill (unpublished until 2017), took Dorothy at her word that theirs had been a chaste relationship.

A less glamorous reminder of the Village in the 1920s met his death, a particularly ugly one, a few months after O'Neill's passing. Max Bodenheim, the poet and friend of O'Neill with whom Dorothy had spent many evenings at the Hell Hole, had reached the end of his tether. In his sixties, lost to alcoholism, evicted from his apartment, reduced to hawking his poems on the street, he turned to the friend he hadn't seen in many years. Dorothy gave him shelter at the Peter Maurin Farm, along with Ruth, his much younger, outrageously flirtatious third wife, but after a few months they wandered back to Manhattan. There they were taken in one night by a young man who had sex with Ruth in his flophouse room with her husband present and, when both Bodenheims were asleep, shot Max and stabbed Ruth to death, claiming when arrested that he should be rewarded with a medal for having killed two Communists.

The tabloids made the most of the lurid story, printing photos of the bodies of "the last of the garret geniuses" and Ruth. It was an ordeal for Dorothy. "How little we were able to do for Max and Ruth," she wrote in a tender remembrance in *The Catholic Worker*. "The bare bones of hospitality we gave them. If only we loved them more, if Ruth had found more love with us. . . . God must listen to our prayers for them." She speculated—hoped—that the horror of their end might serve as sufficient penance for any sins they had committed and that "the gates of eternity" could then be opened for them.

Thirty years earlier, Max Bodenheim had been a Village bohemian, a recognizable type. In 1950s America, he was just a freak, and the real source of his freakishness wasn't his wife who liked the attention of younger men or his devotion to writing poems few people wanted to read. He was a freak in his indifference to squalor, in his acceptance of poverty on a level that meant periodic homelessness and shabby living. He had turned his back on the American Dream.

It always seemed to come back to poverty, to attitudes toward comfort and destitution. The state had more to say about that than ever, with city inspectors showing up on Chrystie Street more frequently and others questioning why the Catholic Worker wouldn't let the city's social workers and mental hospitals take over the people they were better equipped to handle. The fact of the matter, though, was that many of those the Catholic Worker took in were precisely those whom the system had always failed. They were the people no one wanted to acknowledge.

Indeed, one of the hardest tasks Dorothy found in the course of her travels at that time was to convince her audiences that poverty was still a formidable reality in the United States. Unemployment was low, the economy was strong, and jobs were to be had by those willing to work. The latest consumer products were within the reach of more people than ever before, and the suburbs promised an affordable good life. In Dorothy's eyes, *The Grapes of Wrath* remained a meaningful testament to the need for compassion. For most Americans, it was a hefty text on a high school syllabus.

Even two priests in her audience, she wrote after one of her lectures, spoke up to contest her claim that not everyone was able to share in the postwar bounty. The poor were largely undeserving, they argued. If a man couldn't support a family, he shouldn't have one. Opportunities to pull oneself up by one's bootstraps were plentiful. The sin now, in modern America, wasn't hard-heartedness or indifference to the pain of others, it seemed. The sin was poverty.

FIFTEEN

✦ RESISTANCE ✦

THE 1951 NEW YORK STATE DEFENSE EMERGENCY ACT MANDATED that all New York residents take refuge in one of the state's thousands of air-raid shelters should civil defense drills become necessary. By 1955, the threat of nuclear attack was deemed plausible enough to put that stipulation of the act into effect.

On June 15, when the city's more than six hundred air-raid sirens were sounded at midday, all of New York City's streets and buildings were supposed to be emptied of everyone but police, auxiliary police, relevant government officials, and the elderly and infirm. Though many ambulatory people no doubt remained in their apartments with the blinds drawn, the populace in the main complied. The stock market closed for an hour, though ironically the crowds that packed Yankee Stadium for a ball game were allowed to remain in place as it was thought their numbers would make an evacuation too hazardous. Dorothy, Ammon Hennacy, and a number of others from the Catholic Worker—Stanley Borowsky, Eileen Fantino, Mike Kovalak, Mary Ann McCoy, Carol Perry, Mary Roberts, Pat Rusk, and Helen Russell—did not comply, nor did they hide. (Bob Ludlow, Tom Sullivan, and Michael Harrington were no longer with the Worker. Ludlow, burned out, had left the previous year and would soon leave the Church, Sullivan had entered a Trappist monastery the month before, and Harrington was working with the Socialist Party.) They gathered in City Hall Park with more than twenty friends and colleagues from the Fellowship of Reconciliation and the War Resisters League, including A. J. Muste and the civil rights activist Bayard Rustin, and waited to be arrested.

The Off-Broadway actress Judith Malina was a part of Dorothy's group by happenstance. She had been invited by a friend to join the protest, about which she knew very little. She missed the friend in the park and ran into

Ammon Hennacy, an acquaintance, boisterously distributing his newspaper as usual. He introduced her to "a tall woman, strong-boned and sharply molded," wearing a Hopi cross, her white hair in braids twined over the top of her head. Dorothy Day "won all my heart instantly," she remembered. Malina stayed with the Catholic Worker group.

From the pacifist point of view, the drills were part of a larger problem that had to be publicized and decried: the attempt to normalize the nuclear arms race. That was the true madness of the day. Creating a false sense of security among urban populations that they would have the remotest chance of surviving an attack of that nature, either at the time of the blast or in the devastating weeks and months that followed, was allowing the government and the military-industrial complex to render the unthinkable thinkable and therefore less in need of an immediate solution. That, to people who thought like Day, Hennacy, Muste, and Rustin, was intolerable. The form of the protest itself, Dorothy said, had been Ammon Hennacy's idea. In vintage Hennacy style, he had written to the FBI to let the agency know of the group's plans, including a jocular personal note for J. Edgar Hoover: "We are, as you know, subversives, though openly so."

While the Yankee fans watched the end of their game in peace, the protestors seated on benches in City Hall Park were loaded into police vans, their petition to Mayor Robert Wagner ignored, and kept in cramped cells with no food throughout the day and long evening until they were taken in to night court. An irate judge told them that their actions were potentially murderous, but they were released on bail at three in the morning, though not before Judith Malina was carted off to Bellevue Hospital's psychiatric ward for an examination for having engaged in a cheeky outburst against the judge. It was one of the few times Dorothy would accept bail for a demonstration of her political and spiritual values and agree to see her sentence, when she was later found guilty, suspended. The group was making a statement and wanted publicity and public discussion of their actions. She was relieved, however, not to be spending the summer in jail, as Tamar was about to give birth to her seventh child, Martha, an event she did not want to miss, especially as she knew that David Hennessey's drinking was becoming a more serious problem by the month.

The attention given to their actions probably exceeded the protestors' hopes. Several major newspapers from around the country took note of their arrest, either that week or at the time of the subsequent hearing several weeks later. The front-page headline in the *Baltimore Sun* was pleasingly relevant: DEFIANCE OF DRILL RAISES BIG ISSUES. The attorney for the protestors claimed that the state had violated the group's right to peaceable assembly. Other legal experts noted that the government's authority to abrogate the right to peaceable assembly was legitimate during an actual national emergency, but was a drill an emergency? Not really. Everyone who had been involved in the protest promised to be back on the park benches if the government ordered another drill (which, in fact, happened five more times before the absurd practice ended with a final drill in 1960). They would not participate in state-sponsored "psychological warfare," as the Catholic Worker's statement to the press termed the drills, and they would continue indefinitely to refuse to participate, terming their defiance also an act of penance to Japan for the US attacks on Hiroshima and Nagasaki. The latter observation infuriated more than a few veterans.

The Catholic Worker did not make friends in high ecclesiastical or political places by challenging the Defense Emergency Act, insisting that Truman's decision to drop the bomb had been immoral and delivering a letter to the Japanese consul every August asking forgiveness for the wrong the United States had done in using the bomb. Pronouncements by the Church hierarchy about nuclear armament had always been vague, far from the emphatic anti-nuclear position Dorothy was hoping for. That would have to wait until the next pope and the bracing air of Vatican II. Indeed, the following year, Pope Pius XII issued a statement condemning conscientious objection among Catholics in wartime. If called upon to fight the Communists, the pope asserted, Catholic young men incurred no sin in taking up arms. That, to Dorothy, was a deeply disturbing position. Had the pope been apprised of Dorothy's arrest, he would surely have wanted her reprimanded. Cardinal Spellman had nothing to say. ("Some of the bishops are on your side. I am not committed," he had at one time commented to Dorothy.) *Commonweal* was the only Catholic publication to remark favorably on the value of the Workers' act of civil disobedience. City Hall and the federal government likewise did not look kindly on the protestors.

The following spring brought the inevitable consequence: the IRS reinstituted its longtime harassment of Hennacy on suspicion of owing back taxes and having "hidden assets" (a mirthful proposition to anyone who knew him), and Dorothy received a summons to appear in court on charges of being a slumlord and, after a recent fire at the house in which one man had died of smoke inhalation, of running a facility that was a health hazard. Since June, she had been receiving fines that she had not paid. She had repeatedly asked someone from the city to come to Chrystie Street to better understand the unique purpose and needs of the facility, but no one came. When she showed up to answer the summons, she discovered that there was nothing to explain or argue. An order to vacate the building within a week had already been issued by the city, and furthermore, she was informed that she was being fined $250. Her first thought was to protest the fine and go to jail, but she had to acknowledge that spending time in a cell as a protest was not going to be helpful to the many people at the house who now had to be looked out for.

Once again the press came to the aid of the Catholic Worker, not so much by a direct advocacy of her position but simply by publicizing a newsworthy situation. The city was going after a charitable organization that was serving the most destitute of its citizens and intended to close it down: Who thought that was a meritorious state of affairs? A few days later, on her way back to court to plead for an extension to her eviction notice, Dorothy was approached by a scruffy-looking man. Despite his disheveled appearance, which made her assume at first glance from a distance that he was a new resident at the house, she recognized the craggy face when he came closer. She knew him from Hélène Iswolsky's Third Hour salon evenings. W. H. Auden lived on St. Mark's Place in the East Village and had long been an admirer of Dorothy. He bounded up to her on the street, told her he had read about the fine in the *Times*, and handed her a check for the full $250. Dorothy remarked later that their conversation was rushed and she thought she was being given a check for $2.50. Only on the subway did she discover, to her delight and disbelief, the sum Auden had provided her.

It was a good day in court, too. The judge had read the newspapers and taken the trouble to learn more about what the Catholic Worker actually did and agreed to give it the necessary time to bring the building up to code—and to raise the $28,000 that such work would require, including fireproofing. More than $23,000 came in over the next few weeks as a result of more media attention, especially through the broadcasts of several friendly radio commentators. Some of those funds came, once again, from the same generous British poet, who appeared on a local television quiz show for the express purpose of winning some prize money to send to the Catholic Worker. Wystan Hugh Auden was a wonderfully quirky man, and the *New York Times* gave front-page coverage to the episode.

The adage that any publicity is better than no publicity was not a saying Dorothy subscribed to, though, and certainly not when it pertained to herself, to the particulars of her own life. When Dan Wakefield, just out of college, wrote a laudatory article about the Catholic Worker for *The Nation* in February 1956, entitled "Miracle on the Bowery," he couldn't understand why Dorothy, with whom he thought he'd established a friendship of sorts, wouldn't speak to him when he stopped by. A friend filled him in: he had committed the ultimate faux pas by quoting in his article Malcolm Cowley's remarks from *Exile's Return*. What Wakefield saw as exciting and interesting, an "achievement" that a woman in her younger days could drink some rough-and-tumble Village guys under the table, Dorothy saw as something she never wanted to hear about again. Weeks passed before she warmed to him again.

A similar development, but considerably worse, followed not long after. Caroline Gordon's ninth book, *The Malefactors*, was published in 1956. The months leading up to that novel's release involved some seriously unpleasant fulminations and negotiations. Dorothy had kept abreast of the careers of her old friends, Caroline and her husband, Allen Tate, and been thrilled at their conversion to Catholicism in the 1940s. At the end of the summer of 1955, she visited the couple when they were living in Princeton and attended a reading of Tate's poetry. She probably didn't know then that their marriage was drifting into a difficult place again (they had divorced once before, in 1946, but remarried the following year), a situation that would have distressed her, but she had much more to be distressed about when she first got wind of Caroline's novel.

The first Dorothy heard about it was when Caroline told her she had finished a new book and wanted to dedicate it to her. Dorothy declined the honor and thought no more about it. Soon after, Sue Light, the old friend from the Village who had thwarted her suicide attempt, got in touch. She had been shown the galleys by a friend at Caroline's publishing house,

Harcourt, Brace and Company. She suggested that Dorothy read the book, which she promptly did. Sue had been rather startled by some of what she read and presumably alerted the publisher to the possibility of litigation. What Dorothy read left her speechless.

The novel tells the story of a Lost Generation–era couple struggling to find themselves in middle age, and a fairly banal, meandering tale it is. What mattered, what made Sue Light as well as Caroline Gordon's editor uneasy, was that Dorothy Day was all too obviously the character of Catherine Pollard, a woman who was "unrestrained" in her Greenwich Village days, had once participated in a black Mass, and was now a monomaniacal Catholic, living (as one character put it) like a "medieval abbess, with her own chapel and her own priest and her own butcher and baker." That character in the novel, Marcia Crenfew, expresses great skepticism not only about Pollard's flophouse in the Bowery, which takes in anyone and everyone (Marcia's idealistic daughter wants to work there, and she is afraid the girl will be brainwashed into a cult), but about "Joseph Tardieu," a French-born prophet who preaches a "green revolution" and the benefits of a rural, communal life. When he makes a brief appearance late in the novel, he is a dotty old man.

From Dorothy's point of view, it was hard to know what was more upsetting: that Peter Maurin should be written about as a ridiculous crank or that she should be depicted as debauched and blasphemous in her youth. There was also a suggestion that the Dorothy character was much closer to Hart Crane at his most crazed than Dorothy had ever implied was the case in real life. That she might have been the book's dedicatee was past comprehension. What in the world was Caroline Gordon thinking? she wondered.

Under no circumstances would Dorothy have sued the publisher or the author or tried to halt publication of the book. She made that abundantly clear to everyone. That was not her way. She did indicate her grave displeasure with the parts of the text that dealt with her, she wanted that on the record, and she certainly wanted the mention of participating in a black Mass deleted. (One wonders, naturally, if that was a real feature of the never-to-be-discussed time in unholy Paris in 1921.) She told Caroline's editor that the best solution in her mind would be to burn all the copies, but she knew that wasn't going to happen. The chagrined editor told his author that changes would have to be made. Caroline Gordon was not pleased.

About the emphasis on Hart Crane's homosexuality in the novel, Dorothy commented that it was probably fair and suited Caroline's plot needs, though she herself found regrettable any mention of that "most loathsome of sins." The reference to the "most loathsome of sins" is interesting. Though Dorothy had comfortably socialized with gay men—e.g., Charles Demuth—in New York in her younger days and surely knew about the sexual orientation of W. H. Auden and Bayard Rustin (no secret even then), her beliefs about homosexuality by the 1950s were strictly in line with the most conservative of Church teachings. Homosexuality was not merely a moral lapse, an occasion of sin, an unfortunate condition for a person of faith to have to struggle with, it was "loathsome." The many—very many—gay men and lesbians who worked at the various Catholic Worker houses over the years knew not to raise the subject, which made her uncomfortable.

At the same time, Dorothy liked at odd moments to show that she could be worldlier than the young people around her thought she was, if the moment was a private one. One resident of the farm, John Stanley, recalled a young Italian American man who had fled an abusive family in the city and come to stay in Newburgh for a while. He and one of the Workers, Joe Fratelli, liked to wrestle on the lawn. One day Dorothy saw the two of them sitting shirtless in the summer sun and remarked to John Stanley, in a tone that sounded to him complacent enough, "D. H. Lawrence knew about all that." The famous homoerotic Gerald–Rupert wrestling scene in *Women in Love* hadn't shocked the author of *The Eleventh Virgin*.

The area of secular, political life in which Dorothy was more emphatically in line with the liberal elements of her time had to do with race, not sexual orientation. She had written a column in 1954 with the acerbic title "Southern Hospitality," describing the harassment and arrest in Shreveport, Louisiana, of a New York friend of hers who, on a visit to Louisiana, had shared lodgings with some black friends, and the following year, the murder of Emmett Till was a heinous crime she wanted publicized. She asked Robert Steed, a newcomer to the Worker, to make that the subject of his first article for the paper ("Murder in Mississippi" appeared in the October 1955 issue), and she solicited Dan Wakefield, who had reported on the trial of Emmett Till's murderers for *The Nation*, to lead one of the Friday-night discussion sessions on that topic.

In April 1957, Dorothy went south herself to visit and stay at an interracial farming community in the countryside of southern Georgia. The Koinonia Farm in Americus had been founded several years earlier by a Baptist minister, Clarence Jordan (an uncle of Hamilton Jordan, President Jimmy Carter's White House aide), and had somehow managed to avoid coming to the attention of the more aggressive white residents of the area. By 1956, though, that period of benign neglect was over, and outbreaks of violence were increasing in number and intensity. The farm's market, essential to its survival, was damaged by a stick of dynamite, rifle fire had destroyed the community's fuel pump, some of its hogs had been shot, the farmhouse had been raked with machine-gun fire, and the Ku Klux Klan had paraded by the property and burned two crosses, intimating worse to come. Dorothy wanted to see for herself what the brave people of Koinonia were up against.

Her experience there confirmed her most pessimistic assessment of race in the United States. When she went with the minister's wife to several stores in search of seeds for planting, they were met with brutal invective about "nigger lovers" and "Communist whores." During Easter week, Dorothy took a turn as one of the night sentries at the farm, sitting in a station wagon under a floodlight near the entrance drive. A car sped by in the middle of the night and a shotgun was fired, hitting the vehicle but not its occupants. The solicitor general of the county expressed his view that all of the incidents reported by the Koinonia Farm tenants were fictitious, designed to create sympathy for the farm, and publicly suggested that the use of a buggy whip might stop "race mixers" and Communists from further polluting the state.

Dorothy returned to New York to write at length about her two weeks in Americus, helping with the cooking and meeting the residents, discouraged but impressed with the fortitude of Reverend Jordan, the sixty other members of his community, and their few allies in the neighborhood.

One southern Catholic who should have known better was not especially gracious in her reaction to Dorothy's appearance on behalf of civil rights in her state. "All my thoughts on this topic are ugly and uncharitable," Flannery O'Connor wrote to a friend, "such as: that's a mighty long way to come to get shot at, etc." She professed great respect for Dorothy Day but not enough to exempt her from the disdain she felt for any northern agitators on the race issue.

* * *

Three months later was the occasion for the next nuclear air-raid drill and arrest. Dorothy, Hennacy, and several others including Stanley Borowsky (a participant the year before) and Deane Mowrer, a former college teacher new to the Worker who was gradually losing her eyesight, gathered this time in Washington Square Park. They were duly arrested, declined bail, and spent five days in jail. The protest of the following year, with the arrests taking place on Chrystie Street, was a different matter. The presiding judge meant business, and he had no intention of suspending sentences, as has been the case in 1955, or handing out a five-days-behind-bars slap on the wrist. The sentence was thirty days. The men and women, including Judith Malina and Deane Mowrer, were taken to their respective houses of detention while the one minor who had joined the group, an enthusiast named Karl Meyer, was sent to the juvenile wing at Rikers Island.

It probably hadn't helped Dorothy's cause that an article in *The Catholic Worker* had vehemently defended the *Daily Worker* the year before when the offices of the Communist Party's paper had been illegally padlocked by the IRS for failure to pay taxes, though, in fact, no tax bill had been sent. It certainly didn't do her any good that she, A. J. Muste, and Bayard Rustin had been invited to the annual convention of the Communist Party of America in New York City in February. They had gone as guests of a breakaway faction of the party that was hoping American Communists could distance themselves from Moscow. Party hard-liners were not thrilled about seeing non-Party members at their gathering, but the "special observers" had eagerly accepted the invitation. J. Edgar Hoover's agents took note. The more dangerous any association with communism in the 1950s became, the more Dorothy was inclined to dig in her heels. She could not abide being told what to do by a government that ignored its own Constitution.

Her thirty days in the Women's House of Detention were a hellish experience. There was the vaginal and rectal cavity search, so aggressive that Dorothy had to be treated for excessive bleeding. There was the lack of privacy when using the shower or the toilet. There were the disdainful guards, the noise, the suffocating heat, the nonstop shouted obscenities from the inmates, the ever-present threat of violence. Judith Malina remembered, "We shared a cell. She asked to be put in the cell with me in order to protect me." Some of the obviously lesbian women on their floor had been vocal about their interest in Malina, an attractive thirty-year-old, and wanted her placed with them. One woman was particularly insistent, and Dorothy was adamant that that was not to happen.

A "theologically interesting" coda to this situation, as Malina termed it, developed when Dorothy later heard that the woman, a drug addict, had shot herself after her release. Dorothy wanted everyone at St. Joseph House to pray for the deceased and worried that she should not have interfered with the guards' original plan to place Malina in her cell. It was possible, Dorothy believed, that Malina could have helped her. (Not surprisingly, Malina was uncertain about that vote of confidence.) "Dorothy felt this was a lesson in not interfering. She very much felt it was her fault," Malina wrote, "and said that she should have let me go." Self-protectiveness, or even the desire to protect others, was from that perspective a presumption and a danger. Perhaps God meant us to embrace risk, knowing that it could lead to beneficent results we could never foresee. A person in anguish—meaning "one of the least of these"—meaning Christ himself—had been left to suffering and degradation, failed by more stable people who could have provided a shoulder to lean on. Dorothy wrote her account of that painful episode in the December 27, 1957, issue of *Commonweal*.

Judith Malina recorded in her journal, published three years after Dorothy's death, another aspect of her time with Dorothy in their shared cell. She was struck over the course of the month by Dorothy's manner toward the other women, who started to come by in the evening when their cell doors were opened for a few hours. They wanted to know about the breviary and the rosary beads she had with her. They wanted to tell her their stories, hear about her beliefs and the strangeness of where she lived and with whom she lived. It would appear that Dorothy provided a calming presence on the floor, unpitying and nonjudgmental. "What she did remains the mystery of sanctity," Malina concluded. Her cellmate was also taken with Dorothy's honesty when talking to her about the difficulties of the path she had chosen, how hard it had been to do without marriage, both companionship and intimacy, and how it did not come naturally to her to live with some of the more disturbed people she sheltered downtown. But following one's natural bent was not always what God intended for us, Dorothy seemed to suggest. "Such piety as is hers does not swerve one away from one's own faith," Malina, who was Jewish, wrote. "Rather, in her faith I strengthened my own and through her saw how far a trust in God can take one."

*   *   *

Events of that fall only reinforced Dorothy's sense that her country was on a deadly downward spiral. The launching of Sputnik in October provoked a kind of hysteria across the United States; by November, a second launch by the Soviets with a larger payload suggested to the West that the USSR would have the potential in the not-too-distant future to land nuclear missiles on US soil within thirty minutes of their launch time. The United States' effort to follow suit the next month was a major embarrassment, with its missile rising several feet into the air before exploding and consequently being dubbed in the press "Flopnik," "Stayputnik," and "Kaputnik." The arms race was about to take a different, more worrisome turn, while critics of the escalation such as the Catholic Worker protestors were seen as playing, yet again, into the hands of the Soviets. It was a tired litany by now.

An opportunity to put politics aside for a time presented itself when a priest Dorothy knew in Minnesota, a friend from the 1930s, Father Leo Neudecker, invited her to accompany him and fifteen of his parishioners on a pilgrimage to Mexico City. Their destination was the Shrine of Our Lady of Guadalupe on the outskirts of the capital, the site of an appearance in 1531 of the Virgin Mary to a Mexican peasant, Juan Diego. Like Veronica's veil, the burlap cloak, or *tilma*, Diego wore and filled with miraculously blooming Castilian roses to present to his bishop had been imprinted with the face of the Virgin, who proclaimed herself the protectoress of the Mexican Indians. Diego's *tilma* now hangs behind the high altar of the basilica built on the site of the visitation and, then and now, is one of the most visited shrines in Christendom.

Dorothy met up with her fellow pilgrims in Kansas City and then traveled the rest of the way with them by train. It had been almost thirty years since her sojourn in that troubled country, and this was a chance to see firsthand the extent to which the state's anticlericalism was still in force. "Sad to say," she wrote in her account of the trip for *The Catholic Worker*, "there are huge areas where there are still no priests and the churches have fallen into decay." Some churches had been made into restaurants and garages, and priests wore a tie rather than the Roman collar on the street. Given that ordinations were still not allowed in Mexico, the shortage of priests was an obvious problem.

On the other hand, elsewhere on the journey, she could report that she saw "churches being rebuilt in town after town, and new churches going up." There was reason to assume that the worst had passed. What the trip reinforced most strongly was that it was the people themselves, hungry to keep their faith alive, who had—absent any strong or centralized leadership, in the face of governmental opposition—taken charge of their own fate.

Archbishop Miguel Dario Miranda y Gómez, who had been imprisoned and then exiled during the worst of the anti-Catholic purges of the 1920s, met with Dorothy and Father Neudecker on their last day in Mexico. In the course of their conversation, he made the salient observation that the racial problems besetting American Catholics were not anything the Mexican hierarchy had to worry about. Intermarriage had long since taken care of that.

As a seasoned journalist, Dorothy was by that time highly conscious of her audience. She knew that she wrote for some people to whom she did not have to explain the point of a pilgrimage, found nothing embarrassing in the Catholic approach to relics and holy sites, believed in miracles, and understood Mariology—the veneration of Mary—as a sustaining pillar of faith. She also knew that some readers of *The Catholic Worker* took a different view of those matters, believing in the creed and the Mass but choosing to imagine a wide gulf between themselves as "modern Catholics" and the thousands of unsophisticated Mexican peasants bending devotedly before holy images or crawling on bloody knees across the plaza to the basilica. In her two columns about her trip for *The Catholic Worker* and in a column for *Commonweal*, Dorothy aimed to make crystal clear that her affinities were not with the skeptics and the sophisticates.

"God means us to use material things as aids," she wrote. "He clothed the sacraments with bread and wine, with water, with oil, with the accompaniments of all [the] beauty of ritual, music, color, odor of flowers and beeswax and incense. The Indians, too, say, 'With this body, I thee worship,' coming on their knees to the shrine, singing hymns to El Señor, in lamentation and petition, in joy and thanksgiving . . . they kneel before the picture of Our Lady by the hour." Though she herself found it difficult to enter fully into the mystical experience of the shrine because of the size of the crowds and the low-level noise all around her, she was renewed by the bracing passion and absolute certainty—the evidence of a life-transforming, unshakable faith—of the men, women, and children around her.

* * *

At home the travels continued relentlessly: more bus rides, more houses of hospitality and college campuses to visit, more groups to address. With the young, the reaction could sometimes be just what Dorothy hoped for; Abbie Hoffman, a junior at Brandeis University in 1958, was thrilled to hear a message that questioned the status quo so vigorously. Yet that was also the period that saw some of the greatest—and most freely expressed—hostility to Dorothy's message and to the bearer of the message herself when she was on the road.

In Memphis, as a guest of Helen Caldwell Day at the racially integrated Blessed Martin House (a problem in itself for many area residents), Dorothy gave her customary talk about our moral obligations to help the needy, the premise behind the Catholic Worker's labors, and the risks involved in amassing great wealth. In the Q&A period afterward, she was met with what was becoming a familiar barrage of hostile questions from audience members: Did she think there was something particularly holy about dirt, rats, and cockroaches? Did she think God's love didn't extend to the man who just works hard and takes care of his family? Doesn't charity begin at home? Is it actually sinful to be rich, is that what she was suggesting? Wasn't the Catholic Worker encouraging indolence by feeding people who could be taught, or forced, to take care of themselves?

There is no particular holiness attached to poverty and dirt, Dorothy explained, by no means, nor was she implying that everyone was morally bound to embrace voluntary poverty, certainly not to the degree she had. People had to find their own way, to know themselves and their own workable level of commitment to the Cross. But, she insisted, there is a grave danger of moving far *from* holiness if we harbor any level of disdain for the poor or for poverty itself, which Americans too often seem to do, and think largely (or, worse, exclusively) about our own homes, families, comfort, and financial security. A flight from suffering can be a flight from God.

That was a scene—moments of belligerence from an angry audience, an attempt at clarification, frustration on all sides—repeated more than a few times every year now as the universal pain of the Depression faded into distant memory.

The last time Dorothy spoke in Vermont, in the late 1950s, she was heckled so loudly and abusively by a man in the audience that she vowed never to lecture in that state again, a vow she kept, according to her granddaughter.

Attacks in print from conservatives such as the columnist William F. Buckley (who described Dorothy as good-hearted but "slovenly, reckless, intellectually chaotic," even at heart anti-Catholic) meant nothing to her, but disparaging words from the common run of the faithful were difficult to take.

Even in a setting where one might have thought she would have found herself in the presence of naturally sympathetic listeners, such as a Catholic college, Dorothy discovered that the opposite could be true. The attendees were young people with no firsthand knowledge of breadlines, evictions, Hooverville shanties. She was asked by a skeptical Fordham University student after a lecture to an unenthusiastic audience there in 1958 if she didn't think her movement would be more successful if it weren't so demanding in its philosophy and expectations, which were "kind of hard to take." One can imagine the stare that remark was met with. The gospels, when you come down to it, Dorothy dryly pointed out to the young man, are "kind of hard to take."

Broad as her shoulders were, such criticisms, implicit and explicit, took a toll that left her both sad and angry. The letters to the editor in myriad papers announcing a "discovery" of a subversive Communist past, the questioning of her patriotism and personal morals, the insinuations about her morbid attachment to poverty, the threats from city agencies: it could all become too exhausting for a woman of sixty who was feeling her years.

During times of stress, Dorothy found solace in the rosary and her attendance at daily Mass, of course, and from conversations with her confessor and those people—not a large number at that period, especially considering the controversial issues with which she was embroiled—who understood her point of view. She took heart from the young people who kept showing up to join the Catholic Worker. There was joy in visiting Tamar, who had relocated her family to a farm in Perkinsville, Vermont. There was delight in seeing her grandchildren, now numbering eight, with the birth of Hilaire Peter Hennessy, named for Hilaire Belloc and Peter Maurin.

She had yet another resource, though, cultivated in adolescence, that lasted throughout her long life and never failed her: namely, her passion for the great novelists. She kept up with contemporary American fiction all her days—reading John Updike, J. D. Salinger, Mary McCarthy, Flannery O'Connor, Walker Percy, James Baldwin, and her special favorite, Saul Bellow—but she was at heart a devoted Anglophile. (The Russians were for spirituality, she felt; the British were for great storytelling.) Settling into a seat on a dingy Greyhound bus, relaxing under a tree at the farm, or climbing into bed at night after a difficult day and spending time with Jane Austen, the Brontës, Dickens, Anthony Trollope, George Eliot, Conrad, Galsworthy, or D. H. Lawrence or opening new books by Dorothy Sayers and Graham Greene provided refreshment, time away from the *Sturm und Drang* of Worker life. It was an especially vital respite in the 1950s and 1960s.

Her love of those novelists speaks to two other aspects of Dorothy's personality as well.

There was, first, before middle age, a plausible and healthy envy. How satisfied she would have been to have joined that company, to have written and seen published a novel, quite unlike the unskillful *The Eleventh Virgin*, that was respected for its craft and spoke to her vision of modern life. But that wasn't to be. Her devotion to secular literature also tells us that Father's Hugo's stringent influence had its limits. Those who accused her of scorning the here and now, of failing to see value in anything but religion and allowing her piety to overtake all other aspects of her life, were wide of the mark. Like her feeling for Wagner and Rouault, her appreciation of the great British novelists was emblematic of a person who loved striving and beauty in various guises.

A word in this context should be said specifically about Aldous Huxley, all of whose many books Dorothy seems to have read. Despite their obvious differences in background and the fact that the British writer had no interest in the Vatican nor Dorothy in mescaline as a path to heightened consciousness, the similarities between the two are striking, more so than between the founder of the Catholic Worker and any other novelist of the twentieth century.

Huxley's early, satirical works were used on one occasion by Dorothy to rebuke Forster in an angry letter, with Dorothy telling her lover that he was just like the sarcastic author of *Crome Yellow* (1921) and *Antic Hay* (1923)—i.e., lordly, cynical, acting as if he lived on a higher plane than ordinary mortals. (That was a fair characterization of Huxley's persona based on those first books.) Huxley's subsequent novels, though, are more laments about the direction of modern life and the need to seek an enlightenment that science, rationalism, and consumerism will not provide. Dorothy and Huxley shared a Cassandra-like outlook on the West's steamroller interest in developing the technology of pleasure, and the protagonist's cry of protest in *Brave New World* (1932)—"But I don't want comfort. I want God, I want poetry, I want real danger"—in the face of a secular, anesthetizing, machine-driven society was very much in spirit with her concerns.

Huxley's analysis of the failure of radical politics to give sufficient meaning to life, a theme Dorothy well understood, was treated in *Eyeless in Gaza* (1936). She saw *After Many a Summer Dies the Swan* (1939) as offering a cautionary portrait of the hell that originates in the urge toward uncontrolled sex and sadism. "There is no such thing as seeing how far one can go without being caught," she wrote in the same 1963 *Catholic Worker* column that alluded to that novel and was one of her most honest statements about her own youth. The plot of *Time Must Have a Stop* (1944) is centered on the conflicting paths of hedonism and spirituality, and many of Huxley's later essays, steeped in the mystics of various faiths (including Catholicism), are about the search for God and an ultimate reality that transcends what we think of as "reality" in our earthbound consciousness.

Aldous Huxley and Dorothy Day were also in full agreement about prayer as an act of mortification, a "dying to self." They were in agreement about the lust for power and pleasure as, in Huxley's apt words, "God-eclipsing things." Huxley sent an encouraging note to Dorothy and made a small contribution to the Catholic Worker at some point in the 1940s.

It was also possible by the end of the 1950s for Dorothy to look back on twenty-five years at the Catholic Worker and take some satisfaction in considering the number of people whose lives she had influenced, men and women who had left the Worker to do God's work in another capacity. Joe and Alice Zarrella were in Tell City, Indiana, where Joe worked as a labor organizer. Julia Porcelli, married and raising a family, was a sculptor receiving Church commissions for her statues of saints, her art inspired by study with Ade Bethune. Nina Polcyn had opened a Catholic bookstore in Chicago that was regarded as the best of its kind anywhere. John Cort was a significant figure in labor activism, as were John Cogley and Jim O'Gara in Catholic journalism. Arthur Sheehan authored biographies of Pierre Toussaint, the black Catholic philanthropist, and Rose Hawthorne Lathrop, Nathaniel Hawthorne's daughter, a nun who ran a cancer hospice. Jack English had become a monk, while Tom Sullivan had become a teacher. Eileen Fantino, Mary Ann McCoy, and Helen Russell—the last a nun who had left her convent in California to come to St. Joseph House—were three of the most indefatigable women who ever set foot on Chrystie Street; all of them were arrested in the first nuclear air-raid drill. They had taken an apartment in East Harlem and on their own initiative opened a day care center for the Latino children of that neighborhood.

The fruit of a well-articulated personalism was found in the activism many of the former Workers displayed after their time with Dorothy, going out into the world to utilize their talents in a distinctive way. It wasn't acolytes who were going to bring the gospels to life, Dorothy knew, but young people charged with the spirit of Christ and the self-confidence to act on it.

Yet in a hand-to-mouth enterprise such as the Catholic Worker, light-years away from the world of power and pleasure, the struggle to keep the doors open just would not end. The city informed Dorothy that, under the law of eminent domain, 223 Chrystie Street was being slated for demolition as part of a subway expansion program on the Lower East Side. The Workers had several months to vacate, but the prospects for finding a similar building were not good. She and Robert Steed began to look into all the possibilities in that part of Manhattan, the only area of the city that would conceivably accept a group like the Catholic Worker. The best that could be found was a rental property at an affordable $100 a month that came with some serious drawbacks.

The huge loft at 39 Spring Street could be subdivided into usable spaces for offices, a clothing room, and a dining and discussion area, but it was up a long flight of stairs, which would not be easy to manage for the elderly or visitors with bad legs, and it had no room for sleeping quarters. Apartments in the neighborhood would have to be found for the men and women who were staying on Chrystie Street in buildings that would accept more than several people to a unit. That announcement gave rise to an understandable fear that after twenty-five years of continuous operation largely under one roof, the community *as a community* was about to be dissolved, but Dorothy insisted that the Worker would hold itself together for as long as it took to find another building to purchase. The paper would still come out—in Steed, Dorothy felt she had again a superb editor—and the poor would still be fed, clothed, and sheltered. The move to Spring Street was completed at the start of the new year.

An all-too-human despair and an invincible optimism: both, by this time, were a part of Dorothy's character and something everyone at the Catholic Worker was used to. The death of the pope was a forceful example of the latter. Eugenio Pacelli's passing in 1958 marked the end of an era; whatever disagreements Dorothy had with the pontiff (his lack of support for conscientious objection and unconditional pacifism and his blanket condemnation of communism foremost among them) counted for nothing. She never wanted to hear any criticism, then or later, of Pius XII. Loyal Catholics did not openly criticize the Vicar of Christ. The election of Angelo Roncalli as the new pope—John XXIII—represented an unknown for everyone, but in what is always a potentially traumatic moment for the faithful, the end of one papacy and the beginning of another, she was uncertain but hopeful. How appropriate that hopefulness turned out to be was made clear soon enough.

Evidence could also be found that a subtle shift was taking place in the nature of the US clerical community, a shift that Dorothy regarded as an especially positive development. In February 1959, Dorothy noted in her diary that she was reading Thomas Merton's *The Seven Storey Mountain*. The Trappist monk's sharply honest "autobiography of faith," first published in 1948, had been the surprise best seller of mid-twentieth-century publishing, and it is odd that Dorothy hadn't read it long before. Perhaps she meant that she was rereading it. A communication began that winter with Merton that lasted until his death almost a decade later, and he published several articles in *The Catholic Worker*, though the two never met. At one point in their epistolary relationship, Merton wrote to Dorothy, "If there were no Catholic Worker and such forms of witness, I would never have joined the Catholic Church."

Merton's autobiography touched chords in Dorothy: how much they had in common as they stumbled their way toward faith and the Catholic Church. What Thomas De Quincey had been to the bookish Dorothy in her teens, William Blake had been to Merton. Both young people had immersed themselves in a highly unconventional writer, a social critic who presented a caustic outlook on life that later became an unexpected gateway to belief. Both had had a flirtation with communism and a freewheeling sexual period, and Merton's friendship with the painter Reginald Marsh in New York and various Cambridge friends faintly echoes Dorothy's time with Mike Gold and Eugene O'Neill. Both had been drawn to Catholic worship before they

had the least understanding of its meaning and ramifications. Merton wrote
movingly of the awkwardness of the new convert's situation, and his journey from a bright, restless, self-absorbed intellectual adolescence to his "new
freedom" in Christ was quite similar to Dorothy's.

Merton became a meaningful figure to a generation of young men and
women interested in a more contemplative, less doctrinally rigid approach
to Catholicism, an outlook that didn't seek to debate or undermine the *mag-
isterium* but presented a view of religion that was inward and prayerful rather
than fiercely dogmatic. Yet Dorothy had a criticism to make about Merton
based solely on her experience of the memoir, namely, that he had "plunged
himself so deeply in religion that his view of the world and its problems [was]
superficial and scornful." That opinion changed quickly when Merton wrote
to express support for the Catholic Worker's stand on the nuclear air-raid
drills. Over the next few years, he was only too happy to express himself on
the subjects of peace and war and social justice until his Cistercian superiors
instructed him in 1962 to cease writing.

That spring saw another jail sentence after another nuclear drill protest. Dorothy was just back from Conyers, Georgia, where she had happily
attended the ordination of Jack English, now a Trappist. Ammon Hennacy
wasn't with her at the protest, as he, Karl Meyer, and others, were busy being
arrested in Nebraska for a trespassing protest at the Strategic Air Command
center in Omaha. Nor was Charles Butterworth with her. A Harvard Law
School graduate and convert, Butterworth had come to New York to work
at the house as business manager and to write for the paper. He was a committed celibate at the time (to the dismay of some women at the Worker)
but a bit of "an innocent walking through a mine field," in the estimation of
one friend. Getting arrested was by that time almost a rite of passage for the
younger Catholic Workers; Butterworth felt guilty that he had never been in
jail. He solved that problem by being taken into custody by the FBI for alert-
ing a soldier who had gone AWOL and was staying at St. Joseph House that
the authorities were after him. Robert Steed bailed him out, and, probably to
his disappointment, Butterworth received a six-month suspended sentence
from a sympathetic judge.

Not many people felt sympathetic to the aims of the Catholic Worker
in that period. Eleanor Roosevelt had answered a letter from Dorothy that
spring, presumably soliciting support for the group's refusal to take shelter,

but the former first lady wasn't having any of it. She tersely answered that she was "at a loss" to know what Miss Day had been thinking when she had defied the government under circumstances meant to protect the civilian population. Allies weren't always found where one expected them.

Nor was compassion always found where it should have taken root. By now, Dorothy had seen enough of the inside of jail—and heard enough stories from Ammon Hennacy, who had clocked more time in more prisons around the country than anyone she knew, and had printed enough personal incarceration narratives in *The Catholic Worker*—to know that something was very wrong with the US penal system. She readily accepted an invitation from the New York State Legislature to testify in 1959 about prison conditions for women, in particular those suffering from drug addiction. The New York City prison commissioner, Anna Kross, who preceded her at the hearing, initially impressed Dorothy as she talked about the need for the state to go after the drug lords more aggressively than the users of the drugs, but that good impression evaporated when she went on to observe that she didn't think the women she was responsible for found their experience particularly trying and that the withdrawal symptoms most inmates displayed were largely simulated. "Her total lack of sympathy for the women in her charge . . . was horrifying," Dorothy wrote.

Dorothy had a different story to tell. Leaving heroin addicts to go "cold turkey," banging their heads against the walls of their cells, lying in their own vomit, and screaming their lungs out at night, was neither humane nor conducive to recovery. She thought that the state could do a great deal more to make prison conditions less demeaning, but, in particular, she argued that more had to be done to treat addiction. When released, the women simply, naturally, went back to their old ways. Several months later, when Judith Malina and Julian Beck staged a play about addiction, *The Connection* by Jack Gelber, which became a notable work in Off-Broadway history, Dorothy and Hennacy went to the Living Theatre to see it, and Dorothy wrote about Gelber's intense, innovative drama for the paper. The production was dedicated, she was pleased to note, to Thelma Gadsden, a heroin addict whom Malina and Dorothy had befriended in their month at the Women's House of Detention two years earlier. After she had been released, Gadsden had visited Dorothy at St. Joseph House but, sadly and predictably, soon after died of an overdose.

A death closer to home awaited Dorothy. In the fall, Forster called to say that the woman he had lived with for the last thirty years, Nanette, had cancer and that the doctors had done all that they could. He pleaded for her help. Dorothy's relationship with her former lover was problematic. He had never done his part, financial or otherwise, in raising Tamar, nor had he ever accepted Dorothy's commitment to the Catholic Church, but she still harbored some affection toward him at times. To her surprise, he had shown up in 1957 to stand with other protestors on her behalf on the street outside the Women's House of Detention. He was now living in Florida but was distraught when he talked about the tragedy that was looming. He needed to be near his sister, Lily, and—he hoped—someone as steady and practical as the mother of his child.

Dorothy canceled most of her speaking engagements for the fall of 1959 when Forster and Nanette came to New York and rented a cottage near hers on Staten Island. She began to spend weekdays there, cooking and cleaning and comforting the distraught Nanette, while Lily came on weekends so that Dorothy could go back to Spring Street to catch up on her writing and correspondence. It was evident that Nanette wouldn't last more than a few months and that Forster was entirely unable to cope on his own. "One would think he is taking up where he left off with me, or that I have always been with him, as Lily has," Dorothy confided to her diary. "I am a part of him." About that neediness, which would become more desperate and childlike by the week as Nanette's health declined, Dorothy felt considerable ambivalence, sometimes rage, yet she regarded it as right that she should be there, assisting as best she could.

Other troubles intruded that autumn. Dorothy had to rush to Vermont when Tamar was taken to the hospital with what her doctor feared was appendicitis or an inflamed gallbladder. Dorothy arrived to find the house in complete disarray, with Eric at twelve years of age and Susie at thirteen having to care for the little ones and David, alternating between irrational outbursts and sullen silence, on the verge of a complete breakdown. When she visited her sister on her way home in the hope of a break, that didn't go any better. Della's own marriage was in trouble, and when Dorothy wanted to talk about her daughter, at thirty-four pregnant with her ninth child, Della's response homed in on the obvious: Tamar had had too many children. It had been a mistake not to talk to her about birth control. Dorothy walked out on Della.

Turning sixty-two that November, Dorothy busied herself when not with Nanette by trying to learn French, playing Beethoven on the record player Forster had given her, rereading her favorite parts of *The Idiot*, and visiting Marge Hughes and her family, who lived nearby on Staten Island. By Thanksgiving, Nanette talked angrily of wanting to commit suicide. The colostomy, the swelling, the pain and decay were too much to endure. All Dorothy could do was sit by her bedside for longer periods and try to distract her. By Christmas, Forster was paralyzed with grief, weeping and bemoaning his fate most of the day. A nurse who volunteered in her spare time at St. Joseph House came out to help. Nanette was given morphine in her final days and baptized, as she wished. Crushed by his loss, Forster the lifelong atheist made no comment about that decision. After two days of agony, Nanette died peacefully on January 8, 1960. Forster and Lily were on their own.

As quickly after the funeral as she could leave, Dorothy departed for a four-month speaking tour. She wanted to visit Ammon Hennacy, who was about to be released from federal prison in Minnesota, and reconnect with her national audience. Time spent in Detroit, Chicago, St. Paul, Madison, and Fargo, at a Sioux Indian mission in South Dakota, in Seattle, Spokane, Portland, San Francisco, Fresno, Los Angeles, Albuquerque, New Orleans, and St. Louis—among so many other cities—meant a flight from Forster and awkward memories, from Spring Street and debilitating conflicts, from the needs of others that could never be satisfied. Yet there was no real escape. "Traveling in a bus is like traveling with a slum always with you," Dorothy wrote to Deane Mowrer. It was a statement that has the air of both a complaint and an affirmation.

SIXTEEN

❧ PACEM IN TERRIS ❧

ONE WONDERS: WHAT DID THE STUDENTS AT ST. JOHN'S UNIVERsity in Minnesota in 1960 make of Dorothy's statement that it would be better to die in a nuclear attack than to retaliate and slaughter so many innocents with our own missiles? What did the students at the College of the Holy Cross in Massachusetts think of her condemnation of President John F. Kennedy a few weeks after the Bay of Pigs fiasco in the spring of 1961 and her claim that the US government should be giving aid to Cuba, not provoking bloodshed? What did any student audience think of her observation—an insistent theme now in campus talks—about "the mortal sin" that had been committed by the United States in incinerating the people of Hiroshima and Nagasaki?

The first years of the new decade occasioned three momentous and unexpected developments in the world: the election of a Roman Catholic to the White House, the breakdown of the United States' relations with its onetime ally Cuba, and the opening of the Second Vatican Council. The first of these was a source of satisfaction to millions of American Catholics (though not to Cardinal Spellman, known to be a supporter of Vice President Richard Nixon). To Dorothy, Kennedy was a Cold Warrior who had made much during his campaign of an alleged missile gap with the Soviet Union, a senator who had never taken a stand against Joseph McCarthy or spoken up for civil rights, i.e., not a leader from whom she could expect much. She surely suspected that his Catholicism was of the thinnest kind. Nuns might line up by the dozens at polling places, but she had no more intention of voting in that election than in any other. The Cuban missile crisis would confirm her belief that Kennedy was just another occupant of the Oval Office in the dangerous spirit of Truman and Eisenhower.

The last year of the Eisenhower administration was a rocky one. The defense budget had grown astronomically over the last decade, the domino theory was in the ascendant, relations with the Soviet Union were precarious, and not everyone was at ease with where that momentum was taking the country. Writing to Karl Meyer, still in jail but now based in Chicago and making a name for himself as a peace activist and Hennacy-like tax resister, Dorothy expressed her approval for his work and for the demonstrations that were taking place abroad as the United States expanded its military bases around the world. She was glad that massive Japanese protests had forced the cancellation of Ike's trip to Japan after the signing of a mutual defense treaty that many Japanese wanted no part of.

In May, the annual nuclear air-raid drill was held in New York—and what a different experience it was for those opposed to this charade than it had been in 1955. Several hundred people, including mothers with strollers, turned up in City Hall Park to protest. Joining Dorothy, Ammon Hennacy, A. J. Muste, and the Catholic Worker crowd were Dwight Macdonald, Norman Mailer, *Village Voice* columnist Nat Hentoff, and the novelist Kay Boyle. By that time, the mainstream press was in agreement that the drills served no purpose (the *New York World-Telegram* headlined its editorial "An Exercise in Futility"). The police carted off a few dozen of the younger demonstrators but refused to touch Dorothy and her associates, obviously under instructions from their superiors to leave the more newsworthy elders alone. A woman whose work had been covered by *Time* magazine and who had appeared the year before on Mike Wallace's television interview program was not someone any judge really wanted to see in his court now. Dorothy did show up in court, however, to show solidarity with those who had been arrested and arraigned.

The Catholic Worker crowed in its July issue, probably underestimating the size of the crowd, "500 Defy Civil Defense Drill in NYC." Thereafter, Hennacy and a new face at the Worker, twenty-six-year-old Mary Lathrop, began to picket the city's civil defense office on Lexington Avenue for two hours each day. Hennacy was relentless in stirring the pot.

What was perceived as Dorothy's quirkiness in other areas still irked some of the paper's subscribers. That fall, she returned a check to the city for $3,579, the interest owed on the city's long-delayed purchase of 223 Chrystie Street, as a statement of the Worker's opposition to usury and the principle of interest—and then broadcast that news on the front page of the paper under the title "The Money Is Not Ours." Letters arrived at Spring Street berating her for her folly in urgently appealing to readers for donations every year and then rejecting a hefty amount that, in the view of most Americans, was rightfully hers. "We do not believe in the profit system," she wrote to the city treasurer, "and so we cannot take profit or interest on our money. . . . Please be assured that we are not judging *individuals*, but are trying to make a judgment on the *system* under which we live." Either you opposed the core of capitalism, or you didn't.

In October, Dorothy published what would be her penultimate book. It had an exceptionally long gestation. Even before finishing *The Long Loneliness*, she had decided that she wanted to write about St. Thérèse of Lisieux. The "Little Flower," as she is known, is one of the most popular saints in modern Catholicism, though hers was one of the least dramatic of lives and she died young, a French Carmelite nun, claimed by tuberculosis at twenty-four in 1897. Throughout the 1950s, Dorothy determinedly worked on her manuscript in a piecemeal fashion.

It is easy to see why the subject interested Dorothy. No Joan of Arc deciding the fate of nations, no Catherine of Siena lecturing popes, Thérèse Martin saw herself as a "little flower" in God's garden, and, long before the Vatican's verification of a fantastic number of posthumous miracles achieved in her name and her subsequent canonization in 1925, she was accepted by the laity worldwide as a symbol of laudable self-surrender, the redemptive power of renunciation, contentment in daily worship, and "the little way," the quiet way. She was a saint for the masses whose lives were simple, obscure, devout, unheroic. In the New York of the 1930s, she might have been one of the many nuns who came to Mott Street to honor the commitment to service and humility that characterized the Catholic Worker at its best.

It is also easy to see why Dorothy's editors at Harper were less enthusiastic, feeling that a book about Thérèse of Lisieux might find a decent readership by way of a religious press but was unlikely to do so on a mainstream trade publisher's list. Moreover, they kept telling the author, not always so gently, that each revision she showed them was simply too bland, too colorless, for them to believe it would ever be worth publishing. One editor suggested that she travel to France to see if she could pick up some of the atmosphere of Normandy and the convent where her subject had lived in the hope that she might produce a more inspired text, but of course Dorothy had neither the time nor the money to do so. In truth, she had no special flair as a biographer and, at one point, acknowledged, "I am faced with the humiliating fact that I can write only about *myself*."

Her awareness of the Little Flower went back some decades. It was when she had been in the maternity ward of Bellevue Hospital in 1926 that a woman in another bed had told her about the saint who had died the year Dorothy was born and, when she heard that Dorothy was going to name her new baby Tamar Teresa, had given her a medal of St. Thérèse that she had in her purse. After Dorothy's conversion in 1928, Father Zachary of the Church of Our Lady of Guadalupe on West 14th Street had given her, among other books, a copy of *The Little White Flower: The Story of a Soul*, Thérèse's posthumously published autobiography, which had come out in English two years before. She didn't think much of it. The book was "pious pap," she concluded, a judgment many would agree with today. In 1958, she had published in *The Catholic Worker* an equivocal review of a new translation of the book.

For several years, Dorothy spent time on her bus rides studying all the other accounts in print. There was plenty to read. St. Thérèse of Lisieux is hardly an understudied topic in Church history. Sheed & Ward had even published two biographies about her, and Frank Sheed had translated a volume of her letters. So how does Dorothy's book compare to its forerunners? It isn't as saccharine as John Beevers's *Storm of Glory* or as ponderous and propagandizing as Hans Urs von Balthasar's account. Frances Parkinson Keyes's popular *Written in Heaven* is on a par with her many articles in *Good Housekeeping*, and Henri Ghéon's *The Secret of the Little Flower* is a slapdash affair. Vita Sackville-West's *The Eagle and the Dove: A Study in Contrasts* juxtaposes Teresa of Ávila with Thérèse of Lisieux and is written with a novelist's skill, though it has myriad quirks. The one exception to this dubious list would be Dorothy's favorite, Ida Görres's *The Hidden Face*, ably translated from the German into English in 1959 and more deeply analytical than anything else written in Dorothy's lifetime but excessively long.

Indeed, compared to most of the competition, Dorothy was rather harsh in her judgment of her own effort, which avoids the sentimentality many of Thérèse's other biographers succumbed to and makes a more plausible case for seeing the young nun as someone who might actually have something to say to a modern believer. Titled simply *Thérèse*, her account of the life of the

Little Flower was published by Fides Press of Notre Dame. It failed to garner much attention beyond the loyal readership of *The Catholic Worker*, though. Even *Commonweal* and *America* declined to review it.

The book came out at a less-than-propitious moment in the history of religious biography, certainly. American Catholics who might have been reasonably well informed about the lives of saints in previous decades were considerably less interested in the subject in the 1960s. Veneration of saints seemed to many young people the least compelling or explicable aspect of Catholicism. Not so in Dorothy's mind. For more than thirty years, she read biographies of those whose lives she found instructive about the different paths to holiness, the saintly and the venerable—e.g., Augustine, Francis of Assisi, Teresa of Ávila, Ignatius of Loyola, Philip Neri, Francis de Sales, Vincent de Paul, Cardinal Newman, Rose Hawthorne Lathrop. Thérèse of Lisieux, she was convinced, was more relevant to the twentieth century than many other religious figures. "In these days of fear and trembling of what man has wrought on earth in destructiveness and hate," she wrote in her preface, "Thérèse is the saint we need."

Fear and trembling: That meant Cuba. That meant Nikita Khrushchev banging his shoe on the table in front of him at the United Nations, proclaiming to the non-Communist world, "We will bury you." That meant a government in Washington insisting that it could not live indefinitely with a political system ninety miles from Miami of which it did not approve. That meant "Better dead than Red" and models of concrete family air-raid shelters displayed on public squares in midsized cities.

Americans in the early 1960s had more leisure time, more discretionary income to spend on leisure activities, and more access to material comforts than ever before. It was easy to pretend that the world had not become more dangerous than at any previous moment in human history. White middle-class Americans alive at that time are more likely today to remember an era of ease and amusement: a fashionable first lady, the end of Hollywood censorship, color televisions, big-finned cars fresh from Detroit, the family trip to Disneyland. In truth, though, there was cause for serious anxiety, and much of that had to do with the proximity of Cuba to the United States and what might happen there.

The task of articulating to the fullest extent the Worker's view of the Cuba-US situation had been handed to Dave Dellinger in the first month of the Kennedy administration while, unbeknown to the public, the Bay of Pigs invasion was in its final planning stages. A conscientious objector during the war, Dellinger was one of the most noted peace advocates of his generation (he would be one of the infamous Chicago Seven in 1968), and he and his wife became friends with Dorothy in the 1950s; in fact, his wife gave birth to one of their children at the Peter Maurin Farm. Dorothy thought highly of him as a writer and an activist. His February 1961 article in The Catholic Worker, "America's Lost Plantation," reviewed in copious detail the left-wing understanding of the reasons behind the United States' relationship with Cuba, which had soured so suddenly and completely.

As Dellinger outlined the situation, summarizing a view that Dorothy completely supported, the overthrow by Fidel Castro's rebels in 1959 of the US-backed Fulgencio Batista, as reprehensible a dictator as any in Latin America, was an opportunity for a realignment in US foreign policy in the Western Hemisphere. Castro was, at first, a potential new ally. He spent several days in New York City, charming reporters and onlookers, and met with Vice President Nixon. The United States' surprise that he meant what he said about land reform and the nationalizing of Cuba's industries ended any possibility of a comfortable relationship. He intended to improve the living conditions of his country's impoverished majority, however ruthless he had to be in the process, and put an end to foreign investors who took more than they gave back, to the brothels and casinos American tourists had long patronized, to the American crime syndicates' influence on the island, to a capitalist economy that had done nothing for most Cubans. His decision to sign a trade agreement with the Soviet Union and meet with Khrushchev was unacceptable to Washington. He quickly became a nemesis of the Eisenhower administration and its Camelot successor. Plans for covert CIA action to topple Castro were just that—covert—though the escalating government and mainstream press rhetoric was anything but muted.

The Sunday Visitor, a publication with a circulation that was vastly greater than that of The Catholic Worker and that had the advantage of being distributed after Sunday Mass in hundreds of Catholic churches across the country, laced into Dellinger that winter, and Dorothy knew what she was now up against in defending a nation that was looking toward Moscow for help. She went out on the most dangerous of limbs when acknowledging that the persecution of the Church in countries such as Cuba was both "deserved and undeserved." The understandable aspect of peasants' anger at bishops and local pastors was what it had always been: the Catholic Church was viewed in the popular mind as far less concerned with social justice than with preserving its self-serving ties to the ruling class. Still more forcefully, she wrote of the revolutionaries' position: "If religion has so neglected the needs of the poor and of the great mass of workers and permitted them to live in the most horrible destitution while comforting them with the solace of a promise of a life after death when all tears shall be wiped away, then that religion is suspect."

By the spring of 1962, Dorothy decided that she wanted a firsthand experience of Cuba. She enrolled in a Berlitz crash course in Spanish. "I want to see the collective farms, the education system, the condition of religion," she told Thomas Merton. She knew what others were going to say. "The fervent Catholic in [the] U.S. feels that a loyal Catholic must hate everything Fidel stands for, must hate Marxism-Leninism (without understanding in the least what that 'pernicious doctrine' stands for)," she noted in her diary just before her departure. At bottom, she didn't care. She was going to see for herself, and no one could talk her out of it. The division of the world into two irredeemably oppositional camps wasn't any longer—certainly not in a nuclear age—a sustainable approach to life, she believed. "I go to see Christ in my fellow brother, the Cuban," she wrote in her diary, "the revolutionary as well as the counter-revolutionary."

Getting a passport to travel to Cuba proved to be easier than expected, but the US trade embargo had commenced and US ships were no longer permitted to sail there, so Dorothy booked passage on a Spanish ship in September. (She dreaded the thought of having to look at pictures of Generalissimo Franco's face every day in the ship's dining room.) It wasn't as if she set out oblivious to the fact that the overthrow of Batista had not been nonviolent, that it was anything but a testament to Gandhian *satyagraha*. She knew about the ongoing reprisals against the vestiges of the old regime. Bob Ludlow, her old editor, told her that it was disappointing that she had turned her back on pacifism, a charge she denied. She wanted more patience brought to any public discussion of Castro and what he had wrought. She wanted the rush to judgment stopped. The United States had never had a problem with Batista amassing a fortune on the backs of his people, half of whom were illiterate, and running a vicious police state. Now the nation was up in arms because a new leader had deported all priests and nuns who refused to refrain from criticizing communism, frozen out US investors and seized their assets, and was ready to forge an alliance with the Soviet Union.

To be exacting about all that, though, and fair to Ludlow, Cuba *did* provoke a modification in Dorothy's views on pacifism. She wasn't as critical, as absolute, about the taking up of arms to change an oppressive social order as she had been in the past. Some sentences in her columns—fleeting, ambiguous at moments—tilt in a different direction. Her hope, rather, was that that phase of the revolution would be over quickly and that "the grace of God will grow in [Castro]," who was after all a baptized Catholic, leaving the Church free to function and the poor to be succored, as only he—not Batista or his ally to the north—had promised to do.

Once in Cuba, Dorothy did her best to observe and learn what she could on a one-month visa. She obtained press credentials and hoped for an interview with Fidel or Raúl Castro or Che Guevara, but the closest she came was hearing them speak in public. US journalists of any stripe were now considered undesirable in Havana. She dropped off the medical supplies she had brought for the National Hospital and, sometimes with a guide and often all on her own, set about to meet people to interact with, in the capital, at Guantánamo near the US base, in smaller villages. She visited nursery schools, state farms, hospitals, fishing cooperatives, literacy classes. She insisted that despite the new restrictions on the Church, she had been able to find a place at which to attend Mass each day, both in Havana and in the countryside. Catholics enjoyed complete freedom of speech, she maintained (in what was perhaps her most dubious contention), and alcoholism was nonexistent. What a contrast to the Bowery! She was pleased to note that birth control was condemned and that the man in charge of a large mental hospital she toured had been one of Castro's soldiers and was a devout Catholic who said the rosary each day and had even done so when fighting with Castro in the Sierra Maestra. Permission to meet with political prisoners had been denied, and she was saddened to note the increasing poverty that the US embargo was inflicting on the Cuban people. Food was rationed; machine parts were impossible to find. The United States was going to squeeze those people back into the orbit of "the free world."

Dorothy's journalistic objectivity was open to question, of course. She went hoping to see noble suffering and progress of a kind she could applaud. Personal memories were no doubt at play. Havana was a city her father had spent a good deal of time in—had taken her younger brother John to for his initiation in his adolescence—a playground of brothels, casinos, and race-tracks. John Day was the kind of American who had enabled Batista and his followers to flourish. Now Dorothy could write about a land where the traces of that selfishness and debauchery were being expunged, and that was the thrust of many of her columns. She left Cuba on October 11, coincidentally the day that the first session of the Second Vatican Council convened in St. Peter's Basilica in Rome.

Dorothy's route back was circuitous, extreme even for her: by ship to Veracruz to Mexico City to San Antonio, then north to speak at the University of Minnesota, St. John's University, North Dakota State College, Marquette University, and finally the University of Chicago. At every stop, she felt in her audiences, or among those she was meeting at dinners and parish visits, an intense interest in the subject of Cuba, whether, she noted, "it takes the form of wishing to invade or to overcome the barriers between us and resume friendly relations." Her intention at that point was to do everything she could to further the latter outlook. She wanted her countrymen to know that they had more to fear from their own government's saber rattling than from Castro's proletarian revolution. She insisted, no matter what anyone else wanted to believe, that she had not come upon one closed church in her travels there and that the nuns she had met in Mexico City seemed to live under more government-imposed restrictions than did the women in religious orders in Havana. Having heard Fidel Castro speak on four occasions, she claimed that his voice, manner of expression, tendency to repetition, loquaciousness, and concern for the poor reminded her of—Peter Maurin.

Few public statements that Dorothy had made since the time of the Spanish Civil War and Pearl Harbor elicited so little approval as her remarks about Cuba. *Naive* was the word used by some friends and allies. More evidence, if any was needed, of her Communist sympathies and her deplorable judgment: that was the verdict of skeptics and critics.

Despite the predictable angry letters from subscribers, who could never forgive Castro for placing any restrictions on the Church, *The Catholic Worker*'s circulation figures remained steady in this period, around 65,000, and there were a few people who were firmly in her corner. Karl Meyer, whose politics aligned perfectly with Dorothy's, was one, as was A. J. Muste. Thomas Merton was another. To Daniel Berrigan, a like-minded Jesuit, Merton described Dorothy's articles on Cuba as "moving in their honesty and earnestness and in their wonderful Gospel sweetness." Writing to a friend that fall, he was downright testy: "The next time I hear anything about the iniquity of Cuba and the righteousness of the U.S., I am going to throw a bowl of soup at somebody."

Within a week of Dorothy's return to New York, the Cuban missile crisis brought the world to the brink of Armageddon. About that near disaster, every civilized person's worst fear, Dorothy saw little to praise in the actions of Washington or Moscow—or Havana, for that matter. It was almost impossible to believe: mankind had drifted so far from God, from grace and sanity, that it could actually contemplate the extinction of life on the planet over a political system on one island in the Caribbean that elicited conflicting responses between two superpowers. Change and technological advancement had not brought progress, as hopeful social critics had promised at the turn of the century; they had brought the stuff of nightmares.

Change seemed to accelerate at the Catholic Worker as well. A new house to purchase was found at 175 Chrystie Street in 1961, so the inconveniences of the Spring Street rental could be left behind and Dorothy could give up her own small apartment on Ludlow Street, but the new space was cramped and dingy. Turnover of staff was considerable, too, in the early and mid-1960s. Judith Gregory, a few years out of Radcliffe, drove to New York in 1959, handed over the keys to her car to the Catholic Worker, and stayed for several years, helping produce the paper, selling it on the street, and managing at times both the house and the farm. Though she knew that it would be wise not to discuss her sexual orientation with Dorothy, she and Dorothy got along well, and Dorothy felt close enough to Gregory to make her the executrix of her will. On the other hand, Gregory's close friend Robert Steed, one of the best editors the paper had but no fan of the more visible displays of piety at the house, felt it was time to leave by 1964, as he had found a boyfriend and didn't want to live any longer under the pressure of an enforced silence, keeping secret the romantic side of his life.

Ed Forand, an ex-Marine in his thirties who knew and respected Father

Hugo (a rare and significant asset in Dorothy's eyes), came to the Catholic Worker in 1961 and stayed all the rest of his days, outliving Dorothy and proving a mainstay at running the house. His first contributions to the paper were sensitive articles about the neighborhood, the more poverty-stricken of the resident guests at the house, and the ravages of urban renewal. (The planned World Trade Center, which tore apart a downtown area of small shops, was a prescient subject.) In November of the same year, Jim Forest, recently discharged from the navy after declaring himself a conscientious objector, arrived to work on the paper but stayed only four months. Tom Cornell and Chris Kearns were young men in their twenties who showed up to offer their services on the paper. (Cornell, Kearns, and Forest became leaders of the Catholic Peace Fellowship, a protest organization, in 1964.) Cornell had first heard of Dorothy when he had read a roommate's copy of *The Long Loneliness* at Fairfield University several years earlier and came into the city to attend one of the Friday-night sessions. It was a recurrent pattern: old-timers left, but the young kept coming.

The most significant departure from the house in that era was Ammon Hennacy's. He wasn't one to be tied down, and Dorothy probably sensed that his conversion was not going to last. He could never let up with his criticism of the clergy for their attachment to convention and comfort. Yet difficult as he was to get along with, he had acquired a mythic presence at the Catholic Worker. He could wrangle speaking invitations from the most unlikely places, he probably sold more copies of the paper than anyone else, and he liked nothing better than to corner a priest who spoke up in favor of capital punishment or against pacifism to argue him into submission or stupefaction. Celibacy, which life at St. Joseph House called for, was not for him, though, and he began a hectic courtship of Mary Lathrop. He suggested that she join him in setting up a house of hospitality, to be called the Joe Hill House after the famed IWW martyr, in Salt Lake City.

In flight from a dysfunctional, aggressively anti-Catholic family, Lathrop had made her way to the Catholic Worker at the suggestion of a family friend, Caroline Gordon, and found in Dorothy a surrogate mother who appreciated her exuberance and felt a measure of responsibility for her. Dorothy was of two minds about the proposed union. The forty-year age difference was only half of the problem. Hennacy was an erratic personality with a roving eye, and Dorothy invited her young protégée to accompany her on a car trip through the South and Southwest. On the road, as Dorothy intended, Lathrop made a decision: she would join her suitor out west as a friend and coworker, but theirs wouldn't be a marital bond. Dorothy accepted that it was time for Hennacy to break away, though she knew she would miss his feistiness and rebelliousness. She was also relieved that even if Mary Lathrop was joining him in his Utah endeavor, she wouldn't be making the mistake of marrying him. A Tamar-David disaster was avoided.

The opening of a Catholic Worker–style house in Salt Lake City was not welcomed by the bishop there, Joseph Federal, and the New York Chancery had told Federal, when he inquired, that in no way did the Catholic Worker "enjoy ecclesiastical approval in this Archdiocese." Hennessy and Lathrop made gracious overtures to their new bishop; all were rebuffed.

A new breed of young person was showing up at the house at this time that was every bit as feisty and rebellious as Hennacy but a good deal less pleasing to Dorothy, the people Thomas Merton liked to call Dorothy's "beatniks." It was a term she pleaded with him to avoid. Allen Ginsberg visited the farm and occasionally gave readings on discussion nights, but that was one thing; he was a man of the social fringe, but he was also a serious poet and an individual of spiritual inclinations. The "beatniks" were anything but serious. They brought their girlfriends or boyfriends to sleep over in the extra apartments the Catholic Worker rented, freely indulged in their drugs of choice, and showed up to work at St. Joseph House when and if they felt like it or when they wanted a free meal. Dorothy directed Charles Butterworth and Ed Forand to speak to the more egregious offenders. They were told to mind their own business. The apartments were eventually padlocked and the rent payments stopped.

One intermittent visitor to the house, an NYU student named Ed Sanders, along with a few mischievous Catholic Worker friends, pushed things a little further down the anti-establishment path. The group put out a mimeographed erotic poetry review to distribute in the Village—produced, it jokingly claimed in its pages, by the Catholic Worker—entitled *Fuck You: A Magazine of the Arts*. Dorothy's reaction was predictable (she was irate), and her fear that a copy would come to the attention of the cardinal wasn't unreasonable. Sanders had "a diabolic sense of humor," Dorothy told a friend, "and his aim was to affront us as much as he could." He had succeeded. That episode led to what the young people at the office thereafter referred to as "the Big Stomp": everyone involved with the publication of *Fuck You* or anyone who even spoke up for Sanders was sent packing.

Not that Dorothy couldn't "enjoy the comic aspects of things," Judith Gregory insisted. When she heard that some of the same unruly crowd had been taken in by the American Friends Committee, where they had changed the name of their publication to *Fuck Thee*, she thought that was quite funny. But she didn't want to see Sanders and his friends on her territory ever again.

The issues that had always mattered to *The Catholic Worker* continued to be raised in the paper by the new generation of writers. Alleviating involuntary poverty would never become a marginal concern—and Dorothy greeted with pleasure the publication in 1962 of Michael Harrington's *The Other America*, his best-selling study of poverty in the United States (read by President Kennedy, his brother Robert, and his brother-in-law Sargent Shriver) that is credited with providing data and inspiration for the federal government's War on Poverty.

Harrington acknowledged in his preface that "it was through Dorothy Day and the Catholic Worker movement that I first came into contact with the terrible reality of involuntary poverty and the magnificent ideal of voluntary poverty." She was reading George Orwell's *The Road to Wigan Pier* and *Down and Out in Paris and London* that summer. Finally an American had spoken up as authoritatively and persuasively about the great unmentionable in the land of plenty as Orwell had in Great Britain in the 1930s. That was her Michael. (The fact that Dorothy didn't believe in interfering with her book reviewers is evidenced by the sharp-tongued review of the book that appeared in the June issue: Judith Gregory had high literary standards and was not one to mince words.)

Racial injustice was likewise a theme *The Catholic Worker* was not ever going to soft-pedal. The paper printed reports on the experiences of the Freedom Riders and the damning results of its own survey on the discriminatory policies of hotels on the Lower East Side of Manhattan. In the summer of 1963, Dorothy joined a group of marchers in Danville, Virginia, after being asked to speak there on behalf of integration and faced down some of the most threatening police officers she had ever encountered. Similarly, labor disputes were still given space in the paper—though admittedly somewhat less than in the past—and Dorothy publicized her disappointment with Fordham University, which was still, in 1962, refusing to allow its lay faculty, secretaries, and maids to form a legitimate union with full bargaining power.

Yet there was an issue that overshadowed all others in this tumultuous decade, and the brinkmanship of the Cuban missile crisis had made that clear. Ending poverty and racism and the exploitation of workers would mean nothing if the future brought mushroom clouds of atomic particles, the end of agriculture, and millions of unburied dead on the streets of every major city. Some readers of *The Catholic Worker* complained that the paper was becoming monotonously top-heavy with articles about war, pacifism, and the nuclear threat, but Dorothy regarded that criticism as profoundly misguided.

The burgeoning peace movement was bringing Dorothy into closer contact with a fuller range of activists now, with people as notable in their way as A. J. Muste, Bayard Rustin, Dave Dellinger, and Thomas Merton. Eileen Egan, a Welsh-born woman in her late forties who became one of Dorothy's traveling companions in the 1960s, had been on the Catholic Worker scene intermittently for the better part of two decades, occasionally writing for the paper and stopping by the house to work in the kitchen or attend a discussion evening when she was in town. Her full-time work was with missions for Catholic Relief Services in postwar Europe, in India with Mother Teresa, and elsewhere, and with the founding of the American Pax Association, where she partnered with another respected antiwar activist, Gordon Zahn. Other sponsors of Pax included Hélène Iswolsky and Arthur Sheehan.

Zahn, a sociologist and teacher, was someone Dorothy especially admired; he had first written for *The Catholic Worker* during the war, when he had attacked the Allied saturation bombing of Cologne and described the plight of American conscientious objectors. His were the kind of books she believed in: *Another Part of the War* described the experience of imprisoned COs in wartime camps in New England, which Zahn knew about firsthand; his *German Catholics and Hitler's Wars* was a disturbing, well-researched indictment of Catholics' passivity during the rise of Nazism (when the hierarchy's prudence became, in effect, capitulation), a book that scuttled his career at Loyola University in Chicago; and his biography of Franz Jägerstätter was an important work about an unsung hero. Jägerstätter was an Austrian farmer and devout Catholic who, despite the urging of his local pastor and bishop that he be mindful of his patriotic duty, refused to serve in the Nazi army. He was beheaded by the Germans in 1943 at the age of thirty-seven and has since been beatified. His grave in the 1960s was already becoming a site of pilgrimage for the young. Jägerstätter's was a perfect martyrdom narrative for the antiwar movement. Dorothy enthusiastically reviewed Zahn's biography, aptly titled In Solitary Witness.

Her friendship with Gordon Zahn also provided Dorothy with something of a proper "cover." Though courtly and mild-mannered, he had emphatic opinions, and he could—and did—offer sharp critiques of the Church hierarchy and its dismal record on the subjects of peace and war, critiques of a bluntness that Dorothy did not always want to make herself in a public way. To Zahn she confided, "I never expected much of the bishops."

Yet—in a development Dorothy had long been waiting for—the new pope, the very un-Pius-like Angelo Roncalli, suggested that maybe all that was about to change, that the Vatican's disapproval of conscientious objection and support for the "just war" theory and obsession with fighting communism might be revised or mitigated by John XXIII. That prospect thrilled Dorothy Day and everyone else at the Catholic Worker.

Pope John XXIII's encyclicals were generous, warmhearted, and challenging to conservatives—and they spoke to Dorothy more than any previous papal statement had. Mater et magistra in 1961 observed that, although spiritual salvation was the primary concern of the Church, the magistra of Catholicism had a duty to offer guidance concerning "the exigencies of man's daily life, with his livelihood and education, and general, temporal welfare and prosperity." The encyclical affirmed the principle "that the remuneration of work is not something that can be left to the laws of the marketplace . . . a decision left to the will of the more powerful." It called for wages that would allow all workers "to live a truly human life and to fulfill their family obligations in a worthy manner." It decried "the spirit of hedonism abroad today" and the investment of resources to create "terrible instruments of ruin and death." No one would suggest that encyclicals from earlier popes, notably Leo XIII and Pius XI, had been silent on the theme of labor relations and justice to workers (and John XXIII's encyclical alluded frequently to his predecessors' encyclicals), but there was an exhilarating quality to an updated, extensive, and explicit critique of the capitalist system and such a clear attack on "unbridled luxury," on the "privileged few [who lived] in violent, offensive contrast to the utter poverty of the majority." That was, after all—had always been—the ethos of the Catholic Worker.

Pacem in terris in 1963 was even more to Dorothy's liking. For the first time, a pontiff recognized that the very nature of war had changed. Nuclear weaponry had altered the terms of armed conflict, and a tired reiteration of the "just war" theory was woefully inappropriate at a time when governments, including that of the United States, were speculating about the utility of limited nuclear strikes and the inevitability of massive numbers of civilian deaths. (The encyclical raised several other issues and included the crucial observation that the role of women in society had changed and that women would rightly no longer "tolerate being treated as mere instruments.") The arms race, the concept of deterrence through mutual assured destruction, racism, and nationalism were condemned, while the importance of individual conscience—a vigorous nod to the pacifists—was affirmed. As one historian of the nonviolence movement in America wrote, "*Pacem in terris* heralded a new approach to warfare and a revolution in the meaning of Catholic peacemaking."

Not everyone in the Curia was pleased with that development. Not everyone among the religious orders was pleased, either. Thomas Merton was directed to cease writing essays on the topic—though he was told he could continue to pray for peace. In a letter to Jim Forest, he summarized his situation: someone in the intelligence service had told his Trappist superiors that he was publishing in "a communist-controlled publication (The Catholic Worker)." He could joke about it to Forest—"You didn't know you were communist-controlled, did you?"—but the narrowness of that outlook troubled him, as it did Dorothy.

It was the right moment, then, Dorothy decided, to be present in Rome as the Vatican Council continued to debate those very issues. In April 1963, she set sail from New York to meet up in Italy with fifty other women from various countries—Catholic women, women of different faiths, women of no faith at all—to be present for any public functions to which they could be admitted and present a petition to the Holy Father. "Mothers for Peace" was a disparate and impassioned group that wanted to bear witness, and the Catholics among them participated in a fast. It was clear that they would not enjoy a private audience with the pontiff, whose health was declining by the week and whose cancer diagnosis was now public knowledge. The fact that a few of the mothers, including Dorothy, were suspected of belonging to left-wing political groups might have been a factor in what they saw as their marginalization, though at his weekly public audience the pope did laud the "Pilgrims for Peace" who had come to the Eternal City, and that was recognition enough for the delighted mothers. They were sure then that their petition had, in fact, reached him.

That packed, hectic month in Italy included side trips for Dorothy to Florence, Siena, Assisi, and Monte Cassino. In Milan, she was asked to speak to a group of university students with a translator by her side, and at that gathering met the renowned theologian and teacher Father Luigi Giussani. She gave a talk to American seminarians in Rome, prayed at the tombs of the last four popes, and was allowed a private interview with Cardinal Augustin Bea, a prominent member of the Curia, who assured her he knew of the good work being done by the Catholic Worker. (Whether Gordon Zahn had ever mentioned it is not known, but Cardinal Bea was the prelate who had attempted to block the publication in Germany of his *German Catholics and Hitler's Wars*.) Her more general impression, though, was that the clergy she met, Father Giussani excepted, did not know much about lay organizations concerned with social justice—how many churchmen still thought in terms of "their" Church, "their" leadership—but Dorothy was sure that that approach to the faith was changing. John XXIII had set something in motion that would not be easily sidetracked.

Dorothy felt acutely the pain of John XXIII's death, which occurred the very day she returned to New York, as she did a few weeks later of another religious figure closer to home. Joseph McSorley, the Paulist priest who had seen her through her early struggles with the hierarchy, who had watched her back when the Chancery and local priests were most agitated about the tone and philosophy of *The Catholic Worker*, passed away. "How gentle and how saintly a man," she wrote in her July–August column. Few were left who remembered the 1930s and the suspiciousness that the Catholic Worker had engendered at its inception.

Though President Kennedy's assurance in a televised interview with Walter Cronkite the summer before his assassination satisfied some people that the United States was not about to become involved in a major war, others were less confident. In August, Tom Cornell and Chris Kearns had staged the first anti–Vietnam War protest. Dorothy, too, was concerned that her government was about to flex its muscles in the jungles of Southeast Asia. Invited two months later to go to England to be a speaker at the British Pax conference at Spode House, a Dominican retreat center outside Birmingham, Dorothy happily accepted the invitation, even though she had been abroad already that year and took Eileen Egan with her.

Upon her arrival in London, Dorothy told Egan that she wanted to make one stop before heading north. She wanted to see her British counterpart, whom she had met in New York many years before. Seventy-nine years old, a Protestant from a privileged background who had given away her money and taken to living in the East End slums among those she helped, Muriel Lester was a Christian socialist, a pacifist, a Tolstoyan, a friend of Gandhi—"a Baptist Dorothy Day," as one religious scholar called her. Egan thought they were "uncannily alike" with their chiseled features and high cheekbones, and they shared reminiscences of their arrests, their travels, their hopes for peace in the world.

At the Pax conference, Dorothy gave an extended address, "Fear in Our Time," that dealt with all the reasons people are naturally afraid to stand up for what is right: fear of bodily harm and adverse employment consequences, fear of humiliation and ostracism, fear even of making a mistake, of not always being right. Yet she had plenty of examples to offer of the admirable boldness of specific individuals—Rosa Parks, Dr. King, Bayard Rustin, Peter Maurin, the black and white people running the Koinonia Farm in Georgia, Cuban Catholics—and entire movements, Catholic Workers and early Communists alike. Her speech was an affirmation of risk taking, a call to make a more determined effort to overcome our unease about suffering, controversy, and criticism. The times demanded it. Perhaps because she was out of the country, Dorothy also used the Pax conference forum to display a level of honesty she sometimes shied away from at home, naming those bishops who had been obstructive over the years and insisting that it was a mistake for Catholics always to wait for the hierarchy to provide leadership on moral issues. When Peter Maurin had first told Dorothy, back in 1933, that he saw her as a potential Catherine of Siena instructing Church leaders, he had not, after all, been so wide of the mark.

As always, Dorothy fit more into one brief trip than most people would even attempt. She made excursions to Oxford, Cambridge, Southhampton, Greenwich, and Tunbridge Wells, spoke to the Anarchist Society in London, had tea with Eric Gill's brother in Cardiff, visited the poet Emily Coleman (a convert for whom Jacques Maritain had served as godfather) at Stanbook Abbey, and attended a dinner and reception at the house of Victor Gollancz, the left-wing publisher who had brought out Orwell's *Down and Out in Paris and London*. She ran into the now-famous Michael Harrington on the street, looking "young and happy," she thought. Then, before their departure, the two women received an unexpected invitation to lunch from the opposite end of the class spectrum from that occupied by Muriel Lester in the slums of London: Frank Pakenham, the seventh Earl of Longford, a convert and one of the few Catholic peers in the United Kingdom, asked Dorothy and Egan to dine with him at the House of Lords. They looked at each other in some astonishment. "Oh, why not?" Dorothy said.

Her journals from that trip are no longer extant, and to have been a fly on the wall at that repast would have been satisfying. The earl, father of the writer Lady Antonia Fraser, was one of the great eccentrics of his age, reviled by the British press more regularly than Dorothy had been by the American press. Living well into his nineties, he was an Anglo-Irish aristocrat who served in Parliament with the Labour Party, much of the time to the dismay of Labour Party leaders. He was the kind of man who had fought for the Wolfenden Report, which recommended the decriminalization of homosexuality, yet had a monomaniacal abhorrence of that orientation. He was a wide-eyed, wild-haired, bombastic original Dickens would gladly have made use of. Like many well-informed European Catholics and as a friend of Evelyn Waugh, the earl had heard about the accomplishments and controversies of the Catholic Worker.

Last, Dorothy made a stop her critics at home would have made much of: she went to Highgate Cemetery in north London to pay her respects at the grave of Karl Marx. She even shocked the young man from Pax who had accompanied her there, and probably Eileen Egan as well, by directing him to steal some flowers from a nearby grave and place them on that of the author of *Das Kapital*: another tweak at J. Edgar Hoover, Senator McCarthy, and the architects of the Bay of Pigs invasion.

* * *

One last book of original prose and one last attempt at fulfilling Peter Maurin's dream of a pastoral institute occupied Dorothy in the last months of 1963 and the first months of 1964. *Loaves and Fishes* was advertised by Harper & Row as a sequel to *The Long Loneliness*, which it is in a way, though it is really more a history of the Catholic Worker—the paper, the houses and farms, the protests. It gave Dorothy another opportunity to explain the importance of Peter Maurin in her life and the concept of holy poverty and to extol in print innumerable friends and allies: Robert Steed, Judith Gregory, Charles McCormack (whom she praised as the best manager of the house ever), Charles Butterworth, Ed Forand, Deane Mowrer, Marge Hughes, Marge's son-in-law Ed Turner, and Marge's daughter Johanna Hughes Turner, Dorothy's goddaughter. She was willing to acknowledge now more boldly than ever an affiliation with the Communist Party before her conversion ("I had been a Communist in the early twenties," she wrote, and later in the text she explicitly called herself an "ex-Communist" at the time she met Peter Maurin). Let the chips fall where they might.

Dorothy was unhappy, though, with the final product, which had been heavily cut and reshaped. Assorted editors had felt that the manuscript was far too long and meandering to reach the market they were hoping for, and even a favorite chapter about her experiences in the American South was dropped. It was a "hodge-podge," she complained. She must have dug in her heels about keeping her chapter on the Bodenheims' murder, which is an interesting but eccentric addition to the book, and she was adamant about not deleting her affectionate chapter about Ammon Hennacy (entitled "Picture of a Prophet") along with some loving pages about Mary Lathrop, maternally described as "always ready for an adventure." Ironically, though, despite her reservations, *Loaves and Fishes* is her most readable book and garnered a fair number of good reviews. The prose is limber, and the portraiture is evocative. *Commonweal* called it, somewhat oxymoronically, a work of "modest yet aggressive passion" written by "the most admired sign of contradiction in American Catholicism."

The purchase in the new year of a derelict estate in upstate New York more than made up for any disappointment with the book. Estimates of its acreage vary widely, but the property, on a bluff overlooking the Hudson River, was certainly the largest the Catholic Worker had ever owned, bought for $25,000 down on a $78,000 purchase price, a sum that pretty much emptied the Worker's bank account for the moment. Just north of Bard College outside the town of Tivoli, the nineteenth-century Italianate house with a wide veranda had originally been the mansion of John de Peyster, a writer and Civil War general, and in more recent times a school, Jehovah's Witness summer camp, and a hotel. Two structures, providing plenty of space for a dormitory and a chapel, and a huge swimming pool had been added over the years. With three buildings in total (all in need of one degree or another of repair, of course), ample grounds, and breathtaking views of the river, Dorothy felt, at last, that she had secured a site for the purposes that most mattered to her. Given the slope of the land and the rocks, the amount of arable land was minimal, but at that point that was evidently the least of her concerns.

As soon as the deed was signed, Dorothy arranged for a retreat to be run by her good friend Father Marion Casey, a pacifist priest from Minnesota (and the man who had the distinction of being the only priest Ammon Hennacy could find nothing to complain about), followed by a Fourth of July conference about the ongoing Harlem rent strike and worsening conditions in New York's slums. Deane Mowrer, whose sight was now all but gone, needed to get out of the city, so it was decided that she would move upstate and write about the activities at Tivoli for the paper. Hans Tunnesen, a Norwegian seaman and cook who had been with the Worker for three decades, would settle in to man the large kitchen, Marge Hughes would work her bread-making magic, and Marty and Rita Corbin and their three children—a family who had been with the Catholic Worker for several years—would reside there year-round and see to the management of the house while Marty continued to edit the paper long distance. John Filligar would keep the grounds and raise the vegetables. It was going to be an ideal setting for the first American Pax conference that summer. Hélène Iswolsky could have her own room to write when she decided to retire. "We've moved into the mansion class," Stanley Vishnewski commented.

Begun in a spirit of great optimism, Tivoli as "agronomic university," or conference center or site of spiritual retreats, would within a decade prove as heartbreaking to Dorothy as the earlier such ventures had been. It wasn't just the inadequate well, the liquor store that opened up in the village, the freeloaders who happened to mistake the place for a hotel, the health code violations. The times were changing in ways no one could have foreseen.

SEVENTEEN

⚛ BURNING ⚛

MECHANIZED FIRE—THE SEARING OF HUMAN FLESH—BECAME AN accepted part of warfare early in the twentieth century. The flame-throwers introduced in the Great War had one disadvantage, though: gasoline burned too quickly to do damage on any but a limited scale. Not so with napalm. Employed extensively during World War II, it is a form of jellied gasoline in which the thickening agents of naphthenic and palmitic acid better produce the long-range, long-lasting effect its users desire. A single bomb can engulf a 2,500-square-yard area, melting the skin off anyone it touches. Though it had been used in Southeast Asia on a small scale in the closing days of the Kennedy administration, napalm raining from the skies over Vietnam only became widespread, and its impact on the civilian population widely known, in 1965.

On November 6 and 9, 1965, Americans saw different images of fire-based destruction on the nightly news. On the sixth, less than three months after Congress had passed a law making the destruction of draft cards a crime, an antiwar rally was held in Union Square. Dorothy Day was at the podium with A. J. Muste and other notables in the pacifist movement. "I speak today," she told a crowd of two thousand, "as one who is old and who must endorse the courage of the young who themselves are willing to give up their freedom." Theirs was a struggle, she insisted, for "full freedom and human dignity," a vital protest against the "cruelty and hysteria of war." She spoke of other successful struggles "begun by courage, even in martyrdom," referring to the emerging nations of Africa, Asia, and Latin America and the black civil rights movement. She concluded with a prayer from St. Francis: "O Lord, make me an instrument of your peace. Where there is hatred, let me sow love." Following her remarks, four Catholic Worker young men including Tom Cornell joined her on the platform and burned their draft cards. (Cornell had to ask the Selective Service office for a duplicate of his card as he had burned the original at an earlier action.) Hecklers from the other side of the street screamed abuse at "Moscow Mary," a traitor and Communist, and called out to the young men to torch themselves, not their draft cards. One man with a fire extinguisher reached the foot of the stage, spraying Dorothy, Cornell, and the others. "It should have been acid, not water," one of the counterprotestors yelled.

Three days later, a young man named Robert LaPorte, reported to be associated with the Catholic Worker, sat down on the pavement in front of the Dag Hammarskjöld Library of the United Nations, composed himself in the Buddhist position of prayer, doused himself with gasoline, and struck a match. He lived for another twenty-four hours, over 90 percent of his body destroyed by second- and third-degree burns, and spoke from his bed at Bellevue Hospital about his motives. Like the young man who had committed the same act in front of the Pentagon earlier in the year, he was taking a stand against a war he saw as unjust that was escalating rapidly by the month, led by a president who had been elected the previous year by promising that the United States would not fight in Asia.

Massive napalm bombings by the US Air Force, draft card burnings, a fiery suicide: all disturbing events to contemplate, but only one registered extensive and prolonged anger with the American people, and it wasn't the peeling flesh of Vietnamese children or the charred form of a twenty-one-year-old former Trappist novice smoldering on a Manhattan sidewalk; it was the audacity of the young men who defied their government's order that they register for the draft and assist in a war effort they regarded as profoundly immoral. This was the new America Dorothy felt she was facing, a country that saw itself as a beacon of democracy and the leader of the free world even as it was committing atrocities abroad, its troops blessed by prelates of her own Church, dissent regarded as treason.

Dorothy Day's awareness of the problem of Vietnam long predated the United States' involvement, though. In May 1954, after reading several books on the topic, she had written a historical sketch for *The Catholic Worker* about the West's relation to Indochina (with a lengthy reflection about a martyred French Catholic missionary there, Théophane Vénard), expressing dismay over the French postwar occupation and the lack of respect that European nations, with an avaricious eye on the area's natural resources, had always showed toward the indigenous culture. Hers was an implicit warning of the dangers of a US commitment to a land war in the jungles of Vietnam, even as the French were seeking just that aid from President Eisenhower in the midst of the catastrophe of Dien Bien Phu. And with more insight and prescience than any officials in the State Department or the Pentagon, she had raised the possibility that North Vietnam might merely be another Yugoslavia—a repressive, anti-Christian, Communist state but *not* a part of any vast Soviet or Chinese bloc that represented a falling-domino juggernaut threat to the rest of the world.

There were others, of course, outside government circles who were of a similar mind. The year after her *Catholic Worker* column, Dorothy had read *The Quiet American*, Graham Greene's novel that suggested how easily the United States' rabid anticommunism, good intentions, and naiveté about the region could lead to disaster. But the skeptics and protestors were a minority in the fifties and early sixties, and by 1965, that disaster was well under way. The United States' role in Vietnam became the ultimate heartbreak for Dorothy Day the citizen as well as Dorothy Day the Catholic, shattering hopes formed fifty years earlier that her country would ultimately use its power and prestige for greater ends.

The reactions to LaPorte's death were troubling on several fronts. His suicide was not an action the Catholic Worker supported, and there was even some confusion as to how involved the young man had been with anything taking place on Chrystie Street. Few people remembered his being there very often. Dorothy had seen him only a few times and hadn't spoken with him personally, to the best of her recollection. She offered the most generous assessment of his shocking decision that she could, terming him a "victim soul" and suggesting that although "it has always been the teaching of the Catholic Church that suicide is a sin . . . mercy and loving-kindness dictate another judgment." It was "a sad and terrible act," not a sound or healthy one, she agreed, but "Roger's attempt was to love God and his brother."

Fingers were sharply pointed in her direction, though. A *National Catholic Reporter* editorial suggested that radical pacifist rhetoric could have a dangerous effect on "young and tender consciences," strongly implying that the Catholic Worker, a movement that had "never been well-grounded intellectually," must shoulder some of the blame for LaPorte's death and needed to be more careful in its statements. At New York University's Catholic Center,

Dorothy attended a gathering of angry students fired by such hostility that she was momentarily concerned for her physical safety. Two bomb threats were received at the Catholic Worker. William F. Buckley had been warning in his syndicated columns for some time that "deluded young men having fallen under the otherworldly influence of Miss Dorothy Day" were apt to come to just such horrific ends. Thomas Merton's response, which came in the form of a telegram to Dorothy, caused her the greatest discomfort (and anger) as he, too, pointedly questioned the extent to which the Catholic Worker might be responsible or even have extended implicit approval for such a terrible act. Stung, Dorothy wrote back to insist that the opposite was true. "If anyone ever dreamed he contemplated such an action," she assured Merton, "he would have been watched day and night" by his peers. "None of us can understand what has happened." She asked for Merton's prayers.

As the social fabric of the United States began to fray in unprecedented ways, Dorothy could at least take some sustenance from developments in Rome. Earlier that fall, she and Eileen Egan had flown to Italy, once again as "peace lobbyists," to be present for the closing session of Vatican II, during which they began an arduous ten-day fast at a convent there, subsisting entirely on water—a great trial to Dorothy's no longer iron constitution. (During that fast, Egan remembered, Dorothy had pains "she had never had before, pains in her very bones.") She had been thrilled by the Vatican's announcement definitively reversing Pope Pius XII's statement about conscientious objectors and, a few months later, an unequivocal statement condemning nuclear war, two of the many fruits, she felt, of the great council the late pope had set in motion. Popes John XXIII and Paul VI had never shared their predecessor's opposition to statements of conscience in wartime, and it was a particular relief to know at last that young Catholic men who chose that option would not need to feel any qualms that they were acting against Church authority. In pre-Christmas talks given in Providence, New Haven, and Philadelphia, and in New York City at Fordham University and Yeshiva University, Dorothy felt there was as much hopeful news to share as there was concern about the future and the widening war.

Other positive signs came from a geographically opposite direction. In California, Cesar Chavez, cofounder in 1962 of the National Farm Workers

Association, was organizing his followers in ways that were unprecedented for a community that had long been assumed to be in a hopeless economic position because of its migrant status, lack of community ties, lack of political clout, and invisibility in the press. *The Catholic Worker* had been one of the few publications in the nation to address with any regularity the plight of the nation's grape and lettuce pickers. By 1964, Chavez had brought more than a thousand members into his new union, which won its first strike and pay raise in 1965. That cause itself would have elicited Dorothy's backing under any circumstance, but meeting Chavez when he came to New York in April 1966 had left a warm personal impression. Here at last was a labor organizer who was a devout Catholic, lived humbly, supported the cause of nonviolence, and believed that his was a spiritual and not merely an economic mission. "He looks just like his pictures," she happily observed. It had been years since she had met a labor leader about whom she felt such confidence. She let him know she would always be ready to help his cause.

That spring saw Dorothy away from New York again for an extended period. A speaking tour and visits to houses of hospitality took her to cities in Ohio, Indiana, Illinois, Wisconsin, Minnesota, and Missouri. Before leaving for the Midwest, she had accepted an invitation to talk at an Episcopal church, St. James', in Hyde Park, not far from Tivoli. She felt welcomed, but one of the pastors there let it be known that he thought her views on the war in Vietnam were completely wrong. She heard the same thing from a Jesuit from India who had stopped by to visit in New York the week before. India would one day fall to the Communists, he assured her, if the United States failed to check North Vietnamese aggression now: communism was monolithic, its intention was world conquest, and Dorothy was a political naif. That was the never-finished residue of pre-sixties American anticommunism. Stalin and McCarthy were dead, the Korean War was long over, and Alger Hiss and Whittaker Chambers were names from the past. Yet the domino theory was alive and well, J. Edgar Hoover was warning President Lyndon Johnson that Communist sympathizers (from Martin Luther King, Jr., to Theodore White) had infiltrated every corner of American life, and ministers of God were less worried about indiscriminate bombing and mounting casualty figures than that Ho Chi Minh should be stopped at the 17th parallel.

How refreshing to spend time with people who thought otherwise. In Chicago, toward the end of her monthlong trip, Dorothy had dinner with

Saul Alinsky at the home of his protégé and her friend Monsignor John Joseph Egan. A well-known community organizer and left-wing radical, Alinsky was a longtime supporter of the Catholic Worker. He and Dorothy had met once before, and their regard was mutual. The fact that Alinsky was an agnostic mattered a good deal less than his mentorship of Monsignor Egan in his important community work, his authorship of the brash *Reveille for Radicals*, and the fact that he had been instrumental in the 1930s in revitalizing the blighted Chicago neighborhood that was the setting of Upton Sinclair's *The Jungle*. He was a stern critic of Sargent Shriver, who headed Lyndon Johnson's much-hyped "war on poverty," an effort that seemed to him to be founded on a form of colonialism and the dubious premise that throwing large amounts of money, helter-skelter, at urban poverty was going to change anything. Ironically, it was always a source of pride to Sargent Shriver, a devout Catholic, that he had been Dorothy Day's host at a Saint Thomas More Club Communion breakfast at Yale in 1938.

Alinsky's disdain for "big government" paternalism and the smugness of the bureaucrats he met who knew better than the people they were supposed to serve made for a special bond with Dorothy, who agreed that community-level, "from the bottom up," activism was the only kind that was going to produce results. Alinsky also knew Cesar Chavez quite well, though he ultimately did not share Dorothy's hopefulness about his long-range leadership qualities.

The most painful part of any homecoming now was observing Tamar's family troubles. The Hennessys had been a family in crisis for far too long. Since David had left home, nothing had improved for him, and his alcoholism and inertia were now completely out of his control. When Dorothy's grandson Eric took the bus to New Jersey as an adolescent to see his father, then living with a woman in a run-down part of Atlantic City, he found him passed out on a park bench, too inebriated to recognize his eldest son. Eric was "crushed . . . shocked by what he had found," Tamar remarked. Desperate to support the six of her offspring who still ranged in age from six to seventeen, Tamar was struggling with the demands of a rigorous nursing program when twenty-one-year-old Becky and eighteen-year-old Eric announced their intention of dropping out of school—Becky walking away from a full scholarship at the University of Vermont, Eric leaving a technical school. Becky was going to get married, she informed the family, and indeed she did, providing

Dorothy with her first great-grandchild by the end of the year. Eric's decision carried more ominous consequences, as he would lose his student deferment and become eligible for the draft. In 1966, for men of his background, that almost automatically meant being called up for duty in Vietnam.

Even more upsetting to Dorothy on her visits to Vermont each summer and each Christmas were her daughter's fragile emotional state—the Valium she needed to take to get herself to her job, the periods of incapacitating depression—and dwindling religious faith. None of that made its way into Dorothy's columns, which always offered a cheerful picture of family life in Vermont. But it shocked Dorothy that Tamar had no interest in seeing that any of her children attended Mass or observed the holy days and she herself was expressing equivocal thoughts about the faith she had been raised in. By the end of the year, Tamar would cease attending church and would openly admit that she was no longer a practicing Catholic. She believed in the Catholic Worker, she maintained; she did not believe in any of the rest of it—the liturgy, the creed, the piety, the papacy. For her mother, that was an appalling, heartbreaking reality to assimilate.

Dorothy saw no alternative but to accept Tamar's decision, hope and pray that she would one day change her mind, and immerse herself all the more energetically in her own work. If she could admit to herself that she had made grave errors in raising Tamar, it was too late to do anything about them.

The American Pax conference at Tivoli that summer was, as such events usually were, an energizing week of conversations and workshops with information shared by old friends and new acquaintances about the peace movement worldwide. Tivoli had not yet begun to fall apart. A separate daylong conference was held concerning racial issues in the United States with a few African American and Puerto Rican participants, and Dorothy spent a day in August at a Dominican retreat house in Schenectady where the weighty pile of documents that had come out of Vatican II was being carefully studied. She was invited to Fairfield University in Connecticut to address a large gathering of the Christian Family Movement where thousands of children sprawled across the campus, watched over by local nuns, while three hundred couples and fifty priests listened to Dorothy on the topic of "Loving the Poor in Deed" and attended a Mass celebrated by New York's famous auxiliary bishop Fulton Sheen.

All of that was well and good. Yet when men called to Christ seemed to take an equivocal position on weighty matters such as the Fifth Commandment, there was reason to feel anything but hopeful. A talk before seminarians in Rochester, New York, was "disappointing," Dorothy noted in her diary. The young men she encountered might as well have been working for the Johnson administration. According to their worldview, Chinese communism, the gravest threat to democracy and Christianity, was the real force behind the trouble in Vietnam and had to be stopped by any means necessary. People such as Dorothy Day were obtuse on that subject and vaguely offensive in their naiveté. "It is hard to be treated so coldly," she observed, at a seminary no less. Her spirits were raised by an invitation to speak across town. Thankfully, the students at the Newman Club at the University of Rochester had, from her perspective, a more informed understanding of what was happening in Southeast Asia, where nothing that could be called a "democracy" existed in South Vietnam and where Ho Chi Minh wanted as little to do with Mao Zedong and the Chinese as he could manage.

The meeting with the seminarians rankled, but it bothered her more when men of high profile and significant influence, leaders who were supposed to have the most authentic understanding of Christ's teachings, took an insensitive approach to violence and suffering and even encouraged their continuance in the name of a presumed higher goal. On those occasions, optimism could collapse into bitterness and discouragement.

In late December, to Dorothy's horror, Cardinal Spellman flew to South Vietnam to praise the US struggle there and, in a Christmas Day sermon, urge the troops on to "total victory." In previous columns in *The Catholic Worker*, Dorothy had in a vague way praised the cardinal for spending time with US troops abroad in dangerous areas. His words on that trip, though, were cause for grave concern. Anything less than total victory, he insisted to the fighting men, was "inconceivable," as they were fighting for "the cause of righteousness, the cause of civilization, God's cause." A negotiated settlement with the godless Viet Cong and North Vietnamese, of the kind the Vatican firmly endorsed, would be the equivalent of defeat. En route home, Spellman stopped in Manila to visit with dictator Ferdinand Marcos and his wife, Imelda, who lived lavishly amid one of the most poverty-stricken populations on Earth.

Dorothy wasn't alone in her dismay at that turn of events and at the cardinal's hyperbolic words. The editors of *Commonweal* had by now turned against the administration, branding the war in Vietnam unjust and immoral. The noted newspaper cartoonist Pat Oliphant skewered Spellman in a widely reprinted, vitriolic cartoon. Oregon senator Wayne Morse publicly denounced the cardinal's sermon. A few days later, Pope Paul VI let it be known that he did not approve the New York prelate's views. Spellman's fellow US bishops remained silent, though. It was several months before any criticism of US policy in Southeast Asia began to be heard from that quarter, and a few weeks after the pope's rebuke, Spellman called President Johnson, eagerly accepting an invitation to lunch at the White House and insisting that he was sure the pope hadn't really meant what he'd said.

The frustration Dorothy often felt about the obstacles the Church hierarchy put into the path of the faithful was painfully reinforced by the Spellman episode. She used her January column in *The Catholic Worker* as an occasion to express her grief when she wrote about the danger of demonizing one's adversaries and ignoring the toll armed conflict inevitably takes on civilians. A demand for "total victory" over negotiation, "going against even the Pope," was an ethical lapse. "Words are as strong and powerful as bombs, as napalm," she insisted.

The next month she was equally explicit, and perhaps more tart, in her judgment when she described the recent arrest of twenty-three antiwar protestors, including ten college professors, during Mass at St. Patrick's Cathedral. They had been seized by the police for waving placards (THOU SHALT NOT KILL) intended to remind Spellman of his moral duty. She would not have joined them in a demonstration in a house of worship, she wrote, but she did permit her name to be used to raise funds for their defense.

As far as one can tell, the cardinal never responded to those columns.

Old warriors were passing away. A. J. Muste died suddenly and unexpectedly on February 11, 1967, and was honored by Dorothy with a laudatory notice in *Commonweal*, and Mike Gold, who had just turned seventy-three, was gone a few weeks later, the subject of a deeply loving remembrance by Dorothy in her column in *The Catholic Worker*. Later in the year, she included a respectful mention of the death of Che Guevara. Her critics took note.

Muste and Gold were formidable figures in their prime, and it was sometimes hard to see who was going to take their place. She appreciated the fact that many of the younger generation were less career oriented and less complacent about the wrongs of the world than their older siblings and parents had been, but that didn't mean that leadership and moral fervor—not as she expressed it, not as she lived it—were to be found emerging confidently from every direction of the counterculture.

From the point of view of a woman who was soon to turn seventy, too many of the college-age young she met—both the men and the women— were, in the main, a pretty self-regarding, hedonistic, rude, unwashed, and unreliable bunch. There was reason to wonder if their attacks on establishment America were founded in deeply felt beliefs about social justice, a late-adolescent wish to shock their elders, who still paid their college bills, or some indefinable combination of the two. (Of course, the same could be said about all youthful radicalism: How much of Dorothy's own early life had been about saying, I will not be what John Day wishes me to be, and I want him to know it?) In sum, Dorothy's view of the radical youth of the United States in the 1960s was anything but starry-eyed. Her letters and diary entries throughout that decade are filled with acerbic comments about the long-haired, sexually active, drug-indulging young men and women she encountered so frequently in New York and on her travels.

Increasingly, examples could be found close to home, too. Reluctant as she was to demand that a volunteer leave Catholic Worker premises, she did insist that two young men, one an ex-seminarian, had to go, as they were sleeping with their girlfriends in the house, which they seemed to regard as a rent-free dormitory, when they could easily afford rooms of their own elsewhere. The men protested Dorothy's sternness. "I could only explain that people were not sending us money to support them, but to support the destitute," she told Thomas Merton. Likewise, the drug crowd had to be told to go. St. Joseph House was not a sanctuary for users of illegal substances, at least not when the offenders were caught. The same scenario was played out repeatedly, yearly, well into the 1970s, and the evictees were always incredulous.

Nor did she want the name of the Catholic Worker to be even remotely associated with the libertarian excesses of the day. The style of provocation of Ed Sanders—he of *Fuck You: A Magazine of the Arts*—was beyond the pale, she felt. But even admirers, even the well intended, could drive her to distraction. Ever since he had first heard her speak at Brandeis University when he was a student there, Yippie Abbie Hoffman had found inspiration in Dorothy's statement of her values. Living in New York, he stopped by St. Joseph House from time to time. She was "the original hippie," he liked to say (and said repeatedly). Yet when the woman who had so inspired him picked up his *Revolution for the Hell of It*, a classic of sixties nihilism and sarcasm, she was dismayed. It was "a terrifying book," she noted in her diary, full of "bitterness, hatred, hell unleashed." Anti-establishment fervor came in many forms, and Hoffman's was not one Dorothy wanted anything to do with.

The huge anti–Vietnam War protest rally held in Central Park in the spring of 1967 gave similar cause for concern about selfishness and immaturity. On the one hand, it was satisfying that the number of Americans willing to stand up and say to a government they no longer trusted, "Enough killing, enough lying," was increasing by the month. Yet she disliked the tone those important events had acquired: the rage and the obscenities, the irreverence and smugness, the lack of humility. She was particularly offended by the sight of buttons blazoning the message DRAFT SPELLMAN. To her mind, it was entirely possible to be in the right politically and in the wrong spiritually, and many of the protestors exemplified, for Dorothy, that dichotomy. She attended the rally in the Sheep Meadow, she noted, but kept to the side. "I hate contempt and ridicule," she wrote to Frank Donovan, the new business manager of *The Catholic Worker*, about the experience.

By that time, Dorothy Day had become a truly confusing figure to many. How, more and more people asked, could one of the most challenging, anti-establishment voices in the United States—in the modern world—care about protecting Cardinal Spellman's dignity and profess such ardent loyalty to an institution most non-Catholics in the West saw as profoundly reactionary? It was not a source of confusion to her.

First, as she had always insisted, she believed without doubt in the reality of God, the divinity of Christ, the inspirational, intercessional capacity of the Virgin Mary and the saints, confession and absolution, and the apostolic Church to which she belonged. That belief was something she wished all human beings could share in some form; it was the bedrock source of any Catholic's humanity and morality. That such a deep faith would be impossible to sustain outside an organized, hierarchical community of faith was a truth of which she was convinced. Yet none of that meant that she lived with an ahistorical mind-set or a blinkered sense of the world she lived in.

That some popes were less Christlike than others, that too many bishops aligned themselves with the powers-that-be and evinced scant interest in holy poverty, that too many priests were more preoccupied with personal comfort and the minutiae and complacency of parish life—none of those were realities that Dorothy had ever passed over lightly. She knew, too, that some bishops had wished over the years that she were a less opinionated, less questioning daughter of the Church. No more or less than anyone who loves his or her family or country ever feels that attachment in an uncritical way, so she loved the Catholic Church—authentically and critically. She wished it to be judged, as Karl Adam had suggested in *The Spirit of Catholicism*, that crucial text she had read in 1928, by its finest achievements and highest aspirations rather than by the lapses and missteps occasioned by fallible men. Those achievements and aspirations, divinely inspired, precluded rage and obscenity, ridicule and contempt, regard for self before others.

But there was even more to Dorothy's understanding of Catholicism, elements of which were necessarily not going to appeal to—or even be understood by—a culture that had made its own gods out of skepticism, rationalism, democracy, and perfect liberty. Postwar America didn't merely honor individuality and the rights of man but gave them absolute pride of place. Postwar America often equated reverence with religiosity, viewed mysticism as humorous eccentricity, disdained holy silence, and invested inconceivable fortunes in spectacle and entertainment. That was not the kind of society, she well knew, that was likely to embrace the Sermon on the Mount. With each passing year after her first meeting with Peter Maurin, Dorothy wished to distance herself from anything that might lessen the force of those words, the astonishing originality of the call to regard "the least of these" as the embodiment of God toward whom we should show infinite love.

Dorothy's "cultivation of worldly failure," as the historian James Terence Fisher fairly termed her lifelong quest, did indeed come to have a Jansenist aspect to it; there was at times what could be called a fetishizing of poverty in her refusal to seek under any circumstances a normal modicum of comfort (e.g., her determination to find not merely a modest hotel on her travels but the cheapest, most spartan one in town). Yet at many more times, it was simply the means by which she, and those who chose to follow her example, could feel the living presence of Jesus in their daily lives and more fruitfully obey his commands.

So, too, her belief in obedience to episcopal authority. Having experienced firsthand when she was young the raw pleasures and dangers of sex—more than she wanted most people to know—she certainly agreed by the 1930s with the Church's teachings on abortion, birth control, masturbation, and premarital sex. There was no reluctant acquiescence involved in that stance. Moreover, obedience to religious authority itself became a virtue, not only as a matter of belief but as a *spiritual gesture* that needed to be practiced from time to time, a means by which to humble the ego and circumscribe one's individuality. If a healthy ego and a strong sense of self, sacred notions in the West, were obstacles to knowing God, they must cease to be all-important. Those ideas were not easy to convey to the young people she was surrounded by in the whirlwind of the sixties.

Nowhere did Dorothy feel that her conversion, subsequent struggles, and life choices had been more rightly made than when she was in Rome. In October, a few weeks before her seventieth birthday, she and Eileen Egan set off for Italy again, this time for the third World Congress for the Lay Apostolate. She traveled east by boat, as she always had, but came home by air, astonished at the ease, speed, and cheaper fares of a mode of transportation she had nervously resisted for twenty years. A skeptic returned from Italy a confirmed flyer.

The congress included workshops, speeches, lunches, dinners, café conversations on the fly with members of the clergy and the laity, and an address by the pontiff. Tom Cornell, Dorothy Weston Coddington—her first coeditor of the paper, back in 1933—and the blustery Catherine de Hueck Doherty were in attendance as well. Unlike the two previous congresses, at which Dorothy Day had not been present, this one did live up to its name: it was a gathering led more by the laity than the hierarchy. Following a week of meetings, the congress's final public resolutions included a unanimous condemnation of racism ("totally unacceptable . . . and contrary to the Christian faith"), a statement of concern about the plight of the Palestinian refugees, suggestions that women be given a larger role in Church affairs and greater tolerance be shown for marriages between men and women of different Christian faiths, and some rather general remarks condemning war that, probably to Dorothy's annoyance, made no direct mention of the one war that was raging on the planet and showed no signs of stopping.

The drift of opinion Dorothy heard about one topic surprised her— namely, the Church's stance on birth control. Pope Paul VI had been seeking counsel on the matter for some time. For her part, Dorothy hardly assumed that there was much to discuss. Instead, she learned that more than a few cardinals, and numerous priests from many countries, were ready to advocate for a change they regarded as long overdue, implying that the basis in natural law for the Church's prohibition of contraception was questionable and suggesting that it was time to allow married Catholic couples to decide the matter themselves. She was relieved that many congress participants were not of the same mind. It was a timely topic, though. Only six months earlier, *Time* magazine had run a jubilant cover story on "the pill," entitled "Freedom from Fear." Her concern presumably was that the growing strength of the pro-contraception forces, some within the Curia itself, would influence the pope to announce an about-face. (That turned out, of course, not to be the case at all the following year. Quite the contrary.) She would have been happier with a resolution affirming the Church's long-standing view, but there was no consensus on the topic, so the lay apostolate remained silent on one of the most controversial issues of the day. On balance, given the polite factionalism in the air, the resolutions did not seem to please many of the congress's participants, she noted—herself included.

On October 15, the Feast of St. Teresa of Ávila, Dorothy received Communion at the hands of the pope, only one of 150 out of more than 3,000 delegates from a hundred countries (and only one of two Americans) invited to receive that "truly overwhelming honor." In typical fashion, she recorded for her readers in her column in *The Catholic Worker* the people for whom she prayed in those precious moments after receiving the Host in St. Peter's Basilica: the many conscientious objectors in prison in the United States, the late Che Guevara, and Lolita Lebrón, one of the Puerto Rican nationalists in prison for the attack on Congress in 1950, who had recently been writing to her from prison.

Before leaving Rome, Dorothy and Eileen enjoyed an unexpected evening out on the town. Through mutual friends, they went to dinner one night with Ignazio Silone and his wife. Silone's 1936 masterpiece, *Bread and Wine*, had long been one of Dorothy's favorite novels, and meeting the man, an ex-Communist, who had written the most compelling fictional account of Mussolini's Italy, the struggles of peasant life in Abruzzo, the cruelty of the Fascists, and the narrowness of the Communist opposition, was a great thrill. The two shared a similar disillusionment about modern life and politics. Like Dorothy, Silone was hard of hearing in one ear, and they had to rearrange themselves accordingly at the dinner table, but he was a marvelous person to break bread with, telling humorous stories and wanting to know more about the inspiration of her life, Peter Maurin. The novelist was evidently not familiar with Dorothy's personal story, as he asked her if she were a practicing Catholic! He had fallen away from the Church himself long before, though *Bread and Wine* suggests a deep respect for those priests, small in number as they were, who had stood up to Mussolini.

With Eileen Egan off to Israel, two other stops occupied Dorothy before she headed back to New York, taking her in opposite directions: Sicily and England. She had long wanted to meet Danilo Dolci, spoken of by many as Italy's Gandhi or Martin Luther King, Jr., respected by writers like Silone, and known for his work on behalf of the exploited workers of Sicily and his brave fight against the Mafia. Calling out government and ecclesiastical corruption, he was even more a thorn in the side of the Catholic hierarchy in Sicily than Dorothy was in New York. The difference was that Dolci had left the Church, Dorothy was saddened to learn, while she hadn't and never would. Though the language barrier and the inadequacy of their interpreter made conversation difficult during her three-day visit, Dolci made sure his guest not only saw the landscape, the Greek temple ruins, and the picturesque small towns of the island but experienced the opposite end of the spectrum as well. Her tour with Dolci through the slums of Palermo was shocking. The worst villages, she wrote later in *The Catholic Worker*, were "paradises of sun and air" compared to the backstreets of Palermo.

London was a different matter. It always was for an Anglophile. Earlier in the year, Dorothy had immersed herself in Edgar Johnson's satisfyingly fat two-volume biography of Charles Dickens, and she rarely traveled any great distance without a British novel in her bag. After speaking at the British Pax conferences in the capital and at Spode House and visiting several Catholic Worker–style communities, she had time for the British Museum across the street from her hotel, a tour of some of the old synagogues in the East End, and a trip to the Brontës' house in Haworth. She also met a kindred spirit of sorts, the Dominican priest and theologian Herbert McCabe. McCabe had recently been fired from his position as editor of *New Blackfriars* journal for his editorial about a prominent fellow theologian, Charles Davis, who had announced that he was leaving the Catholic Church, repelled as he was by its corruption. McCabe's response was that Davis was being absurd; of course the Church is corrupt, it always was corrupt, it was a product of both base human needs and divine guidance, but that was hardly a reason to turn from Rome. That wasn't exactly the line the *New Blackfriars* board wanted taken on the matter. McCabe was a devout, feisty, quirky individual—not unlike Dorothy herself. He was also a passionate critic of the Vietnam War. Dorothy met up with Egan again, and the two returned to New York, exhausted but elated.

While the travelers were out of the country, they had missed considerable drama in the streets and in the news. Opposition to the Vietnam War at home had grown more heated, resulting in more aggressive activism. Philip Berrigan, a Josephite priest of Dorothy's acquaintance, and three others, moving from dissent to active resistance, had been arrested for pouring blood over draft records at a Selective Service office in Maryland. The trespassing and vandalism of the Baltimore Four were one of the earliest of dozens of draft board actions that occurred across the country over the next few years and resulted in a stiff jail sentence for Berrigan. That same month, the March on the Pentagon saw 100,000 demonstrators, including Dwight Macdonald, Robert Lowell, Norman Mailer, and her good friend from the old days Father Charles Owen Rice, converge on the Department of Defense to make the largest and most public statement to date of opposition to the war machine. Catholic Workers were among the marchers.

The cost of the war took on a poignant personal aspect when the Hennessys had to come to terms with Eric's draft status. The likelihood was that, unemployed and out of school, he was going to be sent to Vietnam. Earlier in the year, Tamar had pleaded with the local draft board in Vermont for an exemption based on her dependence on him as an eldest son in a family with an absent father and numerous younger siblings. She had apparently done so over Eric's objection, but the request had been rejected in any case. Eric was drinking heavily at the time and had recently totaled the family car. He was notified that he was to report to the induction center in Woodstock, Vermont, on January 2, 1968—sad news indeed for his grandmother.

Spending the holidays in Vermont, Dorothy had hoped to have some time with her grandson before his departure, but most of that week, he was out and about with his buddies, who were also being called up. His gifts under the tree remained unopened, left on his bureau when he reported for duty until he returned on his first leave in April. Such was his anger, about which Tamar, his siblings, and his grandmother could do nothing. The whole family dynamic was fraught. Dorothy attended Mass on Christmas Day alone.

Unlike Eric and most men of his age and class, how many Catholic Worker young men who were refusing their draft call were in jail or awaiting sentencing by this time: the number was considerable. And growing. The imprisonment of two men Dorothy especially respected—David Miller and Bob Gilliam—was given coverage in the paper. Yet newcomers, male and female, kept arriving on Dorothy's doorstep. Daniel Marshall and his wife were typical of the kind she had always hoped the movement would attract.

Marshall was a young man about whom Dorothy didn't have to lose sleep fretting over drug use, hedonism, and loutish irreverence. A New Yorker whose parents knew Frank Sheed and Maisie Ward, he had heard Dorothy speak at the Jesuit high school he attended, Regis High School, in 1956 and again at the College of the Holy Cross in Worcester, Massachusetts, when he was an undergraduate. He had eventually drifted to San Francisco and found his way to a Catholic Worker house in Oakland, where he had become converted to the cause and to anarchism and, sometime later, to pacifism under the dynamic influence of Karl Meyer and Ammon Hennacy. He had arranged for Dorothy to give a talk at Berkeley in the midsixties. A conscientious objector who had refused to report back for duty with the Navy Air Reserve, he suspected that the government was on his trail. He also liked what he had heard about the Tivoli community, and, recently married, he and his wife decided in December 1967 to investigate the possibilities there. He spilled out his story to Dorothy when she opened the door of the farmhouse. Her bouncy reply: "Looks like jail for you! Come on in." Another pair of true believers was taken into the fold. Marshall did not, in fact, end up serving jail time but, a green-revolution activist, became a worker at Tivoli for two one-year stints in the 1970s.

The year 1968, possibly the most traumatic in twentieth-century US history, began for the Catholic Worker with the purchase of the 1st Street property it occupies today, which was ready for its residents, after numerous repairs, by midsummer. Yet it was a period that encompassed as much sorrow and anxiety as joy. It was a year of deaths, and not only those of combatants in the mud of Khe Sanh and the streets of Saigon during the Tet Offensive: it was a year marked by the murders of Martin Luther King, Jr., and Robert Kennedy; the accidental death of Thomas Merton, only fifty-three, while at an interfaith conference in Thailand; and the passing of men of principle she admired such as the great liturgical reformer and opponent of Nazism, Father Reinhold, as well as Upton Sinclair, Norman Thomas, and John Steinbeck. Race riots after Dr. King's death wreaked havoc, with entire city blocks going up in flames in the nation's capital, Harlem, Kansas City, Chicago, Detroit, and dozens of other cities.

The US Catholic Church itself seemed about to be torn asunder in the midst of a crucial philosophical and theological divide. The presence of priests and nuns at antiwar marches was for conservatives a sign of a new clerical radicalism they wanted no part of, while Pope Paul's long-awaited encyclical *Humanae vitae*, published in July and definitively insisting on the immorality of any form of birth control other than the rhythm method, led thousands of young people to turn from the Church and thousands of married couples to pay less attention than ever to any statements coming out of the Vatican. Ammon Hennacy published a new edition of his memoirs in 1968, explaining his reasons for leaving the Church.

"On Pilgrimage" for that year touches on some of those tragedies even as Dorothy struggled to find positive topics to write about as well. In her columns, she described with satisfaction Peggy Baird's entrance into the faith— of all the people she had known in Greenwich Village in the 1920s, Peggy would probably have seemed, when she met her, the least likely Catholic convert—eulogized Father Reinhold, whose loss she deeply felt, and wrote a piece, both appreciative and critical, about the inimitable Ammon. She expressed a sense of accomplishment about the appearance of *A Penny a Copy*, the *Catholic Worker* anthology brought out by Macmillan, and wrote about seeing the film of *War and Peace*, adding that the time might be right for her to reread Tolstoy's epic. Opportunities to recommend Tolstoy and Dostoevsky to her readers were always to be seized upon. She took a swipe at the New York archdiocese's new leader, Terence Cooke, when describing a Loyalty Day parade in the city and a counterdemonstration held in Central

Park, a march for peace, suggesting that his failure to appear at the latter event was a missed opportunity.

The major project for the Catholic Worker in the first half of 1968, however, was the move to the new quarters. In August, with the permits and the painting out of the way, with everyone finally settled in on 1st Street, it was time for another extended trip. Marge Baroni, more an epistolary friend than anything else, had asked Dorothy to visit her in Mississippi. The integration battles of the decade had made the situation of Marge—a white woman who socialized with blacks, a Catholic convert who vocally opposed segregation—scarcely tenable. For years, her family had endured a miserable time of it in Natchez, their neighbors ostracizing them, local thugs spewing insults and making threats of violence. Even fellow Catholics turned away from them at the Communion rail on Sundays. Marge needed to see her friend and mentor in person.

En route, Dorothy stopped in Washington, DC, to accept an award from the Liturgical Society, an occasion she used to speak well of the Berrigans, and then drove on to the Trappist monastery in Conyers, Georgia, to see how her old friend Jack English was managing, and then to Selma, to bask in the sight of the famous march, which Tom Cornell was covering for the paper. In Natchez, Mississippi, staying for a week, she had a chance to assess the progress that had been made in the South—integrated parks, integrated restaurants—and how much was left to do in an impoverished area. Most important, she was a shoulder for Marge to lean on. Her most pointed criticism when she wrote about the trip had to do with how little white churches seemed to be doing to ameliorate the social and physical hardships of the region's black residents. As far as she could tell, there was only a thin commitment to racial and economic equality among the clergy there, far too little priestly radicalism. Yet her trip "through our usually violent south" was at least a peaceful experience, she noted in her next column, compared to the horror that had taken place that month on the streets of Chicago at the Democratic National Convention.

In the North, a different picture of priestly radicalism had taken shape and was quickly expanding, with Philip Berrigan and his brother Daniel, a Jesuit priest, at the forefront of this momentous new development. Dorothy had known Dan from the 1940s, when before his ordination he had been teaching school in New York and would bring students by St. Joseph House, especially for the Friday-night "clarification of thought" discussions. When he and eight others burned the draft records in the Selective Service office in the Knights of Columbus building in Catonsville, Maryland, the event made headlines across the nation. At this point, people like Dorothy were forced to ponder the extent to which they could approve of activists like Phil and Dan Berrigan or the Milwaukee Fourteen, a group of fourteen men, including five priests and Jim Forest, who, inspired by the Berrigans, had raided the Milwaukee Selective Service office that fall and used homemade napalm to make a huge bonfire of thousands of draft cards and records. Baltimore's archbishop, Cardinal Lawrence Shehan, for instance, was one of the few Catholic prelates who had doubts about the war and believed in the right to conscientious objection. He understood the Berrigans' intent but firmly deplored their methods.

Ultimately, Dorothy was inclined to agree. An intimidating stance (and surely the invasion of an office was an unnerving experience for the people working there and could involve some degree of physical coercion) and the destruction of property were not part of the Gandhian approach the Catholic Worker espoused. She felt with Gordon Zahn and Thomas Merton that the Catonsville action had probably "frightened more than it edified." Yet she was temperate in expressing those reservations at first, understanding that others believed that more forceful gestures of opposition were needed. Her letters to the Berrigan brothers were scrupulously loving and supportive. They and the many men and women like them who were willing to go to prison were martyrs, she told her readers, offering themselves as "a living sacrifice, hostages" to a nation's murderous policies. She could even call their actions "a kind of prayer."

In October, when the trial of the Catonsville Nine began, she was present for a rally in Baltimore, an emotional event where nuns, seminarians, and college students by the hundreds gathered with veterans of the civil disobedience movement such as Noam Chomsky, Howard Zinn, I. F. Stone, Rabbi Abraham Heschel, Episcopal Bishop James Pike, and Dorothy herself. Her accommodations at a local convent were arranged by Willa Bickham and Brendan Walsh, who were just opening Viva House, a Catholic Worker house (still in existence fifty years later) and whose commitment to the poor of Baltimore Dorothy applauded.

Dorothy struck Francine du Plessix Gray, covering the event for *The New Yorker*, as "statuesque, austere," a little unsteady on her legs, but a charismatic figure who inspired a reverence in the audience quite different from the tumult that greeted the remarks of someone like Bishop Pike, "flamboyant as a peacock," who called for more draft card burnings and dared the government to arrest him as well. Dorothy spoke of the Berrigans' gesture of "peaceful sabotage" as a needed revolutionary act against the state but also an act "against the alliance of Church and state, an alliance which has gone on much too long. Only actions such as these," she proclaimed, "will force the Church to speak out when the state has become a murderer." She also reminded her audience, in the face of the calls so often heard now for more aggressive modes of protest, that the way of Gandhi, Martin Luther King, Jr., and Cesar Chavez was more important than ever. Pacifism was "the most difficult thing in the world," as she well knew, "and the one that requires the most faith." She received a standing ovation.

Asked later by a reporter in Baltimore, "Why has your Church been so silent about the war?" Dorothy's response was an exasperated retort: "What do you think this trial is all about?"

She was equally short with a young admirer who breathlessly approached her to ask if Father Berrigan was a Catholic Worker. "No, Dan isn't a Catholic Worker," she sharply answered Patricia McNeal, the future historian of Catholic pacifism. "He came to us and stole our young men away into the peace movement."

The frustrations of those who felt that the United States had lost its way were only increased in November. The peace movement of presidential candidate Eugene McCarthy, which seemed to blossom early during the primaries, went nowhere, and the dissembling Richard Nixon was elected to the presidency intending only to continue in a different form Lyndon Johnson's Vietnam policies for four more years, despite his campaign announcement of a "secret plan" to end the conflict. Nothing about the rhetoric of the Nixon-Agnew campaign suggested that tensions over race or the war were going to dissipate. It was a dark moment in which to be an American. More than ever, belief in something greater was needed.

EIGHTEEN

❧ JOURNEYS ❧

DURING THE FIRST WEEK OF JANUARY 1970, AMMON HENNACY picketed each day outside the Utah State Capitol in Salt Lake City. Opponents of capital punishment, he and his wife of five years, Joan Thomas, were protesting the imminent execution of two convicted murderers. On the eighth, he was stricken with a heart attack on the street. A week later, he was dead. Dorothy was shaken and in her February column eulogized him, extolling the "romantic Irishman" who had never, to his last day, lost his "love of drama, [his] love of life." "He was an inspiration and a reproach," she wrote mournfully. The same issue printed eulogies by Karl Meyer, Tom Cornell, Michael Harrington, Mary Lathrop, and Joan Thomas.

Though she had probably been flattered by Hennacy's romantic attentions when they first met—reconciling herself to life without a loving partner had been hard—Dorothy knew that theirs would have been a completely unsuitable marriage. It was for his politics and his passion that she held him in such high regard, even after he left the Church. He felt the urgency of their shared mission as intensely as anyone at the Catholic Worker ever had. The year before had represented a hallucinatory unraveling in America: the Chicago Seven trial, the Stonewall riots, Woodstock, the Manson murders, more troops sent to Vietnam—staggering numbers, peaking at *more than half a million men*. To Ammon Hennacy, none of it was surprising. His country had always been a chaotic, even tragic, work in progress, a wayward nation that needed to be reminded of its moral duty by its dissidents. With his passing, a certain kind of radical—unflappable, intransigent, jubilantly ornery, a Gandhian never reconciled to injustice and inequality—was gone.

Experiencing shortness of breath herself that year, a problem soon to be diagnosed as the onset of congestive heart trouble, Dorothy had reason to contemplate her own mortality. Death was erasing the past with some ferocity: Floyd Dell and Max Eastman, the radical leaders of *The Masses*, had both died in 1969, and Peggy Baird, the libertine friend of her youth and a Catholic convert, Malcolm Cowley's first wife, was stoically wasting away with cancer in her bed at Tivoli, to which she had come in her retirement. Dorothy spent hours by her side. "I did not think it would take so long," she told Dorothy. In September 1970, while Dorothy was out of the country, she died. What an admirable example of bravery and composure, Dorothy confided to her diary.

One bright spot in this period: Dorothy's grandson Eric was back from Vietnam, an enormous relief to his mother, grandmother, and siblings. His was an escape from death, though not, as it turned out, from the effects of Agent Orange.

Retrenchment would be the normal course of action for many women feeling their age, past seventy, suffering from high blood pressure, arthritis, and agonizing bouts of sciatica. For Dorothy, the opposite was the case. She commenced a period of more extensive travel than ever before. Some of it had a dizzying quality. More than a few of the trips seemed about *not* being in New York, escaping East 1st Street, as much as being somewhere else. After flying to Utah to attend Ammon Hennacy's funeral, Dorothy went directly to Tallahassee, where she spoke to several history classes at Florida State University, followed by another visit to the Koinonia farm in Americus, the Trappist monastery in Conyers, and Atlanta to meet with some union leaders, then to Detroit and Ann Arbor for speaking engagements, and finally back to New York just long enough to rest for a few days and see that the paper made it to the printer before leaving for Boston (where she was impressed with Haley House, founded in 1967), and Worcester, where she spoke at Assumption College. On one of the stops she had had to consult a doctor because she was feeling so winded and debilitated. In Detroit, a Catholic Worker took her to the hospital for an examination when she complained of chest pains. She had some fluid in the lungs and an enlarged heart, she was told. Some months later, she spent a week in South Dakota on a speaking tour.

Dorothy's appetite for travel had become a lust for travel by this time, and her choices became more adventuresome. She was told by her doctor that the trip to Guatemala she had been pondering was out of the question, given the altitude and its potential effect on her heart, and so she set her few days at the St. Benedict's farming commune Father Heffey ran and then stayed with the Catholic journalist and Pax member Paul Ormonde and his wife in Melbourne. St. Benedict's was in the bush, a rough and beautiful landscape, two hours outside the city, and conditions for the fifty residents, some of whom were Benedictine oblates, were spartan. But there was a spiritual aura to the community that Dorothy appreciated. The residents sang a Gregorian Mass once a week, not something one could picture happening at Tivoli.

In Melbourne, she gave a television interview and a radio interview, spoke to several school groups, and addressed an overflow crowd at the Public Lecture Theatre at Melbourne University. Her rhetoric was as strong as ever: "Our present capitalist, industrialist system is inhuman and wicked." It was up to the young, she said, to fight against economic inequalities, to demand that the obscenity of war be ended, to keep Christ's message alive in a world that paid only lip service to the Sermon on the Mount. She praised Australia's draft resisters. She shared the platform with Jim Cairns, the charismatic Australian Labour Party politician, one of the most outspoken critics of Australia's involvement with the United States in Vietnam and the organizer that year of the largest antiwar demonstration in his country's history—a man obviously after Dorothy's own heart. She repeated her message to a large gathering of theology students at Corpus Christi College.

Australia, as it turned out, had a more progressive side than it was given credit for. It was stirring to contemplate. Reading about the trip in Dorothy's columns when she returned home, though, one would never suspect from the writer's modesty her own stirring impact on her hosts and listeners, though she was judged a better speaker in smaller settings, less dynamic (and less audible) in larger halls. Undoubtedly, a few people following the news reports of her visit, not least the Australian bishops, were dismayed by Dorothy's continued praise of Castro, but one homeless shelter resident neatly summed up the warmth she inspired: "She can drink out of my bottle any time."

India, by way of Hong Kong, was the next stop on their around-the-globe itinerary. A meeting with Mother Teresa, whom Eileen knew well through her work with Catholic Relief Services, was something Dorothy had long been looking forward to. Mother Teresa met them at the airport in Calcutta at midnight to welcome them and deck them with garlands. She asked Dorothy to speak that week to her novices (who were a little shocked at her arrest record), arranged for her to meet with the Missionaries of Char-

sights on a more ambitious, less altitudinally challenging sojourn. S
long wanted to see something of Asia, Africa, and the Soviet Unic
if she had sponsors willing to foot the bills and eager travel compan
Eileen Egan and Nina Polcyn, she was ready to go. The doctors co
what they wanted about that.

In August 1970, Dorothy and Eileen flew to Honolulu, then to /
lia. The airfare for the two women had been paid for by funds raised
Australian priests who also found them lodgings, religious men as
of the mainstream in their country as Dorothy was in hers. Father
Pryke and Father John Heffey had met Dorothy in New York in 194(
they were seminarians, and they liked everything they learned durin
visit about her, her newspaper, the houses of hospitality, and Peter N
They were Catholic Worker evangelists down under—meaning spi
and politically radical, unimpressed by their church's hierarchy, intere
liturgical reform, thrilled by Vatican II, and appalled by what was hap
in Vietnam. They were the kind of priests who inspired in Dorothy 1
to be hopeful about the future of Catholicism.

In Sydney, the travelers spent a week with Father Pryke, who li
several speaking engagements for Dorothy (making sure she met
number of students), including one at the Sydney Town Hall. She
about the Catholic Worker, pacifism, the example of Ammon He
Pryke took his guests to see the Matthew Talbot Hostel run by th
ety of St. Vincent de Paul, a facility that provided beds for as many
hundred men a night, and the house of the Little Sisters of Jesus, ar
ministering to the Aboriginal population. Dorothy and her host woul
had a lot to talk about: his leadership of the Australian Catholics for
the progress of the peace movements in both countries, Australia's l
The Catholic Worker during World War II, homelessness in Sydney an
York, the many times Pryke had been called onto the carpet by his b
their mutual regard for Pope John XXIII. Their one area of disagre
concerned *Humanae vitae*, an encyclical Pryke thought misguided ar
lieved would have disastrous consequences for the Church. Doroth
a far more orthodox Catholic than the priest she was staying with, tl
Pryke was nonetheless convinced that she was "certainly the greatest p
I have ever met."

Heading south to Victoria, Father Heffey's territory, Dorothy stayec

ity Brothers, and gave her a tour of the many houses she had opened in that stricken city. At least several people died each day under the care of her nuns, so dire was their situation when they were taken in. But they didn't die feeling that no one cared about them; that was Mother Teresa's central tenet. "At my time of life, one thinks of death every day," Dorothy remarked in passing to Eileen.

There were similarities between the two women and the houses they had opened, and there were notable differences. Mother Teresa, an Albanian Indian, had founded her own religious order, the Missionaries of Charity, serving the needs in many countries of "the poorest of the poor"—very much like the Catholic Worker—though the people she took in were orphans or, in large numbers, malnourished adults very ill or nearing death due to the ravages of leprosy, tuberculosis, and other virulent diseases. Her nuns lived amid the poor but also, as befit a religious order, lived apart in their sleeping and eating arrangements. Mother Teresa had no interest in fighting the political battles that engaged so much of Dorothy's time, nor would she ever have expressed any criticism of the Church hierarchy. The two accepted donations from very different sources, and she ran a much tighter ship than Dorothy Day the anarchist. Certain kinds of behavior that were a fact of life at the Catholic Worker would never have been tolerated among the residents of her shelters or her nuns. Yet they were two women with a similar outlook on their calling, the need to embrace holy poverty, and the ways in which modern society had turned its back on the message of Christ expressed in the New Testament. Dorothy was made an honorary member of Mother Teresa's order.

Calcutta itself was what Dorothy expected. "The glow of the invisible world, so movingly described by [Cardinal] Newman in one of his sermons, is all around us in this land of the poor, the lepers, the rickshaw drivers," she wrote in her diary. At the same time, "the curse of colonialism is all around. Disruptive village life, trade, buying and selling, profit, made the acquisitive society." She experienced in Calcutta the violence of nature and the violence of man: the monsoon season had ended, but the "mango showers" were just as bad, and she could see the effects of the horrendous downpours in adding to the misery of the lives of farmers and city dwellers alike. On some days, she and Eileen couldn't venture into the streets, the water was so high. They were also told by Mother Teresa to stay indoors on Martyrs'

Day, as the threat of bloodshed, linked to the Maoist Communists known as Naxalites, was real. More than a dozen policemen had been killed in the city that year, wealthy landlords lived in constant fear of attack, and statues of Gandhi had been vandalized. Bombs did go off around Calcutta that day, and three policemen were blinded in an acid attack.

In New Delhi to catch their plane to Africa, Dorothy and Eileen were asked a question by their Sikh cabdriver: What was the story with all of the American hippies descending on India? Who were they, exactly? It was a difficult query to answer. They parted from the driver outside the terminal with a promise on his part to send them a packet with information about his religion, which he knew was little understood in the United States, an offer Dorothy welcomed.

From India, the travelers flew to Tanzania on the east coast of Africa. In Dar-es-Saalam, Dorothy and Eileen stayed at a YWCA where a number of African young women who spoke English were also staying, which allowed for just the kind of conversational exchange they wanted. The two women walked along the beachfront on the Indian Ocean, where they watched the men caulking their dhows and recovered from their considerable jet lag, strolled through the city's parks, sat in on classes at the University of Dar-es-Saalam, where they were interviewed by a student journalist, and spent a day with a well-informed woman who gave them a tour of some outlying villages.

Dorothy's principal reason for making that quick stop on her way home from Asia was her interest in learning more in situ about Tanzania's Catholic president, Julius Nyerere, whose speeches and essays she had been reading with enthusiasm in New York that year. She asked about him everywhere, of everyone she met. Nyerere had been a force in bringing about the independence of his country from British rule (originally Tanganyika; then Tanzania upon the merger of Tanganyika and Zanzibar)—that alone made him an impressive figure—and was an avowed opponent of Ugandan dictator Idi Amin to the north and the white supremacists of Angola, Rhodesia, and South Africa to the west and south. Educated at the University of Edinburgh, he was a modest man who lived simply and a socialist who wanted to end his country's tribal rivalries, dependence on foreign aid and investment, and crushing cycle of poverty. He proselytized for the concept of *ujamaa*, a nationally extended sense of family, an emphasis on communal agriculture, and an end to competition. Talking to his countrymen left Dorothy impressed. What she learned about Nyerere and his plans for the revitalization of Tanzania put her in mind of Cesar Chavez, Danilo Dolci, Coretta Scott King, Ralph Abernathy, and, of course, Peter Maurin.

In truth, not unlike Castro, Nyerere was the kind of revolutionary leader Dorothy was determined to think well of. In a world in which colonialism had not been fully eradicated and European economic hegemony was still a threat, anyone of promise from the opposite camp was to be praised, and the subsequent praise in *The Catholic Worker* was lavish. (The man had also translated two Shakespeare plays into Swahili: no mere politician, he.) With no real background in economics or political science, Dorothy was more concerned with inspiration than details and workability. Later accounts of Nyerere's one-party, press-restricted leadership involve more equivocal judgments than hers, and despite its founder's good intentions, Tanzania remained for decades one of the continent's poorest countries, with distressing rates of malnutrition. Shiva Naipaul, visiting Tanzania in the 1970s, was one of many writers who made a more realistic assessment of Nyerere's less-than-successful brand of African socialism.

Several months later came an opportunity to travel in a different direction, through the Iron Curtain. Dorothy and Nina Polcyn signed on with fifty others (mostly Quakers and Protestants of various denominations, she noted), many of whom were high school or college teachers, for a three-week tour of Eastern Europe and the Soviet Union led by retired Yale theology professor Jerome Davis, the founder of the peace advocacy organization Promoting Enduring Peace. Davis, long persecuted both in and out of academia for his left-wing politics, had been happy to offer Dorothy a travel fellowship funded by the radical philanthropist Corliss Lamont; she was exactly the kind of person his trips had been designed for, an activist who wanted to break down barriers with, and stereotypes about, ideological opponents. (In 1975, Promoting Enduring Peace awarded Dorothy its Gandhi Prize.) Interestingly, Dorothy noted, no one on the tour except Professor Davis, including the one other Catholic woman, had ever heard of the Catholic Worker. The Australians she met had been far better informed.

The group stopped briefly in a few cities, sometimes just for several hours, en route to the Communist capital. Amsterdam was beautiful, Dor-

othy wrote to Della; Brussels, less so; East Berlin was grim. Warsaw, where
they stayed for a long weekend, was the surprise—"benches, parks, flowers
everywhere," most—but not all—sites of Nazi destruction rebuilt. They had
an audience with Prime Minister Piotr Jaroszewicz and spent an afternoon
at Frédéric Chopin's restored château and an evening at the opera, seeing
Claudio Monteverdi's *The Coronation of Poppea*. Dorothy attended Mass
with an overflow crowd and was pleased to see so many ardent worshippers,
though the priest's style was, to her eye, decidedly distant, stiff, his back to
the congregation—a holdover from pre–Vatican II days. After Poland, the
tour proceeded to Leningrad for three days and two nights.

In the former St. Petersburg, the site of the glory days of John Reed and
Louise Bryant in welcoming the Bolshevik Revolution, Dorothy could walk
the streets that had inspired *Ten Days That Shook the World*. She and Nina
Polcyn paid their respects at the graves of Fyodor Dostoevsky, Modest Mus-
sorgsky, and Nikolai Rimsky-Korsakov outside the St. Alexander Nevsky
Monastery and saw the great art collections of the Hermitage, where Dorothy reported that she was most moved by Rembrandt's massive and mag-
nificently painted *Return of the Prodigal Son*. She stared long and hard at the
battered shoes and blistered feet of the repentant son, she said, a reminder of
the condition of so many people the Catholic Worker embraced.

Then it was on to Moscow for five days. Dorothy in Red Square—how
Mike Gold would have enjoyed that image. In the era of Brezhnev, détente,
and cultural exchanges, Moscow offered a blend of the artistic and the political for the travelers to experience. The Tretyakov Gallery was home to a
treasury of Russian art and religious icons, which thrilled Dorothy and Nina,
and their visit to Lenin's tomb, to view the preserved body under glass of
the founder of the Soviet Union, made for its own macabre experience. She
prayed for John Reed, standing before the Kremlin wall where his remains
had been interred, and was disappointed that a pilgrimage to Yasnaya Poly-
ana, Tolstoy's home near Tula, wasn't possible.

Proceeding at a less hurried pace than they had before, the group was
able to interact more directly with some English-speaking residents of the
city, riding the subway and strolling through the GUM department store,
and they benefited from a helpful, conversational guide. To the members of
the Soviet Peace Committee at the House of Friendship, Dorothy—despite
having been told not to disturb the tour by doing so—was unabashed in

speaking up to protest the treatment that Alexander Solzhenitsyn, the author of *Cancer Ward* and *The First Circle*, was enduring in his homeland. She was conciliatory on the subject of how many churches she had come upon that were open for worship now that Stalin's brutal anticlericalism was no longer in force, but it was her defense of the USSR's most recent Nobel laureate, denied the right to travel to Stockholm to receive his prize, that made the strongest impression on her irritated Soviet acquaintances. Yet, as she wrote in her column upon her return to the United States, "Alexander Solzhenitsyn was another of the reasons I wanted to visit Russia, to set foot on the soil that produced the likes of him." She was glad that Hélène Iswolsky had agreed to review his latest novel for *The Catholic Worker*, the first installment of his epic *August 1914*. On the way home, the group caught their breath for a few days at a comfortable hotel on the Bulgarian side of the Black Sea and spent a few days in Sofia and Budapest.

An editor at Dutton expressed interest in publishing a book about Dorothy's impressions of the Soviet Union, but nothing came of the idea. It was "a piece of effrontery," she remarked to some friends, to pretend one knew much about a country after a few weeks as a tourist. A few columns in *The Catholic Worker* were one thing; a book would have been another matter.

The antiwar movement had brought righteous passion to American life, but it dissipated all too soon after the draft ended and a volunteer army was sent to fight the losing war in Asia. New fires were being kindled by the women's movement and the gay rights movement, and activism against racial injustice continued. The violence at Attica Prison in September 1971 rattled all but the most complacent.

Yet in the wake of the Vietnam War protest a new mood was taking hold in the country, a skepticism that the Pentagon Papers and Henry Kissinger's winning a Nobel Peace Prize and Watergate revelations did nothing to lessen. It was a mood that had many roots, though, just as it affected myriad aspects of society, not excepting the Catholic Worker both in its urban home and at Tivoli.

Religion among the young—how seriously it was taken and how much it guided their moral life—was one such shift Dorothy was in a position to note. Even at Catholic colleges, the brightest students weren't reading

St. Augustine and St. Thomas Aquinas with the intentness of undergraduates before them; they were reading Albert Camus, Jean-Paul Sartre, and
Samuel Beckett. Nobel laureate Jacques Monod's *Chance and Necessity*, arguing man's aloneness in the immensity of a random universe, was a surprise
best seller among the more intellectually inclined. Condoms and marijuana
were ubiquitous on many campuses, both Catholic and secular—how different the college experience of 1970 was from that of 1960—and discom-
forting doubt or an educated cynicism was fast becoming the order of the
day. Some of the young people who came to the Catholic Worker to help
were only nominally Catholic, no longer Catholic at all, or so critical of
the Church that Dorothy hated to listen to them air their views. Most were
socially concerned, compassionate, and hardworking, but many didn't want
to hear a good word about Pope Pius XII or *Humanae vitae*. If they received
Communion and cared to go to Mass at all, it wasn't after having gone to
confession the day before. Compline at night after dinner was as alien to
some of them as saying the rosary or reading the Christian personalists.

That wasn't the case with Patrick and Kathleen Jordan, newlyweds
and devout Catholics who became mainstays of the movement and close
personal friends of Dorothy. It also wasn't the case with Jane Sammon, a
twenty-two-year-old who arrived in the East Village in 1972 (and is still
with the Worker in New York today) who was looking for a different kind of
Catholicism than she had known growing up in Cleveland. Or Anne Marie
Fraser, a New Yorker who left her first-grade teaching job in Brooklyn to sign
on with the Worker. And it certainly wasn't the case with Sister Donald
Corcoran, a young Benedictine nun studying and living at Fordham University in the Bronx, who spent a year at St. Joseph House at Dorothy's urging.
"Dorothy leaned on me to be a companion," Sister Corcoran recalled. She
was happy to fill that role. Her steadying presence made Dorothy consider
that having more nuns to help run the house might be a solution to a good
many problems, one that she should have thought of years before perhaps,
but there were no lines of religious women waiting to live in the Bowery.
Indeed, the number of nuns leaving their orders in the early 1970s was staggering, more than three thousand in 1970 alone.

Peter Maurin's counsel, Dorothy needed to remind others (and herself),
was never more relevant: we don't *measure* our success, we don't despair, and
we don't judge; we simply do the work God intends us to do.

Someone who agreed with the outlook of never abandoning the struggle, however uncertain the results, was the indefatigable Daniel Berrigan,
released from the Federal Correctional Institution in Danbury, Connecticut,
in 1972. He was invited to celebrate a Mass of Thanksgiving at St. Joseph
House. He handed Dorothy the fifty dollars he had been given when he
left Danbury, the standard amount issued to prisoners as they began their
post-incarceration life. After the Mass, Dorothy directed one of the young
men to go to her room and bring down the jar of holy water she kept there.
Dipping the bills into the water—filthy lucre from a warmongering state—
she proudly announced, "Now we can use this!"

Dorothy was becoming more irascible than ever. On the occasion of her
seventy-fifth birthday, Bill Moyers interviewed her for a segment of his television program, *Bill Moyers Journal*, which he entitled "Still a Rebel." In
case his public-broadcasting producers and viewers might feel inclined to
coo over a sweet old lady doing good deeds of a spiritual nature, Dorothy
went out of her way to bring a dose of harsh reality into the program. She
talked about one woman who had been brought to the doorstep of St. Joseph
House in Manhattan by the Brooklyn police—*dumped* would be the more
accurate verb—covered with lice from head to foot, smelling of urine, and
with a prolapsed rectum coated with excrement. *That* was what the Catholic
Worker had to deal with, she wanted people to know. Marge Hughes was
interviewed as well and was forceful about "the big lie" in American life, the
myth that dire poverty was a thing of the past. Michael Harrington's book
could be rewritten in each decade.

By that time, Dorothy was a historical figure. Several years earlier, Marquette University had approached her about donating her papers to its archives. That seemed a reasonable idea: the files were starting to take over
her bedroom, the offices of the Catholic Worker, and every corner of the
farmhouse. The less pleasing aspect of an archive, though, was the prospect
of a biography. At some time in the early 1960s, Dorothy had asked Charles
Butterworth to come out to the farm on Staten Island to help with a chore.
When he had returned to Manhattan, he had told Robert Steed just what
that surprising chore had entailed: a day of Dorothy sorting through boxes
and drawers and the two of them carrying piles of papers into the yard to
burn. The mystery of gaps in the documentary account of her life, missing
diaries and letters, is no doubt explained by that conflagration.

Dorothy's prominence was not of a uniform nature, however. When James Finn published *Protest: Pacifism and Politics*, a collection of interviews with thirty-eight of the country's most significant antiwar activists, Dorothy was necessarily among them. Studs Terkel had interviewed her for his best-selling oral history of the Depression, *Hard Times*. Richard Avedon had photographed her, and Harvard psychologist Robert Coles had published a photographic essay tribute on her. Even an edgy downtown New York paper not known to cover religious topics, the *Village Voice*, paid homage, and Dwight Macdonald reaffirmed his glowing opinion in the *New York Review of Books* in 1971, honoring the longevity of her paper, "the Methuselah of little mags," and its founder's indominable spirit. The article was accompanied by a great cartoon by the master caricaturist David Levine. W. H. Auden wrote a positive review of *A Harsh and Dreadful Love: Dorothy Day and the Catholic Worker Movement* in the same publication in 1972 that was as much a birthday card from an admirer as a notice about William Miller's book. *America* celebrated her seventy-fifth birthday by devoting an entire issue to her. That summer, she accepted the prestigious Laetare Medal from Notre Dame University, sharing the stage with Hannah Arendt, who was receiving an honorary degree and later came as a speaker to one of the Friday-night sessions.

At the same time, strange as it may seem, it could be said that in the early 1970s Dorothy and the Catholic Worker were actually less well known among working-class and middle-class mainstream Catholics than ever before. The days when parochial schools ordered bundles of the paper, when nuns stopped by the house in groups and spread the word of the great work they saw taking place, when "labor priests" and the rank and file they supported looked to her as an important ally were in the past or on the wane. It was among an elite audience that her reputation was secured. The general run of American Catholics who had made it into the middle class and moved to the suburbs had no particular interest in someone their own parish priest might have regarded as a zealot and eccentric, if he were even clear as to what the Catholic Worker was really all about.

Dorothy was just as happy not to be the focus of any kind of celebrity. William Miller's desire to write her biography was met with equivocation and evasion, and she let him know she wasn't pleased with the subtitle of his recent book, which she told him should have been *Peter Maurin and the*

Catholic Worker Movement. People who came by St. Joseph House to gaze on a saint were a particular source of annoyance, as was any talk of her special sanctity. Being spoken of as a "saint" in one's own lifetime was the easiest way to be marginalized, Dorothy repeatedly insisted. And she meant it.

Among conservatives, she didn't have to worry about garnering excessive regard. Urging Americans not to prejudge Angela Davis, the black UCLA professor and member of the Communist Party who was being tried as an accessory in a courthouse shooting, pegged Dorothy Day as beyond the pale. Most of white America was convinced of Davis's guilt. (She was, in fact, found not guilty.) The paper's positive references to the Black Panthers raised eyebrows. When Maisie Ward appeared on William F. Buckley's television interview program, *Firing Line,* the very mention of her friend's name caused her host to bristle. Numerous bishops had yet to be won over, and some of her co-religionists expected stronger statements from her about *Roe v. Wade.*

That Court decision was troubling to Dorothy, but she felt that women who made the same mistake she had made fifty years earlier should be the focus of sorrow and forgiveness, not criminality and unrelenting condemnation by the Church. Abortion was to be looked upon as wrong—a grievous sin, a horror—but no one was beyond redemption. (Dorothy was aware that one young Catholic Worker she particularly liked had had an abortion in her early twenties, before they met; she was neither hypocritical nor callous enough to suggest that the woman, pained by her decision, couldn't share fully in the mission of the house.) One reason she would welcome any pregnant unmarried woman who showed up on the doorstep in the city or upstate was her hope that she might think twice about terminating her pregnancy.

At Tivoli, she didn't have to worry about excessive regard, either, and the lack of respect she was sometimes shown there mattered in a very different way. The considerable good that was accomplished on the old de Peyster estate was undeniable. Tivoli served as a conference center, a place for reflection and debate, on many fronts. The gatherings of Pax, the Catholic Peace Fellowship, the War Resisters League, and other groups were important occasions for the participants, recharging them for the good fight. Sometimes as many as two hundred people occupied the house and the grounds when the events took place. One summer Dorothy opened a day care center for the children of migrant workers in the area. Fresh vegetables were sent back to 1st Street by the carload, thanks to John Filligar and a few diligent gardeners. Tivoli also brought Tamar and her children into more regular contact with Dorothy, and her granddaughter Susie's baby, Charlotte, was born and baptized there. Some of Tamar's children have the warmest memories of frolicsome times there.

It was a good place as well for those at the end of their days, such as Peggy Baird. The unknown and the well-known died with dignity there, never alone. The poet Emily Coleman (a truculent personality, by all accounts) had been friends with Djuna Barnes and other avant-garde figures in her youth in Paris in the 1920s. She knew Dylan Thomas and Peggy Guggenheim. She had been a Catholic Worker in New York in the 1950s, had emigrated to England in the 1960s, and had later come to Tivoli, where she died of a brain tumor in 1974. The same love and care were afforded to the elderly Hans Tunnesen, the cook, when his time came.

The problems were at least as noticeable, however, and threatened to scuttle the entire enterprise. Tivoli wasn't merely a refuge for the poor. The drug-addicted or battle-scarred Vietnam War veterans who showed up were especially worrisome. Some of their antics were annoying but harmless. There was one Vietnam War vet who, when no one was looking, kept turning all the books in the house to the wall so that their titles couldn't be read and constantly opened closed windows and closed open windows just to be difficult. One fellow liked to rip the wallpaper off the walls in patches. Others would find ways to get liquor or drugs and could assume a menacing attitude. The Corbins, who had been helping to run Tivoli for a decade, decided that it was no longer a place to raise their children, now teenagers, and Marty Corbin took a job elsewhere.

Thievery was a constant problem. Peggy Baird's body wasn't even in the ground before her room was stripped bare, her clothes and even her books taken. Dorothy's own room was vulnerable; she'd find a book she was reading gone and discover it later under a tree, soaked by rain. Signed copies of works by Maritain and Belloc, books she treasured, disappeared. No one with any sense left valuables on view, if they had any, or wore clothes that might attract attention and envy. One woman volunteered to buy the week's groceries in town, took two hundred dollars, and drove off in one of the Worker's cars, never to be heard from again.

When Mary Lathrop, living back in New York, paid a visit, she thought the whole place full of rather "sinister characters." Robert Steed, who had kept in touch with Dorothy through the years, spent some time at Tivoli and was similarly horrified by the disorder and selfish behavior he witnessed. The "characters" were usually young people who lived a vagabond life, hippies and wanderers who had heard that there was free food and a place to sleep for as long as one wanted at a big ramshackle house on the Hudson, and so, with backpacks and tents, they showed up in significant numbers, especially during the summer months. They'd been told no one was ever kicked out and you could pretty much do whatever you wanted. Coming down to breakfast one day, Dorothy attempted to make conversation with a scruffy young man at the table she hadn't seen before. She had no idea where he came from or when he had arrived. She asked his name. His response: "And who are you, old lady?" That exchange wasn't the only instance of rudeness she had to put up with.

Tivoli struck some as the perfect setting for the exercise of the now much-ballyhooed "free love." It wasn't as if Dorothy were naive about the sexual ways of young people. She knew what went on in the woods, down by the river, or in the house at night. Her grandchildren brought their boyfriends or girlfriends. The problem she was not willing to let slide, which was getting out of hand, was the "open immorality" often thrown in her face. A destitute woman with children had moved in with her husband and child; the husband took up with a seventeen-year-old and let his wife know he wanted a divorce, but he was in no hurry to vacate his free room. Another husband didn't want to divorce his wife but "thinks it is his duty to befriend young girls (the latest only fourteen)" who were camping out on the grounds. Another girl, an alcoholic in flight from an abuser, was crawling into the bed of any available man at Tivoli. Many, when asked to leave, simply ignored Dorothy.

The estate was a "commune," she was informed by some of the crowd, and her values were out of place and outdated. Two gay women holed up in a room together and seemed to come out only at night, piling empty beer cans on the landing outside their bedroom door. An anarchist or libertarian view of authority and a belief in the personalist ethic of leading by example, not by commands or coercion—those values were more sorely tried than ever before under these conditions.

Between the libidinous hippies and the mentally incompetent, tensions could become dire, and Dorothy wasn't immune from the threats posed by the less stable residents. Michael Mok, a former *Life* magazine overseas photographer staying at the Worker, "went out of his mind today," Dorothy wrote in her diary in March 1973. He rushed into her room while she was napping and threw himself on top of her. "Insanity is the bitterest of our trials," she noted. Stanley Vishnewski heard the commotion and raced into the room to pull Mok, a hefty guy in his forties, off the bed before Dorothy suffered any broken bones, but Mok pushed him out and tried to lock the door, and it took more help to deal with the situation than Stanley could manage alone. The police came, and Mok was taken, drunk and ranting, to Hudson River State Hospital, a nearby mental facility. Verbal violence was endlessly tolerated at Tivoli, but physical violence was less acceptable. Yet all Dorothy could think of later were the horrors that Mok had witnessed, and so ably photographed, in Vietnam, Biafra, and the Middle East, images she knew had troubled and unbalanced him.

Another problem was that Tivoli was in danger of becoming a dumping ground. Bishops would send their alcoholic priests there—and the numbers kept growing—as if the farm were a treatment facility, which it most definitely was not, and as if it weren't the responsibility of the Church to set up its own centers to deal with a major problem of long standing. Some of them would say Mass in the chapel, but Dorothy didn't appreciate having a priest consecrate the Host on whose breath she could smell whiskey. Some had sexual histories, heterosexual and homosexual, that made them unsuitable for their parishes. A friend of Shane O'Neill, Eugene O'Neill's second son, asked if Shane could be taken in, but suicidal young men with drug issues suffering from severe depression were not the kind of people the Catholic Worker was equipped to help, either. (Shane O'Neill, like his older half brother, Eugene, Jr., did eventually take his own life.) No one could quite figure out what to do with the young man who liked to set fires on the grounds. This mixture of the needy and impoverished, the angry and the alienated, the committed and the indifferent meant that it was anybody's guess whether Tivoli served a purpose that justified the enormous expense and the labor it took to keep it going or should simply be shut down. Dorothy wondered about that for years.

Yet in sometimes unexpected instances, the farm was just what some people needed. Rachel de Aragon, a niece by marriage of Dorothy's brother

John, was a New York City social worker in the 1970s. She approached Dorothy about lodging one of her clients, a young woman who had suf-fered a breakdown and was doing her best to fight her drug addiction, for a few months. Rachel asked it as a favor, believing that the woman had little chance of recovery if she remained in the city surrounded by bad influences. She was hopeful that the experience of life upstate might be grounding for her. Dorothy was dumbstruck. "Rachel, you really think Tivoli would be 'grounding'?" she asked. Happily, de Aragon knew best: the woman she was working with did join the community and returned to New York several months later, more or less restored and ready to make a fresh start.

In many ways, it was an odd life. Dorothy was both a woman lauded and a woman under duress. To be sure, the honors continued to come in from far and wide: the Eugene V. Debs Award from the Eugene V. Debs Foundation in Terre Haute, Indiana; the Pacem in Terris Peace and Freedom Award from the Davenport Catholic Interracial Council of Davenport, Iowa; the Frederic F. Melcher Book Award from the Unitarian Universalist Associa-tion for *On Pilgrimage: The Sixties*, the collection of her columns from that decade brought out in paperback (the copyright put into Tamar's name); the Saint Vincent de Paul Award from DePaul University in Chicago; the Isaac Hecker Award for Social Justice from the Paulist Center in Boston. She ac-cepted most of them in person. She stuck to her policy of refusing honorary degrees and had no interest in awards from any university with an ROTC program, but the requests kept coming. Hence the satisfaction of being ar-rested with the striking farmworkers of California—one last time to stand in solidarity, imprisoned, with those treated unjustly, one more chance to resist being made respectable, safe, iconic.

As she aged, Dorothy's aesthetic sense didn't lessen; it deepened. She was willing to allow herself more time for the pleasures of art, for the enjoyment of creative accomplishments that a life of voluntary poverty and unrelenting work had sometimes mitigated against. The Saturday-afternoon broadcasts from the Metropolitan Opera became a weekend ritual, and interruptions were resented. Wagner, Verdi, Strauss, and Puccini—how far they could take one from the Bowery and alcoholic priests and "bag ladies" with no teeth who did nothing but complain and Michael Mok climbing on top of her, haunted by the bodies of Vietnamese women and Biafran babies. She lingered over the Rembrandts at the Metropolitan Museum. She read Dante, *The Canterbury Tales*, and Chekhov's and Vincent van Gogh's letters and returned to *A Portrait of the Artist as a Young Man*, grabbed from her hands by Lionel Moise and thrown out the window of the Chicago El.

There were trips to the theater to relish great plays and great acting. She enjoyed Off-Broadway productions of Samuel Beckett's plays, of *Three Sisters* and *Uncle Vanya* (two of her favorite dramas), and a Broadway production of *The Iceman Cometh* starring James Earl Jones. That same winter, Robert Steed took her to see what became a legendary Broadway revival of *A Moon for the Misbegotten* with Colleen Dewhurst and Jason Robards. If ever she had doubted that Eugene O'Neill's vision had been an essentially religious one, that heartbreaking story was one to remind her of what she had known, or sensed, more than fifty years earlier. The tender, virginal Josie Hogan cradling the lost, alcoholic Jamie Tyrone in her arms: the final scene was a veritable Pietà, she wrote to Louis Sheaffer, O'Neill's biographer, who had interviewed Dorothy for his Pulitzer Prize–winning biography. Living and dying in the shadow of despair, her old friend from the Hell Hole had gotten one thing right: we all crave forgiveness of the kind only to be had from an all-knowing, all-loving God.

The part of her daily life that Dorothy found unpleasant, at times intolerably frustrating, was her own incremental physical decline. She had stopped driving early in 1973, to the relief of passengers and pedestrians alike. Each year so much became harder: climbing stairs, standing for long periods, catching her breath after walking, concentrating and staying focused.

Her hearing in one ear started to go. It was all occurring at a moment when the needs at the Catholic Worker were escalating. The men and women who had charge of the paper, the house, and the farm—Patrick Jordan, Jane Sammon, Frank Donovan, Daniel Marshall, old-timers such as Ed Forand and Catholic Worker Arthur Lacey, newcomers such as Anne Marie Fraser and Peggy Scherer—were utterly reliable individuals. Under Jordan's leadership, *The Catholic Worker* was as probing and crisply edited a publication as ever. It went out now to more than 80,000 subscribers. Sufficient funds were at last coming in through generous donations. The IRS had dropped its demand for hundreds of thousands of dollars in back taxes, finally acknowledging that the Catholic Worker was a nonprofit organization, even if unincorporated, and that no one was paid a salary. But the tide of misery wasn't decreasing; it was suddenly increasing.

By the mid-1970s, Dorothy was watching New York City fall apart all around her. Now it wasn't merely the bad neighborhood the Catholic Worker had staked claim to that caused concern; the city itself was running out of money, and a massive social breakdown was well under way. Parts of Midtown, the Upper West Side, and Central Park hadn't been peopled by so many homeless men and women since the Depression, there appeared to be no way to curtail the rising crime and omnipresent graffiti, and city services were being drastically cut back. Drug dealers all but took over Bryant Park and Washington Square Park. The war in Vietnam was over, and one disquieting result was the number of men in army fatigues begging on street corners. Mental hospitals released their patients into an uncertain future on their own. Urban America was beginning to be spoken of as ungovernable. The newspapers were full of speculation about the possibility that New York City, with its tax base shrinking, would eventually have to declare bankruptcy.

Writing in 1974 to a Jesuit friend at Fordham University, Father James Gilhooley, Dorothy expressed concern about the closing of so many city shelters "for the kind of drunken, or out-of-their-mind, street women who sleep in doorways or sit in our dining room until 11 at night hoping to be overlooked when we lock up (and they surrounded with shopping bags— their earthly goods). . . . They are at home with us because we are the off-scouring [too]. They like our atmosphere." A Catholic Worker house, unlike a Salvation Army shelter or a city shelter, would expect nothing, demand nothing, from them. But Dorothy stayed awake at night worrying, fretting: How many more such suffering citizens could the Catholic Worker accommodate, how much more hospitality could it afford to offer? St. Joseph House was approaching its own breaking point.

NINETEEN

❧ ENDINGS ❧

IN THE FALL OF 1974, A RECENT COLLEGE GRADUATE NAMED MARC
Ellis, a son of middle-class Jewish parents, a child of the Miami suburbs,
decided to postpone his graduate school studies and move into St. Joseph
House in New York to see what help he could offer. He had heard Dorothy
speak in one of his history classes at Florida State University, when she had
been invited by his teacher, William Miller, and that experience had been
quietly transformative. Miller was profoundly uneasy when he discovered
that his student was planning not a weeklong or monthlong visit to the
Lower East Side but a stay that might last all of that academic year. He knew
the neighborhood, he knew the residents, he knew how far suburban south
Florida was from the shocking world Ellis would encounter. As it turned out,
Ellis stayed at St. Joseph House for nine months, devoting himself to the
work that had to be done and keeping a diary, which was published by the
Paulist Press in 1978.

A Year at the Catholic Worker: A Spiritual Journey Among the Poor is an unnerving document. The memories of those who were a part of the Catholic
Worker then quite naturally dwell today on warm recollections of Dorothy,
a heartfelt appreciation of one's friends and hardworking peers, the sacra-
mental sense of life one acquired by proximity to her and those who shared
her belief in the power of love and a commitment to Christ's way. Those
thoughts fill Ellis's journal as well. He would never be the same person again
after spending September 1974 to the following spring on East 1st Street in
the most degraded period of that city's twentieth-century history. Yet the
book has the merit of pressing the reader's face into the sights, smells, chaos,
dangers, irrationality, brutality, and satisfactions of the house in a way that
few other chronicles of the Catholic Worker do.

Some of Ellis's observations could have applied to life in the house in the 1930s or 1950s. Its loose structure took some getting used to, as did the lack of any privacy, the odor of people who refused to shower, and the duties that were involved when it was one's turn to "take the house," i.e., to act as house manager for several hours, something almost every Catholic Worker had to do at one time or another. Taking the house meant, among many other things, a willingness to accept violence without retaliation, he was told. One had to learn to defuse and deflect aggression, to be infinitely patient. Aggression, emotional and physical, was omnipresent by the time Ellis arrived, and that was the key difference from an earlier time. On a regular basis, one had to confront threats, abusive language, smashed windows and chairs, fistfights, assaults, knives drawn. It was everywhere, inside and out, far worse than it had ever been. "People were beating each other up just incessantly," Ellis's fellow Worker Lee LeCuyer agreed.

Life on East 1st Street showed the city at its worst. A man was gang-raped on the sidewalk in the middle of the night just down the street from St. Joseph House. Ellis's foul-mouthed, unbathed roommate kept piles of *Screw* magazine under his bed and a jar of urine in the middle of the room as he was too lazy to get up during the night to make a trip to the bathroom down the hall. Cleaning out the room of a hoarder, as the Catholic Workers did every spring, removing her thirty-five bags, sent the woman into a screaming rage. The fellow who ran the clothing donation center was badly beaten. Some men wanted more clothes than they could wear or were entitled to, to sell to used-clothing dealers for money to drink. At that same violent encounter, a seminarian was dragged into the middle of the street by his hair. Ellis himself almost had his jaw broken one night in the foyer by a deranged resident, was kicked in the groin another time, and was sexually catcalled by male residents. A community spirit among the Catholic Workers was hard to come by; it could mean only so much when so many of the young people were transients themselves, as ready to move on after a few weeks or months as some of the nomadic residents.

Yet Ellis stuck it out for the school year he had taken off to be in New York, and much of that had to do with the fellow Workers who were both personally centered and steadying for those around them, such as Patrick Jordan and Anne Marie Fraser. And then there was Dorothy. His impressions of Dorothy were not those of the many people who describe her as standoffish in her later years. He was taken by the fact that she wanted to know his background, why he was there. He was taken by how much she enjoyed youthful company. Her belief that they were doing exactly what God wanted in opening their doors to the neediest, most damaged, and least grateful of humanity, those whom others would gladly cast off, was unshakable, and that was remarkable to him. "Her face is highlighted by high cheekbones and a carved thinness," he wrote. "She is beautiful."

Marc Ellis was aware that he was meeting Dorothy at the beginning of her long, slow decline. Travel had come to an end for her. In 1973, she had made her last trip abroad, to Ireland, accompanied by Jane Sammon. She wanted a look at the lush countryside she had heard so much about, to see for herself just how dire things were in civil war–ravaged Belfast, and, most important, to visit the Catholic activist Michael Cullen and his family in Kerry. A friend of Dorothy, Cullen had recently been deported from the United States after serving a year in prison for his role in destroying draft records with the Milwaukee Fourteen. She also wanted to stop in London to see her favorite niece, Della's daughter Susannah, and to visit one of the "Simon communities," a British version of the Catholic Worker named after Simon of Cyrene, who was compelled by the Romans to carry the cross of Jesus. A few months later, Dorothy made her final extensive US speaking tour, a typical patchwork of Day commitments that included participating in a symposium on poverty with Karl Meyer at DePaul University, appearing in Sioux Falls to show her support for the Native American defendants on trial for their antigovernment protest at Wounded Knee, and delivering a commencement address at St. Joseph's College in Standish, Maine.

It was all too much. Even the visits to Vermont to see Tamar had become too much, too exhausting. The time was coming when it would be necessary to stay put. She was gaunt, her face lined beyond her years. She was hesitant on her feet. A college student, Michael Harank, soon to join the Worker, met her in Boston when she was there to receive the Isaac Hecker Award for Social Justice in 1974 and thought she looked profoundly weary. The deaths of good friends from earlier times—Maisie Ward, Karl Stern, and Hélène Iswolsky—added to that weariness. Della, herself a recent widow, seemed frail, lost at moments, and would eventually move to British Columbia to be near her daughter, who had relocated there. Dorothy took to spending longer stretches of time resting in the quiet of the Staten Island bungalow the Worker had bought earlier in the decade in a beach community called the

"Spanish Camp." It had been bought with $1,800 from a donor, as Dorothy had insisted that no Worker funds were to be used toward its purchase.

Hard to bear as well were the changes that had come to American Catholicism, changes that went beyond the new liturgy (some of which she liked, some of which she didn't) and the abandonment of the kind of prayers and religious music that Dorothy had always loved. When Philip Berrigan left the priesthood without permission in 1973 to marry an ex-nun he had fallen in love with and who would share his life as an antiwar activist, Elizabeth McAlister, the two were excommunicated. They were hardly anomalies. The exodus from rectories and convents quickly reached astonishing levels. What a surprise it had been to hear from Australia that even the devoted Father Pryke, her affable host in Sydney, had given up on the Church and married. Karl Meyer, whom she admired as much as anyone, no longer practiced his faith. Dorothy could see the same wave of disillusionment gathering momentum all around her in New York. She viewed Pope Paul VI as a sound spiritual leader and bristled at any invidious comparisons to his beloved predecessor, but she knew that many young people at the Worker saw him as a disappointment, a pontiff overseeing a gradual chipping away at the promise and excitement of Vatican II.

A fair amount about post-1960s America left Dorothy feeling alienated. The women's movement was a case in point. Dorothy paid very little attention to it and professed not to understand what it was all about or why it was needed. She believed that some gender differences (e.g., a greater maternal tenderness in females) were inherent and that the world would be well advised to remember that. In any event, poverty, race, and religion were the issues that mattered to her, not gender.

The young women around her had to explain that the second wave of feminism wasn't exclusively about sexual freedom, which Dorothy assumed to be the case, but about equal pay, equal opportunity, and an end to sexual harassment. The media attention to bra burning and the pill and the raw language some feminists used didn't exactly convince Dorothy of the merit of that contention. Ti-Grace Atkinson talking about Mary's having been "knocked up" by the Holy Ghost (in a lecture at Catholic University, no less), Kate Millett's attack on D. H. Lawrence, and Shulamith Firestone opining on the barbarism of pregnancy and the male incapacity to love struck her as belonging to another, and not at all desirable, mental universe.

With her energy ebbing, aware that her days of vigor and force were behind her, Dorothy also had to endure the knowledge that plenty of people were ready to embalm her in the pages of history. William Miller, the author of the first lengthy study of the Catholic Worker, was gently persistent about his wish to be her biographer, as was the historian James Finn. She let Miller know that the idea made her uncomfortable, but he wasn't merely an academic on the hunt for a fresh subject. He was a friend of the family now—he had taken in one of her grandchildren in a time of need and had been helpful to Tamar in various ways—and he was a gracious man. She gave him interviews, regretting almost every minute of them, and permission to talk to anyone he wanted to. She gave him a copy of *The Eleventh Virgin* and answered his query that, yes, it was all true, it was the story of her early life—knowing full well that she was to some extent misleading him. (His book, published in 1982, naturally but erroneously took the novel as a roman à clef in every respect.) Several times, she beseeched him not to continue with the project.

Miller was not alone in his archival efforts. Deane Mowrer, among others, had begun as early as the late 1960s taping interviews for posterity, many with those who had known Dorothy before she did—e.g., Peggy Baird, Charles Butterworth, Jack English, Caroline Gordon, Marge Hughes, Julia Porcelli, Karl Stern—and with those who were still on the scene in different capacities—e.g., Tom Cornell, Mary Lathrop, and Stanley Vishnewski. By the late 1970s, the archive at Marquette University was taking shape and a small fund was set up to employ interviewers to continue to fill in the record. Money was solicited from the Rockefeller Foundation to help with the process, but that effort came to an abrupt end when Dorothy angrily threatened to take back her records; she remembered the avaricious John D. Rockefeller and Ludlow strike massacre of 1914 all too well.

Knowing that she was the object of biographical scrutiny, Dorothy could have elected to take any remaining secrets to her grave. Instead she did something surprising: she spoke one day at Tivoli to a trusted Catholic Worker, Daniel Marshall, about something she could not speak of to Professor Miller. Marshall, in his midthirties, was a devout Catholic, a true scholar/worker, a believer in the values of Maurin and Hennacy, and a good listener. Dorothy told him the true story of her abortion in Chicago, the details of which had been changed and glossed over in *The Eleventh Virgin*. Marshall is certain

that she spoke to him with the idea that he would one day, in the right context, share the information after her death. That he did in 2011.

Meanwhile, at the Worker itself, that irregular but vitally important
and nearly inexplicable phenomenon—an infusion of fresh blood into the
house—was taking place. Bill Griffin was a twenty-six-year-old Georgetown
University graduate who had refused induction into the army, gone to Canada for two years, and returned to serve as a medical orderly in the military,
a decision he had come to question. When he happened upon a copy of *The
Catholic Worker* at Left Bank Books in Seattle and read Dorothy's columns
and articles by Patrick Jordan and Tom Cornell, his life changed. "They
squared the circle," he later commented. An obvious intellectual, he struck
Marc Ellis as having "an aura of meditation about him," and once in New
York, he immersed himself in the personalist writers in a way that had to
have pleased Dorothy. He also had a natural affinity for the tenor of the
cause. Ellis was stunned to see him one evening washing the feet of a blood-
ied man who had assaulted him earlier in the day.

Tom Hoey at twenty-six was a returning veteran of the experience. He
had first come to Dorothy's attention as a teenage runaway in 1965. She had
seen that he was housed with a family in the city, and when he approached
her about working at the house, she insisted that he finish high school before joining the community, which he did the following year. She took him
under her wing to be sure he didn't fall victim to drugs and alcohol like some
of the other young men who worked in the house. She knew about his beer
drinking and occasional use of marijuana. She talked to him, maternally but
honestly, about her own use of marijuana in the 1920s, a temptation she
knew young people were prone to and needed to resist. Hoey left in 1968
to marry, but after his divorce and coming out as a gay man, he returned in
1975. He told her about his marriage and his sexual orientation. She simply
answered, "I love you," and neither topic was something he and Dorothy
ever spoke about again once he moved back to St. Joseph House.

That same year, Brian Terrell and Robert Ellsberg came to St. Joseph House.
Terrell, a midwesterner, had seen Dorothy on Bill Moyers's program when he
was in high school and been impressed; Patrick Jordan had invited him to
come to New York for a visit, and he was happy to stay for four years. Ellsberg, a
son of the famed Pentagon Papers whistleblower Daniel Ellsberg, took a leave
of absence from Harvard to spend six months with the Worker that turned into

a five-year stay. Terrell and Ellsberg were both nineteen when they arrived in the East Village. Dan Mauk was a Franciscan friar from the Midwest in search of more demanding service for the poor. Meg Brodhead, a New Yorker and Rutgers University student, decided to leave college at the end of her junior year to join the Catholic Worker. "I welcomed the shock of it," she said.

New faces like theirs were needed in the mid-1970s because the turnover among younger Catholic Workers was becoming more rapid and not all was right with some of the old faces. At some point in that disorganized period, the Worker's longtime lawyer and accountant, John Coster, started to embezzle significant amounts of money from the accounts he had been entrusted with. It isn't clear exactly when his malfeasance was discovered, who else might have known about it or at least suspected, or whether anyone ever told Dorothy. It is quite possible she was kept in the dark, as the details of running the house were something she rarely inquired about anymore. All that seems certain is that the money was never replaced, and the fear of the devastating effect any publicity would have on donations and the Worker's reputation meant that there was no prosecution. A loose leadership style had significant drawbacks.

In January 1976, a second Catholic Worker house officially opened in Manhattan. For years, it had been Dorothy's dream to have a separate house for the women. In the past, when St. Joseph House was full, someone would take latecomers who showed up after dark in the cold over to the Bowery and pay the few dollars that would get them a squalid roof over their heads for the night. Those places, single-room occupancy hotels that had existed for more than a century, were fast disappearing. Residents slept on the floor at St. Joseph House, in the hall, in the basement, in the mail room, violating all kinds of city regulations. An alternative to the dangerous overcrowding, which exacerbated the already considerable tensions there, was essential.

On East 3rd Street between First and Second Avenues, an old music school created out of two adjoining town houses had gone on the market in 1973. The Worker had bought the property, with the Abbey of the Genesee in upstate New York making a large donation toward the $100,000 purchase price, but, given the city's increasingly strict occupancy codes and the renovation costs, it had taken almost two years for the building to be ready for Dorothy, several Catholic Workers, and fifty or so residents to move in.

Finally it passed inspection. Several nuns from various orders (Dominicans, Franciscans, Sisters of the Good Shepherd) whom Dorothy knew—among them, Sister Theresa Murray, Sister Elizabeth Kelliher, and Sister Renee Canitrot—came to the house for the first months to help Dorothy, Frank Donovan, and Anne Marie Fraser get it up and running. With a sprinkler system and a good number of retiled bathrooms, new stairs, and new plumbing, it was a far cry from Mott Street.

Freshly cleaned and painted, Maryhouse, as it was called, might have started out in a passable cosmetic fashion before its inevitable deterioration, but it was clear from the start that peace and quiet were not going to be found on East 3rd Street. A Hells Angels club down the block made a considerable racket with their motorcycles and street parties. Within, things were often no better. Dorothy's room was next to one occupied by Anna, a longtime resident with a terrible odor and a ferocious temper. Anna had ulcerated sores on her legs that caused her no end of pain. She would scream throughout the night, accusing Dorothy Day of being "the cause of my suffering." The newcomer Michael Harank asked Dorothy if she heard her when she was trying to sleep. "Oh, yes," she remarked, "but then I sleep with my deaf ear up."

In August of that year, Dorothy gave her final public talk. She was invited to speak at the National Eucharistic Congress in Philadelphia. The audience of Catholics from across the country was enormous—several thousand people—and the weeklong event, coinciding with the nation's Bicentennial celebrations, was filled with speeches, conferences, workshops, performances, and exhibitions. Dorothy felt her usual trepidation at public speaking in a large, formal setting but forced herself to honor her commitment. She also did something she rarely did: she wrote out her text, permitting herself no ramblings or digressions. She spoke about the Workers' attempts to feed the body and soul of those who came to their houses and about her gratitude to the Church that had brought meaning and direction to her life and hope to the world. But that was not where her remarks ended.

With her white hair wrapped in a kerchief of blue cotton and in a blue cotton dress that hung loosely on her tall, thin frame, ever so gingerly making her way to the podium, Dorothy looked especially frail that day—yet, her friend Eileen Egan wrote in admiration, "not too frail or too old to challenge the establishment." The date was August 6, and across town at the Cathedral Basilica of Saints Peter and Paul a Mass was to be held for members of the armed forces and their families, with the soldiers, sailors, and airmen invited to attend in full military regalia. Sorry as she was to have to take the organizers of the conference to task before she left the stage, Dorothy did just that. Had no one in a position of responsibility remembered that August 6 was a day of shame, she asked, the day on which the United States had incinerated the inhabitants, women and children included, of Hiroshima? Couldn't a military Mass have been scheduled for any other day? She asked that the Mass, and any others offered then, be approached not as an occasion to honor men and women in uniform but as "an act of penance, begging God to forgive us." The audience, which included Mother Teresa, gave her an ovation lasting several minutes.

Attending the National Eucharistic Congress took a great deal out of Dorothy, even more than she had expected it would, both physically and emotionally. Fortunately, she had a chance for an immediate respite. The next month she enjoyed her final retreat led by Father Hugo at a convent outside Pittsburgh, a week of prayer, meditation, and silence that left her feeling, for the first time in a long while, she wrote, "refreshed and strengthened." If there was one person she believed was misunderstood more often than she was, it was John Hugo.

In September 1976, Dorothy suffered a mild heart attack, necessitating more bed rest. She wasn't the easiest of patients. She hated the very idea of hospitals, cardiograms, checkups, and her growing regimen of pills. She was a somewhat better patient once she had a female doctor, Marion Moses, who had known her for several years but became her personal physician only in 1977, after a second, more serious heart attack. Moses had begun her medical career as a nurse with the United Farm Workers of America in California—as good a credential as any for Dorothy Day—and was the one person who seemed able to cajole her difficult patient into following her professional advice. Many people who saw Dorothy on a daily basis were convinced that Moses's care prolonged her life by two or three years. Dorothy also felt comfortable enough with her new doctor to speak with her about her past, the mistakes of her youth, her abortion.

Visitors came to Maryhouse now with the knowledge that they were visiting a cherished friend, mentor, and family member whose time on Earth was limited. Joe and Alice Zarrella and Gerry Griffin stopped by to wish her well and reminisce about the Worker in the 1930s and '40s. Forster, not in the best of health himself, became a more regular presence in the house; Tamar drove down from Vermont once a month. Dorothy's brother John came—her brother Sam, never—and occasionally John's son, Wyatt, the one member of the Day family whose politics most aligned with his aunt's. Wyatt had picketed on behalf of the Fair Play for Cuba Committee in the 1960s and later decamped for three years in Spain to avoid the Vietnam War–era draft. The same activist spirit was evinced in Dorothy's granddaughter Martha Hennessy, who was involved in actions at nuclear plants and unafraid to be arrested for her civil disobedience. It was satisfying to know that, problematic as her family seemed to her at times, the younger generation was not entirely without political convictions.

Some visitors and phone callers were more welcome than others. Mother Teresa and Cesar Chavez, always eager to see her when they were in New York, were more than welcome. Eunice Kennedy Shriver would call from time to time (knowing how tropical New York summers could be, she offered to provide air conditioners for the whole house, a gesture Dorothy appreciated but declined). Dorothy was happy to see Bob Gilliam, one of her favorite young draft resisters from the 1960s; Joe Fahey, a friend who taught at Manhattan College and was a leading figure in the peace movement; and Sister Peter Claver, who had known her for forty years. Mary Lathrop and her new husband, Kevin Pope, came by to read to her. A reconciliation with Philip Berrigan, a husband and father now but still active in war resistance, was effected in that period. Phil's brother Dan, untamed by prison, and Tom Cornell and his wife, Monica Ribar Cornell (two of Dorothy's closest friends since the early 1960s), visited. They were always stimulating companions, people she could disagree with about certain issues but still feel close to. Jacques Travers, the saintly founder of the Arthur Sheehan House of Hospitality in Brooklyn, brought flowers and vermouth. He was a Frenchman of "delicate attentions," Dorothy wrote admiringly in her diary.

The last visit of Catherine de Hueck Doherty, Dorothy's counterpart, so to speak, at Friendship House in Harlem was another story. Theirs was not a friendship that had worn well over time, at least on Dorothy's side. Doherty was warmhearted but loud and brassy, sometimes melodramatic; Dorothy became more reserved as she aged. When asked by Michael Harank if she wanted her guest brought upstairs on her last visit to St. Joseph House, she was quick to answer, "Oh, no, the dining room! Or I'll never get rid of her." It proved to be an awkward visit, as Doherty, who had never approved of Dorothy's style of management, looked about the room and felt moved to comment on how many distressing people they had both had to put up with in their lifetime of service—not a remark Dorothy wanted to hear, not an attitude she appreciated, no matter how comrade-like the spirit in which it was intended.

Figures on the world stage still made their way to Lower Manhattan to pay tribute to a woman whose work for peace long predated theirs. Dorothy was charmed to meet Mairead Corrigan, the Irish activist who had been awarded the Nobel Peace Prize in 1976 at the age of thirty-two. Corrigan asserted that reading about the Catholic Worker in Belfast when she was in her teens and twenties had been a great source of inspiration to her. Ernesto Cardenal, the poet-priest from Nicaragua and one of the leading proponents of liberation theology, brought Dorothy an autographed copy of his most recent book of poetry. Within four months, the US-backed dictator Anastasio Somoza was ousted and Cardenal assumed the position of minister of culture in the new Sandinista government of Daniel Ortega, a leftist political commitment that earned him a severe rebuke from Pope John Paul II a few years later. It was typical of Dorothy Day that she could feel a profound respect for both Father Cardenal and the Polish pope.

Disconcerting to more than a few visitors was the fact that Frank Donovan felt it necessary at a certain point to keep Dorothy's bedroom door locked when she was in there. To some in the house, he was a fierce gatekeeper. Dorothy didn't see it that way; she had always appreciated Donovan's hands-on approach to managing things and especially his protective manner toward her. Visitors thought nothing of heading up the stairs and walking right into Dorothy's room, whether invited to do so or not. That had to stop. Donovan, retired from a job with UPS, in his midfifties, was a shield, her aide-de-camp, Jane Sammon asserted. Dorothy called him "a son in my dotage."

Summarizing his impressions of the house at this time, Michael Harank commented later that he had seen "a group of people, a community of people . . . somewhat polarized, somewhat worn out, very tired, because of the load of work that had to be done and the lack of people to do it. . . . It was a period I would call very strained." Once, there had been an immediate rejuvenation when Dorothy returned from a long speaking tour, a quickening of energy around the house, a sense (not always grounded in reality) that she would sort out differences, take charge, and move things ahead. To whatever extent that had been true in the past, it wasn't now.

Enforced rest was not exactly Dorothy's preferred mode of life. "I'm 'on the shelf' here in this delightful place by the sea," she wrote from the Staten Island bungalow in the summer of 1977 to Nina Polcyn (recently married, now Nina Polcyn Moore). "Collecting rocks, reading, answering mail— moping at my general feebleness. . . . I am not used to it and rebel." She wrote again later in the year to Nina, "Pray I get to be like 'Mother Jones,' [of] I.W.W. fame, a wanderer in her nineties." But she knew her wandering days and time of leadership were done; she *hated* that fact, and her rebellion against the confinement could take the form of targeted crankiness.

That same year a number of Catholic Workers had gone to New Hampshire to occupy the Seabrook nuclear power plant, then under construction. Robert Ellsberg, Dan Mauk, and others were arrested and detained for longer than expected. Brian Terrell, twenty-one at the time, brought Dorothy's dinner up to her at Maryhouse one evening. She stared at him before lashing out, "Why aren't you in jail with your comrades?" "Someone has to do the work here while they're away," he told her. It was reprehensible, she snapped back, that an able-bodied young man should use the demands of the house as an excuse not to go out and do what had to be done at Seabrook.

It took Terrell a while, understandably, to forgive that tongue-lashing, but he soon enough came to realize that Dorothy was speaking more about herself, railing at her own limitations, than judging him. In any case, he was fully vindicated in Dorothy's eyes several months later when he and Robert Ellsberg got themselves arrested at Rocky Flats, Colorado, near Denver, protesting (along with Ellsberg senior, Stokely Carmichael, and hundreds of others) the opening of a plant to manufacture plutonium for use as triggers in nuclear missiles. Ellsberg's "Long Days, Dark Nights in a County Jail," an extended account of the experience, was one of the best incarceration narratives the paper ever published.

If you were young and fit at that stage in the history of the Catholic Worker, Dorothy expected you to be compassionate, forgiving, willing to care for the indigent—and ready to be handcuffed and spend at least a few days behind bars. What would be a source of shame to most middle-class Americans was a sign of favor in Dorothy's eyes and, perhaps, in God's.

Other changes were in the offing. Tivoli had long since served its purpose, and for years Dorothy had considered talking to realtors about selling the property, but the inertia and ambivalence brought on by age and exhaustion had forestalled any definite action. In 1978, Stanley Vishnewski convinced Dorothy that something had to be done and that Peggy Scherer was the person to handle the matter. She agreed. The estate was put onto the market (as it had been more than once before), but then Dorothy changed her mind, took it off the market, and told Peggy only after the fact. Eventually she realized, or was leaned on to realize, that she had to step back from the process. She asked others to contact Scherer, in Mexico at the time after a stay in Guatemala, urging her to return to New York to oversee the sale, which she did. It proved to be a difficult, protracted business, but when it was finally completed, the sale price was enough to pay off the mortgage and allow for the purchase of another, much smaller farm. Scherer, Mauk, and Donovan set out in search of a new place upstate. They found what they were looking for in the town of Marlboro, just outside Newburgh.

There was a determination from the start that the new Peter Maurin Farm, which opened in 1979, was not going to replicate the problems that had bedeviled Tivoli. It was going to be better managed, smaller, and less alluring (no swimming pool, two modest-sized houses, and a barn with plenty of room for crops), with only a dozen of the neediest of the fifty residents of Tivoli moving in. It was going to be a place for older residents and for Workers from the city who needed a respite. No more hippies, no more vagabonds who could manage on their own. From its inception, it worked well, especially under the leadership of Carol Campain, who, with her female partner, made sure that plenty of good food headed down to Manhattan every week and that life among the residents took a more protected, organized form. In the 1990s, Tom and Monica Cornell assumed management of the farm, where they still reside today, their son serving as the master farmer that Peter Maurin had always envisioned.

The closure of Tivoli led to a collective sigh of relief at the Worker, but nervous speculation on other topics was hard to avoid—principally, what would happen to the Catholic Worker once Dorothy was no longer alive. When Kenneth Woodward, the religion editor of *Newsweek*, was writing a profile of Dorothy for the magazine, he bluntly put the question to her, which she looked to Peggy Scherer to answer for her. "We have Dorothy

now, but we will always have the Gospel," said Peggy. Others were less confident. Was there anyone who would step in to fill the vacuum? Could the
movement really manage without such a figure? As the city continued to
collapse around them, it was not unreasonable to wonder even about the
past and the present, about what lasting good had been accomplished over
the years after all the struggle and anguish.

Others not on the scene in New York were speculating along the same
lines. At eighty-one, Father Paul Hanly Furfey published his last book, *Love
and the Urban Ghetto*, in 1978, testifying again, after so many years, to the
"overpowering effect" the Catholic Worker had had on him when he met
Dorothy in 1934. He was less sanguine in his letters that year to Catherine
de Hueck Doherty, suggesting in a mood of despair that too little progress
toward social equality had been made in America, especially on the racial
front, despite the efforts of Dorothy, Catherine, and himself. At moments,
he verged in his letters on a direct criticism of *The Catholic Worker* for not
having raised the subject of racial injustice often enough in its pages, a criticism that, given the overall record, is entirely unfair.

In 1978, Geoffrey Gneuhs came to the Catholic Worker. He had spent
the summer of 1974 there while a Dominican seminarian, living in a basement room at St. Joseph House. (He was the seminarian who had been assaulted and dragged into the street by the men wanting more of the donated
clothing.) After his ordination, to the bewilderment of his superiors, he
had gone back to the Catholic Worker and become the first official chaplain of the house. No longer did Dorothy have to rely on an ever-changing
lineup of priests, some steadier than others: there was a priest living amid
the Workers now, always available to say Mass, hear confessions, and lead
anyone in prayer while helping to serve the needs of the residents. He was
also not averse to public protest, to being arrested when necessary. It was a
comfortable relationship made more secure by the fact that Gneuhs, at the
suggestion of the historian Sydney Ahlstrom, had just written his MA thesis
at the Yale University Divinity School on Peter Maurin. As far as Dorothy
was concerned, if you knew and respected Maurin, dead now for thirty years
and in danger of being forgotten, you were a friend and ally.

Indeed, the legacy of Peter Maurin was a potentially sore subject. The
economic roller coaster of the 1970s, the oil crisis, and the recognition that
the war in Vietnam had been a catastrophic mistake hadn't changed the

direction of Americans' thinking about the country's role in the world as a superpower, their faith in its nuclear arsenal, their support for pro-US dictators, and their primary commitments to growth, commerce, comfort, entertainment, technology, and nationalism. In the decade that saw the building of huge malls in every state, with deforestation and highway building radically altering the American landscape, with massive corporate takeovers accepted as business as usual, no matter the cost to the workers, the personalist and distributist creeds had come to seem little more than quaint to any but true believers. Catholicism was no more synonymous in the public mind with social action and a critique of capitalist excess than it had been in the 1940s.

Gentrification was another sore subject. One weekend when he had to be away, Father Gneuhs asked a fellow Dominican priest with whom he was friends if he would cover for him and say Mass at Maryhouse in his stead. Father Boniface Ramsey agreed. Ramsey also knew a few people who lived nearby on the Bowery in a large, high-ceilinged renovated apartment, two brothers from a comfortable middle-class family and the son of a famous sculptor. He invited them to come by for Mass, and one of the brothers, Hugo Owen, accepted the invitation. After Mass, Ramsey introduced his friend to Dorothy and mentioned his great apartment in the neighborhood. Dead silence ensued. Dorothy just glared at Owen. Father Ramsey was stunned and asked Owen later if he had any idea what had just happened. It wasn't a surprise to him, his friend remarked. Dorothy obviously knew the building in question. We're the gentrifiers, he told Ramsey—the enemy, the ones the Catholic Worker doesn't want in the area, the people they assume will drive them out someday.

That *someday* is a whole other story in itself, as St. Joseph House and Maryhouse remain, four decades after Dorothy Day's death, exactly where they have always been but surrounded now by chic eateries, high-price co-ops, boutique hotels, and chain stores.

The editorship of the paper passed definitively out of Dorothy's hands in the late 1970s, but she had no problem relinquishing that part of her life. She had delegated to the right people, and there was much to be proud of when each issue came off the press. Some issues crossed the 90,000 mark, a number of readers *The Catholic Worker* hadn't reached since before World War II. In 1974, Patrick Jordan had passed the managing editor's baton to Anne Marie Fraser, the first woman to have full editorial authority, who was succeeded in 1976 by Robert Ellsberg, who two years later suggested to Dorothy that Dan Mauk and Peggy Scherer take charge.

In addition to its news coverage, the paper in the last years of Dorothy's life printed essays of considerable length and depth: e.g., Patrick Jordan on Martin Buber, Meg Brodhead on Desiderius Erasmus, Dan Berrigan on life in prison, Eileen Egan on women's roles in the peace movement and the Vatican's history of misogyny, Robert Ellsberg on J. Edgar Hoover's files targeting Dorothy and the Catholic Worker, his father, Daniel Ellsberg, on the nuclear arms race. But there were also issues that led some within and outside the Catholic Worker movement to question the ongoing relevance of the paper in a time of some unexpected social upheaval and debate.

One such issue concerned gay men and lesbians. A letter in the summer of 1978 applauding a recent editorial in the paper condemning anti-Semitism came in one day from a Connecticut subscriber. The young man had a poignant question to ask, though, one that deeply troubled him as gay rights ordinances were being repealed across the country and Anita Bryant's "Save Our Children" campaign was in full swing: "If the Catholic Worker is the gentle enemy of all oppressors of people, the pages of this newspaper have been silent on the increased oppression, discrimination and violence taking place against American gay people." Why is this? he asked. He had read the paper since high school, he noted, and he had learned much about nonviolence and compassion from what he had read there. But silence regarding "the struggle of gay people—many of whom are, I'm sure, friends of the Catholic Worker, as I am—deeply puzzles and saddens me."

A difficult discussion ensued around the table among the editors and writers. Initially, it was felt by most that the letter should be printed. A fair question, appropriately phrased, had been asked. Variously worded responses might suffice. As some liberal clergy were already arguing, one could take a stand against antigay prejudice and violence while still accepting the Church's "natural law" doctrine on the "disorder" of homosexuality. Dorothy herself had once, in response to an insensitive remark about gay men from a Catholic Worker from California, indicated her displeasure with that tone and answered back, "*Someone* has to minister to gay people." She was thinking of Tom Hoey and dozens of other Catholic Workers about whose sexual orientation she was well aware and whose reserve on the subject she respected. Yet Frank Donovan, the house manager, gay himself, argued that the decision about whether or not to publish the letter should first be put to Dorothy. She had almost nothing to do with the paper at this point, it was true, and spent as much time as possible on Staten Island resting, but it was still, in effect, her paper. Dan Mauk went to see her.

Dorothy's initial reaction was not what people such as Peggy Scherer, Father Gneuhs, or Michael Harank (the last two both gay men) were hoping for. At first, somewhat rattled, she quoted St. Paul as she often did: "Let these things be not so much as mentioned among you." (One longtime Catholic Worker, the bohemian Walter Kerrell, had been asked to leave after spending what Dorothy considered an inordinate amount of time on the phone with someone who was obviously his boyfriend. The fact that Kerrell had spoken to his "petit chou" in French hadn't done much to disguise the fact. He was, though, far from the only gay person to leave the Catholic Worker in bitterness and disillusionment on that account.) In effect, "Don't ask, don't tell" had been the Catholic Worker's policy for decades.

Then Dorothy raised a different point with Mauk. Even separate from the matter of Church teachings on the subject of homosexuality, *The Catholic Worker* had never been a paper devoted to every social issue the United States confronted; it had always been selective in its coverage and commentary. In truth, in any context, homosexuality was not a topic Dorothy really wanted addressed in its pages. Mauk understood that. In the end, she shifted her view altogether and told him that the editorial board should do what it wanted. "It's your paper now," she conceded. It was too much for her to have to grapple with.

The board chose not to print the letter, a decision that left a bitter taste among some on the staff and with Tamar, when she heard about it later. Homosexuality and the way gay people were treated, or mistreated, in the United States wasn't a subject that was destined to go away, of course, and became all the more heated in the 1980s as the AIDS crisis overwhelmed the neighborhood and the city.

The new year opened and closed with tragedy, with mounting health concerns and family tribulations in between. In January 1979, Justin, the four-year-old son of Dorothy's granddaughter Becky, was hit by a school bus in Vermont and killed. Dorothy could barely speak for grief, which tore at every member of the Hennessy family. That summer, the Vermont house was destroyed in a nighttime blaze. Tamar and three of her children—Martha, twenty-four; Hilaire, twenty; and Kate, nineteen—were living there with Nicky, who, at thirty, was drinking and becoming increasingly unstable. Asked to leave, Nicky set fire to the house, an act of arson that led to a sentence of two years in jail for Tamar's most troubled child.

Then, in December, Stanley Vishnewski died unexpectedly of a heart attack in his room at Maryhouse. His death was a leveling blow. He had been with Dorothy almost from the beginning. She could rib him mercilessly, telling him (not unjustly) that he did the least work around the house or farm of anyone at the Catholic Worker. She could bark at him about his television watching ("Turn that damn thing off. You know I can't stand the commercials"), but Stanley had an answer for everything. The definition of a martyr, he liked to quip, was someone who had to live with a saint.

He had also been a loving support for Dorothy as she aged, picking up discounted books he thought she might like at the nearby Strand Book Store and providing a strong shoulder to lean on in times of depression and doubt. She could cry openly in front of him in moments of frustration, and he was always willing to make the trip with her to New England to see how the Hennessys were managing. His loss was no less hard on Tamar and her children.

An obituary by Dorothy, her last extended piece for the paper, was entitled "A Knight for a Day." She recalled the time in the 1930s during a strike when he had come between her and the horse of a policeman that was about to crush her against a wall and the day at Tivoli he had saved her from Michael Mok. The eighteen-year-old who had offered to carry her typewriter in 1935 had been devoted to her well-being for forty-five years, and he was buried not far from Peter Maurin at St. John Cemetery in Queens. Stanley left behind a short memoir of life at the Catholic Worker, *The Wings of the Dawn*, that he desperately wanted to see in print but for which he had never been able to find a publisher. His friends at the house saw that it was privately printed a few years after his death.

Throughout 1980, Dorothy felt her strength ebbing away. She insisted on writing her column, afraid that readers would assume she had died, but all she could pass on to the editors were increasingly terse, scattered jottings from her diary. She tried to read, but that once-vital pastime was becoming harder by the week. Her powers of concentration failed her. She complained that if Frank Donovan didn't bring the *New York Times* to her room each morning, she wouldn't have any idea what day it was. The young men and women in the house noticed that she was repeating the same stories over and over and forgetting their names. Events that would have been the subject of earnest commentary in her columns—the Mariel boat lift from Cuba, the founding of Solidarity in Poland, the ascendancy of Ronald Reagan—went unremarked.

By the late fall, Dorothy's energy had dwindled to a shockingly low point. Visitors became an intolerable strain. More than ever, she needed Frank Donovan as a gatekeeper. When she came back from a doctor's visit, he and Tom Hoey, or any other able-bodied young man on hand, had to carry her upstairs in a chair. Deane Mowrer taped the Friday-night discussion sessions for her when she could no longer manage the one flight down to the auditorium. She liked knowing that important occasions for "clarification of thought"—Peter's delightful phrase—were still taking place in the house, and in fact, in the last year of Dorothy's life, the schedule of speakers and the topics under discussion were as robust and probing as they had ever been. *Commonweal* editor Peter Steinfels came to Maryhouse to talk about the emerging neoconservative movement, the peace activist David McReynolds spoke on the arms race, James Finn on V. S. Naipaul, John Cort on Eric Gill, and the controversial theologian Charles Curran on Catholic ethics, while Gordon Zahn introduced a new documentary film about Franz Jägerstätter. But it annoyed Dorothy that she couldn't be there in person, sitting as usual in the front row, taking notes, learning, questioning, eagerly watching others learn and question.

The one positive development for Dorothy as the end neared was the chance to repair, to whatever extent it was possible, her relationship with Tamar. Family was never far from her mind now. Della had died in May: more heartbreak, more regret. Now both mother and daughter wanted to put to rest the issues that had divided them.

Some of those issues were intractable. It was like "a knife wound to my heart," Dorothy had told a friend, that Tamar and all of her children had left the Church. For Tamar, the bitterness that was hard to let go of had to do with her abysmal schooling, with her mother's failure to see that she had even a proper high school education, let alone any preparation for college. She felt that her intellectual potential had never been recognized when she was young, and on that topic Dorothy's guilt prevented her from seeing the justice of her daughter's complaint. Yet there was still space to affirm their love, for Tamar to indicate her deep concern for her mother's well-being, for Dorothy to show tenderness toward a needy child whose deepest needs she had not always answered. "It was only in these last two years," Tamar told Geoffrey Gneuhs shortly before Dorothy died, "that I have been able to be friends with my mother." A long period of emotional distance had come to an end.

On November 8, Dorothy turned eighty-three. The birthday wishes poured in, but Dorothy was aware that she would never see another. With her pulse rate alarmingly low by the end of the month, Dr. Moses insisted that she go to Beth Israel Medical Center, where there was talk of valve surgery, but Dorothy insisted with equal vehemence that she understood that the end had come. She wanted to go home to die. Home was the Catholic Worker.

By Saturday, November 29, everyone in the house knew that the end was rapidly approaching. Dorothy spoke with Eileen Egan on the phone early that afternoon, inquiring about the victims of the earthquake in Italy that had taken place earlier that week and the aid efforts of Catholic Relief Services. "Her voice was strong with compassion," Egan later recalled. That was Dorothy Day's last extended conversation. Maryhouse became that afternoon, for once, a place of silence. Even the more recalcitrant residents, women who badgered one another mercilessly throughout the dinner hour, women who howled their pain and anger on a daily basis, walked about quietly or talked in hushed voices on the stairs or in the yard. Tamar spent the late afternoon by her mother's side.

Just after 5:30 p.m., Tamar called out for help. Dorothy had collapsed in the bathroom down the hall, and Tamar needed help getting her back into her room. She was dead by the time the sheets were smoothed and her head was gently placed upon her pillow.

TWENTY

❦ DEO GRATIAS ❦

Dorothy Day's passage from this world was in the spirit of the Catholic Worker itself: intense, chaotic, spare, sad, passionate, celebratory, anti-institutional, and personalist to the last. Her body was washed Saturday night by Sister Marie Kimball, a recent volunteer whose warmth and humor Dorothy had enjoyed. Sister Kimball had experience ministering to older nuns, and Tamar agreed that her mother was being left in the right gentle, capable, loving hands. It took several hours—until almost midnight—before the death certificate was signed and the undertaker's men came to the house, allowing time for the people closest to Dorothy to take turns keeping a vigil, comforting Tamar, praying the rosary. The house continued to be eerily silent.

The next day, the body was viewed at the funeral parlor on Second Avenue by Frank Donovan, Dan Mauk, and Peggy Scherer, and Dorothy was then brought back to the house in her beloved blue-and-white-checked housedress and bandanna, to rest in a simple open pine coffin on the narrow wooden altar—carved by some artistic friends from the trunk of a hefty cedar tree—in the small second-floor chapel at Maryhouse. The funeral was scheduled for Tuesday morning, December 2, at the Church of the Nativity, only a block away on Second Avenue. That was the church—a squat modernist monstrosity of black brick and unpainted concrete but the only one nearby—where Dorothy had worshipped when she was still able to leave the house. Two of her grandsons and four of her granddaughters came to the city to serve as pallbearers.

The Chancery called on Sunday morning to offer the cathedral on Fifth Avenue for the funeral, but that was out of the question. Dorothy Day would be taken to her grave from a church built among the poor, no matter the architecture, and not from a cathedral. Wherever the service was going to be held, Cardinal Cooke would be happy to celebrate the Mass, his secretary noted, though the hour would need to be moved from 11:00 a.m. to 10:00 a.m. to accommodate a previous commitment. Given the time needed to serve breakfast and clean up at the two houses, everyone who had any say in the matter was adamant: the funeral would start at 11:00 a.m. as announced. As no one really wanted the cardinal to officiate, the excuse seemed diplomatic enough.

Another awkward matter to be straightened out concerned who would in fact say the Mass. Father Hugo was under the impression that he would be the celebrant, as Dorothy had remarked to him once years earlier that that would be the case. Dan Berrigan thought the same, but Tamar's wish, supported by everyone in the house, was that Geoffrey Gneuhs, her mother's chaplain for the last two years, would have that honor, along with Father Pierre Raphael, a priest in the neighborhood from the Little Brothers of Jesus whom Dorothy admired for his work with prisoners at Rikers Island. About Hugo, the man she held more responsible than anyone for the years of alienation from her mother, the priest whose retreats and calls to piety and renunciation had been so painful to her, Tamar remarked, "If he says the Mass, I won't attend."

The wake on Monday afternoon and evening brought together more than eight hundred people who represented the disparate strands of Dorothy's life: Cesar Chavez and I. F. Stone, Michael Harrington and Abbie Hoffman, Eileen Egan and Gordon Zahn, John Cort and Robert Ellsberg, Joe Zarrella and Nina Polcyn Moore, Tamar's children, John Day and his family, peace activists from several states, priests and nuns who had known her for years, Catholic Workers from houses and farming communities in other states, neighbors who respected the work being done in their midst—those paying their respects included the faithful and those with no faith other than in the mission started in 1933 by Peter Maurin and Dorothy Day. The disheveled Frank Sheed stood by the coffin weeping copiously, talking to Dorothy for a length of time that became awkward, causing the line of mourners to stretch down the stairs and into the foyer. The intensity of feeling in the small room was at moments overpowering. Martha Hennessy was shocked to see an old woman, trembling, bend over the coffin and kiss her grandmother on the lips. Others placed small objects in the coffin beside Dorothy. One man who had left the Catholic Worker twenty years earlier showed up inebriated and had to be gently restrained as he seemed to want to climb into the coffin.

After the wake, some of the younger men went out to one of the Ukrainian bars on Second Avenue. They wanted to reminisce, tell their favorite Dorothy stories, marvel at how their lives had been affected by that one mesmerizing, demanding, paradoxical woman. They got drunk, hopelessly drunk—"really smashed . . . not just tipsy," Brian Terrell remembered, "but fraternity-party drunk. Stomping on tables, that kind of thing." The next morning, oddly, no one seemed hung over. It was Dorothy's first miracle, someone said.

On the morning of the funeral, obituaries appeared in almost all major papers across the country. In New York, it was unseasonably mild for early December. The request had been made the night before that only the family follow the procession and the coffin to the church around the corner on Second Avenue, but former Catholic Workers by the dozens had no intention of not being present for every moment of the good-bye to Dorothy Day. "Hell, no," thought Michael Harrington, along with so many others who had given some part of their lives to the Catholic Worker and who now felt that if anyone was "family" to Dorothy, they were. They gathered in the street. The slow walk to the church started. The cross was borne by Ed Forand, the incense censer by Arthur Lacey, the tall paschal candle by Michael Harank, with two women who had worked with Dorothy for several years, Kathy Clarkson and Jeannette Noel, carrying the other candles. They were followed by Father Gneuhs and Father Raphael. The procession was silent; the only noise, the sounds of traffic on the avenue and a boisterous fight between two truck drivers shouting at each other from their cabs. The church bells, growing louder, eventually drowned them out.

As the coffin rounded the corner from East 3rd Street, a classic Catholic Worker moment occurred. A rumpled man standing on the curb, obviously homeless and unwell, came running toward the pallbearers. The grandchildren stopped. The man said nothing. He gently placed his hand on the coffin and then ran off.

Cardinal Cooke was waiting outside the church to offer a blessing. In his red episcopal robes and skullcap, with two clerics nearby, he blessed the coffin and greeted the grandchildren before they carried their grandmother inside. On the landing, the shaken Tamar and Forster stood together,

Tamar's arm through her father's. The cardinal leaned over to Forster, who seemed small and shrunken to most onlookers, and remarked in sympathy, "Your wife was a wonderful woman." To which Forster, anticlerical to his dying day, shot back, "I don't need you to tell me that." Then John Shiel, a peace activist from Washington, DC, who had taken a 4:00 a.m. bus to be present for the funeral, seized the moment—he was famous for confronting bishops on social issues—and put himself into Cooke's path, asking when the archbishop of New York was going to take a public stand against nuclear arms. The cardinal greeted him kindly, ignored the question, and walked to his car.

Several hundred people filled the church, some standing in the aisles. Father Boniface Ramsey and several Dominican priests had taken the earliest train from Washington to be there; they were among many who had to remain on the church steps when they arrived, so large was the crowd inside, filling even the cafeteria below, which had been outfitted with speakers to hear the Mass. Wyatt Day brought his dead aunt to the funeral. Tina de Aragon had died of bone cancer a few months before and been cremated, the ashes stored with Frank Donovan at Maryhouse until her nephew decided what to do with them. That morning, before the service, he had stopped by and collected his aunt's urn, which he brought with him to the Church of the Nativity in a shopping bag. Dorothy had always liked Tina.

Other than the family at the front and the current Catholic Workers at the two houses and Peter Maurin Farm, no pews had been reserved for anyone. The well-known—Chavez, Stone, Harrington, Ward, Episcopal Bishop Paul Moore, Kenneth Woodward of *Newsweek*—and the unknown, past writers for the paper, past and present Catholic Workers sat scattered on the hard seats under the ceiling stained with watermarks or stood in the aisles.

The Mass began. The readings were carefully chosen. Peggy Scherer read from Isaiah 58:6–12 ("Is not this the kind of fasting I have chosen; / to loosen the chains of injustice / and untie the cords of the yoke"), Dan Mauk from 1 John 4:11–18 ("Whoever lives in love lives in God, and God in them"), and Father Gneuhs from Matthew 5:1–12 (the Beatitudes). Gneuhs opened his eulogy by quoting Dorothy from *The Long Loneliness*, "All my life I have been haunted by God," and recounted just where that haunting had led her: to a life of simplicity and poverty among the poor, to solidarity with the scorned and the outcast, to jail in a stand against militarism, to community and love, to an extraordinary pilgrimage that could never have been predicted from her origins and to a life lived in faith as an example to the world.

The mourners exited to the strains of the Lutheran hymn "A Mighty Fortress Is Our God." On the steps of the church, Kenneth Woodward watched a woman approach someone he didn't know but had spoken to when they filed in together; the man had remarked to Woodward that he was a Jew and it wasn't Dorothy's religion but her political beliefs that had inspired him to attend. During the Mass, he had obviously not joined the Catholic worshippers who had chosen to receive Communion. Now the woman handed him a Communion wafer, saying, "Dorothy would have wanted you to have this!"—a strange statement, to say the least, given the meaning to any believer of the consecrated Host.

As Michael Harank neared the door, he noticed in a back pew an older woman, possibly a resident of Maryhouse, stretched out, sound asleep. With that, on the other hand, Dorothy would have had no problem.

A smaller group made the ride to the far end of Staten Island, to Resurrection Cemetery. The opening of the grave had been paid for by the archdiocese, a fact regarded as pleasingly ironic by those who remembered the Calvary Cemetery grave diggers' strike of 1948 and Dorothy's fierce opposition to Cardinal Spellman's decision to break that strike. There Father Gneuhs said the final prayers, and the coffin was committed to the ground. Three greyhounds appeared out of nowhere, gamboling at the edge of the crowd.

A small, square, flat headstone would be placed over the plot a few weeks later, inscribed with the simplest of epitaphs: DOROTHY DAY, NOVEMBER 8, 1897–NOVEMBER 29, 1980/DEO GRATIAS.

After the funeral, mourners who had not gone to Staten Island went back to Maryhouse, where a ten-gallon kettle of pea soup was simmering and loaves of brown bread and baskets of oranges filling a table nearby. There were so many to feed that day.

POSTSCRIPT

In November 1997, on the occasion of what would have been her hundredth birthday, Cardinal John O'Connor, the head of the Archdiocese of New York, announced in a homily from the pulpit of St. Patrick's Cathedral that he was considering a proposal to begin the process that could lead to Dorothy Day's canonization. He invited those who had known her most intimately to offer their views in the coming months. The following February and again in March, a number of people who had worked closely with Dorothy met with the cardinal to share memories and talk about the advisability of proceeding with what is an exacting, time-consuming, expensive, and arcane process. Not long after, the cardinal wrote to the prefect of the Congregation for the Causes of Saints in Rome to do just that.

The long road to official recognition of sainthood for Dorothy Day hadn't originated with O'Connor, though. Rather, soon after his arrival in New York in 1984, he had taken up the cause of his immediate predecessor, the late Cardinal Cooke. It was the Claretians of Chicago, a religious order, that in 1983 first argued the desirability of promoting Dorothy's canonization, soliciting prayers and testimonials and eventually devoting part of their website to that end. But it required someone of O'Connor's stature to advance the initiative, and the longer O'Connor was at the helm in New York, the more he came to feel the wisdom of acting on it.

Eighteen months later, in March 2000, the announcement came from Rome that the cause for the beatification of the founder of the Catholic Worker and, ultimately, her potential canonization had been officially opened. In the terminology the Church employs, she could now, with O'Connor's imprimatur, be called a Servant of God. The next stage, currently under way, involves the Congregation's exhaustive examination of her life for evidence of "heroic virtue," at which time, if it is found, she will be designated the Venerable Dorothy Day. Her subsequent beatification, if that comes to pass, would render her the Blessed Dorothy Day, worthy of veneration in her own diocese, and at her canonization she would become Saint Dorothy Day, a figure to be revered by the entire Catholic world.

The process leading to beatification and canonization is anything but a speedy one, and its intricacies are legendary. Nor is its outcome for any candidate ensured. In 2005, O'Connor's successor, Cardinal Edward Egan, established the Dorothy Day Guild, which raises funds and public awareness, and its efforts are supported by Egan's successor, the current leader of the Archdiocese of New York, Cardinal Timothy Dolan. In 2012, under Dolan's leadership, the United States Conference of Catholic Bishops in a voice vote at its annual meeting expressed its wholehearted support for pursuing canonization.

Finally, in September 2015, Pope Francis I became the first pontiff to comment publicly and explicitly about Dorothy Day, and his remarks were delivered in a setting that guaranteed worldwide attention. Following a trip to Cuba (where he met Fidel Castro and celebrated Mass in Havana) and before traveling to New York to address the United Nations, Francis spoke in the US Capitol before the entire Congress, the Supreme Court, members of President Barack Obama's cabinet, and other dignitaries. In a well-received speech that focused on the challenges of environmental collapse, immigration, poverty, and the family, the pope cited four Americans who offer us "a way of seeing and interpreting reality" that is desperately needed in our time. Those three men and one woman, he asserted, had led exemplary moral lives and could be seen as unique sources of inspiration: they were Abraham Lincoln, Martin Luther King, Jr., Thomas Merton, and Dorothy Day.

Everyone on the Mall that day who gathered before the huge screens broadcasting the pope's address knew the first two names on his list, of course. The better informed of those many thousands of people had heard of the Trappist monk, and some surely had read his best-selling memoir of the path to his vocation, *The Seven Storey Mountain*, a book that in more than sixty years has never been out of print. The name that occasioned puzzlement and questions was Dorothy's. It would hardly have surprised her that she was little known among American Catholics thirty-five years after her passing; no one was less concerned with personal fame or her posthumous reputation.

Since the time of the American bishops' vote and the pope's address, discussion of Dorothy's place in modern Catholicism has been more actively debated by a wide range of people. Unanimity on the subject could hardly have been expected, views of Dorothy having been so divided in her lifetime. A small number of conservative Catholics are to this day horrified at the prospect of canonizing a woman who had an abortion and a child out of wedlock and who condemned capitalism far more frequently and vehemently than she condemned Marxism-Leninism. They vent their spleen unreservedly in the digital world. Another group, which includes some family members and Catholic Workers who knew her in the 1970s, are indifferent or opposed, believing that the institutionalization of Dorothy's memory and life's work would be antithetical to her very uninstitutional, anti-hierarchical approach to spiritual growth and social change. They fear the loss of her radical edge. The archdiocese's suggestion that her body be removed from the Staten Island cemetery where it now rests to a vault in St. Patrick's Cathedral, on the plausible assumption that such a move would advance her cause with the Vatican, has been rebuffed by her grandchildren, whose permission is required. (Tamar died in 2008.)

Yet others who knew Dorothy are equally certain about the value of her canonization. While noting that she had no interest in speculating about her own worthiness, they point to her enthusiastic study of the lives of the saints and the sustenance those examples provided her. As Robert Ellsberg wrote in an essay for *America*, "Dorothy believed that the canonized saints were those who reminded us of our true vocation," i.e., of the Gospel-inspired need to give more thought and energy to charity and justice than to our own happiness and success. Many who knew her at the Catholic Worker have no doubt of the result in the years to come. "Our children will go to Rome to see her canonized," Tom Cornell insists.

Regardless of one's view of canonization, one fact is striking. Dorothy Day's legacy has not disappeared in the twenty-first century. Her books, particularly *The Long Loneliness*, find new readers all the time, and the monthly newspaper she and Peter Maurin founded seventy-five years ago is still sent out several times a year to more than 25,000 subscribers. It remains a steadfast voice for pacifism. More than 150 Catholic Worker houses and farms across the United States remain in operation, feeding and sheltering the needy, and another 29 worldwide. (Some are in more viable shape than others, and no one any longer looks to the New York house for guidance or leadership. A true personalist decentralization is in place.) These efforts exemplify "the little way" of Dorothy's beloved St. Thérèse of Lisieux. They embody the Franciscan ideals of compassion and self-sacrifice and the Benedictine belief in simplicity and prayerful community, all of which meant so much to Dorothy Day. They echo as well Peter Maurin's insistence that, in the end, love, effort, and faith are all that matter.

ACKNOWLEDGMENTS

Dorothy Day's sizable archive—her diaries and journals, manuscripts and correspondence and clipping files, the many oral history transcripts collected over the years—resides in the Special Collections of the Raynor Memorial Libraries at Marquette University in Milwaukee, carefully administered over the years by archivist Phil Runkel. Everyone who has written about Day over the last thirty or more years, including the authors of this book, owes an enormous debt of gratitude to him. As many before us have observed, Phil is a veritable encyclopedia of information, always ready to share that knowledge, about the life and times of the subject of this book. He made sure our visits to Milwaukee were productive. We are pleased to dedicate this book to him.

Many librarians and archivists at archdioceses and universities around the country were helpful to us in our research—a special place in the next world should be reserved for archivists, in our estimation—and we appreciate the leads and information provided by those individuals. Among them are Alison M. Foley of the Archdiocese of Baltimore, Karen Horton of the Archdiocese of Mobile, Heidi Johnson of the College of St. Scholastica in Duluth, Shane McDonald of the archives of Catholic University of America, Kathleen Messier of the Archdiocese of Burlington, Vermont, Julie Motyka of the Archdiocese of Indianapolis, Sarah Ater of the Archdiocese of Cincinnati, Peggy Roske archivist jointly for St. John's University and St. Benedict's College in Minnesota, Gary Topping of the Archdiocese of Salt Lake City, Monsignor Francis J. Weber of the Archdiocese of Los Angeles, and Kenneth White of the Archdiocese of Pittsburgh. Wendy Chmielewski of the Swarthmore College archives; Alan Delozier at the Archives of Seton Hall University in South Orange, New Jersey, where the papers of the Archdiocese of Newark are housed; and Benjamin Panciera at the Lear Center of the Charles E. Shain Library of Connecticut College in New London, repository of the principal Eugene O'Neill collection, were similarly helpful.

Patrice Kane, archivist emerita of Fordham University, deserves a special mention for the help she provided on the very day of her retirement.

The resources of the New York Public Library and the Walsh Family Library of Fordham University in the Bronx were important to our work. We also benefited from examining the Ade Bethune Papers at the Library of St. Catherine's University in Minneapolis; the Emily Coleman Papers at the archives of the University of Delaware; the John Cort Papers and the Paul Hanly Furfey Papers at the archives of the Catholic University of America; the Grace Delafield Day–Katherine Anne Porter correspondence at the McKeldin Library at the University of Maryland; the Dorothy Day, Sheed & Ward, and Nina Polcyn papers at Notre Dame University; the Helénè Iswolsky Collections at the Weinberg Memorial Library at the University of Scranton; the Claude McKay Papers at the Beinecke Library at Yale University; Father Joseph McSorley's papers at the Archives of the Missionary Society of St. Paul the Apostle in New York City; and the Peace Collection at Swarthmore College.

The late Rosalie Riegle Troester's two oral history collections were invaluable in learning more about Dorothy Day, the Catholic Worker, and the antiwar movement. She is a key figure in any study of Dorothy Day. The same must be said for Robert Ellsberg, whose editing of the diaries and letters in the Marquette collection provides an invaluable resource for anyone who wishes to understand this remarkable woman.

Equally crucial to this project, of course, was the opportunity to talk with some of the men and women who were inspired to join the Catholic Worker or who met Dorothy Day under other circumstances, or who knew her or members of her family personally. She is forty years gone now, but the memories she inspired among friends and associates are still vivid. For our conversations and interviews, or for information provided by email or in person, we are grateful to many people: Gerald Adams; Mary Allen; Rachel de Aragon (a niece of John Day, Jr., and Teresa de Aragon Day); Garrick Beck (the son of Judith Malina and Julian Beck); Willa Bickham; Meg Brodhead; Michael Burke (a nephew of Forster Batterham); Maggie Corbin (the daughter of Marty and Rita Corbin); Sister Donald Corcoran, OSB; the ever hospitable Tom and Monica Cornell of the Peter Maurin Farm in Marlboro, New York; Wyatt Day (the nephew of Dorothy Day and son of John Day, Jr.); Ed Egan; Marc Ellis; Robert Ellsberg; Jack Fahey; R. Paul Fitzmaurice; Robert Gilliam;

Bill Griffin; Bishop Thomas Gumbleton; Tom Hoey; George Horton; Kathleen and Patrick Jordan; Anne Marie Fraser Kaune; Betsy Keenan; Mary Lathrop; Daniel Marshall; Dan Mauk; Kathleen McKenna; Karl Meyer; Chris and Joan Montesano; David O'Brien, Henry Presler, Father Boniface Ramsey; Jane Sammon; Peggy Scherer; Dr. Elizabeth Sheehan (the daughter of Arthur Sheehan); Martin Sheen; Carl Siciliano; Robert Steed; Brian Terrell; Johanna Hughes Turner (the daughter of Marge Hughes); Dan Wakefield; Brendan Walsh; and Kenneth Woodward.

Father Geoffrey Gneuhs, who knew Dorothy in her last years, served as her chaplain, and delivered the eulogy at her funeral, was especially helpful, in terms of his own familiarity with Dorothy Day and the philosophy of Peter Maurin (the subject of his Yale MA dissertation in 1978), and in his suggestions for research and interview leads. His friendship and interest in the progress of this book was at all times an added pleasure in this endeavor. Michael Harank went above and beyond the call in finding us other people to interview who knew Dorothy. In a similarly helpful spirit, Martha Hennessy, Dorothy's granddaughter, made herself available for a conversation about her grandmother that was deeply moving and meaningful.

We are grateful, too, to have had the opportunity to talk to Cardinal Timothy Dolan about the Church's view of our subject, the beatification and canonization process, and the Cardinal's own perspective on the importance of Dorothy Day to our time. Professor Harry Murray of Nazareth College shared his research on Peter Maurin, which provided some important information, and it was a pleasure to talk with Jeremy Harmon of the *Salt Lake City Tribune* about Ammon Hennacy and his time in Utah; our thanks to him for sharing Joan Thomas's unpublished biography of Hennacy. Dr. Susan Mountin of Marquette University, who teaches a course on the life and thought of Dorothy Day, provided food for thought. Chloe Lucchesi-Malone examined the Swarthmore College Peace Collection papers for us. Dr. Val Noone of the University of Melbourne, one of Dorothy's greeters on her trip to Melbourne, was key to providing information about Dorothy's visit to Australia in 1970.

Friends such as Lisa Adler, Steven Amarnick, Lucie Andre, Don Babcock, Jack Davis, Candi Deschamps, Lisa Ford, the Farish family, Jeff Kearney, Laura Kirk, Ron Koury, Kevin Lally, Marjorie Mueller McKittrick, Catherine McMenamin, Joyce Slayton Mitchell, Betsey Osborne, Maya

Popa, and Brad Whitehurst formed our ideal readership in our minds. Deane, Blythe's brother, was a great champion of the project and contributed in myriad ways. For much-needed technological assistance along the way, our thanks also extend to Ralph L. Williams and, especially, the indispensable Maya Popa, poet and technocrat.

We were fortunate in that our literary agent, Rob McQuilkin of Massie & McQuilkin in New York City, was enthusiastic about this project from the start and connected us with the right editor, Alice Mayhew at Simon & Schuster. Alice believed that the time was ripe for a new biography of Dorothy Day. At Simon & Schuster, we benefited from the expertise of Amar Deol and Jessica Chin, Carly Loman, and Beth Maglione.

Finally, our personal thanks extend to our respective husbands, Steve Roser (Blythe's better half) and Thomas Orefice (John's), both of whom were patient and supportive and have probably heard more about Dorothy Day and the Catholic Worker than they ever imagined possible.

One can't say that the subject of this book was particularly helpful to the process in that she destroyed plenty of what were no doubt fascinating personal papers from her earlier years—as any individual has the right to do, of course—and was never particularly concerned with an exact sense of chronology in her own writings about her life. Nonetheless, it is doubtful that we will ever encounter another person as challenging and complex as Dorothy Day, as worth the effort to tell a life story of enduring value.

BIBLIOGRAPHY

Ahlmstrom, Sidney. *A Religious History of the American People*. New Haven, CT: Yale University Press, 1972.

Arnold, Hillel D. "A Sign of Contradiction: The Record Keeping Practices of the New York City Catholic Worker." *American Catholic Studies* 121, no. 2 (Summer 2010): 1–29.

Aronica, Michele Teresa. *Beyond Charismatic Leadership: The New York Catholic Worker Movement*. New Brunswick, NJ: Transaction Books, 1987.

Auden, W. H. "Happy Birthday, Dorothy Day." *The New York Review of Books*, December 14, 1972.

Bak, Hans. *Malcolm Cowley: The Formative Years*. Athens: University of Georgia Press, 1993.

Baratte, Linda L. "Eileen Egan: Portrait of the Life, Lifestance, and Pedagogy of a Catholic Prophet of Peace." PhD dissertation, Fordham University, Bronx, NY, 2004.

Barnette, Sean Michael. "Houses of Hospitality: The Material Rhetoric of Dorothy Day and the Catholic Worker." PhD dissertation, University of Tennessee, Knoxville, TN, 2011.

Beck, Garrick. *True Stories: Tales from the Generation of a New World Culture*. Bloomington, IN: iUniverse, 2017.

Bendiner, Elmer. *The Bowery Man*. New York: Thomas Nelson & Sons, 1961.

Berrigan, Daniel. *To Dwell in Peace: An Autobiography*. New York: Harper & Row, 1987.

———. *The Berrigan Letters: Personal Correspondence Between Daniel and Philip Berrigan*. Edited by Daniel Cosacchi and Eric Martin. Maryknoll, NY: Orbis Books, 2016.

Betten, Neil. *Catholic Activism and the Industrial Worker*. Gainesville: University Presses of Florida, 1976.

Burston, Daniel. *A Forgotten Freudian: The Passion of Karl Stern*. London: Karnac Books, 2016.

Clayton, Douglas. *Floyd Dell: The Life and Times of an American Rebel*. Chicago: Ivan Dee, 1994.

Cogley, John. *A Canterbury Tale: Experiences and Reflections, 1916–1976*. New York: Seabury Press, 1976.

Cole, Audrey H. "The Catholic Worker Farm: Tivoli, New York, 1964–1978." *The Hudson Valley Regional Review* 8, no. 1 (1991): 25–42.

Coles, Robert. *Dorothy Day: A Radical Devotion*. Reading, MA: Addison-Wesley, 1987.

———. *A Spectacle unto the World: The Catholic Worker Movement*. New York: Viking Press, 1973.

Cook, Jack. *Bowery Blues: A Tribute to Dorothy Day*. Xlibris, 2001.

Cornell, Tom. "The Catholic Worker, Communism, and the Communist Party." *American Catholic Studies* 125, no. 1 (2014): 87–101.

———, Jim Forest, and Robert Ellsberg, eds. *A Penny a Copy: Readings from "The Catholic Worker."* Maryknoll, NY: Orbis Books, 1994.

Corrin, Jay P. *Catholic Intellectuals and the Challenge of Democracy.* Notre Dame, IN: Notre Dame University Press, 2002.

———. *G. K. Chesterton and Hilaire Belloc: The Battle Against Modernity.* Athens: Ohio University Press, 1981.

Cort, John. *Dreadful Conversions: The Making of a Catholic Socialist.* New York: Fordham University Press, 2003.

———. "My Life at the Catholic Worker." *Commonweal*, June 20, 1980, 361–67.

Covis, Leonardo. "The Radical Next Door: The Los Angeles Catholic Worker During the Cold War." *South California Quarterly* 91, no. 1 (Spring 2009): 69–111.

Cowley, Malcolm. *Exile's Return: A Literary Odyssey of the 1920s.* New York: Penguin, 1994 [1934].

———. *The Literary Situation.* New York: Viking Press, 1958.

———. *The Long Voyage: Selected Letters of Malcolm Cowley, 1915–1987.* Edited by Hans Bak. Cambridge, MA: Harvard University Press, 2004.

Coy, Patrick G., ed. *A Revolution of the Heart: Essays on the Catholic Worker.* Philadelphia: Temple University Press, 1988.

Cunneen, Sally. "Dorothy Day: The Storyteller as Human Model." *CrossCurrents* 34, no. 3 (Fall 1984): 283–93.

Day, Dorothy. *All the Way to Heaven: The Selected Letters of Dorothy Day.* Edited by Robert Ellsberg. New York: Image Books, 2010.

———. *Dorothy Day: Selected Writings.* Edited by Robert Ellsberg. Maryknoll, NY: Orbis Books, 2005.

———. *Dorothy Day: Writings from* Commonweal. Edited by Patrick Jordan. Collegeville, MN: Liturgical Press, 2002.

———. *The Duty of Delight: The Diaries of Dorothy Day.* Edited by Robert Ellsberg. New York: Image Books, 2008.

———. *The Eleventh Virgin.* Chicago: Cottager Press, 2011 [1924].

———. *From Union Square to Rome.* Maryknoll, NY: Orbis Books, 2000 [1938].

———. *Hold Nothing Back: The Writings of Dorothy Day.* Edited by Patrick Jordan. Collegeville, MN: Liturgical Press, 2016.

———. *Houses of Hospitality.* New York: Sheed & Ward, 1939.

———. *Loaves and Fishes: The Inspiring Story of the Catholic Worker Movement.* Maryknoll, NY: Orbis Books, 2003 [1963].

———. *The Long Loneliness.* New York: Harper and Row, 1952.

———. *On Pilgrimage: The Sixties.* New York: Curtis Books, 1972.

———. *Peter Maurin: Apostle to the World.* Edited by Francis J. Sicius. Maryknoll, NY: Orbis, 2004.

———. *Thérèse.* Notre Dame, IN: Christian Classics, 2016.

Day, Helen Caldwell. *All the Way to Heaven.* New York: Sheed & Ward, 1956.

———. *Color, Ebony.* New York: Sheed & Ward, 1951.

———. *Not Without Tears.* New York: Sheed & Ward, 1954.

Dell, Floyd. *Homecoming: An Autobiography.* New York: Farrar and Rinehart, 1933.

Diener, Laura Michele. "The Habit of Being Passionate: Dorothy Day's Radical Mysticism." *Numéro Cinq* 7, no. 8 (August 2016).

Doherty, Catherine de Hueck. *Fragments of My Life: A Memoir.* Combermere, ON: Madonna House Publications, 2007.

Dolan, Jay. *In Search of an American Catholicism: A History of Religion and Culture in Tension.* New York: Oxford University Press, 2002.

Dowling, Robert M. "'Told in Context': Dorothy Day's Previously Unpublished Reminiscence of Eugene O'Neill." *Eugene O'Neill Review* 38, nos. 1–2 (2017): 1–12.

Downey, Jack Lee. *The Bread of the Strong: Lacouturisme and the Folly of the Strong.* New York: Fordham University Press, 2015.

Dvorchak, Paul. "Dorothy Day and the Beginning of St. Joseph House of Hospitality in Pittsburgh, 1936–1941." *Gathered Fragments,* Western Pennsylvania Society of Catholic History.

Egan, Eileen. "The Final Word Is Love: Dorothy Day and the Catholic Worker Movement." *CrossCurrents* 30, no. 4 (Winter 1980–81): 377–84.

———. *Peace Be with You: Justified Warfare or the Way of Nonviolence.* Maryknoll, NY: Orbis Books, 1990.

———. *Such a Vision of the Street: Mother Teresa, The Spirit and the Work.* New York: Doubleday, 1986.

Ellis, Marc H. "The Legacy of Peter Maurin." *CrossCurrents* 34, no. 3 (Fall 1984): 294–304.

———. *Peter Maurin: Prophet in the Twentieth Century.* New York: Paulist Press, 1981.

———. *A Year at the Catholic Worker: A Spiritual Journey Among the Poor.* Waco, TX: Baylor University Press, 2000 [1978].

Ellsberg, Robert. "Five Years with Dorothy Day." *America,* November 21, 2005.

Endres, David, ed. *Remapping the History of Catholicism in the United States.* Washington, DC: Catholic University of America Press, 2017.

Farrell, James J. "Dorothy Day and the Sixties." *Records of the American Catholic Historical Society of Philadelphia* 108, nos. 1–2 (Spring–Summer 1997): 29–37.

———. *The Spirit of the Sixties: The Making of Postwar Radicalism.* New York: Routledge, 1995.

Finn, James. *Protest: Pacifism and Politics.* New York: Vintage, 1968.

Fisher, James Terence. *The Catholic Counterculture in America, 1933–1962.* Chapel Hill: University of North Carolina Press, 1989.

Forest, Jim. *All Is Grace: A Biography of Dorothy Day.* Maryknoll, NY: Orbis Books, 2011.

———. *At Play in the Lions' Den: A Biography and Memoir of Daniel Berrigan.* Maryknoll, NY: Orbis Books, 2017.

Fox, Robert J. Paul. *Dorothy Day's Visit to Montana.* St. Paul, MN: Good Ground Press, 2014.

Garvey, Michael. *Confessions of a Catholic Worker.* Chicago: Thomas More Press, 1978.

Givner, Joan. *Katherine Anne Porter: A Life.* Athens: University of Georgia Press, 1991.

Gneuhs, Geoffrey. "Peter Maurin: The Life and Thought of the Founder of the Catholic Worker Movement." MA thesis, Yale Divinity School, New Haven, CT, 1978.

Gold, Mike. *Mike Gold: A Literary Anthology.* Edited by Michael Folsom. New York: International Publishers, 1972.

Goldweber, David. "Home at Last: The Pilgrimage of Claude McKay." *Commonweal*, September 10, 1999, 11–13.

Gordon, Caroline. *The Malefactors.* New York: Harcourt, Brace & Company, 1954.

Gornik, Vivian. "Dorothy Day at 72: The Dailiness of Grace." *Village Voice*, November 20, 1969, 5–6, 31.

Gray, Francine du Plessix. *Divine Disobedience: Profiles in Catholic Radicalism.* New York: Knopf, 1970.

Greene, Dana. *The Living of Maisie Ward.* Notre Dame, IN: University of Notre Dame Press, 1997.

Gregory, David L. "Dorothy Day, Workers' Rights and Catholic Authenticity." *Fordham Urban Law Journal* 26, no. 5 (1999): 1371–92.

Gregory, Judith. "Catholic Worker Lessons Stayed with Me." *The National Catholic Reporter*, June 20, 1997.

———. "Some Memories of the Catholic Worker." Unpublished essay, 1996 (copy provided by Robert Steed).

Harmon, Katharine E. "Drawing the Holy in the Ordinary: Ade Bethune, the Catholic Worker, and the Liturgical Movement." *American Catholic Studies* 123, no. 1 (Spring 2012): 1–23.

Hebbler, Michael H. *The Sister Karamazov: Dorothy Day's Encounter with Dostoevsky's Novel.* MA thesis, University of Dayton, Dayton, OH, 2009.

Heineman, Kenneth J. *A Catholic New Deal: Religion and Reform in Depression Pittsburgh.* University Park: Pennsylvania State University Press, 1999.

Hennacy, Ammon. *The Autobiography of a Christian Anarchist.* New York: Catholic Worker Books (Libertarian Press), 1954.

———. *The Book of Ammon.* New York: Catholic Worker, 1994 [1953].

Henneberger, Melinda. "In Changing World, Catholic Workers Hew to Their Course." *New York Times*, October 8, 1992.

Hennessey, James. *American Catholics: A History of the Roman Catholic Community in the United States.* New York: Oxford University Press, 1981.

Hennessy, Kate. *Dorothy Day: The World Will Be Saved by Beauty: An Intimate Portrait of My Grandmother.* New York: Scribner, 2017.

Herrmann, Eileen J. "Saints and Hounds: Modernism's Pursuit of Dorothy Day and Eugene O'Neill." In *Eugene O'Neill's Early Contemporaries: Bohemians, Radicals, Progressives and the Avant Garde*, edited by Eileen J. Herrmann and Robert Dowling (Jefferson, NC: McFarland Publishers, 2011), 210–33.

Holben, Lawrence. *All the Way to Heaven: A Theological Reflection on Dorothy Day, Peter Maurin, and the Catholic Worker.* Eugene, OR: Wipf & Stock, 1997.

Isserman, Maurice. *The Other American: The Life of Michael Harrington.* New York: Public Affairs, 2000.

Iswolsky, Hélène. *No Time to Grieve: An Autobiographical Journey.* Philadelphia: Winchell Company, 1985.

James, William. *The Varieties of Religious Experience.* New York: Modern Library, 1929.

Jones, Margaret C. *Heretics and Hellraisers: Women Contributors to "The Masses," 1911–1917.* Austin: University of Texas Press, 1991.

Jonza, Nancylee Novell. *The Underground Stream: The Life and Art of Caroline Gordon.* Athens: University of Georgia Press, 1995.

Jordan, Patrick. *Dorothy Day: Love in Action.* Collegeville, MN: Liturgical Press, 2015.

Klejment, Anne. *American Catholic Pacifism: The Influence of Dorothy Day and the Catholic Worker Movement.* New York: Praeger, 1996.

———. "Dorothy Day and Cesar Chavez: American Catholic Lives in Nonviolence." *U.S. Catholic Historian* 25, no. 3 (Summer 2011): 67–90.

———. "Dorothy Day's Fictionalized Family." *U.S. Catholic Historian* 35, no. 2 (Spring 2017): 103–23.

Krieg, Robert Anthony. *Karl Adam: Catholicism in German Culture.* Notre Dame, IN: Notre Dame University, 1992.

Macdonald, Dwight. "The Foolish Things of the World: I." *The New Yorker,* October 4, 1952, 37–60.

———. "The Foolish Things of the World: II." *The New Yorker,* October 11, 1952, 37–58.

———. "Revisiting Dorothy Day." *The New York Review of Books,* January 28, 1971, 12–19.

Makowsky, Veronica. *Caroline Gordon: A Biography.* New York: Oxford University Press, 1989.

Malina, Judith. *The Diaries of Judith Malina: 1947–1959.* New York: Grove Press, 1983.

Maritain, Jacques. *A Christian Looks at the Jewish Question.* New York: Longmans, Green & Co., 1939.

———. *Exiles and Fugitives: The Letters of Jacques and Raïssa Maritain, Allen Tate, and Caroline Gordon.* Edited by John Dunaway. Baton Rouge: Louisiana State University, 1992.

Martin, James. "Dorothy Day and Abortion: A New Conversation Surfaces." *America,* July 1, 2011.

Marx, Paul. *Virgil Michel and the Liturgical Movement.* Washington, DC: Catholic University of America Press, 1957.

McCarraher, Eugene. "Into Their Labors: Work, Technology, and the Sacramentalism of Dorothy Day." *Records of the American Catholic Historical Society of Philadelphia* 108, nos. 1–2 (Spring–Summer 1997): 13–27.

McDonough, Tom. *An Eye for Others: Dorothy Day, Journalist, 1916–1917.* Washington, DC: Clemency Press, 2016.

McGreevy, John T. *Catholicism and American Freedom.* New York: Norton, 2003.

McKanan, Dan. *The Catholic Worker After Dorothy: Practicing Works of Mercy in a New Generation.* Collegeville, MN: Liturgical Press, 2008.

———. "Inventing the Catholic Worker Family." *Church History* 76, no. 1 (March 2007): 84–113.

McNeal, Patricia. "Catholic Conscientious Objection During World War II." *The Catholic Historical Review* 61, no. 2 (April 1975): 222–42.

———. *Harder than War: Catholic Peacemaking in Twentieth-Century America.* New Brunswick, NJ: Rutgers University Press, 1992.

Meconis, Charles A. *With Clumsy Grace: The American Catholic Left, 1961–1975.* New York: Seabury Press, 1979.

Merriman, Brigid O'Shea. *Searching for Christ: The Spirituality of Dorothy Day.* Notre Dame, IN: Notre Dame University Press, 2001.

Merton, Thomas. *The Hidden Ground of Love: The Letters of Thomas Merton.* Edited by William H. Shannon. New York: Farrar, Straus and Giroux, 1985.

———. *Thomas Merton: A Life in Letters.* Edited by William H. Shannon and Christine M. Bochen. New York: HarperCollins, 2008.

Meyer, Karl. *Positively Dazzling Realism.* Unpublished autobiography. Nashville, TN: privately printed, 2015.

Miller, David. *I Didn't Know God Made Honky Tonk Communists.* Berkeley, CA: Regent Press, 2001.

Miller, Bob. "From 'Militant Christian' to Silent Patriot: Archbishop John T. McNicholas, 1925–1950," Archdiocese of Cincinnati, http://www.catholiccincinnati .org/98975/from-militant-christian-to-silent-patriot-archbishop-john-t-mcnicho las-1925-50/.

Miller, William D. *Dorothy Day: A Biography.* New York: Harper and Row, 1982.

———. *A Harsh and Dreadful Love: Dorothy Day and the Catholic Worker Movement.* New York: Liveright, 1973.

———. *The Spirituality of Dorothy Day.* New York: Doubleday, 1987.

Mize, Sandra Yocum. "Unsentimental Hagiography: Studies on Dorothy Day and the Soul of American Catholicism." *U.S. Catholic Historian* 16, no. 4 (Fall 1998): 36–57.

———. "'We Are Still Pacifists': Dorothy Day's Pacifism During World War II." *Records of the Catholic Historical Society of Philadelphia* 108, nos. 1–2 (Spring–Summer 1991): 1–12.

Moon, Penelope Adams. "'Peace on Earth: Peace in Vietnam': Antiwar Witness, 1964–1976." *Journal of Social History* 36, no. 4 (Summer 2003): 1033–57.

Morris, Charles R. *American Catholic: The Saints and Sinners Who Built America's Most Powerful Church.* New York: Vintage Books, 1998.

Mounier, Emmanuel. *A Personalist Manifesto.* New York: Longmans, Green & Co., 1938.

———. *Be Not Afraid: Studies in Personalist Sociology.* New York: Harper & Brothers, n.d.

Murphy, Brenda. *The Provincetown Players and the Culture of Modernity.* New York: Cambridge University Press, 2005.

Noone, Val. "Dorothy Day in Australia." *Tjurunga* 90 (2017): 59–73.

Novitsky, Anthony. "Peter Maurin's Green Revolution: The Radical Implications of Reactionary Social Catholicism." *The Review of Politics* 37, no. 1 (January 1975): 83–103.

O'Brien, David J. *American Catholics and Social Reform: The New Deal Years.* New York: Oxford University Press, 1969.

O'Connor, June. "Dorothy Day's Christian Conversion." *The Journal of Religious Ethics* 18, no. 1 (Spring 1990): 159–80.

———. *The Spirituality of Dorothy Day: A Feminist Perspective.* New York: Crossroads, 1991.

O'Neill, William L. *The Last Romantic: A Life of Max Eastman.* New York: Oxford University Press, 1978.

Pecklers, Keith F. *The Unread Vision: The Liturgical Movement in the United States of America, 1926–1955.* Collegeville, MN: Liturgical Press, 1988.

Peters, Benjamin T. *Called to Be Saints: John Hugo, the Catholic Worker, and the Theology of Radical Christianity.* Milwaukee, WI: Marquette University Press, 2016.

———. "Ignatian Radicalism: The Influence of Jesuit Spirituality on Dorothy Day." *The Catholic Historical Review* 103, nos. 1–2 (Spring 2017): 297–320.

Piehl, Mel. *Breaking Bread: The Catholic Worker and the Origin of Catholic Radicalism in America*. Philadelphia: Temple University Press, 1982.

Polner, Murray, and Jim O'Grady. *Disarmed and Dangerous: The Radical Lives and Times of Daniel and Philip Berrigan*. New York: Basic Books, 1997.

Pycior, Julie Leininger. "Bearing Witness: Catherine de Hueck Doherty and the 'Gospel of Dorothy Day.'" *U.S. Catholic Historian* 26, no. 1 (Winter 2008): 43–66.

Rademacher, Nicholas K. *Paul Hanly Furfey: Priest, Scientist, Social Reformer*. New York: Fordham University Press, 2017.

———. "'To Relate the Eucharist to Real Living': Mother Teresa and Dorothy Day at the Forty-First International Eucharistic Congress, Philadelphia, Pennsylvania." *U.S. Catholic Historian* 27, no. 4 (Fall 2009): 59–72.

Rauch, R. William, Jr. *Politics and Belief in Contemporary France: Emmanuel Mounier and Christian Democracy, 1932–1950*. The Hague, Netherlands: Martinus Nijhoff, 1972.

Reinhold, H. A. "The Catholic Worker Movement in America." *Blackfriars* 19, no. 222 (September 1938): 635–50.

———. *H.A.R.: The Autobiography of Father Reinhold*. New York: Herder & Herder, 1968.

Rexroth, Kenneth. *An Autobiographical Novel*. New York: Doubleday & Company, 1966.

Rice, Lincoln. *Healing the Racial Divide: A Catholic Racial Justice Framework Inspired by Dr. Arthur Falls*. Eugene, OR: Pickwick Publications, 2014.

Richardson, Richard D. *William James: In the Maelstrom of American Modernism*. New York: Houghton Mifflin, 2006.

Richey, Lance, and Adam DeVille, eds. *Dorothy Day and the Church: Past, Present, and Future, A Conference Held at the University of Saint Francis, Fort Wayne, Indiana, in May 2015*. Fort Wayne, IN: Solidarity Hall, 2015.

Riegle, Rosalie. *Dorothy Day: Portraits by Those Who Knew Her*. Maryknoll, NY: Orbis Books, 2006.

Roberts, Nancy L. *Dorothy Day and the Catholic Worker*. Albany: State University of New York Press, 1985.

Rosenstone, Robert A. *Romantic Revolutionary: A Biography of John Reed*. New York: Random House, 1975.

Segers, Mary C. "Equality and Christian Anarchism: The Political and Social Ideas of the Catholic Worker Movement." *The Review of Politics* 40, no. 2 (April 1978): 196–230.

Sheaffer, Louis. *O'Neill: Son and Playwright*. Boston: Little, Brown, 1969.

Sheed, Frank. *The Church and I*. New York: Doubleday, 1974.

Shipman, Charles. *It Had to Be Revolution: Memoirs of an American Radical*. Ithaca, NY: Cornell University Press, 1993.

Sicius, Francis J. "The Chicago Catholic Worker Movement, 1936 to the Present." PhD dissertation, Loyola University, Chicago, IL, 1979.

———. "Karl Meyer, The Catholic Worker, and Active Personalism." *Records of the American Catholic Historical Society of Philadelphia* 93, nos. 1–4 (March–December 1982): 107–23.

——. "Peter Maurin's Green Revolution." *U.S. Catholic Historian*, no. 3 (Summer 2008): 1–14.

Spicer, Kevin. "Last Years of a Resister in the Diocese of Berlin: Gerhard Lichtenberg's Argument with Karl Adam and His Fateful Imprisonment." *Church History* 70, no. 2 (June 2001): 248–70.

Stoughton, Judith. *Proud Donkey of Schaerbeek*. St. Cloud, MN: North Start Press, 1988.

Stout, Janis P. *Katherine Anne Porter: A Sense of the Times*. Charlottesville: University of Virginia Press, 1995.

Thorn, William, Phillip Runkel, and Susan Mountin, eds. *Dorothy Day and the Catholic Worker Movement: Centenary Essays*. Milwaukee, WI: Marquette University Press, 2001.

Troester, Rosalie Riegle. *Voices from the Catholic Worker*. Philadelphia: Temple University Press, 1993.

Unrue, Darlene Harbour. *Katherine Anne Porter: The Life of an Artist*. Jackson: University Press of Mississippi, 2005.

Valaik, J. David. "American Catholic Dissenters and the Spanish Civil War." *The Catholic Historical Review* 53, no. 4 (January 1968): 537–55.

Valenta, Markha Gabrielle. *The Radical Folly of Love in (Post) Modern America: The Autobiographical Narratives of Dorothy Day*. PhD dissertation, University of Iowa, Iowa City, IA, 1999.

Vishnewski, Stanley. *Wings of Dawn*. Privately printed, 1979.

Wakefield, Dan. *New York in the Fifties*. New York: Greenpoint Press, 1992.

Wald, Alan M. *Exiles from a Future Time: The Forging of the Mid-Twentieth-Century Literary Left*. Chapel Hill: University of North Carolina, 2002.

Walker, Martin. *The Cold War: A History*. New York: Henry Holt, 1993.

Walsh, Brendan. *The Long Loneliness in Baltimore*. Baltimore: Apprentice House, 2016.

Ward, Maisie. *To and Fro: The Sequel to an Autobiography*. New York: Sheed & Ward, 1973.

——. *Unfinished Business*. New York: Sheed & Ward, 1964.

Warren, Donald. *Radio Priest: Charles Coughlin, The Father of Hate Radio*. New York: Free Press, 1996.

Watkins, T. H. *The Hungry Years: A Narrative History of the Great Depression in America*. New York: Henry Holt, 1999.

Webb, Sheila. "Dorothy Day and the Early Years of the 'Catholic Worker': Social Action Through the Pages of the Press." *U.S. Catholic Historian* 21, no. 7 (Summer 2003): 71–88.

Weber, Francis J. "Memories of an Old Catholic Priest." Mission Hills, CA: Saint Francis Historical Society, n.d.

Wild, Robert, ed. *Comrades Stumbling Along: The Friendship of Catherine de Hueck Doherty and Dorothy Day as Revealed Through Their Letters*. New York: St. Paul's, 2009.

Wills, Garry. "Dorothy Day at the Barricades." *Esquire*, December 1983, 228–32.

——. *Head and Heart: A History of Christianity in America*. New York: Penguin, 2007.

——. "The Saint of Mott Street." *The New York Review of Books*, April 21, 1994.

Wolf, Daniel. "Emmanuel Mounier: A Catholic of the Left." *The Review of Politics* 22, no. 3 (July 1960): 324–44.

Woodward, Kenneth. "Dorothy Day." *Newsweek*, December 27, 1976, 61.
———. *Getting Religion: Faith, Culture, and Politics from the Age of Eisenhower to the Ascent of Trump*. New York: Convergent Books, 2017.
———. *Making Saints: How the Catholic Church Determines Who Becomes a Saint, Who Doesn't, and Why*. New York: Simon & Schuster, 1990.
Zahn, Gordon. *Another Part of the War: The Camp Simon Story*. Amherst, MA: University of Massachusetts Press, 1979.
Zurier, Rebecca. *Art for the Masses: A Radical Magazine and Its Graphics, 1911–1917*. Philadelphia: Temple University Press, 1988.
Zwick, Mark and Louise. *The Catholic Worker Movement: Intellectual and Spiritual Origins*. Mahwah, NJ: Paulist Press, 2005.

NOTES

PROLOGUE: ARRESTED: AGAIN

7　*"It appeared that I"*: Dorothy Day's diary (entry for July 30, 1973), CW series, D-4, Box 7, Dorothy Day Collection, Raynor Memorial Libraries, Marquette University.

9　*"We are under lock and key"*: Dorothy Day, "On Pilgrimage," *The Catholic Worker*, September 1973, 1.

9　*"tore at your heart"*: Dorothy Day's diary (1973), D-4, Box 8, no. 2, Dorothy Day Collection, Raynor Memorial Libraries, Marquette University.

9　*Dorothy also took time*: Dorothy Day, *All the Way to Heaven: The Selected Letters of Dorothy Day*, edited by Robert Ellsberg (New York: Image Books, 2010), 517; Forest, *All Is Grace: A Biography of Dorothy Day* (Mary Knoll, NY: Orbis Books, 201T), 258–60.

10　*"warm and loving"*: Day, *All the Way to Heaven*, 515.

10　*"where, with a great crowd"*: Dorothy Day, "On Pilgrimage," *The Catholic Worker*, September 1973, 2.

CHAPTER 1: BEGINNING

11　*John Day was a difficult man*: The Day family history is taken from Dorothy Day, *From Union Square to Rome* (Maryknoll, NY: Orbis Books, 2000 [1938]), 19–38; Dorothy Day, *The Long Loneliness* (New York: Harper and Row, 1952), 15–36; and William D. Miller, *Dorothy Day: A Biography* (New York: Harper and Row, 1982), 1–30.

12　*The family was living*: John Day's peripatetic journalistic career (he worked for at least five papers) is reviewed in *The Fourth Estate*, July 22, 2016, 12.

13　*"Even now," Dorothy wrote*: Day, *From Union Square to Rome*, 20.

13　*"near open fields"*: Ibid., 22.

13　*"I threw things besides"*: Ibid., 23.

13　*"so high that June"*: Dorothy Day, *The Eleventh Virgin* (Chicago: Cottager Press, 2011 [1924]), 4.

14　*"the earth became a sea"*: Day, *The Long Loneliness*, 21.

15　*"great upheaval"*: Ibid., 6.

15　*"She reigned over the supper table"*: Day, *From Union Square to Rome*, 30.

16　*"pathetic in his efforts"*: Day, *The Eleventh Virgin*, 8.

18　*"dim attic"*: Day, *From Union Square to Rome*, 21.

19　*"lofty enthusiasm"*: Ibid., 27–28.

19　*"Only Irish washerwomen"*: Day, *The Duty of Delight*, 661.

19　*"precocious interest in sex"*: Ibid., 33.

20　*"an agony"*: Ibid.

20　*"I had never heard"*: Day, *The Long Loneliness*, 28.

20　*"We never exchanged"*: Ibid., 30.

20   *If school didn't matter:* Dorothy discussed her adolescent reading and the influence of Sinclair, London, and De Quincey in *From Union Square to Rome*, 36–38, 42; in *The Long Loneliness*, 37–38, 42–43; and in many private conversations and in her diaries.

21   *"interminable gray streets":* Day, *The Long Loneliness*, 37.

23   *he was her favorite:* Day, *From Union Square to Rome*, 30.

24   *She worried in a letter:* Day, *The Long Loneliness*, 32–34. As Day discovered this letter to her friend Henrietta among her papers later in life, a lengthy communication she herself described as full of "pomp and vanity and piety," it has to be assumed that she had either decided not to mail it or had copied it out to keep before mailing it. Given its incredible length, either possibility is unusual.

24   *Maggie Tulliver:* Day, *All the Way to Heaven*, 519.

CHAPTER 2: AWAKENINGS

26   *"happy as a lark":* Dorothy Day, *The Long Loneliness*, 40.

26   *When she arrived:* Information about the University of Illinois is from Roger Ebert, ed., *An Illini Century: One Hundred Years of Campus Life* (Urbana: University of Illinois Press, 1967), and Jerome L. Rodnitzky, "The Making of a University in the Progressive Era: Edmund James and the University of Illinois," *The Great Lakes Review* 2, no. 2 (Winter 1976): 1–18. See also Day, *The Long Loneliness*, 40–50.

27   *Dorothy's first home in Urbana:* Dorothy Day, *From Union Square to Rome*, 39–52.

27   *"my child and my brother":* Ibid., 40.

27   *"howling troop of children":* Day, *The Eleventh Virgin*, 64.

29   *"stirred imaginations":* Barbara Sicherman, *Well-Read Lives: How Books Inspired a Generation of American Women* (Chapel Hill: University of North Carolina Press, 2010), 1.

31   *"I felt so intensely alive":* Day, *The Long Loneliness*, 41.

31   *"Even as I talked":* Ibid.

33   *"Deliciously awkward":* Ibid., 47.

33   *"red hair, brown eyes":* Day, *From Union Square to Rome*, 53.

33   *"under the limitless sky":* Ibid., 55.

34   *Dorothy joined:* "Student Life at Illinois: 1910–1919," Student Life and Culture Archives, University of Illinois at Urbana-Champaign, https://archives.library.illinois.edu /slc/research-education/timeline/1910-1919/.

35   *"new adventures":* Day, *The Long Loneliness*, 50.

CHAPTER 3: CAUSES

38   *Chester Wright was a personable:* William Morris Feigenbaum, "Ten Years of Service: A History of the New York Call to Commemorate the Tenth Anniversary of Its Establishment, May 30, 1918," http://debs.indstate.edu/f297t4_1918.pdf, and Tom McDonough, *An Eye for Others: Dorothy Day, Journalist, 1916–1917* (Washington, DC: Clemency Press, 2016). Biographies of John Sloan, Rosa Pastor Stokes, and Mary Heaton Vorse all mention the *New York Call*, which was certainly one of the most interesting New York City publications of its day. See also "Anita Block," Jewish Women's Archive, https:// jwa.org/encyclopedia/article/block-anita; Block is mentioned admiringly in all biographies of Margaret Sanger.

38   *the promised diet squad articles: New York Call*, December 1916, 3, 6, 12, 15, 18, and 27.

39   *She wrote with a byline*: Dorothy Day, "Here's a Home in Which a Girl May Bury Past Woes," *New York Call*, February 5, 1917.

39   *She was also assigned*: The truth of that situation might involve a little more ambiguity than Dorothy's account acknowledges. The historian Jill Lepore noted that Byrne, the first woman to be force-fed in the United States (a gruesome procedure), hadn't in fact had anything to eat or drink for a week, which would have left her in bad shape, and a *New York Tribune* article from the same day described Byrne as barely able to open her eyes and "twitching with pain" as she left Blackwell's Island. It is possible that Byrne, in no mood for questions, just wanted to send the nosey reporter on her doorstep away as quickly as possible. See Jill Lepore, *The Secret History of Wonder Woman* (New York: Knopf, 2014), 92–96. Day's version of this failed interview is in *From Union Square to Rome*, 76. Her four articles on Byrne were published in the *New York Call* in 1917 on February 2, 3, 4, and 6.

41   *Everyone at the city desk*: Day, *The Long Loneliness*, 53. Day also wrote about Weitzonkorn and Radnor in *From Union Square to Rome*, 71–72, and under fictional names in *The Eleventh Virgin*, 114–15.

42   *One was Mary Heaton Vorse*: Dee Garrison, *Mary Heaton Vorse: The Life of an American Insurgent* (Philadelphia: Temple University Press, 1989), 235, 251–52. Other warm appreciations of Vorse can be found in Murray Kempton, *A Part of Our Time: Some Ruins and Monuments of the Thirties* (New York: New York Review of Books, 1998), 214–17, 231–32, and David Glenn, "Bohemian Rhapsodies," *Columbia Journalism Review*, July–August 2007.

42   *"like a warrior scenting battles"*: Quoted in Garrison, *Mary Heaton Vorse*, 235.

42   *A second person Dorothy met*: Michael Gold, *Mike Gold: A Literary Anthology*, edited by Michael Folsom (New York: International Publishers, 1972); Gold's uncompleted memoirs are in the Special Collections of the University of Michigan Library. See also Alan M. Wald, "Inventing Mike Gold," in Wald, *Exiles from a Future Time: The Forging of the Mid-Twentieth-Century Literary Left* (Chapel Hill: University of North Carolina, 2002), 39–70, and Dorothy Day, "Michael Gold (April 12, 1894–May 14, 1967)," *The Catholic Worker*, June 1967.

43   *He was especially thrilled*: Richard Lingeman, *Theodore Dreiser: An American Journey, 1908–1945*, vol. 2 (New York: G. P. Putnam's Sons, 1990), 161.

43   *Having grown up*: Folsom, 297–99.

44   *Three recent acquaintances*: Anne Klejment, *American Catholic Pacifism: The Influence of Dorothy Day and the Catholic Worker Movement* (New York: Praeger, 1996), 18–30.

45   *"Raw-boned, square-jawed"*: Charles Shipman, *It Had to Be Revolution: Memoirs of an American Radical* (Ithaca, NY: Cornell University Press, 1993), 31.

45   *"She chain-smoked"*: Ibid.

46   *"written for the masses"*: The Masses, March 1911, 3.

47   *"John Barrymore of American radicalism"*: Lillian Symes and Clement Travers, *Rebel America: The Story of Social Revolt in the United States* (Boston: Beacon Press, 1972), 282.

47   *"brilliant, untrammeled thinker"*: Quoted in John Loughery, *John Sloan: Painter and Rebel* (New York: Henry Holt, 1995), 179.

48   *"awkward and charming"*: Floyd Dell, *Homecoming: An Autobiography* (New York: Holt, Rinehart and Winston, 1933), 296.

50   *"impishly profane"*: Shipman, *It Had to Be Revolution*, 19.

50   *"spiritual haven"*: Judith Schwartz, *Radical Feminists of Heterodoxy: Greenwich Village*,

1912–1940 (Lebanon, NH: New Victoria Press, 1982), 29. On various aspects of Village life, see Leslie Berkowitz and Rick Beard, eds., *Greenwich Village, Culture and Counterculture: 1920–1930* (New Brunswick, NJ: Rutgers University Press, 1997); Adele Hunter, *1915: The Cultural Moment* (New Brunswick, NJ: Rutgers University Press, 1991); Christine Stansell, *American Moderns: Bohemian New York and the Making of a New Century* (New York: Metropolitan Books, 2000); Ross Wetzsteon, *Republic of Dreams, Greenwich Village: The American Bohemia, 1910–1960* (New York: Simon & Schuster, 2002).

51 *"long-haired, owl-eyed"*: Max Eastman, *Enjoyment of Living* (New York: Harper, 1948), 565.

52 *Relocated to Manhattan*: Brenda Murphy, *The Provincetown Players and the Culture of Modernity* (New York: Cambridge University Press, 2005), is an excellent study of the theater and, of course, its history is covered in detail in every biography of Eugene O'Neill and Susan Glaspell. Jeff Kennedy's website, http://provincetownplayhouse.com, lists the plays produced there, with cast lists, in chronological order. For cast lists, see also Helen Deutsch and Stella Hanau, *The Provincetown: A Story of the Theatre* (New York: Farrar and Rinehart, 1931).

52 *"a house of magic"*: Jeff Kennedy, "Ivan's Homecoming," http://www.provincetownplayhouse.com/ivanshomecoming.html, quoted from the Gold Papers, University of Michigan.

53 *From that fervent period*: Hans Bak, *Malcolm Cowley: The Formative Years* (Athens: University of Georgia Press, 1993), 125–27. Peggy Baird Cowley is discussed in the many Village memoirs and particularly in biographies of Hart Crane, with whom she had an affair shortly before Crane's suicide in 1932. See Clive Fisher, *Hart Crane: A Life* (New Haven, CT: Yale University Press, 2002).

53 *Dorothy was familiar with Louise Bryant*: Virginia Gardner, *"Friend and Lover": The Life of Louise Bryant* (New York: Horizon Press, 1982), 180, 218; Mary V. Dearborn, *Queen of Bohemia: The Life of Louise Bryant* (New York: Houghton Mifflin, 1996), 168.

53 *"She had no right"*: Gardner, *"Friend and Lover,"* 16; from Gardner's interview with Day in 1972.

Chapter 4: Moorings

56 *"creatures of the Plutocracy"*: Jack London, *The Iron Heel* (New York: Penguin, 2006), 181.

56 *On Saturday afternoon*: Day, *The Long Loneliness*, 72–83; Miller, *Dorothy Day*, 87–102. See also Doris Stevens, *Jailed for Freedom: American Women Win the Vote*, edited by Carol O'Hare (Troutdale, OR: New Sage Press, 1995), 121–28.

57 *"burst in like a tornado"*: Quoted in Stevens, *Jailed for Freedom*, 122.

58 *"Splendid!"*: Quoted in William D. Miller, *Dorothy Day*, 97.

58 *"I lost all consciousness"*: Day, *The Long Loneliness*, 78.

59 *"I hate being Utopian"*: Ibid., 88.

60 *Gold had taken it*: David Roessel, "'What Made You Leave the Movement?,'" in Eileen T. Hermann and Robert M. Dowling, eds., *Eugene O'Neill and His Early Contemporaries* (Jefferson, NC: McFarland & Co., 2011), 234–49.

60 *"the short and simple"*: Quoted in Miller, *Dorothy Day*, 106.

60 *Years later, Dorothy maintained*: Day wrote about her relationship with O'Neill only

briefly and circumspectly, though it is discussed in every biography or biographical study of O'Neill. See, e.g., Robert Dowling, *O'Neill: A Life in Four Acts* (New Haven, CT: Yale University Press, 2014), 157–58; Barbara and Arthur Gelb, *Eugene O'Neill: By Women Possessed* (New York: G. P. Putnam's Sons, 2016), 206; and Louis Sheaffer, *O'Neill: Son and Playwright* (Boston: Little, Brown, 1968), 403–04. Day insisted to Louis Sheaffer when he interviewed her in the 1950s that her bond with O'Neill had been a chaste friendship. On the other hand, a friend of Day, the Catholic writer Joseph Dever, noted in *Cushing of Boston* (Boston: Bruce Humphries, 1965), "It was fairly well-known that, as a budding young dramatist, Gene O'Neill was the lover of then-Bohemian but now austere and saintly Dorothy Day," 231.

61 *"couldn't really love anybody"*: Quoted in Brenda Murphy and George Montiero, eds., *Eugene O'Neill Remembered* (Birmingham: University of Alabama Press, 2016), 72.

61 *"a quality about it"*: Mary Heaton Vorse, "Eugene O'Neill's Pet Saloon Is Gone," *New York World*, May 4, 1930.

61 *Village bookstore owner Samuel Roth*: Maxwell Bodenheim, *My Life and Loves in Greenwich Village* (New York: Bridgehead Books, 1954), 252. As was often the case with Roth's anecdotes, the essence sounds true while the details sound somewhat hyperbolic. It is generally assumed that Bodenheim's "memoir" was actually penned by Roth.

61 *The literary critic Malcolm Cowley*: Malcolm Cowley, *Exile's Return: A Literary Odyssey of the 1920s* (New York: Penguin, 1994 [1934]), 69.

63 *One night O'Neill*: Sheaffer, *O'Neill*, 403.

63 *Dorothy herself believed*: Steven A. Black, *Eugene O'Neill: Beyond Mourning and Tragedy* (New Haven, CT: Yale University Press, 1999), 205.

64 *Accounts of what happened*: Agnes Boulton, *Part of a Long Story*, edited by William Davies King (Jefferson, NC: McFarland, 2011), 76–80; Emily Farnham, *Charles Demuth: Beneath a Laughing Mask* (Norman: University of Oklahoma Press, 1971), 107–08; Gelb and Gelb, *Eugene O'Neill*, 102–05; Miller, *Dorothy Day*, 113–17; Sheaffer, *O'Neill*, 410–11.

66 *"She had had enough"*: Miller, *Dorothy Day*, 117.

66 *One, appearing in*: Dorothy Day, "Marching Men," *The Liberator*, March 1918, 34–35.

66 *The other piece*: Dorothy Day, "A Coney Island Picture," *The Liberator*, April 1918, 46.

67 *"a scene out of Alice in Wonderland"*: Floyd Dell, "The Story of the Trial," *The Liberator*, June 1918, 11. The *Masses* trial is also covered in Douglas Clayton, *Floyd Dell: The Life and Times of an American Rebel* (Chicago: Ivan Dee, 1994), 162–69; Floyd Dell, *Homecoming: An Autobiography*, 313–19; Max Eastman, *Love and Revolution: My Journey Through an Epoch* (New York: Random House, 1964), 58–63; Morris Hillquit, *Loose Leaves from a Busy Life* (New York: Macmillan, 1934), 224–30; Art Young, *On My Way* (New York: Liveright, 1928), 292–300; and Rebecca Zurier, *Art for the Masses: A Radical Magazine and Its Graphics, 1911–1917* (Philadelphia: Temple University Press, 1988), 59–64.

67 *"a scholar and a gentleman"*: Dorothy Day, *From Union Square to Rome*, 91.

69 *The first patient*: The description of nursing at Kings County Hospital is from Day, *The Eleventh Virgin*, 23–73, which Dorothy claimed was an accurate account, and from Day, *The Long Loneliness*, 88–93.

69 *"We had to change"*: Day, *From Union Square to Rome*, 97.

69 *"We were far"*: Day, *The Long Loneliness*, 94.

71 *"just a young boy"*: Day, *The Eleventh Virgin*, 244.

72 *his politics were*: *The Fourth Estate*, April 10, 1920, 19. In the spring of 1920, Moise took a leave from his job at the *Chicago Evening Post* to go to Nebraska to help organize General John Pershing's unsuccessful Republican primary campaign, not a move any left-wing friends would have approved of.

Chapter 5: Ardor

73 *"massive mind"*: Kenneth Rexroth, *An Autobiographical Novel* (New York: Doubleday & Company, 1966), 182.

74 *One eighteen-year-old*: Carlos Baker, *Ernest Hemingway: A Life Story* (New York: Charles Scribner's Sons, 1969), 35. In the 1950s, Hemingway disputed the idea that Moise had influenced him, but his former colleagues in Kansas City thought otherwise, and all Hemingway biographers (e.g., Mary V. Dearborn, Kenneth Lynn, Jeffrey Meyers) comment at least in passing on Lionel Moise's personality and influence on Hemingway. It is possible that Moise hadn't influenced Hemingway's ideas about writing (an assertion that always annoyed Hemingway) but did impress him with his macho demeanor. On Moise himself, see Miller, *Dorothy Day*, 125–43, and Robert Steed, "Who Was Lionel Moise?," *The Catholic Worker: Odds and Ends*, July 9, 2008. Rexroth, *An Autobiographical Novel*, offered some interesting observations, and Robert J. Casey's anecdotal memoir of Chicago journalism, *Some Interesting People* (Garden City, NY: 1945), devoted a chapter to him thinly disguised as "Lyman Moose."

74 *"Let your conscience"*: Dorothy Day, *The Eleventh Virgin* (Chicago: Cottager Press, 2011 [1924]), 268.

75 *"Why do you ask"*: Ibid., 273.

75 *"The life of the flesh"*: Dorothy Day, *The Long Loneliness*, 85.

75 *Lionel insisted*: Dorothy Day, *The Duty of Delight*, 640.

75 *Some of his articles*: e.g., Moise, "Poets Who Toil," *New York Tribune*, December 15, 1918.

75 *"companions in revelry"*: Quoted in Hans Bak, *Malcolm Cowley*, 130. On helping Cowley when he was ill, see William D. Miller's interview with Cowley, Dorothy Day Collection, Marquette University Archives: W-9, Box 1, and Malcolm Cowley, *The Literary Situation* (New York: Viking Press, 1958), 163.

76 *But if he was contemplating*: Jackson R. Bryer, Travis Bogard, Edna Kenton, and Bernadette Smyth, "The Provincetown Players and the Playwrights' Theatre," *The Eugene O'Neill Review* 21, nos. 1–2 (Spring–Fall 1997): 97, 102; Jeff Kennedy, "The Squealer by Mary F. Barber," http://www.provincetownplayhouse.com/squealer.html. Passing notices of Lionel's acting appeared in *The Greenwich Village Quill*, March 1919, 7, and *The Modernist: A Monthly Magazine of Modern Arts and Letters* 1, no. 1 (1919): 42.

79 *"fat, dirty, and furtive"*: James Martin, "Dorothy Day and Abortion: A New Conversation Surfaces," *America*, July 1, 2011. See also Hennessey, *American Catholics*, 27–29. On Ben Reitman, see Frank O. Beck, *Hobohemia: Emma Goldman, Lucy Parsons, Ben Reitman and Other Agitators and Outsiders in 1920s/30s Chicago* (Chicago: Charles Kerr Publishers, 2000), 56–61. He is also discussed in all biographies of Emma Goldman.

79 *In search of a place*: Bak, *Malcolm Cowley*, 136.

80 *"Another strange character"*: William D. Miller, interview with Cowley, W-9, Box 1, Marquette University Archives, Milwaukee, WI.

80 *the two were married*: Almost every book on Dorothy Day speculates on a different date for her wedding and subsequent trip to Europe, but "Marriage Records Index, 1897–1966," CT State Library, https://ctstatelibrary.org/tag/marriage-records-index/, now provides both the date and location of the civil wedding.

80 *The newlyweds didn't remain*: Miller, *Dorothy Day*, 144–47. On meeting Epstein and Duchamp in Europe, see "Recent Correspondence Between Robert Steed and Gregory Beardall," March 31, 2007, and "Berkeley Tobey," December 2, 2009, on Steed's website, The Catholic Worker: Odds and Ends. Note: In some sources (e.g., Miller's biography of Day), Tobey's first name is spelled "Barkeley." In others, such as the masthead of *The New Review*, it is spelled "Berkeley," as it is in Rexroth, *An Autobiographical Novel*, 69, and Kate Hennessy, *Dorothy Day: The World Will Be Saved by Beauty: An Intimate Portrait of My Grandmother* (New York: Scribner, 2017).

81 "*The six months I spent*": Day, *The Long Loneliness*, 94.

84 *the Russian composer joked*: Robert Steed, "The Young Dorothy Day," The Catholic Worker: Odds and Ends, March 20, 2014.

85 "*the beautiful, beloved*": Rexroth, *An Autobiographical Novel*, 137.

85 "*meant only one thing*": Day, *The Long Loneliness*, 100.

85 "*as ugly an experience*": Ibid. See also Day, "Girls in Jail," *The New Masses*, July 1928, 14–15.

86 *That friend was Charles Phillips*: Charles Shipman, *It Had to Be Revolution*, 144. Phillips also went by the names Charles Shipman and Manuel Gomez and is referred to by the latter name in Day, *The Long Loneliness*, 103, 105. Shipman's political exploits are chronicled in *It Had to Be Revolution*; his account of rescuing Dorothy from jail is slightly different from hers. A summary of his antidraft work can be found in Craig Saper, *The Amazing Adventures of Bob Brown* (New York: Fordham University Press, 2016), 125–26.

86 *he was afraid*: Ibid.

87 *His own days at the* Evening Post: Cowley, *The Literary Situation*, 163.

88 "*in her disorderly life*": Day, *The Long Loneliness*, 108.

89 *Dorothy also wrote*: Dorothy Day, "Girls and Boys Come Out to Play," *The Liberator*, November 1923, 30–31.

90 *She wrote to Margaret Sanger*: Day, *All the Way to Heaven*, 2–3.

CHAPTER 6: CONTENTMENT

91 "*surely the most civilized spot*": Quoted in Louise McKinney, *New Orleans: A Cultural History* (New York: Oxford University Press, 2006), 72.

91 "*lovely time*": Dorothy Day, *All the Way to Heaven*, 8.

91 "*huge appetite for a 'good time'* ": Dorothy Day, *The Long Loneliness*, 108.

91 "*lots of pretty boys*": Day, *All the Way to Heaven*, 8.

92 *Her most extensive work*: Scanned copies of her articles with a byline for the *New Orleans Item* are in the Dorothy Day Collection, Rayner Memorial Libraries, Marquette University Archives, Milwaukee, WI.

93 *He also got a complaint*: Dorothy Day, "About Mary," *Commonweal*, November 5, 1943, online edition.

94 "*honest womanhood*": Day, *All the Way to Heaven*, 7.

94 *Indeed, in later years*: Day, *The Duty of Delight*, 646.

94 "*some expectation*": Quoted in Forest, *All Is Grace*, 65.

95 *Post-Lionel, post–New Orleans*: William D. Miller, interview with Malcolm Cowley, W-9, Box 1, Dorothy Day Collection, Raynor Memorial Libraries, Marquette University Archives, Milwaukee, WI.

96 *In the New-York Evening Post*: Hans Bak, *Malcolm Cowley: The Formative Years* (Athens: University of Georgia Press, 1993), 308.

96 *"adolescent"*: Quoted in Miller, *Dorothy Day*, 163.

96 *"not much to get excited about"*: *Detroit Free Press*, August 10, 1924.

96 *"woven her story weakly"*: *Pittsburgh Press*, April 4, 1924.

96 *"bad taste"*: *Indianapolis Star*, October 19, 1924.

96 *a rambling novel*: *St. Louis Star and Times*, May 31, 1924.

96 *"slender but definite"*: *Hartford Courant*, May 11, 1924.

96 *"total inability"*: *The New Republic*, June 25, 1924, 139.

96 *"of a female moron"*: *Oakland Tribune*, April 20, 1924.

96 *Her few favorable reviews*: *Honolulu Star-Advertiser*, August 3, 1924; *Houston Post*, April 13, 1924; *Chicago Tribune*, April 4, 1924.

96 *Interestingly, the abortion scene*: Meg Gillette, "Modern American Abortion Narratives and the Century of Silence," *Twentieth-Century Literature* 58, no. 4 (Winter 2012): 663–87.

98 *"citadel of amateurs"*: Quoted in Robert A. Rosenstone, *Romantic Revolutionary: A Biography of John Reed* (New York: Random House, 1975), 304.

98 *"We were young"*: Quoted in Thomas A. Underwood, *Allen Tate: Orphan of the South* (Princeton, NJ: Princeton University Press, 2003), 108.

99 *"wild people"*: Caroline Gordon, *The Southern Mandarins: Letters of Caroline Gordon to Sally Wood, 1924–1957*, edited by Sally Wood (Baton Rouge: Louisiana State University Press, 1984), 17.

99 *Another potential complication*: William D. Miller, *Dorothy Day*, 169.

101 *"I have been passing through"*: Day, *The Duty of Delight*, xiv.

102 *"We despise anyone"*: William James, *The Varieties of Religious Experience* (New York: Modern Library, 1929 [1902]), 359.

104 *It was the life*: *Miami Daily News*, June 11, 1925.

105 *"My desire for you"*: Day, *All the Way to Heaven*, 17.

106 *"It stands to reason"*: Day, "What Price Love?," *Chicago Herald Examiner*, June 15, 1924.

CHAPTER 7: CALLED TO GOD

110 *"With [the chapter entitled]"*: Robert D. Richardson, *William James: In the Maelstrom of American Modernism* (New York: Houghton Mifflin, 2006), 400.

110 *One day she plunged*: Day, *From Union Square to Rome*, 138–42.

111 *"There was a hard row"*: Ibid., 139.

111 *Having organized a party*: Day, *The Long Loneliness*, 144.

112 *She's never going to make*: Quoted in James Hennessey, *American Catholics: A History of the Roman Catholic Community in the United States* (New York: Oxford University Press, 1981), 44.

114 *"day of grief"*: Dorothy Day, "On Pilgrimage," *The Catholic Worker* (July–August 1977), 2.

114 *"I do love you"*: Ibid., 46.

115 *"I remember very clearly"*: Graham Greene, *A Sort of Life* (New York: Simon & Schuster, 1971), 169.

115 *"It was like a curtain"*: Authors' interview with Mary Lathrop.

115 *Charles Yale Harrison expressed the view*: William D. Miller, *Dorothy Day*, 198.

115 *"Such a strange end"*: Katherine Anne Porter, letter to Della Day, n.d. [marked "before July 1929" in Della's handwriting], Katherine Anne Porter Papers, University of Maryland.

117 *"Creaking up the stairs"*: Quoted in Joan Givner, *Katherine Anne Porter: A Life* (Athens: University of Georgia Press, 1991), 178.

119 *"Having a Baby"*: Dorothy Day, "Having a Baby," *The New Masses*, June 1928, 5–6.

119 *"gentle, understanding soul"*: Day, *The Long Loneliness*, 155.

120 *Even George Orwell*: Robert Anthony Krieg, *Karl Adam: Catholicism in German Culture* (Notre Dame, IN: Notre Dame University, 1992), 47.

123 *"Life in this place"*: Quoted in Jim Forest, *All Is Grace*, 90.

123 *"occasion for sin"*: Ibid., 158.

123 *"uncomfortable situations"*: Quoted in Miller, *Dorothy Day*, 212.

124 *"the fiercest persecution"*: Graham Greene, *The Lawless Roads* (New York: Penguin, 2006 [1939]), 15.

125 *"steady storm of blossoms"*: Dorothy Day, "Spring Festival in Mexico," *Commonweal*, July 16, 1930, 297.

125 *"a huge man"*: Quoted in Miller, *Dorothy Day*, 216.

125 *In February, Dorothy met up*: Dorothy Day, "Picture of Mary Heaton Vorse," unpublished notes, Mary Heaton Vorse Collection, Walter Reuther Library Archives, Wayne State University, Detroit. On Vorse's view of Mexico, see Vorse, "Mexico the Beautiful," *Good Housekeeping*, April 1931, 42–43, 234–41.

128 *Porter hated it*: Givner, *Katherine Anne Porter*, 238; Darlene Harbour Unrue, *Katherine Anne Porter: The Life of an Artist* (Jackson: University Press of Mississippi, 2005), 126.

128 *Porter also nursed a grudge*: Katherine Anne Porter, *The Letters of Katherine Anne Porter*, edited by Isabel Bayley (New York: Atlantic Monthly Press, 1990), 572.

128 *"highly drunk, tottering"*: Givner, *Katherine Anne Porter*, 225.

129 *Porter told Della*: Thomas F. Walsh, *Katherine Anne Porter and Mexico* (Austin: University of Texas Press, 1992), 137.

129 *"burning and imperishable epic"*: Quoted in De Garrison, 238.

CHAPTER 8: PURPOSE

130 *"A man who finds his way"*: G. K. Chesterton, *The Collected Works of G. K. Chesterton*, vol. 20, edited by James V. Schall (San Francisco: Ignatius Press, 2001), 71–72.

130 *The article took*: Dorothy Day, "Communism and the Intellectuals," *America*, January 28, 1933, 401.

131 *"was in a state"*: Dorothy Day, "Hunger Marchers in Washington," *America*, December 24, 1932, 277–79.

133 *"She had a Spaniard's courtesy"*: Joseph A. Brieg, "Apostle on the Bum," *Commonweal* April 29, 1938, 12.

133 *"a short, broad-shouldered"*: Quoted in Miller, *Dorothy Day*, 227.

134 *"dissenter against modernity"*: Ellis, *Peter Maurin*, 19.

134 *He was also*: Dorothy Day, *Loaves and Fishes: The Inspiring Story of the Catholic Worker Movement* (Maryknoll, NY: Orbis Books, 2003 [1963]), 28.

134 *Born in 1877*: Biographical information about Maurin, with the sources generally consis-

tent with one another, can be found in the biographies by Marc H. Ellis, Arthur Shee-han, and Francis J. Sicius (a book based on Dorothy's notes for the biography she never wrote), and in the chapters devoted to him in William Miller, *Dorothy Day*. See also Brieg, "Apostle on the Bum," 9–12. Brieg, an admirer, called him "gnarled and shabby and disreputable" in appearance.

136   *it is entirely possible*: Peter Maurin's death certificate (no. 30376), issued by the New York State Department of Health and dated May 16, 1949, lists congestive heart failure as the immediate cause of death and names "antecedent causes, giving rise to the above cause" as carditis (inflammation of the heart) and syphilis.

137   *The Chestertonian style*: Dorothy Day, *From Union Square to Rome*, 141.

138   *Personalism, on the other hand*: The literature on personalism is vast, but some of the most accessible accounts are to be found in Mounier's own *A Personalist Manifesto* (New York: Longmans, Green & Co., 1938) and *Be Not Afraid: Studies in Personalist Sociology* (New York: Harper & Brothers, n.d.) and in Joseph Amato's *Mounier and Maritain: A French Catholic Understanding of the Modern World* (Ypsilanti, MI: Sapientia Press, 1975), as well as in R. William Rauch, Jr.'s, hagiographic biography *Politics and Belief in Contemporary France: Emmanuel Mounier and Christian Democracy, 1932–1950* (The Hague, Nether-lands: Martinus Nijhoff, 1972). The Mounier of the post–World War II years is more critically discussed in Tony Judt, *Past Imperfect: French Intellectuals, 1944–1956* (New York: New York University Press, 2011).

139   *"material comforts can effect"*: Mounier, *A Personalist Manifesto*, 62.

139   *"If you wish to astonish"*: Ibid., 42.

139   *"fragile curtain"*: Ibid., 128–30.

139   *"zeal for the family"*: Ibid., 137.

141   *Peter could be more*: Dorothy Day, *Peter Maurin: Apostle to the World*, edited by Francis J. Sicius (Maryknoll, NY: Orbis Books, 2004), 65–66.

143   *"If the police don't want"*: *The Catholic Worker*, May 1933, 1.

144   *"Man proposes. Woman disposes"*: Day, *Loaves and Fishes*, 21.

144   *Joe Bennett was sent uptown*: "Overcrowded Harlem Hospital Disgraces City of New York," *The Catholic Worker*, June 1934, 7.

144   *When Arthur G. Falls*: Lincoln Rice, *Healing the Racial Divide: A Catholic Racial Justice Framework Inspired by Dr. Arthur Falls* (Eugene, OR: Pickwick Publications, 2014), 55.

145   *she reprinted Carter's own editorial*: "A Negro Protestant Looks at Catholicism," *The Catholic Worker*, September 1934, 4.

145   *Dorothy's own assessment*: "We Have Sinned Exceedingly": *The Catholic Worker*, July–August 1934, 1, 2.

146   *"no end of trouble"*: Dorothy Day's FBI file, October 24, 1941, copy in the Dorothy Day Collection, Raynor Memorial Libraries, Marquette University.

146   *"sooner or later secure"*: Robert Wild, ed., *Comrades Stumbling Along: The Friendship of Catherine de Hueck Doherty and Dorothy Day as Revealed Through Their Letters* (New York: St. Paul's, 2009), 37.

146   *Cardinal Patrick Hayes*: Miller, *A Harsh and Dreadful Love*, 143.

146   *Dorothy didn't make it*: "The Catholic Worker Case for the Child Labor Amendment," *The Catholic Worker*, March 1934, 3.

146   *"The Mayor Objects"*: *The Catholic Worker*, September 1934, 2.

146   *"You may think"*: *The Catholic Worker*, December 1933, 2.

147   *None of that was to the point*: "God on Broadway," *The Catholic Worker*, February 1934, 2.

147   *To his publisher, Bennett Cerf*: Sheaffer, *O'Neill*, 426.

148   *The past was evoked*: Cowley, *Exile's Return*, 69; Louis Sheaffer, interview with Malcolm Cowley, Eugene O'Neill Collection, Lear Center, Charles E. Shain Library, Connecticut College, New London, CT.

CHAPTER 9: HOSPITALITY

149   *By the time Franklin Delano Roosevelt*: T. H. Watkins, *A Narrative History of the Great Depression in America* (New York: Henry Holt, 1990), 60–61, 70.

149   *Several early issues*: e.g., "House of Hospitality, No Evictions, Urge Unemployed," *The Catholic Worker*, October 1933, 8; "Call for Catholic Houses for Needy Women and Girls," *The Catholic Worker*, November 1933, 1.

150   *With the rental*: "Catholic Worker Has Entire House on Charles Street," *The Catholic Worker*, April 1935, 1, 3.

152   *"We did not need"*: Quoted in Day, *Peter Maurin: Apostle to the World*, 119.

152   *The houses Catherine ran*: A copy of Catherine de Hueck's "constitution" and thoughts on Dorothy and the need for rules can be found in the Paul Hanly Furfey Papers, Catholic University of America, Washington, DC.

153   *"a madhouse"*: Deane Mowrer, interview with Thomas Barry, Summer 1969, W-9.4, Box 1, file 2, Dorothy Day Collection, Raynor Memorial Libraries, Marquette University, Milwaukee, WI.

153   *"at the moment"*: Robert Wild, ed., *Comrades Stumbling Along*, 2. On Mr. Breen, see also Dorothy Day, *Loaves and Fishes: The Inspiring Story of the Catholic Worker Movement*, 38.

154   *In The Seven Storey Mountain*: Merton, *The Seven Storey Mountain* (New York: Houghton Mifflin Harcourt, 1998 [1948]), 169.

154   *So who were the young people*: Many of the early volunteers are discussed in Stanley Vishnewski's posthumously published memoir, *Wings of Dawn* (1979). On Mary Sheehan as "a sharp-tempered soul," see *The Catholic Worker*, November 1946. Julia Porcelli's Woolworth experience is referred to in the November 12, 1937, Box 5, file 22, Paul Hanly Furfey Papers, Catholic University of America, Washington, DC. Ade Bethune recorded her arrival at *The Catholic Worker* in her memoir. Tom Coddington's correspondence with Father Furfey (Coddington file, Paul Hanly Furfey Papers, Catholic University of America, Washington, DC) sheds light on the early days of the house and the paper.

156   *One slightly demented*: A copy of "The Catholic Worker Organization," a seven-page single-spaced typed document prepared by an unnamed member of the St. Francis Monastery, 135 West 31st Street, New York City, listing every imaginable complaint against the group and the newspaper, can be found in Box 5, folder 22, Paul Hanly Furfey Papers, Catholic University of America, Washington, DC.

156   *Albert Coddington*: A passing reference in the *The Catholic Worker*, October 1933, 8. John Cort published his own autobiography, *Dreadful Conversions: The Making of a Catholic Socialist* (New York: Fordham University Press, 2003).

158   *"The bug bit me"*: Rosalie Riegle, *Dorothy Day: Portraits by Those Who Knew Her* (Maryknoll, NY: Orbis Books, 2006), 11.

158   *It didn't escape*: Nancy L. Roberts, *Dorothy Day and the Catholic Worker* (Albany: State University of New York Press, 1985), 94.

161   *"one of those martyr-figures"*: Paul Marx, *Virgil Michel and the Liturgical Movement* (Washington, DC: Catholic University of America Press, 1957), 376.

161   *If Father Michel had*: Keith F. Pecklers, *The Unread Vision: The Liturgical Movement in the United States of America, 1926–1955* (Collegeville, MN: Liturgical Press, 1988), 89; David J. O'Brien, *American Catholics and Social Reform: The New Deal Years* (New York: Oxford University Press, 1969), 147.

162   *Not everyone at the Worker*: "Why We Recite Compline Together," *The Catholic Worker*, February 1937, 3.

162   *"It was love at first sight"*: Quoted in Nicholas K. Rademacher, *Paul Hanly Furfey: Priest, Scientist, Social Reformer* (New York: Fordham University Press, 2017), 3.

162   *"I didn't just write"*: Quoted in Brigid O'Shea Merriman, *Searching for Christ: The Spirituality of Dorothy Day* (Notre Dame, IN: Notre Dame University Press, 2001), 69.

163   *"captivated the young men"*: Day, *Loaves and Fishes*, 44–45.

164   *"Each pictured the commune"*: Ibid., 49.

164   *Nina Polcyn was nineteen*: Rosalie Riegle, interview with Nina Polcyn, DD-CW, W.9.4, Box 6, file 17, Dorothy Day Collection, Raynor Memorial Libraries, Marquette University, Milwaukee, WI.

165   *Nor did the Benedictine nuns*: "Militant Catholic Champions Cause of Laboring Classes," *The Scriptorium*, April 28, 1937, 1.

165   *At the College of Saint Catherine*: Abigail McCarthy, *Private Faces, Public Places* (New York: Doubleday, 1972), 24, 98; Dominic Sandbrook, *Eugene McCarthy: The Rise and Fall of Postwar American Liberalism* (New York: Knopf, 2004), 12–13. See also Marx, *Virgil Michel and the Liturgical Movement*, and Marx, "Dom Virgil Michel, OSB, the Liturgical Movement, and the Catholic Worker," in Mark and Louise Zwick, *The Catholic Worker Movement: Intellectual and Spiritual Origins* (Mahwah, NJ: Paulist Press, 2005), 58–74.

165   *Bishop Joseph Busch of St. Cloud*: *The Catholic Worker*, February 1935, 3.

166   *Invited to speak*: Janice Brandon-Falcone, "Experiments in Truth: An Oral History of the St. Louis Catholic Worker, 1935–1942," in Patrick G. Coy, ed., *A Revolution of the Heart* (Philadelphia: Temple University Press, 1988), 19.

166   *When several students*: Roberts, *Dorothy Day and the* Catholic Worker, 114–15.

166   *Sister Peter Claver*: William D. Miller, interview with Sister Peter Claver, November 19, 1976, W-9.4, Box 1, file 27, Dorothy Day Collection, Raynor Memorial Libraries, Marquette University, Milwaukee, WI.

166   *A noted Jesuit professor*: Dorothy Day, letter to Joe Zarrella, August 15, 1938, Thomas Merton Center, digital archives, Bellarmine.

167   *By the end of 1933*: Circulation figures in its early years for a paper such as *The Catholic Worker* are difficult to authenticate, but a good guide is provided in the appendix ("The Circulation of the *Catholic Worker*, 1933–1983") in Roberts, *Dorothy Day and the* Catholic Worker, 179–82.

Chapter 10: Challenge

168   *Faint glimmerings*: John Loughery, *Dagger John: Archbishop John Hughes and the Making of Irish America* (Ithaca, NY: Cornell University Press, 2018), 227.

170   *the Worker found a new home*: "Moving to Mott Street," *The Catholic Worker*, May 1936, 3. Other descriptions of 115 Mott Street, firsthand and otherwise, abound; see, e.g., John Cogley, *A Canterbury Tale: Experiences and Reflections, 1916–1976* (New York: Seabury Press, 1976), 15–22. Miller's and Dorothy's own accounts are in Dorothy Day, *House of Hospitality* (New York: Sheed & Ward, 1939), and Day, *Loaves and Fishes*.

170   *"When I first saw her"*: Rosalie Riegle, *Dorothy Day: Portraits by Those Who Knew Her* (Maryknoll, NY: Orbis Books, 2006), 1.

171   *"Bullshit!"*: Ibid.

171   *"a stage set"*: John Cort, "My Life at the Catholic Worker," *Commonweal*, June 20, 1980, 362.

171   *"We violated"*: Rosalie Riegle Troester, *Voices from the Catholic Worker* (Philadelphia: Temple University Press, 1993), 8 (from Troester's interview with Zarrella).

172   *"you could throw"*: Cort, "My Life at the Catholic Worker," 364.

174   A Catholic Worker *subscriber*: Day, *Loaves and Fishes*, 49–50.

175   *"As farmers, we were"*: Ibid., 53.

176   *"shaking like a leaf"*: Cort, *Dreadful Conversions*, 17.

177   *Passing through Memphis*: Nancylee Novell Jonza, *The Underground Stream: The Life and Art of Caroline Gordon* (Athens: University of Georgia Press, 1995), 168–69.

177   *"I think Dorothy began"*: Deane Mowrer, interview with Caroline Gordon, W-9, Box 1, folder 35, Dorothy Day Collection, Raynor Memorial Libraries, Marquette University, Milwaukee, WI.

177   *In reality*: Paul Hanly Furfey, letter to Dorothy Day, December 18, 1935, 39, Box 5, file 22, Paul Hanly Furfey Papers, Catholic University of America, Washington, DC.

178   *"some Catholic woman"*: Forest, *All Is Grace*, 137.

179   *"changed and reformed"*: Quoted in Kenneth J. Heineman, *A Catholic New Deal: Religion and Reform in Depression Pittsburgh* (University Park: Pennsylvania State University Press, 1999), 122.

179   *Once in Flint*: "CW Editor Calls on GM Strikers in Plant at Flint," *The Catholic Worker*, March 1937, 1, 4.

179   *"apostles of labor"*: *The Catholic Worker*, March 1937, 4; also quoted in Day, *House of Hospitality*, 221.

180   *"Dorothy Day was then"*: Cogley, *A Canterbury Tale*, 11.

180   *"I'd rather be seen"*: Quoted in Francis J. Sicius, "The Chicago Catholic Worker Movement, 1936 to the Present," PhD dissertation, Loyola University, Chicago, IL, 1979, 100 (from Sicius's interview with Sullivan).

181   *"At the last minute"*: Cogley, *A Canterbury Tale*, 12.

181   *Speaking to the student body*: San Francisco *Foghorn* (student paper of the University of San Francisco), November 12, 1937, 1.

182   *"a group that has worked"*: *Democrat and Chronicle* (Rochester, NY), May 5, 1938.

182   *"I believe the aims"*: Quoted in the *Reading* (PA) *Times*, September 24, 1937.

182   *Like Father Michel, Reinhold*: Jay Corrin, "Social Catholicism and the Career of H. A. Reinhold," in his superb study *Catholic Intellectuals and the Challenge of Democracy* (Notre Dame, IN: Notre Dame University Press, 2002), 236–71, provides an excellent overview of Reinhold.

183   *"fight the hardened bourgeois mentality"*: H. A. Reinhold, "The Catholic Worker Movement in America," *Blackfriars* 19, no. 222 (September 1938): 640.

183   *Bishop John Noll of Fort Wayne, Indiana*: Corrin, *Catholic Intellectuals and the Challenge of Democracy*, 276.

183   *The strictures of one critic*: John LaFarge, "Peter the Agitator Quotes the Prophets of Israel," *America*, August 1, 1936, 395; "Some Reflections on the Catholic Worker," *America*, June 26, 1937, 271; "The Catholic Worker," *America*, July 24, 1937, 371.

CHAPTER 11: PRELUDE

186 *Maritain, Mauriac, and Bernanos*: Bernard Doering, "Jacques Maritain and the Spanish Civil War," *The Review of Politics* 44, no. 4 (October 1982): 485–522. See also chaps. 12 and 13 in Jay Corrin, 292–377, and J. David Vailak, "American Catholic Dissenters and the Spanish Civil War," *The Catholic Historical Review* 53, no. 4 (January 1968): 537–55.

186 *"disgusting spectacle"*: Quoted in Corrin, 350.

186 *The Church hierarchy*: Vailak, "American Catholic Dissenters and the Spanish Civil War."

187 *"a wolf in sheep's clothing"*: Letter to the editor from Henry Guiltinan, *The Catholic Worker*, June 1939, 5.

187 *"camouflaged with Catholic paint"*: Quoted in Miller, *A Harsh and Dreadful Love: Dorothy Day and the Catholic Worker Movement*, 142.

187 *One episcopal attack*: Monsignor Matthias Heyker, letter to Dorothy Day, September 12, 1938, RG1.5 Archbishop John T. McNicholas, Chancery files, Box 88, folder Day, Dorothy (CW). See also Bob Miller, "From 'Militant Christian' to Silent Patriot: Archbishop John T. McNicholas, 1925–50," Archdiocese of Cincinnati, http://www.catholiccincin nati.org/98975/from-militant-christian-to-silent-patriot-archbishop-john-t-mcnich olas-1925-50/.

188 *"We were torn apart"*: Quoted in Nancy L. Roberts, 119 (from her 1981 interview with Zarrella).

189 *"Oh, once you get"*: A line that appears in many Workers' reminiscences; see, e.g., Betty Keenan, quoted in Rosalie Riegle Troester, *Voices from the Catholic Worker* (Philadelphia: Temple University Press, 1993), 72.

189 *What Tom Coddington and Dorothy Weston wanted*: William D. Miller, interview with Joe Zarrella, W-9.4, Box 2, file 28, Dorothy Day Collection, Raynor Memorial Libraries, Marquette University, Milwaukee, WI; Deane Mowrer, interview with Barry Thomas, Summer 1969, W-9.4, Box 1, file 2, Dorothy Day Collection, Raynor Memorial Libraries, Marquette University, Milwaukee, WI. (Thomas Barry was blunt: "Tom Coddington was one of those in which nothing took.") See also Nicholas K. Rademacher, 114, 137–38.

190 *"Johnsonian figure"*: *The Catholic Worker*, July–August 1953, 2.

190 *The matter of Dorothy's*: Belloc continued to be given a pass on the extent of his anti-Semitism and his indifference to Falangist atrocities in Spain long after his and Dorothy's deaths; see, e.g., A. N. Wilson, *Hilaire Belloc* (New York: Atheneum, 1984).

191 *Was she aware*: Donald Warren, *Radio Priest: Charles Coughlin, The Father of Hate Radio* (New York: Free Press, 1996), 104–05.

191 *"Communist in sympathy"*: Day, *From Union Square to Rome*, 147.

192 *"Even the most hardened"*: Ibid., 131.

193 *"The year has been hard"*: Day, *The Duty of Delight*, 45.

194 *Some opinion polls*: Hadley Cantril, ed., *Public Opinion, 1935–1946* (Princeton, NJ: Princeton University Press, 1951), 381–83.

194 *Street violence against Jews*: Stephen H. Norwood, "Marauding Youth and the Christian Front: Anti-Semitic Violence in Boston and New York During World War II," *American Jewish History* 91, no. 2 (June 2003): 233–67; James Weschler, "The Coughlin Terror: War in the Streets of New York," *Wisconsin Jewish Chronicle*, August 11, 1939.

194 *Karl Adam*: Kevin Spicer, "Last Years of a Resister in the Diocese of Berlin: Bernard Lichtenberg's Conflict with Karl Adam and his Fateful Imprisonment," *Church History* 70, no. 2 (June 2001): 248–70. Adam's *The Spirit of Catholicism* never ceased to be a book Dorothy thought highly of, though: she gave a copy to Ammon Hennacy when he decided to convert (see Hennacy, *The Book of Ammon* (New York: Catholic Worker, 1994 [1953]), 288). Adam's biographers are not exactly a stringent group of commentators on this sad aspect of the theologian's life and career. John Connelly, in his excellent *From Enemy to Brother: The Revolution in Catholic Teaching on the Jews* (Cambridge, MA: Harvard University Press, 2012), minces fewer words (19–22).

195 *That view conveniently ignored*: James Carroll, *Constantine's Sword: The Church and the Jews* (New York: Mariner Books, 2002), and John Cornwall, *Hitler's Pope* (New York: Penguin Books, 2000), probably contain the best-known accounts of the Vatican's mixed response to German anti-Semitism, but David Kertzer's scholarship covers a broader canvas; see his *The Popes Against the Jews: The Vatican's Role in the Rise of Modern Anti-Semitism* (New York: Knopf, 2001), 264–91, and *Mussolini and the Pope* (New York: Random House, 2015). Connelly, *From Enemy to Brother*, treats this topic as well.

196 *formation of the Committee*: "Catholics in Fight on Anti-Semitism," *New York Times*, June 12, 1939; Giuliana Chamedes, "Catholics, Anti-Semitism, and the Human Rights Swerve," The Immanent Frame, June 29, 2015, https://tif.ssrc.org/2015/06/29/catholics-anti-semitism-and-the-human-rights-swerve/.

197 *"shows evidence"*: Marie Bellem, letter to Father Joseph Gannon, December 17, 1939, Gannon Papers, Box 10, file 25, University Archives, Walsh Family Library, Fordham University, New York.

197 *Harry McNeil was told*: Harry McNeil, letter to Father Joseph Gannon, August 19, 1940, ibid.

197 *In the November 1939 issue*: The anomalies of Maritain's book, which is the printed version of a lecture he gave in Paris and New York, demonstrated the problem of Catholicism and anti-Semitism in the 1930s quite well; *A Christian Looks at the Jewish Question* was admirably blunt about what was happening in Europe while whitewashing the papacy of any involvement in anti-Jewish practices, even to the extent of pointing a damning finger at Polish Catholics and then expressing concern that Polish readers might take offense.

197 *"his activities on behalf of Jews"*: Ibid. Gannon used the identical phrase several times in letters to angry correspondents in 1942.

197 *"The Catholic Worker is"*: *The Catholic Worker*, May 1936, 8.

198 *"stepped into a hornet's nest"*: "Editor to Speak," an article about Callahan speaking with Father Rice in Pittsburgh in the *Pittsburgh Post-Gazette*, November 16, 1937, alludes to the convention the previous year.

198 *Dorothy knew*: Patrick G. Coy, "Conscription and the Catholic Conscience in World War II" (48–63), and Francis J. Sicius, "Prophecy Faces Tradition: The Pacifist Debate During World War II" (65–76), in Klejment. See also Piehl, 189–204; Roberts, 139–67.

198 *"To fight war"*: *The Catholic Worker*, September 1939, 1.

198 *"listened [to] with great respect"*: Day, *All the Way to Heaven*, 148.

199 *"encyclical"*: Quoted in Francis J. Sicius, "The Chicago Catholic Worker Movement, 1936 to the Present," PhD dissertation, Loyola University, Chicago, IL, 1979, 193 (from Sicius's interview with Sullivan).

200 *"a dictator's methods"*: Quoted in Miller, *A Harsh and Dreadful Love*, 169.

200 *"a pagan brute force"*: Ibid.

200   *"Surely it is"*: Quoted in Dana Greene, *The Living of Maisie Ward* (Notre Dame, IN: University of Notre Dame Press, 1997), 107.

200   *Maisie told Catherine de Hueck*: Robert Wild, ed., *Comrades Stumbling Along*, 89.

201   *"I hope you do not feel"*: Quoted in Paul Dvorchak, "Dorothy Day and the Beginning of St. Joseph House of Hospitality in Pittsburgh, 1936–1941," Gathered Fragments, Western Pennsylvania Society of Catholic History.

201   *That ended for the moment*: Kenneth J. Heineman, *A Catholic New Deal: Religion and Reform in Depression Pittsburgh* (University Park: Pennsylvania State University Press, 1999), 196.

201   *"deserve formal discussion"*: John Ryan, *Social Doctrine in Action: A Personal History* (New York: Harper & Bros., 1941), 216.

201   *"there is nothing"*: Wilfrid Parsons, "Can a Catholic Be a Conscientious Objector?," *Commonweal*, June 27, 1941, 226.

201   *"Men are not ready to listen"*: Quoted in Zwick, 260.

201   *Pray for Poland, pray for England*: Day, "We Are to Blame for the War in Europe," *The Catholic Worker*, September 1939, 1.

CHAPTER 12: WAR

203   *"of great health and vigor"*: "Sigrid Undset," *The Catholic Worker*, February 1941, 4.

203   *Hélène Iswolsky, just escaped*: Iswolsky, Hélène, *No Time to Grieve: An Autobiographical Journey* (Philadelphia: Winchell Company, 1985), 234–35.

204   *"Hélène, you have fallen"*: Authors' interview with Robert Steed, who edited *The Catholic Worker* in the 1950s, knew Iswolsky from her visits to the house, and heard the story from Dorothy.

207   *Religious retreats for Catholics*: For an excellent overview of this topic and its meaning for *The Catholic Worker*, see Brigid O'Shea Merriman, *Searching for Christ: The Spirituality of Dorothy Day*, 131–69.

208   *"At the very least"*: Paul Hanly Furfey, *Fire on the Earth* (New York: Macmillan, 1936), 127.

208   *"I am completely sold"*: Dorothy Day, letter to Gerry Griffin, June 18, 1940, DD-CW, W-73, Box 1, folder 2, Dorothy Day Collection, Raynor Memorial Libraries, Marquette University, Milwaukee, WI.

209   *"a disappointment"*: Quoted in Rosalie Riegle Troester, *Voices from the Catholic Worker* (Philadelphia: Temple University Press, 1993), 31.

211   *"envy the pagans"*: Stanley Vishnewski, *Wings of Dawn*, privately printed, 1979, 215.

211   *Julian Pleasants*: Rosalie Riegle, *Dorothy Day: Portraits by Those Who Knew Her* (Maryknoll, NY: Orbis Books, 2006), 84.

211   *Dorothy Gauchat*: Ibid., 85.

212   *"that this individual"*: This statement in the FBI file is dated April 3, 1941; the interview with Father McIntryre, October 24, 1941; the placement of Dorothy in Group 2, February 3, 1942; the interviewing of other priests, April 8, 1942; the search of Maryfarm, May 20, 1943; the examination of the bank accounts, March 17, 1944; the request of the assistant attorney general, January 26, 1943.

213   *"tolerated by Bishop [Kearney]"*: A copy of Dorothy Day's FBI file, running to more than five hundred pages, is in the Dorothy Day Collection, Raynor Memorial Libraries, Marquette University, Milwaukee, WI. This entry is dated August 25, 1943.

213   *Her beloved friend Nina Polcyn*: Dorothy Day, letter to Nina Polcyn, February 19, 1942, DD-CW, W-17, Box 2, Dorothy Day Collection, Raynor Memorial Libraries, Marquette University, Milwaukee, WI.

213 *"I do not believe"*: Dorothy Day, telegram to Nina Polcyn, DD- CW, W-17, Box 2, Doro-
       thy Day Collection, Raynor Memorial Libraries, Marquette University, Milwaukee, WI.

214 *Thirty-two-year-old Arthur Sheehan*: Obituary by Dorothy Day, *The Catholic Worker*, Sep-
       tember 1975, 2, 8. Other information about Sheehan was provided to the authors by his
       daughter, Dr. Elizabeth Sheehan.

214 *David Mason joined*: Obituary by Dorothy Day, *The Catholic Worker*, October 1969, 1, 4.

214 *"I had to walk"*: Quoted in Ann Hulbert, *The Interior Castle: The Art and Life of Jean
       Stafford* (New York: Knopf, 1992), 138.

215 *space was regularly allotted*: Marie Conti, "Race and Religion," *The Catholic Worker*,
       March 1942, 3.

215 *printed three sonnets*: *The Catholic Worker*, July–August 1945, 4.

216 *"I saw a bit of Germany"*: Day, *The Catholic Worker*, June 1942, 1.

216 *"righteous rage"*: Day, "For These Dear Dead," *The Catholic Worker*, November 1946, 1.

217 *the writer J. F. Powers*: Powers, "A Day in the County Jail," *The Catholic Worker*, August
       1943, 6.

218 *Her January 1943 editorial*: Dorothy Day, "If Conscription Comes for Women," *The
       Catholic Worker*, January 1943, 1.

218 *When Bishop Gerald Shaughnessy*: "Western Bishop Pleads for Morality in War," *The
       Catholic Worker*, May 1944, 1, 6.

219 *The FBI continued*: Dorothy Day's FBI file, May 3, 1943.

219 *Before it closed, though*: Ibid., May 20, 1943.

219 *Another person*: Day, *Loaves and Fishes: The Inspiring Story of the Catholic Worker Move-
       ment*, 165. An example of Dorothy's scattered memory for details by the time she was in
       her sixties is the fact that, when she mentioned the visit in her 1963 book, she had to
       be reminded exactly which Kennedys had visited.

221 *"This protest on my part"*: Day, *All the Way to Heaven*, 180.

221 *"Do pray she gets over it"*: Ibid., 183.

222 *"The career I think"*: Ibid., 187.

222 *"I know you are happy"*: Ibid., 189.

223 *On April 19, 1944*: Kate Hennessy, *Dorothy Day: The World Will Be Saved by Beauty: An
       Intimate Portrait of My Grandmother*, 150–52.

224 *"He may grow"*: Day, *All the Way to Heaven*, 196.

224 *"all usual canons of beauty"*: Jacques Maritain, *Georges Rouault* (New York: Abrams &
       Pocket Books, 1954), n.p.

225 *"He was against"*: *The Catholic Worker*, March 1945, 1.

225 *Though the Catholic Worker*: Dorothy Day's FBI file, July 3, 1945.

225 *"but none so stupid"*: *The Catholic Worker*, July–August 1945, 2.

226 *"Mr. Truman was jubilant"*: "We Go on Record," *The Catholic Worker*, September 1945, 1.

226 *"the primary duty"*: Quoted in Patricia McNeal, *Harder than War: Catholic Peacemaking in
       Twentieth-Century America* (New Brunswick, NJ: Rutgers University Press, 1992), 1.

Chapter 13: Burdens

227 *Modigliani eyes*: Garry Wills, "Dorothy Day at the Barricades," *Esquire*, December 1983,
       228.

229 *Just as seriously, but*: A trenchant account of Mounier in the postwar period and the
       double standard that *Esprit* applied to US and Soviet actions can be found in Tony Judt,
       Past Imperfect: French Intellectuals, 1944–1956 (New York: New York University Press,
       2010).

229   *Two weeks before*: Professor Harry Murray of Nazareth College located Maurin's draft card, now in the archives at Marquette University; see Murray, "Peter Maurin on War and Peace," paper presented at the Sanctity of Dorothy Day Conference at St. Thomas University, March 7, 2014.

231   *Disagreements among the fractious Workers*: Miller, *Dorothy Day: A Biography*, 375.

233   *"fiendish pride"*: Day, *All the Way to Heaven*, 210.

233   *"I should be used to"*: Ibid., 212.

234   *Arrested with another*: Irene Naughton, "Jersey Police Arrest CW's," *The Catholic Worker*, October 1947, 1.

234   *"The common man"*: Irene Naughton, "The Responsible Workman," *The Catholic Worker*, February 1948, 1.

235   *"Things Worth Fighting For?"*: *Commonweal*, May 21, 1948, 136–37.

236   *"If we could achieve"*: Dorothy Day, letter to Hélène Iswolsky (July 1949), Hélène Iswolsky Collections, Day correspondence file, McHugh Special Collections, Weinberg Memorial Library, University of Scranton, Scranton, PA.

237   *John Cogley published*: John Cogley, "Storefront Catholicism," *America*, August 21, 1948, 447–49.

237   *"batty aunt"*: Kate Hennessy, 184.

237   *"to [go to] the slums"*: Evelyn Waugh, *The Letters of Evelyn Waugh*, edited by Mark Amory (New York: Ticknor & Fields, 1980), 290.

237   *"Perhaps to tease"*: Martin Stannard, *Evelyn Waugh: The Later Years, 1939–1966* (New York: Norton, 1992), 228.

238   *In December 1948*: Day, *All the Way to Heaven*, 218–20; Forest, *All Is Grace*, 189–90; William D. Miller, *A Harsh and Dreadful Love: Dorothy Day and the Catholic Worker Movement*, 222–24; Piehl, 92–94. See also David L. Gregory, "Dorothy Day, Workers' Rights, and Catholic Authenticity," *Fordham Urban Law Journal* 26, no. 5 (1999); Arnold Sparr, "'The Most Memorable Labor Dispute in the History of U.S. Church-Related Institutions': The 1949 Calvary Cemetery Workers' Strike Against the Catholic Archdiocese of New York," *American Catholic Studies* 119, no. 2 (2002): 1–33; and "Gravediggers Take Anti-Red Oath," *New York Times*, March 5, 1949, 1.

239   *"their dignity as men"*: Day, *All the Way to Heaven*, 219.

240   *"a loss in dignity"*: Dorothy Day, "Cardinal Brings an End to NY Strike," *The Catholic Worker*, April 1949, 2.

241   *"No matter what"*: Day, *All the Way to Heaven*, 227.

242   *"not coming out"*: Dorothy Day, "Beyond Politics," *The Catholic Worker*, November 1949, 4. See also Day, "The Case of Father Duffy," *The Catholic Worker*, December 1949, 1, 4.

243   *"He had not smiled"*: Dorothy Day, "Peter Maurin," *The Catholic Worker*, June 1949, 1, 2.

243   *"like granite"*: Dorothy Day, *The Duty of Delight*, 129.

CHAPTER 14: REVIVAL

246   *"no sound of traffic"*: Dorothy Day, *The Catholic Worker*, January 1950, 1.

246   *"just another Italian gangster"*: Quoted in Forest, *All Is Grace*, 198.

246   *"polite animosity"*: Dwight Macdonald, "The Foolish Things of the World: I," *The New Yorker*, October 4, 1952, 37–60.

247   *With oil heat and more bathrooms*: Dorothy Day, letter to Ammon Hennacy, July 19, 1950, in Day, *All the Way to Heaven*, 237.

249   *"to run the risk"*: Dorothy Day, "Letter: Blood, Sweat, and Tears," *Commonweal*, December 29, 1950, 300–01.

249 *Gaffney's demand caused*: Day, *The Duty of Delight*, 167–69. Dorothy's letter is quoted on p. 169.

251 *"most of them have"*: Quoted in Daniel Burston, *A Forgotten Freudian: The Passion of Karl Stern* (London: Karnac Books, 2016), 77.

251 *"You must suffer terribly"*: Ibid., 91–92.

251 *"This is a school"*: Authors' interview with Robert Steed.

252 *"All I knew"*: Harrington, 18. Harrington's relationship with Dorothy Day, time at *The Catholic Worker*, and waning faith are well described in "The Life of a Saint," in Maurice Isserman, *The Other American: The Life of Michael Harrington* (New York: Public Affairs, 2000), 68–104.

253 *To her astonishment*: Ammon Hennacy, *The Book of Ammon* (New York: Catholic Worker, 1994 [1953]), 285.

253 *"When I'd first wake up"*: Quoted in Isserman, *The Other American*, 101.

253 *Heaven, Hell, Purgatory*: Ibid., 104.

254 *"If she had operated"*: Quoted in Day, *All the Way to Heaven*, 240.

255 *"more womanly"*: Ibid., 269.

255 *"When writing in haste"*: Ibid., 254.

255 *"a big bourgeois firm"*: Ibid., 263.

256 *"love letter"*: Quoted in Roberts, 102.

257 *"You wouldn't want"*: Ibid.

257 *"a bit weary"*: H. A. Reinhold, "The Long Loneliness of Dorothy Day," *Commonweal*, February 29, 1952, 521–22.

257 *"truly great man"*: Dorothy Day, "On Pilgrimage," *The Catholic Worker*, September 1954, 2.

257 *"would probably horrify"*: *Chicago Tribune*, March 1, 1953.

258 *"Like so many people"*: Quoted in Isserman, *The Other American*, 90.

258 *"Many people think"*: Quotations from the two-part profile are found in Dwight Macdonald, "The Foolish Things of the World: I," *The New Yorker*, October 4, 1952, 37–60, and "The Foolish Things of the World: II," *The New Yorker*, October 11, 1952, 37–58.

259 *"painful and agonizing"*: Dorothy Day, letter to Jack English, August 20, 1954, in Day, *All the Way to Heaven*, 296.

260 *"quietly imposing"*: Dan Wakefield, *New York in the Fifties* (New York: Greenpoint Press, 1992), 85.

260 *"Told in Context"*: Robert M. Dowling, "'Told in Context': Dorothy Day's Previously Unpublished Reminiscence of Eugene O'Neill," *Eugene O'Neill Review* 38, nos. 1–2 (2017): 1–12.

261 *"How little we were able"*: Dorothy Day, "On Pilgrimage," *The Catholic Worker*, April 1954, 3, 7–8.

262 *Even two priests*: Dorothy Day, "Where Are the Poor?," *The Catholic Worker*, January 1955, 1.

CHAPTER 15: RESISTANCE

263 *On June 15*: Dorothy Day, *The Catholic Worker*, July 1955; Ammon Hennacy, *The Book of Ammon* (New York: Catholic Worker, 1994 [1953]), 309–13; Judith Malina, *The Diaries of Judith Malina: 1947–1959* (New York: Grove Press, 1983), 368–75.

264 *"a tall woman"*: Malina, *The Diaries of Judith Malina*, 368.

264 *"We are, as you know"*: Quoted in James J. Farrell, *The Spirit of the Sixties: The Making of Postwar Radicalism* (New York: Routledge, 1995), 22. See also Dorothy Day's FBI file, August 8, 1950.

265   DEFIANCE OF DRILL: *Baltimore Sun*, July 24, 1955, 1. "U.S. Powers Will Be Tested by 28 Who Defied Raid Siren" was the similar headline of the *Cincinnati Enquirer*, July 25, 1955, 12. Several other major papers also picked up the story.

265   *"Some of the bishops"*: Quoted in Frank Sheed, *The Church and I* (New York: Doubleday, 1974), 175.

265   *The following spring*: Miller, *A Harsh and Dreadful Love*, 250.

266   *A few days later*: Day, *Loaves and Fishes*, 189; Forest, *All is Grace*, 217.

267   *Wystan Hugh Auden was*: Will Lissner, "Poet and Judge Assist Samaritan," *New York Times*, March 2, 1956, 1.

267   *"Miracle on the Bowery"*: Dan Wakefield, *New York in the Fifties* (New York: Greenpoint Press, 1992), 94.

267   *The first Dorothy heard*: Nancylee Novell Jonza, *The Underground Stream: The Life and Art of Caroline Gordon* (Athens: University of Georgia Press, 1995), 226–337; Veronica Makowsky, *Caroline Gordon: A Biography* (New York: Oxford University Press, 1989), 206–10; Miller, *Dorothy Day*, 453.

268   *"medieval abbess"*: Caroline Gordon, *The Southern Mandarins: Letters of Caroline Gordon to Sally Wood, 1924–1957*, edited by Sally Wood (Baton Rouge: Louisiana State University Press, 1984), 73.

268   *She told Caroline's editor*: Jacques Maritain, *Exiles and Fugitives: The Letters of Jacques and Raïssa Maritain, Allen Tate, and Caroline Gordon*, edited by John Dunaway (Baton Rouge: Louisiana State University, 1992), 57.

268   *Caroline Gordon was not pleased*: Ibid.

269   *"most loathsome of sins"*: Quoted in Miller, *Dorothy Day*, 454. In a diary entry dated September 9, 1975, Dorothy grappled further with the issue as two friends had recently come out to her as lesbians. She wrote that she was torn between Christ's admonition not to judge and St. Paul's more clear-cut strictures. She recalled attractions she had had to female peers when she was young; she noted that, indeed, "There is no record of Jesus ever having taken up the subject" (Day, *The Duty of Delight*, 587), but obviously she did not feel calm about or confident in pondering the topic any further. Her prison diary for 1959 (ibid., 265) contains many reflections on the extent of lesbianism in the Women's House of Detention, which she found disconcerting, repellent, and poignant. In her 1960 biography of Thérèse of Lisieux, she made reference to schoolgirl crushes that could lead to "depths of evil," 87.

269   *In April 1957, Dorothy went*: In "Fear in Our Time," Dorothy's 1963 speech to Pax, the British peace organization, she recounted her visit to Koinonia Farm in detail (copy in the Dorothy Day Collection, Raynor Memorial Libraries, Marquette University Archives, Milwaukee, WI).

270   *"All my thoughts"*: Flannery O'Connor, *The Habit of Being: Letters of Flannery O'Connor*, edited by Sally Fitzgerald (New York: Farrar, Straus and Giroux, 1988), 218.

271   *It probably hadn't helped*: Hennacy, *The Book of Ammon*, 357.

271   *It certainly didn't do*: Jervis Anderson, *Bayard Rustin: Troubles I've Seen* (New York: HarperCollins, 1997), 202.

271   *There was the vaginal*: Malina, *The Diaries of Judith Malina*, 444–45.

271   *"We shared a cell"*: Quoted in Rosalie Riegle, *Dorothy Day: Portraits by Those Who Knew Her*, 52.

272   *Judith Malina recorded*: Malina, 443–62, includes a lengthy, fascinating, and detailed account of that month in jail with Dorothy.

273 *An opportunity*: Dorothy wrote about her time in Mexico in her columns in the February and March 1958 issues of *The Catholic Worker* and in "Pilgrimage to Mexico," *Commonweal*, December 26, 1958, 336–38.

275 *The last time Dorothy spoke in Vermont*: Hennessy, 209.

276 *"slovenly, reckless, intellectually chaotic"*: William F. Buckley, "The Catholic in the Modern World," *Commonweal*, December 16, 1960.

276 *Even in a setting*: Fordham Ram, May 1, 1958.

276 *She had yet another resource*: This list of admired authors might imply that aside from the many religious texts she read, Dorothy's reading was exclusively highbrow, an English major's syllabus. In fact, it should be noted that she read plenty of the mass-market best sellers of her day as well, including *Marjorie Morningstar*, *Kon-Tiki*, and any number of detective novels.

277 *Huxley's early, satirical works*: Hennessy, *Dorothy Day*, 59.

278 *"There is no such thing"*: Dorothy Day, *On Pilgrimage: The Sixties* (New York: Curtis Books, 1972), 159 (from *The Catholic Worker*, September 1963).

278 *Huxley sent an encouraging note*: Stanley Vishnewski, *Wings of Dawn*, 219.

280 *"If there were"*: Thomas Merton, *The Hidden Ground of Love: The Letters of Thomas Merton*, edited by William H. Shannon (New York: Farrar, Straus and Giroux, 1985), 278.

281 *"plunged himself so deeply"*: Day, *The Duty of Delight*, 258.

281 *"an innocent walking"*: Authors' interview with Robert Steed.

281 *He solved that problem*: "Catholic Worker Staff Member Arrested by FBI," *The Catholic Worker*, April–May 1959, 1. See also Day, *Loaves and Fishes*, 146–47.

282 *"at a loss"*: Eleanor Roosevelt, letter to Dorothy Day, April 21, 1959, W-6-3, Box 1, Catholic Worker Collection, Raynor Memorial Libraries, Marquette University, Milwaukee, WI.

282 *"Her total lack of sympathy"*: Dorothy Day, "Reflections on the Connection," *The Catholic Worker*, July–August 1960, 2, 7.

283 *A death closer to home*: Nanette Batterham's death is discussed in Day, *The Duty of Delight*, 275–96; Miller, *Dorothy Day*, 457–59.

283 *"One would think*: Day, *The Duty of Delight*, 278.

284 *"Traveling in a bus"*: Dorothy Day, *All the Way to Heaven*, 335.

CHAPTER 16: *PACEM IN TERRIS*

285 *One wonders: What did*: The Record, St. John's University, February 3, 1960, and *The Heights*, College of the Holy Cross, November 21, 1961.

286 *Writing to Karl Meyer*: Dorothy Day, *All the Way to Heaven*, 339–40.

287 *"We do not believe"*: Ibid., 342–43.

287 *In October, Dorothy published*: In the literature about Dorothy Day, not a great deal has been written about her biography of St. Thérèse of Lisieux; extended interpretive accounts, though, can be found in Brigid O'Shea Merriman, *Searching for Christ: The Spirituality of Dorothy Day*, 191–97, and J. Leon Hooper, "Dorothy Day's Transposition of Thérèse's 'Little Way,'" *Theological Studies* 63 (2002): 68–86.

288 *"I am faced"*: Quoted in Daniel Ellsberg, foreword to Day, *Thérèse* (Notre Dame, IN: Christian Classics, 2016), viii.

289 *"In these days"*: Day, *Thérèse*, xviii.

290 *His February 1961 article*: Dave Dellinger, "America's Lost Plantation," *The Catholic Worker*, February 1961, 1, 4–6.

290 The Sunday Visitor: Dorothy Day, *On Pilgrimage: The Sixties*, 69 (from *The Catholic Worker*, July–August 1961). (In 1972, a paperback edition of Dorothy's columns from the 1960s was published; quotations from her columns in that decade are taken from that book.)

291 *"deserved and undeserved"*: Ibid., 71 (from *The Catholic Worker*, July–August 1961).

291 *"If religion has"*: Ibid., 101 (from *The Catholic Worker*, September 1962).

291 *"I want to see"*: Day, *All the Way to Heaven*, 370.

291 *"The fervent Catholic"*: Day, *The Duty of Delight*, 338.

291 *"I go to see Christ"*: Ibid., 337.

291 *She wanted more patience*: Day, *On Pilgrimage: The Sixties*, 76 (from *The Catholic Worker*, July–August 1961).

292 *To be exacting*: Ibid., 93, 100 (from *The Catholic Worker*, July–August 1962).

292 *"the grace of God"*: Ibid., 100 (from *The Catholic Worker*, September 1962).

293 *"it takes the form"*: Ibid., 111 (from *The Catholic Worker*, November 1962).

293 *reminded her of—Peter Maurin*: Ibid., 109 (from *The Catholic Worker*, October 1962).

293 *Few public statements*: Roberts, 155–57. Dorothy's columns on Cuba appeared in the July–August 1961, July–August 1962, October 1962, November 1962, February 1963, and September 1963 issues; articles disputing the US view of Cuba were published in *The Catholic Worker* by other writers as well.

293 *Karl Meyer, whose politics*: Authors' interview with Karl Meyer.

294 *"moving in their honesty"*: Thomas Merton, *The Hidden Ground of Love: The Letters of Thomas Merton*, edited by William H. Shannon, 76.

294 *"The next time"*: Thomas Merton, *The Road to Joy: The Letters of Thomas Merton*, edited by Robert E. Daggy (New York: Farrar, Straus and Giroux, 1989), 324.

294 *Judith Gregory*: Gregory's "Some Memories of the Catholic Worker" (provided to the authors by her friend Robert Steed) is a sixteen-page, single-spaced typed memoir, the kind of textured, highly specific document one wishes many more veterans of the Catholic Workers had produced.

294 *Ed Forand*: Authors' interview with Geoffrey Gneuhs.

295 *The most significant departure*: Authors' interview with Mary Lathrop; Day, *Loaves and Fishes*, 106–21.

296 *"enjoy ecclesiastical approval"*: Joseph P. O'Brien, Vice Chancellor, letter to Bishop Joseph Federal, July 21, 1961, Archives of the Archdiocese of Salt Lake City. Hennacy's letters to Federal, warm and hopeful, are also in the Archives of the Archdiocese of Salt Lake City.

296 *"a diabolic sense of humor"*: Day, *All the Way to Heaven*, 364.

297 *"enjoy the comic aspects"*: Gregory, Judith, "Some Memories of the Catholic Worker," 5.

297 *"it was through Dorothy Day"*: Michael Harrington, *The Other America* (New York: Macmillan, 1962), n.p.

297 *Similarly, labor disputes*: "'Company Union' Charged at Fordham Univ.," *The Catholic Worker*, May 1962, 1, 8.

298 *Eileen Egan*: Linda L. Baratte, "Eileen Egan: Portrait of the Life, Lifestance, and Pedagogy of a Catholic Prophet of Peace," PhD dissertation, Fordham University, Bronx, NY, 2004, is the most extensive treatment of Egan's career. See also Egan, *Peace Be with You: Justified Warfare or the Way of Nonviolence* (Maryknoll, NY: Orbis Books, 1990).

299 *Though courtly and mild-mannered*: An example of Zahn's bluntness would be his article in the May 1971 *Catholic Worker*, "The Church as Accomplice"; see Tom Cornell,

Jim Forest, and Robert Ellsberg, eds., *A Penny a Copy: Readings from "The Catholic Worker"* (Maryknoll, NY: Orbis Books, 1994), 186–90, which articulates a highly critical view that Dorothy might have shared but would not have expressed so stridently in print. See also Michael Gallagher, "Let Us Now Praise Gordon Zahn," Catholic Peace Fellowship, 2003, http://www.catholicpeacefellowship.org/downloads/gordon_zahn.pdf.

299   *"I never expected"*: Day, *All the Way to Heaven*, 451.

300   *"Pacem in terris heralded"*: McNeal, 95.

300   *"a communist-controlled publication"*: Thomas Merton, *Thomas Merton: A Life in Letters*, edited by William H. Shannon and Christine M. Bochen (New York: HarperCollins, 2008), 255.

300   *It was the right moment*: Dorothy chronicled her trip to Rome in her May and June 1963 columns; see *On Pilgrimage: The Sixties*, 137–49.

301   *"How gentle and how saintly"*: *The Catholic Worker*, July–August 1963, 7.

302   *"a Baptist Dorothy Day"*: Glen Harold Stassen, *A Thicker Jesus: Incarnational Discipleship in a Secular Age* (Louisville, KY: Westminster John Knox Press, 2012), 38.

302   *"uncannily alike"*: Egan, *Peace Be with You*, 289.

303   *"young and happy"*: Day, *On Pilgrimage: The Sixties*, 163 (from *The Catholic Worker*, November 1963). This column gives the fullest account of Dorothy's trip to England.

303   *Frank Pakenham*: Peter Stanford's aptly titled *The Outcasts' Outcast: A Biography of Lord Longford* (City: Stroud, U.K. Sutton Publishing, 2003) is the principal source about this Catholic nobleman's life.

303   *"Oh, why not?"*: Rosalie Riegle, *Dorothy Day: Portraits by Those Who Knew Her*, 38.

303   *Last, Dorothy made*: Riegle, *Dorothy Day*, 150. In her account, the ever-discreet Eileen Egan left out the flower-stealing part.

304   *"I had been a Communist"*: Day, *Loaves and Fishes*, 8, 21.

304   *"hodge-podge"*: Day, *All the Way to Heaven*, 374. Dorothy's anger at the extensive editing was such that she even complained about it in her Pax speech in England that fall.

304   *"always ready for an adventure"*: Ibid., 116.

304   *"modest yet aggressive passion"*: *Commonweal*, December 6, 1963, 322.

305   *"We've moved into"*: Quoted in Kate Hennessy, 231.

CHAPTER 17: BURNING

306   *"I speak today"*: Quoted in Jim Forest, *All Is Grace*, 245.

307   *In May 1954*: Dorothy Day, "Theophane Venard and Ho Chi Minh," *The Catholic Worker*, May 1954, 1, 6.

308   *The reactions to LaPorte's death*: Authors' interview with Tom Cornell and Robert Steed; see also Rodger Van Allen, "More Information on Roger LaPorte: Postscript to an Article," *American Catholic Studies* 117, no. 4 (Winter 2006): 70–72.

308   *"young and tender consciences"*: Quoted in Miller, 482.

309   *William F. Buckley had been warning*: Buckley, *Pittsburgh Post-Gazette*, October 23, 1965, 4.

309   *"If anyone ever dreamed"*: Dorothy Day, letter to Thomas Merton, November 16, 1965, quoted in Day, *All the Way to Heaven*, 408, and Anne Klejment, *American Catholic Pacifism: The Influence of Dorothy Day and the Catholic Worker Movement*, 114.

309   *"she had never had"*: Rosalie Riegle, *Dorothy Day: Portraits by Those Who Knew Her*, 36.

310   *"He looks just like"*: Dorothy Day, *On Pilgrimage: The Sixties*, 299 (from *The Catholic Worker*, May 1967).

310   *Before leaving for the Midwest:* Ibid., 264 (from *The Catholic Worker*, April 1966).

310   *How refreshing to spend time:* Ibid., 271–72 (from *The Catholic Worker*, May 1966).

311   *Alinsky also knew Cesar Chavez:* Nicholas von Hoffman, *Radical: A Portrait of Saul Alinsky* (New York: Nation Books, 2010), 163.

311   *"crushed . . . shocked":* Hennessy, *Dorothy Day*, 219.

312   *She was invited:* Bridgeport Post, August 20, 1966, 20.

313   *A talk before seminarians:* Day, *The Duty of Delight*, 402.

313   *"the cause of righteousness":* Spellman's trip was covered extensively in the press; see the *St. Louis Post-Dispatch*, December 27, 1966 (photo with President and Imelda Marcos).

314   *"Words are as strong":* Day, *On Pilgrimage: The Sixties*, 289 (from *The Catholic Worker*, January 1967).

315   *"I could only explain":* Dorothy Day, letter to Thomas Merton, June 24, 1965, quoted in Day, *All the Way to Heaven*, 400–01, and Klejment, *American Catholic Pacifism*, 113.

316   *"a terrifying book":* Day, *The Duty of Delight*, 447.

316   *"I hate contempt and ridicule":* Day, *All the Way to Heaven*, 432.

317   *"cultivation of worldly failure":* James Terence Fisher, *The Catholic Counterculture, 1933–1962* (Chapel Hill: University of North Carolina Press, 1989), 246.

318   *The congress included:* The Lay Apostolate Bulletin, 1967, a complete report of the activities and resolutions of the conference, is available online; see also Day, *On Pilgrimage: The Sixties*, 317–23 (from *The Catholic Worker*, November 1967).

318   *"totally unacceptable":* The Lay Apostolate Bulletin, 1967, 12.

319   *"truly overwhelming honor":* Day, *On Pilgrimage: The Sixties*, 318 (from *The Catholic Worker*, December 1967).

319   *Through mutual friends:* Ibid., 324–29 (from *The Catholic Worker*, January 1968).

320   *"paradises of sun and air":* Day, *The Catholic Worker*, December 1967, 6.

321   *Spending the holidays in Vermont:* Hennessy, 254.

322   *"Looks like jail for you!":* Authors' interview with Daniel Marshall.

322   *The year 1968, possibly:* The books about the political tumult of the mid- to late sixties fill entire library shelves, of course, but most of the major studies (e.g., Gitlin, Anderson, Viorst) do not mention Dorothy Day at all; among the very few that do, and by far the best, is James Farrell, *The Spirit of the Sixties: The Making of Postwar Radicalism* (New York: Routledge, 1995).

324   *"through our usually violent south":* Day, *On Pilgrimage: The Sixties*, 343 (from *The Catholic Worker*, September 1968).

324   *Dorothy had known Dan:* George M. Anderson, "Looking Back with Gratitude: A Conversation with Daniel Berrigan," *America*, July 6, 2009.

325   *"frightened more than it edified":* Quoted in Jim Forest, *At Play in the Lions' Den: A Biography and Memoir of Daniel Berrigan* (Maryknoll, NY: Orbis Books, 2017), 122.

325   *"a living sacrifice":* Day, *On Pilgrimage: The Sixties*, 344 (from *The Catholic Worker*, October 1968).

326   *"peaceful sabotage":* Quoted in Francine du Plessix Gray, *Divine Disobedience: Profiles in Catholic Radicalism* (New York: Knopf, 1970), 161.

326   *"Why has your Church":* Ibid., 155.

326   *"No, Dan isn't":* McNeal, 261.

CHAPTER 18: JOURNEYS

327   *"romantic Irishman":* Dorothy Day, "Ammon Hennacy: A 'Non-Church' Christian," *The Catholic Worker*, February 1970, 8.

328   *"I did not think"*: Dorothy Day, *The Duty of Delight*, 506.

328   *What an admirable example*: Ibid.

329   *In August 1970, Dorothy and Eileen*: Dorothy wrote about their trip around the world in her columns in the September, October, and December 1970 issues of *The Catholic Worker*. Eileen Egan wrote about the India part of their trip in "Calcutta: Scourged City" in the December 1970 and January 1971 issues of the paper. For further information, see "Remembering Dorothy Day's Visit 40 Years Ago," CathNews: A Service of the Australian Catholic Bishops Conference, April 6, 2010, http://www.cathnews.com/archives/cathblog-archive/14542-cathblog-remembering-dorothy-days-visit-40-years-ago; Francis Ravel Harvey, *Traveler to Freedom: The Roger Pryke Story* (Sydney: Freshwater Press, 2011); Eileen Egan, *Such a Vision of the Street*, 176–92; and Val Noone, "Dorothy Day in Australia," *Tjurunga* 90 (2017): 59–73.

329   *"certainly the greatest person"*: Quoted in Harvey, *Traveler to Freedom*, 312.

330   *"Our present capitalist"*: Quoted in Noone, "Dorothy Day in Australia," 68.

330   *"She can drink"*: Quoted in ibid., 69.

331   *"At my time of life"*: Eileen Egan, "Calcutta: Scourged City, II," *The Catholic Worker*, January 1971, 3.

331   *The two accepted donations*: The Catholic Worker would not take money from the government, foundations, or wealthy conservatives with suspect political ties; Mother Teresa's funds came from a less restricted list, so to speak. Her contact with the Duvaliers of Haiti, for instance, is not something Dorothy would have countenanced on behalf of the Catholic Worker.

331   *"The glow of the invisible world"*: Day, *The Duty of Delight*, 513.

333   *In truth, not unlike Castro*: Dorothy Day, "On Pilgrimage," *The Catholic Worker*, December 1970, 2, 5. See also the January 1971 issue, 1, 6.

333   *Shiva Naipaul, visiting Tanzania*: Shiva Naipaul, *North of South: An African Journey* (New York: Simon & Schuster, 1979), 197–248. Naipaul visited Tanzania six years after Dorothy, and his book is a sad account of the costly failures of *ujamaa*. See also Martin Meredith, *The Fate of Africa: A History of the Continent Since Independence* (New York: Public Affairs, 2011), 249–59.

333   *Several months later*: Dorothy wrote about the trip in her columns in the July–August, September, and October–November issues of the paper, all in 1971, and discussed it in a taped interview, "Russia (August 1971)," in the Dorothy Day Collection, Raynor Memorial Libraries, Marquette University Archives, Milwaukee, WI. The Peace Collection at Swarthmore College, Swarthmore, PA, also contains files in the Jerome Davis Papers from "Promoting Enduring Peace" that describe the itinerary of the trip.

334   *"benches, parks, flowers everywhere"*: Dorothy Day, *All the Way to Heaven*, 489.

335   *"Alexander Solzhenitsyn was another"*: Dorothy Day, "On Pilgrimage," *The Catholic Worker*, September 1971, 8.

335   *"a piece of effrontery"*: "Russia," taped interview with Dorothy Day, August 1971, Dorothy Day Collection, Raynor Memorial Libraries, Marquette University, Milwaukee, WI.

336   *"Dorothy leaned on me"*: Authors' interview with Sister Corcoran.

337   *"Now we can use this!"*: Daniel Berrigan, *The Berrigan Letters: Personal Correspondence Between Daniel and Philip Berrigan*, edited by Daniel Cosacchi and Eric Martin (Maryknoll, NY: Orbis Books, 2016), 87.

337   *On the occasion*: Transcript of *Bill Moyers Journal*, W-9, Box 1, folder 16, Dorothy Day Collection, Raynor Memorial Libraries, Marquette University, Milwaukee, WI.

338   *Even an edgy downtown*: Vivian Gornick, "Dorothy Day at 72: The Dailiness of Grace," *Village Voice*, November 20, 1969, 5–6, 31.

338   *"the Methusaleh of little mags"*: Dwight Macdonald, "Revisiting Dorothy Day," *The New York Review of Books*, January 28, 1971, 12–19.

338   *W. H. Auden wrote*: Auden, "Happy Birthday, Dorothy Day," *The New York Review of Books*, December 14, 1974, 3–4.

339   *When Maisie Ward appeared*: Graham Greene, *A Sort of Life* (New York: Simon and Schuster, 1971), 192.

339   *not criminality*: Brian Terrell, "Dorothy Day: 'We Are Not Going into the Subject of Birth Control, as a Matter of Fact,'" *National Catholic Reporter*, September 30, 2015.

340   *The poet Emily Coleman*: The letters between Coleman and Dorothy in the University of Delaware archive indicate an often tense relationship; Coleman was a hypercritical person, not especially well suited to life at the Catholic Worker in its Chrystie Street days.

340   *The problems were*: Authors' interviews with Robert Gilliam; Geoffrey Gneuhs; Martha Hennessy; Mary Lathrop; Daniel Marshall; and Robert Steed; among others.

341   *"sinister characters"*: Authors' interview with Mary Lathrop.

341   *"And who are you, old lady?"*: Authors' interview with a Catholic Worker from the 1970s, who wished not to be named.

341   *"thinks it is his duty"*: Day, *The Duty of Delight*, 523.

342   *"went out of his mind today"*: Ibid., 560–61.

342   *A friend of Shane O'Neill*: Dorothy Day, diary, February 21, 1973, D-4, Box 8, no. 2, Dorothy Day Collection, Raynor Memorial Libraries, Marquette University, Milwaukee, WI.

342   *Yet in sometimes unexpected instances*: Authors' interview with Rachel de Aragon.

344   *the final scene was* : Day, *All the Way to Heaven*, 528.

344   *The IRS had dropped*: Authors' interview with Tom Cornell.

345   *Writing in 1974*: Dorothy Day, letter to Father Gilhooley, December 27, 1974, Dorothy Day file, Fordham University Archives, Walsh Family Library, Fordham University, New York.

CHAPTER 19: ENDINGS

346   *In the fall of 1974*: Authors' interview with Marc Ellis; See also Marc H. Ellis, *A Year at the Catholic Worker: A Spiritual Journey Among the Poor* (Waco, TX: Baylor University Press, 2000 [1978]).

347   *"People were beating each other up"*: Deane Mowrer, interview with Lee LeCuyer, March 21, 1979, W-9.4, Box 2, folder 6, Dorothy Day Collection, Raynor Memorial Libraries, Marquette University, Milwaukee, WI.

347   *At that same violent encounter*: Authors' interview with Geoffrey Gneuhs.

348   *"Her face is highlighted"*: Ellis, *A Year at the Catholic Worker*, 51.

348   *she looked profoundly weary*: Authors' interview with Michael Harank.

350   *Money was solicited*: Dorothy Day, letter to William Miller (1/26/76), in Day, *All the Way to Heaven*, 551.

350   *she spoke one day*: Authors' interview with Daniel Marshall.

351   *Meanwhile, at the Worker*: Authors' interviews with Bill Griffin; Tom Hoey; Dan Mauk; Brian Terrell; Bob Ellsberg; and Marc Ellis.

351   *"They squared the circle"*: Authors' interview with Bill Griffin.

351   *"an aura of meditation"*: Ellis, *A Year at the Catholic Worker*, 66.

351   *"I love you"*: Authors' interview with Tom Hoey.

352   *"I welcomed the shock"*: Authors' interview with Meg Brodhead.

352   At some point: If there is one topic Catholic Workers alive today, who were at the house in the 1970s, are not comfortable talking about, it is John Coster's criminal activity, even if almost everyone acknowledges that it took place. Estimates (guesses?) on their part of the amount embezzled range from tens of thousands of dollars to $300,000. Coster, never prosecuted, died not long after Dorothy.

353   *"Oh, yes," she remarked*: Authors' interview with Michael Harank.

353   In August of that year: Eileen Egan, "Dorothy Day: Pilgrim of Peace," in Patrick G. Coy, ed., *A Revolution of the Heart: Essays on the Catholic Worker* (Philadelphia: Temple University Press, 1988), 69–71; Nicholas K. Rademacher, "'To Relate the Eucharist to Real Living': Mother Teresa and Dorothy Day at the Forty-First International Eucharistic Congress, Philadelphia, Pennsylvania," *U.S. Catholic Historian* 27, no. 4 (Fall 2009): 59–72.

353   *"not too frail"*: Egan, "Dorothy Day: Pilgrim of Peace," 69.

354   *"refreshed and strengthened"*: *The Catholic Worker*, September 1976, 2.

355   *"delicate attentions"*: Day, *The Duty of Delight*, 662.

355   The last visit: Authors' interview with Michael Harank.

356   *"a son in my dotage"*: Authors' interviews with Mary Lathrop and Jane Sammon.

356   *"a group of people"*: Marc Ellis, interview with Mike Harank, May 1978, W-9.4, Box 1, folder 36, Dorothy Day Collection, Raynor Memorial Libraries, Marquette University, Milwaukee, WI; also authors' interviews with Harank.

357   *"I'm 'on the shelf'"*: Dorothy Day, letter to Nina Polcyn, August 11, 1977, W-17, Box 2, folder 2, Dorothy Day Collection, Raynor Memorial Libraries, Marquette University, Milwaukee, IL.

357   *"Pray I get to be"*: Dorothy Day, letter to Nina Polcyn, December 27, 1977, W-17, Box 2, folder 2, Dorothy Day Collection, Raynor Memorial Libraries, Marquette University, Milwaukee, WI.

357   Brian Terrell: Authors' interview with Brian Terrell.

357   Ellsberg's *"Long Days"*: Robert Ellsberg, "Long Days, Dark Nights in a County Jail," *The Catholic Worker*, July–August 1978, 1, 4, 8.

358   *"We have Dorothy now"*: Kenneth Woodward, "Dorothy's Way," *Newsweek*, December 27, 1976, 61.

359   *"overpowering effect"*: Paul Hanly Furfey, *Love and the Urban Ghetto* (Maryknoll, NY: Orbis, 1978), 113.

359   In 1978, Geoffrey Gneuhs: Authors' interview with Geoffrey Gneuhs.

360   One weekend when: Authors' interview with Father Boniface Ramsey.

361   *"If the Catholic Worker"*: Daniel Chura, letter to *The Catholic Worker*, August 24, 1978, Dorothy Day Collection, Raynor Memorial Libraries, Marquette University, Milwaukee, WI.

361   A difficult discussion: Authors' interviews with Geoffrey Gneuhs; Michael Harank; Dan Mauk; and Peggy Scherer.

361   *"Someone has to minister"*: Troester, 526.

363   *"Turn that damn thing off"*: Authors' interview with a Catholic Worker who chose not to be identified.

364   *"a knife wound to my heart"*: Day, *The Duty of Delight*, 533.

Chapter 20: Deo Gratias

366   *Dorothy Day's passage*: Information about the wake and funeral is taken from authors' interviews with Robert Ellsberg; Geoffrey Gneuhs; Bill Griffin; Michael Harank; Tom Hoey; Patrick and Kathleen Jordan; Martha Hennessy; Mary Lathrop; Dan Mauk; Boniface Ramsey; Jane Sammon; Peggy Scherer; Robert Steed; Brendan Walsh; and Kenneth Woodward. See also Riegle, 181–89; Colman McCarthy, "The Final Tribute," *Washington Post*, December 3, 1980.

369   *"Your wife was a wonderful woman"*: Authors' interview with Bill Griffin.

Postscript

371   *In November 1997*: Information about the canonization process is taken from Jim Forest, *All Is Grace*, 304–15; Kenneth Woodward, *Making Saints: How the Catholic Church Determines Who Becomes a Saint, Who Doesn't, and Why* (New York: Simon & Schuster, 1990), 29–36; and authors' interviews with Cardinal Timothy Dolan; George Horton, the vice postulator of Dorothy's cause; and numerous members of the Dorothy Day Guild.

INDEX

ABOUT THE AUTHORS

JOHN LOUGHERY is the author of several award-winning and *New York Times* Notable Books, including *Alias S.S. Van Dine* (the winner of an Edgar Award for Biography), *John Sloan: Painter and Rebel* (a finalist for the Pulitzer Prize in Biography), and *The Other Side of Silence: Men's Lives and Gay Identities, A Twentieth-Century History* (the winner of a Lambda and Randy Shilts Award for Gay Male Studies). His most recent biography is *Dagger John: Archbishop John Hughes and the Making of Irish America*. He teaches English, American Studies, and art history at the Nightingale-Bamford School in New York City.

BLYTHE RANDOLPH is a native of Richmond, Virginia, and a graduate of Hollins College and the University of Virginia. She is the author of previous biographies of Amelia Earhart and Charles Lindbergh. She lives in Atlanta, Georgia, with her husband and three rescue dogs.